Building New Bridges
Bâtir de nouveaux ponts

Building New Bridges
Bâtir de nouveaux ponts

Sources, Methods, and Interdisciplinarity
Sources, méthodes et interdisciplinarité

Edited by
Sous la direction de

Jeff Keshen
Sylvie Perrier

University of Ottawa Press
Les Presses de l'Université d'Ottawa

This book has been published with the help of financial contributions from the Social Sciences and Humanities Research Council of Canada and the University of Ottawa Faculty of Arts.

University of Ottawa Press gratefully acknowledges the support extended to its publishing program by the Canada Council for the Arts and the University of Ottawa.

We also acknowledge the Government of Canada for its financial support of our publishing activities through the Book Publishing Industry Development Program.

Library and Archives Canada Cataloguing in Publication

Building New Bridges: Sources, Methods, and Interdisciplinarity / edited by Jeff Keshen, Sylvie Perrier = Bâtir de nouveaux ponts : sources, méthodes et interdisciplinarité / sous la direction de Jeff Keshen, Sylvie Perrier.

Papers presented at a conference held at the University of Ottawa, Ottawa, Ont., May 8-9, 2004.

(Actexpress) Text in English and French. Includes bibliographical references.
ISBN 0-7766-0593-3.   ISSN 1480-4743

1. Social sciences--Methodology--Congresses. 2. Humanities--Methodology--Congresses. I. Keshen, Jeff, 1962- II. Perrier, Sylvie, 1966- III. Title: Building New Bridges.

H61.B855 2005   300'.1   C2005-902204-3E

University of Ottawa Press / Les Presses de l'Université d'Ottawa

Books in the ACTEXPRESS series are published without the University of Ottawa Press's usual editorial intervention. The editorial process for *Building New Bridges / Bâtir de nouveaux ponts* has been ensured by the editors and their contributors.

All rights reserved. No parts of this publication may be reproduced or transmitted in any form or by any means, electronic or mechanical, including photocopy, recording, or any information storage and retrieval system, without permission in writing from the publisher. Copyright clearance available from Access Copyright, 1 Yonge St., Suite 1900, Toronto, Ontario M5E 1E5. 416.868.1620 / 1.800.893.5777 / www.accesscopyright.ca

Cover: Brady Typesetting & Design (Laura Brady)
Proofreading: Lyne's Word (Lyne St-Hilaire-Tardif)

ISBN 0-7766-0593-3. ISSN 1480-4743.

© University of Ottawa Press, 2005
542 King Edward Avenue, Ottawa, Ontario K1N 6N5 Canada
press@uottawa.ca / www.uopress.uottawa.ca

Printed and bound in Canada

Contents
Table des matières

	Introduction *Jeff Keshen/Sylvie Perrier*	1
1	Vellum and *Vaccinium*: Documentary and Archaeological Evidence in the Study of Medieval Produce *Charlotte Masemann*	5
2	Talking Numbers: Deconstructing Engineering Discourse *James Hull*	17
3	Model Behaviour: A Material Culture Approach to the History of Anatomy Models *Susan Lamb*	29
4	Re-disciplining the Body *Lisa Helps*	49
5	The Uncooperative Primary Source: Literary Recovery versus Historical Fact in the Strange Production of *Cogewea* *Robert Strong*	63
6	Reading Books/Reading Lives: Culture, Language, and Power in Nineteenth-Century School Readers *Barbara Lorenzkowski*	73
7	Rigueur et sensibilité dans un parcours historien *Hubert Watelet*	91
8	Inside Out: The Use and Inadvertent Misuse of Oral Histories *Laura E. Ettinger*	103
9	Les sources juridiques au service de l'histoire socio-culturelle de la France médiévale et moderne *Kouky Fianu/Sylvie Perrier*	113
10	Revisiting Quantitative Methods in Immigration History: Immigrant Files in the Archives of the Russian Consulates in Canada *Vadim Kukushkin*	125

11 Réflexions sur la question identitaire d'après les recensements informatisés : l'exemple des « Suisses » en Ontario (1871-1881)   143
    Samy Khalid

12 The Politics of Sources and Definitions   159
    Cristina Bradatan

13 Reporting the People's War: Ottawa (1914-1918)   171
    Jeff Keshen

14 Documents in Bronze and Stone: Memorials and Monuments as Historical Sources   185
    Jonathan F. Vance

15 The Evidence of Omission in Art History's Texts   197
    Katherine Romba

16 Images : mode(s) d'emploi   207
    Mélanie De Groote

17 What do the Radio Program Schedules Reveal? Content Analysis versus Accidental Sampling in Early Canadian Radio History   225
    Anne F. MacLennan

18 Television as Historical Source: Using Images in Cultural History   239
    Caroline-Isabelle Caron

19 *"Wie es eigentlich gewesen?"* Early Film as Historical Source?   249
    Michel S. Beaulieu

20 Evidence of What? Changing Answers to the Question of Historical Sources as Illustrated by Research Using the Census   265
    Chad Gaffield

Contributors/Collaborateurs   275

Introduction

Jeff Keshen/Sylvie Perrier

Interdisciplinarity, a term scarcely known as recently as a decade ago, today seems all the rage within academe. Cutting edge research is now often perceived as synonymous with interdisciplinarity. Bringing together scholars from different disciplines, often for team-based research, projects are now being tackled by experts from a variety of perspectives and, as often claimed, at a depth beyond the capacity of a single researcher. Melding older, often traditional, disciplinary-based approaches and utilizing sources in novel ways, interdisciplinarity has supposedly taken scholarship to a higher level, yielding fresher, more nuanced, and ultimately more sophisticated analyses.

The practitioners of interdisciplinarity are many, and their growing numbers show no signs of abating. Among the plethora of places encouraging this trend is the Washington-based Committee on Facilitating Interdisciplinary Research which "provide[s] findings, conclusions, and recommendations as to how ... interdisciplinary work can be facilitated by funding organizations and academic institutions,"[1] and the Interdisciplinary Research Institute in Lille, France, which is "designed to foster interactions between biologists, computer scientists, mathematicians, physicists, chemists and engineers."[2] The fruits from such work are now appearing in relatively new publications such as the *Journal of Interdisciplinary History*, *Journal of Intercultural Studies*, *Science Communication*, and *ProtoSociology*, sources dedicated to the dissemination of scholarship crossing the boundaries of a single discipline.

Canadian academics and academies have participated with vigour in this trend through new institutes, scholarly programs, and forums for the exchange of ideas, such as the Alberta-based Centre for Interdisciplinary Research in the Liberal Arts which sponsors an annual colloquium and "provid[es] Internet resources to scholars engaged in interdisciplinary research."[3] Granting agencies are also moving in this direction, most notably the Social Sciences and Humanities Research Council of Canada [SSHRC]. In transforming itself - as it began advertising in early 2004 - from a "Granting Council to Knowledge Council," SSHRC announced its intention to promote the interchange of ideas and methods across disciplines to produce results of greater utility, particularly in areas that will challenge Canadians in the years to come like the "new economy," healthcare, sustainable development, the environment, and the maintenance of a "civil society that reflects [Canadian] values and diverse heritages."[4]

Canadian university calendars point to an expanding corpus of interdisciplinary programs that, advocates contend, will produce graduates with the breadth of knowledge to truly understand and effectively address the

---

[1] http://www7.nationalacademies.org/interdisciplinary/
[2] http://www.dr18.cnrs.fr/iri/
[3] http://www.augustana.ab.ca/cirla/
[4] http://www.sshrc.ca/web/whatsnew/initiatives/transformation/consultation_framework_e.pdf

complexity of issues. Some domains are longer established, but have broadened significantly in recent years such as Canadian Studies (where students now delve into History, Geography, Sociology, English, Lettres françaises, Philosophy, Religious Studies, and Political Science) and Women's Studies (which now involves Criminology, Education, English, History, Human Kinetics, Law, Lettres françaises, Nursing, Pastoral Studies, Political Science, Religious Studies, and Sociology). Newer combinations are further expanding the parameters of inquiry, often to address current issues such as Globalization (the study of which now typically covers Political Science, History, Economics, Geography, Religious Studies, Sociology, and Law), and Population Health (which includes Health Administration, Human Kinetics, Law, Microbiology, Immunology, Nursing, Psychology, and Rehabilitation Science).

But not everyone is sold, and from several quarters, cautions have been issued. Often heard is that disciplines have their own internal logic, and that to mix methodologies, perhaps to satisfy the latest fad, will produce work of dubious quality. Many ask who, in fact, is expert enough to determine which disciplines are truly complementary. Others wonder whether new interdisciplinary institutes and the trend toward collaborative research will stunt creativity by forcing artificial connections, creating an extra level of bureaucracy, and defining more rigidly the boundaries of inquiry to respect the team approach. And then there is the matter of what students actually learn, namely, will they truly master any area of study or come away with a superficial smattering of knowledge?

Such concerns should be kept in mind when utilizing this collection of papers which are the product of a May 2004 conference held at the University of Ottawa entitled "Bâtir de nouveaux ponts : sources, méthodes et interdisciplinarité / Building New Bridges: Sources, Methods, and Interdisciplinarity." The goal of the gathering was to bring together established scholars, newer professors, and graduate students from different disciplines to share knowledge. Over sixty participated from across North America and Europe and together their work covered a vast range – temporally, geographically, methodologically, and evidentiary. Participants came from domains that included Sociology, Demography, Philosophy, History, Fine Arts, Native Studies, Music, Kinesiology, Archaeology, Lettres françaises, English, Canadian Studies, Women's Studies and African-American Studies. With generous funding from SSHRC and the University of Ottawa's Faculty of Arts, it became possible to publish a selection of these presentations.

The editors hope that this collection can be used as something akin to a primer for courses in methodology. It seeks to introduce readers to the possibilities for interdisciplinary research, the potential application and effective utilization of sources, as well as to stimulate debate on the merits of melding approaches from different branches of scholarship.

* * * * * * * *

Qu'ils inventent, avec l'apport d'autres disciplines, de nouvelles sources ou qu'ils repensent l'utilisation de documents de facture plus traditionnelle, les auteurs de ce collectif invitent la communauté des chercheurs à sortir des sentiers battus. Osons! Voilà leur message commun. La nature expérimentale de plusieurs des contributions indique que les auteurs ont relevé le défi lancé par les organisateurs du colloque et se sont aventurés en terrains moins familiers, traçant ainsi de nouvelles voies pour la recherche. Ces pistes ne sont pas entièrement débrousaillées, loin s'en faut. Par ailleurs, le caractère interdisciplinaire des textes présentés est visible dans les approches préconisées par plusieurs chercheurs, mais fonctionne aussi comme un dialogue entre les auteurs puisque leurs préoccupations se recoupent au fil des contributions, malgré des horizons académiques différents.

Les premières contributions du recueil mettent les sources textuelles en perspective et montrent qu'elles peuvent être éclairées par d'autres approches et complétées par divers types de documents. L'archéologie est ainsi depuis longtemps la partenaire de l'histoire et c'est grâce à la paléo-ethnobotanique que Charlotte Masemann réussit à dévoiler les secrets de la culture maraîchère à la période médiévale. Ce faisant, elle nous amène à repenser le régime alimentaire des Européens et toute la dynamique de l'économie agroalimentaire médiévale. C'est dans une toute autre direction que nous entraîne ensuite James Hull, qui étudie pour sa part les standards techniques utilisés en génie. Les chiffres et les formules mathématiques deviennent ainsi un discours rationnel à décrypter, discours qui définit à la fois une discipline scientifique et une activité économique. Sources fascinantes s'il en est, les modèles anatomiques analysés par Susan Lamb dévoilent une facette méconnue de l'histoire de la pédagogie médicale et invitent à une réflexion sur notre relation au corps à travers les époques. C'est dans cette même veine que reprend ensuite Lisa Helps qui appelle à une théorisation du corps comme source de connaissance.

Le dialogue parfois difficile entre littérature et histoire est l'objet du texte de Robert Strong. L'histoire a ainsi contribué à la réinterprétation d'une oeuvre importante pour la culture des premières nations aux États-Unis, mais le débat reste largement ouvert. Barbara Lorenzkowski nous convie pour sa part à la relecture des manuels scolaires des jeunes Canadiens d'origine allemande du XIXe siècle. Elle construit ainsi un pont entre histoire des pratiques pédagogiques et histoire des communautés ethniques canadiennes.

Les textes suivants sont le fruit d'une réflexion de certains auteurs sur leur propre parcours de recherche. Hubert Watelet fait le constat que si la pluridisciplinarité fait partie intégrante de l'histoire depuis plusieurs décennies, le réflexe interdisciplinaire n'est pas l'apanage de tous les domaines d'enquête. Il plaide ainsi pour une histoire renouvelée des sentiments qui allierait une exigence de rigueur à une approche pluridisciplinaire. De son côté, Laura E. Ettinger offre une réflexion sur le rôle de l'interviewer dans les enquêtes d'histoire orale en prenant l'exemple de sa propre expérience. Elle insiste sur la position centrale de l'observateur dans le processus d'enquête et sur la nécessité pour ce dernier de se situer franchement par rapport à son sujet, suggérant que cette démarche devrait être commune à tous les historiens vis-à-vis de leurs sources. Pour leur part, Kouky Fianu et Sylvie Perrier se sont livrées à une expérience comparatiste à partir de leurs recherches respectives sur les pratiques sociales de la justice aux époques médiévale et moderne. Si elles adhèrent pleinement à la notion de pluridisciplinarité, elles soulignent également les mérites d'une démarche intradisciplinaire pour contrôler la validité de certaines hypothèses.

Le quantitatif est au coeur des trois contributions suivantes. Tout d'abord, Vadim Kukushkin propose un traitement sériel des dossiers d'immigrants conservés dans les archives des consulats russes. Malgré leurs défauts, ces documents constituent une source précieuse de renseignements sur l'immigration au Canada au tournant des XIXe et XXe siècles. C'est aux migrants suisses que s'intéresse quant à lui Samy Khalid. Dans son article, il s'interroge sur la notion d'identité en s'appuyant sur des exemples tirés de deux recensements canadiens successifs. Cristina Bradatan nous montre par ailleurs que les événements politiques du siècle passé ont influencé la définition des catégories utilisées dans les sources démographiques, ce qui peut remettre en question certaines théories qui font actuellement autorité dans ce domaine.

C'est Jeff Keshen qui entame la dernière section de cet ouvrage collectif, partie consacrée aux médias et aux représentations. À travers les journaux majeurs de l'époque, il nous décrit la vie d'une communauté, celle de la ville d'Ottawa, durant la Première Guerre mondiale. Les monuments consacrés à cette guerre forment d'ailleurs le point de départ de la contribution de Jonathan F. Vance qui analyse la valeur des monuments commémoratifs comme source historique. L'interprétation des monuments artistiques est cependant au coeur de nombreux débats, comme nous le montre ensuite Katherine Romba qui explore le concept d'omission dans les textes interprétatifs d'histoire de l'art. S'intéressant elle aussi aux méthodes d'interprétation de l'art, Mélanie De Groote nous propose un processus méthodologique en partant de l'exemple d'une murale gigantesque illustrant l'histoire de l'Université de Louvain-la-Neuve.

Les ondes de la radio sont des sources plus difficiles à saisir, aussi Anne F. MacLennan a-t-elle eu recours aux horaires de programmation pour reconstituer l'histoire des premières années de radio-diffusion au Canada en y appliquant des méthodes d'analyse de contenu très rigoureuses, avec une approche qui renouvelle l'historiographie du sujet. De son côté, Caroline-Isabelle Caron s'est intéressée à la télévision et prône une utilisation accrue des sources télévisuelles comme mode de compréhension d'une société. Elle montre tout le potentiel de cette démarche en procédant à l'analyse de l'émission *Star Trek / Patrouille du Cosmos* dans le cadre de la culture du Québec contemporain. Michel S. Beaulieu se livre quant à lui à une défense passionnée, et convaincante, du film comme source historique majeure pour l'histoire du XXe siècle, incitant les historiens à adopter ces documents qui peuvent s'avérer de véritables portes vers le réel.

Finalement, cet ouvrage collectif se termine par une réflexion générale offerte par notre collègue Chad Gaffield. En se fondant sur l'analyse des recensements canadiens du XIXe siècle, il insiste sur la plasticité des sources, sur leur caractère malléable. En effet, dans les dernières décennies, l'interprétation des recensements a évolué selon les méthodes d'exploitation disponibles, selon les apports d'autres disciplines et selon les questionnements développés par les chercheurs. Il s'agit donc d'une invitation à la créativité et à l'esprit d'aventure, avec les rigueurs méthodologiques qui s'imposent. La diversité rafraîchissante des contributions de cet ouvrage collectif inspirera, nous l'espérons, d'autres chercheurs à suivre cette voie.

Vellum and *Vaccinium*
Documentary and Archaeological Evidence in the Study of Medieval Produce

Charlotte Masemann

The systematic study of gardens as *loci* of food production during the Middle Ages has largely been overlooked by agrarian historians. Economic agrarian history is based epistemologically on the idea that human actions can best be understood through their economic foundations and consequences, and methodologically on the idea that the best and most accurate conclusions can be reached from a base of quantifiable and documented evidence. This strong epistemological and methodological base has resulted in a large body of excellent and rigorous work. Its focus on numbers and documents has, however, largely obscured the economic importance of cultivation carried out beyond large grain fields.

Leaving gardens and their produce out of the history of European agriculture has resulted in a distorted view of the medieval diet, because the focus on grains and livestock in the existing literature has led to the impression, deliberate or not, that the medieval population was not getting its fruits and vegetables.[1]

The studies carried out by agrarian historians show the importance of the documentary base for this research, namely manorial documents recording grain production on manors and demesnes. In contrast, the study of the food supply for the medieval city generally relies on urban records keeping track of small-scale land transactions, and also on the records of cities' efforts to regulate market activities within their walls. These records are generally preserved on vellum, or scraped animal hide, a common medieval form of paper. Two medieval cities in particular, Ghent and Lübeck, offer considerable documentary evidence on urban agriculture and horticulture.

The development of the discipline of palaeoethnobotany, or the study of archaeological plant remains, over the last thirty years, also offers an important resource for the researcher interested in medieval garden produce.

---

[1] Considerable debate has occurred about the relative health of the European population, particularly before and after the Black Death. Michael Postan argues that before the Black Death, much of the English rural population was living very near the subsistence level. Michael Postan, *The Medieval Economy and Society* (London: Weidenfeld and Nicholson, 1972), 34. Slicher van Bath argues that the Black Death struck a population already weakened by undernourishment. B. H. Slicher van Bath, *The Agrarian History of Western Europe 500-1850*, trans. Olive Ordish (London: Edward Arnold Ltd., 1963), 89. Christopher Dyer notes that garden produce would have provided an important supplement to the diet, and that peasants were subject to "an annual cycle of temporary indulgence and *real* deprivation." Christopher Dyer, *Standards of Living in the Middle Ages: Social Change in England, c. 1200-1520* (Cambridge: Cambridge University Press, 1989), 157, 160.

Palaeobotanists are able to identify plant remains from archaeological digs dating from the Middle Ages with a precision simply not available in written documents. For example, the *Vaccinium* that appears in the title of this essay is a genus of wild berries. The species most commonly found in Lübeck was *Vaccinium myrtillus*, or blueberry. *Vaccinium* was selected not only because of its alliterative properties with vellum, but also because it illustrates a number of things about archaeological evidence. First, it shows the extent to which archaeologists can identify the types of seed they find. The Lübeck archaeobotanists could identify *Vaccinium myrtillus* quite easily, but identifications of other species of this genus remain provisional. Second, the case of *Vaccinium* shows how the archaeological record preserves items that might be derived from wild plants. Wild plants rarely, if ever, make an appearance in documentary evidence. Thus the combination of the more traditional study of documents and the examination of archaeological evidence provides a more complete picture than either can offer on its own. This essay will examine how both documentary and archaeological evidence contributes to a picture of garden produce in medieval Ghent and Lübeck.

The documentary picture of Lübeck's garden produce comes from four types of records: records of land transactions, tithe records, records of rents paid on gardens to the city, and the regulations of the gardeners' guild. The records of land transactions were generally preserved in one of two sources: the *Oberstadtbuch*, a record of transactions of movements of property, mortgages and rents within and, to some extent, outside the city of Lübeck,[2] and the *Niederstadtbuch*, a record of all sorts of transactions between citizens of Lübeck.[3] Tithe records provide a snapshot of the land that was tithed just outside the Mühlentor, the gate at the southern end of the city. The records cover the years 1428, 1444, and an unspecified year after 1451.[4] The third body of documents that provide information on gardens outside the city is the *Wette* garden books. They consist of a series of records of rents paid to the *Wette*, a police-like institution that was composed of two members of the city council called the *Wetteherren*. The *Wette* also enforced the guild regulations recorded in the *Ältestes Wettebuch*, beginning in 1321.[5] An additional responsibility was the collection of the income from gardens and meadows outside the city wall.[6]

The fourth type of document is the *Willkür der Gärtner*, or the regulations of the gardeners' guild. It is undated. Correspondence concerning the existence of the gardeners' guild from 1677 remarks that the guild is at least

---

[2] H. Bickelmann, "Oberstadtbücher," *Kanzlei Findbuch* (Archiv der Hansestadt Lübeck, n.d.), 9.
[3] Ibid., 3.
[4] Paul Hasse and Carl Wehrmann, eds., *Lübeckisches Urkundenbuch (LUB)*, Vols. 1-11 (Lübeck: Friedrich Aschenfeldt; Ferdinand Grautoff; Edmund Schmersahl Nachf.; Lübke & Nöhring, 1843-1905). *LUB* VII, 283 (1428); VIII, 271 (1444); IX, 73 (after 1451).
[5] Georg Fink, "Die *Wette* und die Entwicklung der Polizei in Lübeck," *Zeitschrift des Vereins für lübeckische Geschichte und Altertumskunde* 27 (1934): 212.
[6] Georg Fink, "Beiträge zur Geschichte des Lübecker Friedens von 1629. Die Lage von Michael Festers Garten vor dem Burgtor," *Zeitschrift des Vereins für lübeckische Geschichte und Altertumskunde* 26 (1932): 147.

300 years old and claims that its *Willkür* was written down in the so-called *Aeltestes Wettebuch*, kept from 1321.[7]

These regulations cover many aspects of the life of the guild and its members, including admission of new members, sale of produce, cultivation of produce, land management, fencing, wages, and transportation, among others. This document also expands the list of plants known to have been grown in Lübeck. These are onions (*cypollen*), garlic (*knuflok*), turnips (*roven*), carrots (*moren*), red cabbage (*roden kol*), and green vegetables (*groene warmoos*).[8] It is one of the very few early documents that prove that people in Lübeck sold produce to other people in Lübeck.[9] This document forbade anyone to have more than one stall in the market during Christmas and at Easter, and thus shows us that gardeners cultivating produce outside the city brought it into the city for the purposes of commerce.

All of the records examined here demonstrate that there were plots of land called gardens by the people who kept records. The gardens that appear in these records are located just outside the walls of the city and in the villages of the surrounding area, known as the *Landwehr*. Citizens of Lübeck, men and women, members of the city elite and artisans, were engaged in paying tithes on them, paying rents from them to the city, and engaging in various other transactions involving them. They ranged in size from small to large; an absolute determination of size is not possible. The primary crop of these gardens was hops; these records also mention apples, cabbages and other vegetables, and berries. Tithe records show that items grown in gardens changed over time, and that some gardens went out of production and became bleaching grounds. The *Wette* garden books show that the average income paid to the city from gardens outside the city walls remained fairly constant throughout the approximately 200-year period covered by these records.

Questions regularly asked by agrarian historians will generally go unanswered by the documents concerning Lübeck gardens that appear here. Little quantitative material is available, and no records allow us to calculate the productivity of these gardens or to assess if crop rotation took place. Hops and fruit trees obviously do not lend themselves well to such farming systems. The tithe records show that land use did change over time; the reasons behind these changes are not clear, but could have been made based on analysis of prices. Figures for hop and cabbage prices during the fifteenth century are unfortunately not available. The documents also do not specify cultivation techniques; one must assume that hard work with a shovel and hoe was the primary method of cultivation.

While records concerning gardens in Lübeck do not address well the use of technology, crop rotations, or yields of these parcels of land, they do reveal that plots of largely unknown size, often called gardens, existed outside the city walls and were cultivated for both industrial and food crops. They appear to have been a normal part of the life of the city and its inhabitants.

---

[7] *AHL (Archiv der Hansestadt Lübeck) ASA* Interna, Ämter, Gärtner 1/3.
[8] *LUB* III, 771.
[9] *AHL ASA* Interna Markt 9/1 and 9/2 deal with apple-sellers (1614) and the sale of garden produce in the market (1669), respectively.

The documentary evidence for garden produce in the city of Ghent is somewhat different. Empirical evidence of production of crops around Ghent is drawn from a variety of sources. Some tithe evidence enters the picture here as well, though it involves records of disputes over the payment of the so-called green tithe, paid on garden produce and animals. Rent records, concerning land both inside and outside the city, are useful here as well. Records of the sale of fruit to fruiterers within the city provide evidence about trade in garden produce.

Records of tithe disputes provide the names of some of the types of vegetables grown around Ghent, particularly in the Akker at Ekkergem, an area now within the city limits.[10] These vegetables included various types of cabbages, members of the onion family including garlic, leeks, parsley, parsnips and carrots, as well as the seeds of turnip, rape, onion, and cabbage. The dye plants madder and weld, used for red and yellow dyeing, were also grown. *Pachtcontracten*, or lease contracts, also provide evidence for the cultivation of various food crops around the city of Ghent.[11] Payments in kind included in these contracts reveal that fruit, vegetables, and flax, as well as various animal products and animals were produced in the city of Ghent to a distance of about thirty-five kilometres. Apples, pears, peas, beans, rapeseed, and flax were all paid as part of lease payments, in all cases along with a cash payment. The most common form of payment in kind was in flax, since the linen industry in Ghent had begun to flourish at the end of the thirteenth century.

Material relating to the use of land within the city is found in the so-called *landcijnsboeken*, records on the payment of leases on land within the city to the city government.[12] These records specify land use to some extent; they reveal that rent was to be paid on a garden, for example, or a house. There are many examples in which rent was paid on gardens, walled or unwalled, and with or without houses. However, these records do not state the use to which the garden was put. We are left to wonder whether these were pleasure gardens, with flowers and a place to sit, or small orchards and vegetable plots within the city?

Records of sale show that fruit was sold by residents of the surrounding villages to fruiterers in Ghent.[13] Over twenty-five varieties of apples and over twenty varieties of pears were sold and consumed within the city of Ghent. Nuts and cherries were also sold. The prices of these commodities fluctuated a great deal. Contracts were struck throughout most of the year, but fruit delivery mainly took place in October and November, revealing a trade in seasonal fruit. The people selling fruit within Ghent were

---

[10] *RAG (Rijksarchief Gent)* O1771 1425 August 9.

[11] A. de Vos, *Inventaris der Landbouwpachten in de Gentse Jaarregisters van de Keure. Verhandelingen der Maatschappij voor Geschiedenis en Oudheidkunde te Gent* (Ghent, 1958).

[12] *SAG (Stadsarchief Gent)* Reeks 152.2.

[13] *SAG* Reeks 301. Most of these records were identified by Victor van der Haeghen, a past archivist of the city of Ghent. *SAG*, Nota's van der Haeghen.

often identified as fruiterers and as such would have been members of the corresponding small guild.[14]

The documentary material discussed above will be familiar territory for many medieval historians. While documentary sources can provide useful information on cultivation, the range of plants that appears in them is often quite restricted. Archaeological evidence can expand this range considerably and add to our knowledge of plant consumption.

Palaeoethnobotany is the study of plant remains that survive in an archaeological context, and their relationship to human behaviour. Palaeobotany and archaeobotany are its synonyms. These plant remains can take the form of macrofossils, also called macroscopic plant remains (e.g., pieces that are visible to the naked eye) and microfossils (those that have to be examined under a microscope).

Palynology studies plant micro-remains, or pollen. The pollen of most plants is distinctive and individual, and therefore can be identified to genus, and in many cases to species level, under the microscope. Palynology has been very useful in assessing changes in vegetation over long periods of time; reduction of tree pollen and increases in cereal pollen can suggest the expansion of arable agriculture, while changes in types of tree pollen can suggest a change in the local environment for reasons of climate change or water level, for instance.[15] Pollen evidence in Ghent and Lübeck is rare; only one urban ecclesiastical site in Lübeck was analysed by a palynologist.[16]

By far the bulk of the material excavated in Ghent and Lübeck involved plant macroremains, or pieces of plant material visible to the naked eye. These typically consist of seeds, and less frequently root, stem, and leaf fragments. Left to themselves, plant remains will generally either rot, as in the case of roots or leaves, or sprout, as in the case of seeds. Both of these natural processes can be retarded by humidity or heat. Plant macroremains can be preserved quite well through carbonization, which occurs when they are in the presence of an oxygen-starved fire.[17] A fire with sufficient oxygen will

---

[14] Their guild was suppressed and merged into the guild of the grocers in 1540, and their guild hall, called the *Coelsteen*, which was at the corner of the Korenmarkt and the small Korenmarkt, was confiscated and sold. Maurice Heins, *Gand, sa vie et ses institutions, Tome III* (Gent: Maisons d'Éditions et d'Impressions, 1921-1923), 522. The suppression was part of a range of reforms instituted by Emperor Charles V as a punishment for Ghent's revolt in 1539-1540. For a thorough assessment of the relationship between Charles V and Ghent, his place of birth, see Marc Boone, "Le dict mal s'est espandu comme peste fatale: Karel V en Gent, stedelijke identiteit en staatsgeweld," *Handelingen der Maatschappij voor Geschiedenis en Oudheidkunde te Gent* 54 (2000): 31-63.
[15] Suzanne K. Fish, "Archaeological Palynology of Gardens and Fields," in Naomi F. Miller and Kathryn L. Gleason, eds., *The Archaeology of Garden and Field* (Philadelphia: University of Pennsylvania Press, 1994), 45.
[16] Fritz Rudolf Averdieck,"Botanische Bearbeitung von Proben der Grabungsplätze Heiligen-Geist-Hospital und Königstrasse in Lübeck," *Offa* 46 (1989): 307-31.
[17] Udelgard Körber-Grohne, *Nutzpflanzen in Deutschland. Kulturgeschichte und Biologie* (Stuttgart: Theiss Verlag, 1994), 16.

consume the remains, rather than preserve them.[18] Carbonization generally occurs as a result of human agency, for example an accidental fire during processing or food preparation. It can preserve details of seeds very well indeed, although shrinkage of about ten per cent tends to occur and some surface detail is lost in some cases.[19] Soft plant tissue usually undergoes more drastic changes, such as expansion or shrinkage, deterioration, or in some cases loss of delicate matter; this can interfere with the scientist's ability to compare archaeological material to current samples.[20] Plant material can also be preserved in clay that has been fired; no such material appears in the present study.[21] Much of the material in Ghent and Lübeck was not preserved in carbonized form, but was instead waterlogged.

A consistently moist environment, particularly when accompanied by a low level of acidity, can also preserve plant macroremains. Low levels of oxygen are present in waterlogged remains, and this provides favourable conditions for preservation of plant material.[22] These remains are in effect sub-fossils. Stems, roots, seeds, and seed-capsules are most often preserved; blossoms and leaves rarely survive. The outer husk survives the longest, while the organic material contained within the structure (germ, chlorophyll, etc.) breaks down much more quickly.[23] Areas with a high degree of organic content can also have a preserving effect. For this reason, cesspits and wells tend to be good sources of plant macro- and micro-remains.

Three considerations are valuable when examining palaeobotanical evidence: taphonomy, survival, and use of plants. It is important for the palaeobotanist to know how plant material came to arrive in the site that is being excavated, that is, its taphonomy. Pals, in his discussion of the taphonomy of plant material in wells, distinguishes between local, extralocal, and regional elements brought to the well in a natural way (i.e., not by human agency). This classification applies well to other types of sites and need not be restricted to wells. Local material consists of that growing immediately around or in the well while the well was in use, and the same type of plant growth in the period after the well went out of use. Extralocal material consists of elements from the surrounding agrarian landscape. Regional material would be that carried a further distance on the wind. Usually this material is tree pollen, and can be identified as regional only if there is external proof that that species was not part of the local vegetation.[24] An additional mechanism of dispersal is, of course, human or animal agency. Plant material can be brought to a site for processing (cleaning food, trimming wood) or for consumption (eating,

---

[18] J. P. Pals, "Reconstruction of Landscape and Plant Husbandry," in W. Groenman-van Waateringe and L. H. van Wijngaarden-Bakker, eds., *Farm Life in a Carolingian Village* (Assen: Van Gorcum, 1987), 53.
[19] Körber-Grohne, *Nutzpflanzen*, 16.
[20] Jon G. Hather, *An Archaeobotanical Guide to Root and Tuber Identification*. vol. I *Europe and South West Asia* (Oxford: Oxbow Books, 1993), vii.
[21] Körber-Grohne, *Nutzpflanzen*, 16-17.
[22] James Greig, *Archaeobotany. Handbooks for Archaeologists Number Four* (Strasbourg: European Science Foundation, 1989), 12-13.
[23] Körber-Grohne, *Nutzpflanzen*, 17.
[24] Pals, "Reconstruction," 55-57.

building). A great deal of plant material is preserved in cesspits as part of fecal material.

It is important to be able to establish whether the plant material is from the period of primary usage, or from a later period. A cesspit is a good example of the former; since it was used as a dumping ground, the plant material in it is likely to come from that very use. Wells, however, while they may contain material from plants growing around the edge during their period of use, may also contain plant material from the matter used to fill them after they went out of use.[25] In the cases of Ghent and Lübeck, most of the botanical finds come from cesspits and wells. Cesspits in particular provide evidence for consumption, since they are collecting points for both human and kitchen waste.[26] Although preservation condition in cesspits are usually good, the plant material found there can be damaged by mastication, processing (e.g., milling of grain), and the action of the human digestive system. Fruit stones are usually very well-preserved in cesspits, and can give insight into changes in the species consumed over centuries, as well as giving an indication of when new species were introduced into the diet. These new species can either be imported fruits, or fruit newly going into local cultivation.[27]

Another consideration to keep in mind when examining the results of palaeobotanical analysis is the use of the plant, and its relative number of seeds. The seeds of plants that are used for those seeds (hazel or poppy, for example) will survive in greater numbers than the seeds of plants used for their leaves or roots, like cabbage or carrots. Similarly, seeds of fruits that have their seeds embedded in them and are therefore part of the package will also make their way into cesspits at a greater rate; examples of such fruits are strawberries (*Fragaria vesca*), cherries (*Prunus avium*), and damsons (*Prunus insititia*). Another consideration is the number of seeds produced by each fruit. A single cherry produces one stone, while a single fig can produce thousands of seeds.

The third consideration is the survivability of plant remains. Pollen grains, seed, wood, and fruit-stones are the most resilient to rot, and are therefore most likely to survive. Root, stem, and leaf fragments are much less likely to survive, although some interesting work has been done on identification of waterlogged specimens.[28] Grains, legumes, and leaf and root vegetables are rarely well-preserved.[29] The material recovered in Ghent and Lübeck is almost entirely made up of seeds and fruit-stones, except for some

---

[25] Francis J. Green, "The Archaeological and Documentary Evidence for Plants from the Medieval Period in England," in W. van Zeist and W. A. Casparie, eds., *Plants and Ancient Man. Studies in Palaeoethnobotany* (Rotterdam, Boston: A. A. Balkema, 1984), 101.
[26] Karl-Heinz Knörzer, "Aussagemöglichkeiten von paläoethnobotanischen Latrinenuntersuchungen," 331-38.
[27] Ibid., 331.
[28] P. R. Tomlinson, "Vegetative Plant Remains from Waterlogged Deposits Identified at York," in Jane M. Renfrew, ed., *New Light on Early Farming. Recent Developments in Palaeoethnobotany* (Edinburgh: Edinburgh University Press, 1991), 109.
[29] Knörzer, "Latrinenuntersuchungen," 333-36.

roots found in the Korenmarkt in Ghent.[30] It would be incorrect to assume, however, that these seeds give an accurate representation of all the plants grown in these areas. Although no plant remains were found of the genus *Allium*, to which belong onions, leeks and garlic, the regulations of the Lübeck gardeners' guild show that cultivation of *Allium* occurred in Lübeck. Comparison of lists of plants found in digs and lists of plants mentioned in contemporary documents can thus prove illuminating.

It is clear, therefore, that direct correlations between botanical macro-remains and the type and number of plants consumed in the area cannot be established through excavation. One must always keep in mind the plant remains that may have been excreted or thrown into the cesspit, but which rotted or sprouted; the plants which were used before they set seed; and the plants which produce many seeds per fruit.

As noted above, material from cesspits, and to a lesser extent, wells, can provide good information on some of the plant material consumed and processed by humans. It is much less useful in telling us about production of that material. In the case of Ghent and Lübeck, there are three options for the provenance of this plant material. First, it could have been produced locally, either within the city or a short distance away. The local pollen record can be of some assistance in establishing this, although palynology in many cases is unable to be this specific. Documents with information on local production can be far more helpful. Plant macro-remains of hops (*Humulus lupulus*), combined with local records of rents of hop gardens, suggests that these hops were produced locally.

Second, the material could have been imported. In some cases, this is easy to establish, as in the case of exotic species such as figs, pepper, and coconuts.[31] These plants are too tender to grow in the northern climates of Ghent and Lübeck. It is, however, impossible to assess whether fruits or vegetables that grew in the area were imported from towns in the same general area with the same climatic conditions without additional documentary evidence.

The third possibility is that the plant macro-remains come from plants that grew in the area but were not cultivated. Many of the species found in cesspits come from plants that grow wild, but can also be cultivated. These include strawberries, apples, pears, raspberries, and blackberries. The question of whether the fruits of these plants were gathered from the wild or cultivated also remains open without more information, either from documents or from assessing the extent of available wild habitat in and around the city.

While the city of Ghent has an archaeological program, it has not engaged in the same depth of palaeobotanical analysis of its excavations as has the city of Lübeck. Much of the material published is relevant to a later time period. One exception is a find of dye plants in the Korenmarkt. Excavations in Ghent have turned up findings of dye plants, consisting of both weld and

---

[30] Jan Bastiaens, "Verven met weld en meekrap. Archaeobotanisch onderzoek van de Korenmarkt te Gent," *Stadsarchaeologie* 22, no. 2 (1998): 43-50.
[31] N. A. Paap, "Palaeobotanical Investigations in Amsterdam," in van Zeist and Casperie, *Plants and Ancient Man*, 340. No coconuts were found in Lübeck.

madder. These finds date from the late twelfth century, according to the coins that were buried in earlier layers. The macro-remains of weld consisted of whole stems with pieces of root attached (consistent with the practice of pulling the plant up from the roots); the stems had a great number of seeds attached and were therefore harvested after blooming.[32]

Fragments of madder also formed part of the find in the Korenmarkt in Ghent. This find consisted of root fragments, which had dyed the soil around them red. The first attested madder production in Flanders is from 1173, and by the thirteenth and fourteenth centuries the growth of madder in the clay coastal soils of Flanders and Zeeland seems to have been flourishing.[33] Madder production later declined as a result of the troubles of the Ghent textile industry. Regulations governing the sale of madder in Ghent stipulated the cleanliness of the roots to be sold, restricted its sale to those who had been granted the right to do so, and controlled the marking of madder sold, among other details.[34]

These finds are useful in buttressing the information gleaned from the tithe record of 1425, and show that madder and weld were cultivated outside Ghent and sold within the city, as regulations of the sale of dye plants also attest. Unfortunately, few palaeobotanical investigations of medieval sites within Ghent have been published.[35] This fact means that any analysis of production, sale, and consumption of plant produce is weighted heavily towards production and sale. There are few clues to tell us what plant foodstuffs were consumed by the different population strata of Ghent. Accounts of the abbeys of St. Peter and St. Bavo provide some of these clues. Evidence for consumption of wild plants such as berries is non-existent, because of the paucity of archaeological data. Our knowledge of garden produce in Ghent is effectively limited to that gleaned from documentary sources, and thus to a relatively restricted number of species.

---

[32] Bastiaens, "Verven," 43-44.

[33] Erik Thoen, "Technique agricole, cultures nouvelles et economie rurale en Flandre au bas Moyen Âge," *Flaran* 12 (1990): 56.

[34] *SAG Voorgebod* 1353.11.10 and *Ordinantie* from 1368. I am grateful to Leen Charles for drawing my attention to these items and for sharing her notes with me.

[35] Palaeobotanical investigations have been carried out in other settlements in Flanders; in the interests of methodological consistency, however, I have not examined this evidence here since it does not reveal anything about consumption in medieval Ghent. See Marnix Pieters, Brigitte Cooremans, Anton Ervynck and Wim van Neer, with Martine Hardy, "Van akkerland tot Heilige Geestkapel. Een kijk op de evolutie van de bewoningsgeschiedenis in de Kattestraat te Aalst (prov. Oost-Vlaanderen)," *Archeologie in Vlaanderen* 3 (1993): 299-329; Anton Ervynck, Brigitte Cooremans, and Wim van Neer, "De voedselvoorziening in de Sint-Salvatorsabdij te Ename (stad Oudenaarde, prov. Oost-Vlaanderen). 3. Een latrine bij de abtswoning (12de-begin 13de eeuw)," *Archeologie in Vlaanderen* 4 (1994): 311-22; Werner Wouters, Brigitte Cooremans, and Anton Ervynck, "Landelijke bewoning uit de volle middeleeuwen in Herk-de-Stad (prov. Limburg)," *Archeologie in Laundered* 5 (1995/1996): 159-77; Anton Ervynck, Brigitte Cooremans, and Wim van Neer, "De voedselvoorziening in de Sint-Salvatorsabdij te Ename (stad Oudenaarde, prov. Oost-Vlaanderen). 4. Een beer- en afvalput uit het gastenkwartier (1350-1450 AD)," *Archeologie in Vlaanderen* 45 (1995/1996): 303-15.

The case of Lübeck provides a significant contrast in this respect. Much of the evidence for consumption of garden produce in Lübeck is derived from the ambitious archaeological program undertaken since the Second World War by the city of Lübeck. This archaeological program has produced many site reports; six of these analyse plant remains found during the course of excavation.

A total of thirteen sites have been excavated within the city walls of Lübeck. Two of these are located in the artisans' quarter of the city, seven are from the merchants' and seafarers' section, and four are from ecclesiastical sites, namely monasteries and hospitals. Excavations in the market place have uncovered no botanical remains.[36] The botanical evidence recovered in the digs dates from the period before settlement to the seventeenth century. Evidence from the twelfth century to before 1615 is most relevant to the medieval historian. A total of seventy-one[37] types of macro-remains of useful[38] plants were found.

As a general rule in medieval Lübeck, people tended to live in an area with others of their socio-economic class, sometimes to the extent of residing in close proximity with those who followed their profession. Street names in Lübeck, such as Fleischhauerstrasse (Butcher Street) bear witness to this practice. A closer look at the evidence from sites in three different socio-economic areas of the city is revealing. St. Johanniskloster, a Benedictine monastery and thus an ecclesiastical site, was founded after 1173 on the eastern side of the peninsula, between Fleischhauerstrasse and Hundestrasse, next to the Wakenitz. Botanical analysis was done on samples taken from cultural layers from Period II that date to the beginning of the thirteenth century.[39]

A merchant site, an area that included the lots at the corner of the streets Alfstrasse and Schüsselbuden, was excavated in 1985.[40] A well at Alfstrasse 5 probably supplied water to the residents, both animal (suggested by the presence of straw and grain seeds) and human. The first stone building appeared in the early thirteenth century and is thought to have been one of the earliest secular buildings in the city. This large lot was subdivided in the early fourteenth century, as the area began to be filled in by the closely-built gable houses characteristic of this period.[41]

The excavations at Hundestrasse 9-17, an artisanal site, were carried out from 1974 to 1976. Hundestrasse itself runs east-west from Königstrasse to

---

[36] See Doris Mührenberg, "Der Markt zu Lübeck. Ergebnisse archäologischer Untersuchungen," *Lübecker Schriften zur Archäologie und Kulturgeschichte* 23 (1993): 83-154.
[37] This number does not include cereal plants. Nine cereal species were identified.
[38] This term is roughly translated from the German *Nutzpflanzen*. "Cultivated plants" is an inadequate translation, since some of the food plants were gathered from the wild.
[39] Almuth Alsleben, "Archäobotanische Untersuchungen in der Hansestadt Lübeck. Landschaftsentwicklung im städtischen Umfeld und Nahrungswirtschaft während des Mittelalters bis in die frühe Neuzeit," *Offa* 48 (1991): 332.
[40] Marianne Dumitrache and Monika Remann, "Besiedlungsgeschichte im Lübecker 'Kaufleuteviertel'," *Lübecker Schriften zur Archäologie und Kulturgeschichte,* 17 (1988): 108.
[41] Ibid., 110-111.

the Wakenitz. The street and its name date to the thirteenth century.[42] The high level of humidity in the ground meant that a great deal of plant material was preserved and many samples were taken from cultural layers, cesspits, and garbage dumps.[43] Building occurred on the site from the early thirteenth century, and buildings gradually took up a larger proportion of the area as the piece of land was divided into the properties Hundestrasse 9-17.[44] This building activity did not cover the entire surface area of the lots, and a certain amount of open land was left. Some of it was used for cesspits, at what would be the bottom of the garden.[45] This open land, and the cesspits in it, form the basis for the botanical evidence concerning Hundestrasse 9-17. The macroscopic plant remains of thirty-five samples were analysed.

Archaeological evidence shows that a wide range of fruits and vegetables were consumed on all three sites. Little disparity exists in the evidence from the thirteenth century on all three sites, suggesting that the standard of living at that time was fairly consistent across social levels. The St. Johanniskloster site does not present later evidence. Some of the evidence from St. Johanniskloster and Hundestrasse was slightly surprising. Archaeologists found very little herb evidence in an area thought to be a monastery garden; one would expect herbs to be plentiful in this area in light of documentary evidence from other sites. This anomaly may be due to preservation conditions or the fact that it is the leaves of many herbs that are dried and used, rather than their seeds. The monastery gardeners therefore would have had an incentive to see that their leafy herbs did not go to seed.

Evidence from Hundestrasse also presents something of a puzzle. Material found from the thirteenth century to before 1615 shows a consistently wide range of plant material, including fig seeds that must have been imported. This appears on a site that was known to be the home of a poorhouse. This evidence suggests that the poor may have been eating rather better than one assumes. Documentary evidence shows that the residents of Hundestrasse were primarily middle-class artisans[46]; the archaeological evidence suggests that this class of person ate a varied diet of locally available produce.

Material from Alfstrasse/Schüsselbuden dating from the thirteenth century does not differ markedly from that found at the other two sites. The real difference appears in the evidence from the sixteenth century; this is the only site in Lübeck containing significant numbers of exotic spices such as pepper and coriander. This evidence suggests a high standard of living for the

---

[42] Doris Mührenberg, "Archäologische und baugeschichtliche Untersuchungen im Handwerkerviertel zu Lübeck Befunde Hundestrasse 9-17. Mit einem botanischen Beitrag zu den spätmittelalterlichen und frühneuzeitlichen Pflanzenresten von Henk van Haaster," *Lübecker Schriften zur Archäologie und Kulturgeschichte* 16 (1989): 234.

[43] Hans-Georg Stephan, "Archäologische Ausgrabungen im Handwerkerviertel der Hansestadt Lübeck (Hundestrasse 9-17) -- ein Vorbericht," *Lübecker Schriften zur Archäologie und Kulturgeschichte* 1 (1978): 75.

[44] van Haaster, "Pflanzenresten," 271.

[45] See site diagrams in Mührenberg, "Handwerkerviertel," 262-70.

[46] Rolf Hammel, "Hauseigentum im spätmittelalterlichen Lübeck. Methoden zur sozial- und wirtschaftsgeschichtlichen Auswertung der Lübecker Oberstadtbuchregesten," *Lübecker Schriften zur Archäologie und Kulturgeschichte* 10 (1987): 130.

residents, as well as the possibility that the site was used by an importer of spices.

The botanical evidence derived from the archaeological digs in Lübeck records a wide variety of plants. The useful plants preserved there range from fruits, both wild and cultivated, nuts, vegetables, herbs, spices, and those used for flavouring beer, for fibre, and for oil. Some of these plants, such as hops and raspberries, are found throughout the city, in ecclesiastical, merchant, and artisanal sites. Others are found only in a very few places during a very short time period, such as the peppercorns found only in the merchants' area. In many cases, the evidence provided by plant remains is the only proof that exists that certain types of plants were grown or consumed within the city. This is one of the great boons offered to the historian by the archaeological evidence; it can throw open a window and show a much wider range than appears in the documentary evidence.

The case of Lübeck also reveals how this archaeological evidence can confirm what is known from the documents. Several of the plants found in the archaeological record, such as apples, hops, and cabbages also appear in the documents. This evidence suggests that produce grown outside the city was consumed within it, and that rural growers supplied the urban market.

The evidence from Lübeck shows not only what people of different economic and social status were consuming, but also how well documentary and archaeological evidence combine to provide a more complete picture than either can on its own. Study of medieval foodstuffs has relied for a long time on a variety of documentary sources. Research on grain production on large estates is based on the accounts of those estates. Urban records, such as tithe and rent payments, as well as land transfers are useful to the historian interested in food production and consumption in the city. The relatively new discipline of palaeoethnobotany can amplify the picture provided by these records a great deal. A comparison between Ghent and Lübeck amply illustrates this point; archaeological evidence from Lübeck adds more than fifty species unattested in the documentary records. Continued excavation and palaeobotanical analysis are thus crucial to the study of medieval foodstuffs.

- 2 -
Talking Numbers
Deconstructing Engineering Discourse

James Hull

Consider the following:

(j) For columns reinforced with both longitudinal steel and spirally wound hooping when the volume of hooping is equal to at least one per cent of the volume of the enclosed concrete and the longitudinal reinforcement is not less than one per cent, and not more than four per cent of the cross sectional area, the safe load shall be computed as follows:

Safe load (in pounds) = 650 (Ac + 15 As).

Ac = Net cross sectional area of concrete enclosed in hooping in square inches
As = Cross sectional area of longitudinal reinforcement in square inches[1]

This is an excerpt from a typical example of a technical standard. It has, partly incidentally and partly intentionally, an appearance of objectivity, rationality and factualness. As a product of engineering science – the derivation of technical rules from natural laws – it is ultimately rooted in the mechanical worldview of the Scientific Revolution which imagines the cosmos as composed of real world analogues of mathematical objects. The social meaning with which it is freighted draws more immediately on the Enlightenment's belief that that which is natural is rational but also moral.[2] Defined as "precise statement[s] of a set of requirements to be satisfied by a material, product, system, or service that also indicates the procedures for determining whether each of the requirements is satisfied,"[3] technical standards have conditioned the development of productive technology for the past hundred years. Our material culture is, usually invisibly, shaped by these standards. They are a form of engineering discourse, a way for engineers to talk with each other and to tell others what to do. Like other types of professional discourses they serve a hegemonic purpose, enabling the controllers of the discourse to exercise not just control of natural or human made objects but also

---

[1] Excerpted from By-Law 6107, City of Toronto Council, *Minutes* (1912), Appendix B, 468.
[2] See Tore Frängsmyr et al., eds., *The Quantifying Spirit in the 18th Century* (Berkley: University of California Press, 1990).
[3] *What is ASTM?*, undated and unpaginated pamphlet.

a measure of social control. As historians we wish to know how to eavesdrop on that discourse.[4]

At the very end of the nineteenth century large and complex firms such as the Pennsylvania Railroad in the United States and Siemens in Germany, operating in national, sometimes continental, scale markets began developing extensive in-house standards for their own usage. The companies imposed these standards on their multitudinous suppliers and helped prompt the formation of national standards-setting bodies for industry, including the American Society for Testing and Materials (ASTM), the British Engineering Standards Association and the German *Normalienausschuß für den deutschen Maschinenbau*. The same era saw the formation of capstone national scientific bodies such as the *Physikalisch-Technische Reichsanstalt*, Britain's National Physical Laboratory and the U.S. National Bureau of Standards, institutions devoted in large part to the techniques of exact measurement and the determination of physical constants and other work which underlies industrial standards. In Canada, the Canadian Engineering Standards Association (CESA) and the National Research Association were founded almost simultaneously during World War One.[5] Three trends abetted the penetration of technical standards into the industrial order. As part of its legitimating function, the State's regulation of industry, giving an appearance of democratic control over production, often took the form of highly technical codes and standards.[6] The secondary organization of industry encouraged a high-volume exchange of technical data amongst firms seeking security of enterprise via a flight from competition. Trusts, cartels, *zaibatsu*, *Interessengemeinschaften*, as well as freight car pools, power grids, patent pooling, and cross-licensing rested in part on a common base of both economic and technical information.[7] Finally their professional ambitions led to an increasing desire and practice by younger, university-trained engineers to use in contract specifications language similar to that which they had learnt in the classroom.

The economic role of standards is straightforward. Technical standards can resolve or obviate disputes between buyers and sellers of

---

[4] Albert Batik, *The Engineering Standard* (Ashland:Bookmaster/El Rancho, 1992) makes the point that standards are principally a means to communicate information. An excellent general guide to the world of technical and scientific practitioners is Bruno Latour, *Science in Action: How to Follow Scientists and Engineers through Society* (Milton Keynes: Open University Press, 1987).

[5] Samuel Krislov, *How Nations Choose Product Standards and Standards Change Nations* (Pittsburgh: University of Pittsburgh Press, 1997); Henry J. Stremba and Wayne P. Ellis, *Plain Talk* (Philadelphia: ASTM, 1990); *Memorial Volume Commemorative of the Life and Lifework of Charles Benjamin Dudley* (Philadelphia: ASTM, 1911); and David Cahan, *An Institute for an Empire* (Cambridge: Cambridge University Press, 1989).

[6] See Christopher Armstrong and H.V. Nelles, *Monopoly's Moment* (Philadelphia: Temple University Press, 1986).

[7] Thomas K. McCraw, ed., *Creating Modern Capitalism* (Cambridge: Harvard University Press, 1997); James P. Hull, "'The Surest Augury for Ultimate Success': The Release of Proprietary Technical Knowledge by U.S. Firms in the Early Twentieth Century," *Canadian Review of American Studies* 24 (Spring 1994): 61-86.

products, thus reducing transaction costs.[8] Parts standardization can also significantly reduce inventory costs. These are not abstract matters; high rates of throughput and stock turnover are critical markers of managerial success.[9] Firms eager to do business with one and other can consume costly time negotiating over fractions of an inch when not using common standards and can even end up being unable or unable fully to consummate a transaction. A standard can also play a role in reducing the cost of acquiring information crucial to the timing and extent of diffusion of best practice and further innovation.[10] Conversely, standards can tend towards conservatism, freezing existing practice rather than promoting advance. Standards may be adopted for reasons having more to do with market power or negotiating skills than technical excellence.[11] Standards can be and have been used in anti-competitive ways by firms against rivals and by governments as non-tariff barriers to trade.[12]

To study standards is to study a linguistic activity the key to which is its non-locality.[13] *Standardspeak*, we might call it, evolved as an engineering argot during the first half of the twentieth century, enabling engineers of similar training but diverse origins to communicate across both geographic and temporal barriers. Contracts written in the first decade of that century variously used references to brand names and trade catalogues and language which was either vague - "sand shall be clear and sharp and free from all loam or other earthy matter"[14] - or excruciatingly detailed:

> *Shaft 3 5/16" cases attached to draft chest by 3-7/8"cap screws & 1-7/8" through bolt at top. Gate shaft 1 ¾" net, 16 ft long. Gate stand bored 2 3/8 + 5/128". Gate brackets drilled for clamp holes not regular so no template kept. Bore*

---

[8] Janet T. Knoedler and Anne Mayhew, "The Engineers and Standardization," *Business and Economic History* 21 (1994): 141-51.

[9] Chandler of course argues that transaction costs were internalized within integrated corporations, though that is only one solution. Alfred D. Chandler Jr. *The Visible Hand* (Cambridge: Harvard University Press, 1977).

[10] Nathan Rosenberg, *Inside the Black Box* (Cambridge: Cambridge University Press, 1982), 20.

[11] North American colour television standards and the bar code provide egregious examples. Walter Kaiser, "The PAL-SECAM Colour Television Controversy," *History of Technology* 20 (1998): 1-16. Alan Q. Morton, "Packaging History: The Emergence of the Uniform Product Code (UPC)," *History and Technology* 11 (1994): 101-11.

[12] Notably, the American Society of Mechanical Engineers' boiler code created an effectively protected continental market for North American manufacturers of pressure vessels. Wilbur Cross, *The Code* (New York: ASME, 1990). More general discussions of the economics of standards are given in Donald J. Lecraw, "Some Economic Effects of Standards," *Applied Economics* 16 (1984): 507-22, and Charles Kindleberger, "Standards as Public, Collective and Private Goods," *Kyklos* 36 (1983).

[13] Drawing on Wittgenstein, this is the point made by Simon Schaffer in his "Modernity and Metrology," in Luca Guzzetti, ed., *Science and Power* (Luxemburg: OOPEC, 2000), 71-93.

[14] Archives of Ontario (hereafter AO), James Lewis Morris Papers, MU 4830, Pembroke Electric Light Co. Specifications, 1906.

> *2 3/8" Ptn. Spd. Extra set out to suit wall thimbles already set. 4 – ¾" cap screws. Gate arm spd. marked 30 & 36" hor. Gate rods ¾". Gate pins 7/8" std. btm.3/4" Std.* taps. *Gate blocks std Rack Std. 42"*[15]

The use of standards and the ability to refer to published standards allowed for an apparent economy and precision of language. Thus an Ontario Department of Highways form stated that sampling and tests of aggregates must be "in accordance with the following current A.A.S.H.O. methods" and that organic impurities were "subject to the sodium hydroxide colorimetric test [which] shall not produce a color darker than Figure 2 Plate 1 or the standard color in the current A.S.T.M. Standard Method c.40."[16] Similarly, the buyer and seller of a transformer could simply agree that it "will be tested in accordance with the A.I.E.E. rules."[17] Under a mature standards regime a contract could simply state that "[u]nless otherwise expressly provided in the specifications all goods and materials supplied shall conform to the specifications" of the CESA or if not of Canadian origin then "the recognized standards association of that country shall apply."[18] Perforce, this meant that only those who are *au fait* with the use of standards could be involved in contracting.

For all their vaunted objectivity, a closer look at the discourse surrounding standards shows that their creation and use involved negotiation, promotion, persuasion, and special pleading of all sorts. Moving from brand name or catalogue specifications to standards appeared to substitute engineering knowledge for commercial advantage but this could be deceptive and it could be contested. Seemingly objective standards could in fact be written so that only a single firm could meet them and manufacturers of highly regarded products could object to the allowance of substitutes in standards as something which would degrade best practice.[19] An advertising booklet of Robert W. Hunt & Company, a Montreal-based firm of engineers, assured potential users that they "can have [quality] cast iron pipe if you order according to the specifications of the American Water Works Association," adding "if you employ as your Inspectors, the Robert W. Hunt & Co. Ltd."[20] The booklet prints the 1908 standard specifications of the AWWA and the

---

[15] AO, MS 233, Barber Turbine & Foundries Ltd. Records, 17 December 1909 Delhi Light & Power Ltd.
[16] AO, MS 4036, D.H.O. Form no. 503, April 1946. (AASHO is the American Association of State Highway Officials)
[17] AO, Ferranti-Packard Papers, G.L. Simpson Canadian Container #5, Ferranti Transformer Specification Lectromelt Furnaces Ltd. to Frank T. Wyman 7 June 1926. (AIEE is the American Institute of Electrical Engineers)
[18] AO, RG15-55-1, vol. 25, St. Thomas Hospital contract file.
[19] AO, MU 772, Box 10, W.S. Leslie of A.C. Leslie & Co. Montreal to F.A. Dallyn, 3 September 1929. The A.C. Leslie Company's "Queen's Head" Copper Bearing Sheets enjoyed an excellent reputation among engineers and had long been specified by name in contracts.
[20] AO, MU 772, Box 10, Booklet Robert W. Hunt & Co. "Cast Iron Pipe Inspection" (Montreal, 1926), 3.

standard specification of United States Cast Iron Pipe & Foundry Company. In turn, a booklet of the latter firm noted that its products were "approved by the Underwriters' Laboratories of the National Board of Fire Underwriters" and prints the company's specifications which "are based upon the United States Government Master Specifications for ... Pipe."[21] The National Iron Corporation, Canadian manufacturer of such pipes, forwarded those two booklets to Frederick A. Dallyn, a prominent Ontario sanitary engineer, being desirous of quoting on a tender for a waterworks project in Colborne, Ontario.[22] As a working engineer Dallyn on a daily basis had to deal with standards issues. He was one of those who carried standards based ultimately on laboratory investigations out into the sewers of rural Canada.[23] His correspondence helps unveil this process. Thus we find him telling the Public Utilities Commission of Ingersoll that flouting the Canadian Fire Underwriters' Association's tough standards for municipal water supply did "not appear to have greatly influenced insurance rates."[24] Elsewhere he reassured the Commissioner of Works for York Township as to the safety of concrete pipe, thanks to ASTM standards, and disparaged the standards of the Ontario Department of Health as too conservative. Perhaps they were, but in assessing Dallyn's views and the Department's very public firing of him some years earlier they are worth keeping in mind.[25]

Standard testing procedures supposed to obviate disputes between parties by making commercial contentions technical issues to be resolved scientifically, themselves engendered passionate disputes precisely because commercial questions turned on them. Usually this went on out of sight of any but the parties involved and we must turn to engineers' papers to find them. Richard Hearn, future head of Ontario Hydro and first Chancellor of Brock University, did not hesitate to use his position as Chair of the Hydraulic Power Committee of the National Electric Light Association (NELA) to back a method for gauging velocity of water flow and testing water wheels introduced early on by Hydro at Niagara. This was at a time when the issue was being debated among several engineering and trade associations.[26] A 1925 dispute over steel for crane girders at the Riordon Pulp Company's power house involved Riordon, the engineering firm constructing the power house, an inspection firm, a firm of consulting engineers (for whom Hearn was working), and Ontario Hydro. At issue was whether the steel supplied did or did not meet

---

[21] Idem , "Handbook of de Lavaud Centrifically Cast Iron Pipe" (1928), 9.
[22] Idem , T.W. Hudson to Dallyn, 4 March 1931.
[23] James P. Hull, "Raising Standards: Public Works and Industrial Practice in Interwar Ontario," *Scientia Canadensis* XXV (2001): 7-30.
[24] AO, MU 765, Box 3, Dallyn to Public Utilities Commission of Ingersoll, 18 March 1929.
[25] AO, MU 769, Box 7, F.B. Goedike to Dallyn [sic], 10 June 1927, Dallyn to Goedike, 17 June 1927. See also Jamie Benidickson,, "Ontario Water Quality, Public Health and the Law, 1880-1930," in G. Blaine Bohr and Jim Phillips, eds., *Essays in the History of Canadian Law,* vol. 8 (Toronto: Osgoode Society, 1999), 115-41.
[26] AO, MU 8667, Box 32, File "National Electric Light Association." Also see editorial in *Canadian Engineer,* "New Method of Hydraulic Measurement," 16 September 1920, 357.

specifications. According to a variety of physical and chemical tests it did or it did not. Further, did the outcome of the tests mean that the steel was defective or the specifications wrong?[27] Trying to find an agreement on a source of water for the Ontario village of Glencoe depended on a disputed test of water which involved the village, Dallyn as consulting engineer, the Milton Hersey Company of Montreal doing chemical tests, the Ontario Department of Health, which by law had oversight over municipal waterworks, Professor E.G.R. Ardaugh of the University of Toronto Department of Chemistry in an advisory capacity, and the Canadian National Railway wanting water for the boilers of its locomotives stopping at Glencoe.[28]

Most usually however, similarly trained engineers used the language of standards comfortably as part of their daily work and in their communication with one and other. When involved in the purchase of a transformer from the Packard electrical equipment manufacturing company, Hydro's Chief Engineer, F.A. Gaby, wrote to C.W. Baker of Packard's Transformer Department drawing attention to the "Westinghouse Bulletin titled 'Hottest Spot Indicators for Transformers'" and asked Baker to "follow this procedure." In his notes on the calibration of the indicator, Baker recorded "[a]dd 10°C to this to conform to AIEE conventional Hot Spot temperature" and ordered a thermocouple "to check the thermometer by means of a galvanometer in Hydro's possession."[29]

Although noted for being particularly demanding in their specifications, Ontario Hydro's engineers had to negotiate their application of standards. This could be quite explicit, as when Hydro's Director of Engineering, J.R. Montague, was told that the Commission's "detailed material and test requirements" for a type of electrical cable "have been evolved in co-operation with several cable manufacturers."[30] When the specifications for Ontario Hydro's turbines at Ear Falls were being developed, the Commission's Test and Inspection Department's Chief Hydraulic Engineer, Dr. Otto Holden, had no qualms about identifying what one purpose of standards was, suggesting "[t]he inclusion of clauses in addition to those contained in the specifications for steel castings and forgings which we believe to be desirable and which will serve to eliminate disputes between the inspectors and the manufacturers." He further advised a change in specification for a grade of bronze used in a turbine so as to oblige the manufacturer to accept the argument that it was an industry standard in practice if not in name.[31] Holden also counselled use of CESA instead of ASTM specifications "for the purpose of recognizing the work of C.E.S.A., and to eliminate the criticism from Canadian manufacturers which in

---

[27] AO, MU8673, Box 38, File "Riordon, Concrete - P.H. (Power House).
[28] AO, MU 764, Box 2, File "Glencoe - water supply - correspondence, 1928-29," 32.
[29] AO, Ferranti-Packard papers, Container #10, Gaby to Baker [n.d.] and Baker "Notes," 25 March 1929.
[30] Hydro One Networks Inc., Archives, GSI Collection, Accession #91-209, Bin #3-11, Box 9314, Aug 1950, F.H. Chandler to J.R. Montague, Specification #C491001 "For Thermoplastic Control Cable for 600 Volt Service."
[31] Hydro One Networks Inc., Archives, ORR, Material Specifications for Turbines, Remarks of O. Holden, 18 February 1939.

all probability would result if the specification was not used."[32] This was not always possible; a proposed change to CESA from ASTM specifications for materials for transmission towers ended up using general CESA steel standards but ASTM standards for steel bolts. Some suggested improvements were rejected as not practical though good in principle. Others were needed on the grounds that the existing standards, while very good, were "not readily enforceable." [33] In examining these few examples of technical negotiations we can see how standards derived not so much from the requirements of the physics of materials but from commercial, professional, political, and practical pressures.

We can and should penetrate more deeply into the sociology of standards. Historians and sociologists of science and technology have in recent years done much to clarify our understanding of a set of issues relating to measurement and quantification. Technical standards are increasingly being recognized as an important part of this.[34] Engineers and scientists wish to have standards regarded "as properties of nature rather than contingent outcomes of cultural work." However their precision in particular "is the result, rather than the cause, of consensus."[35] Further, modern sociologies of knowledge have problematized the very factualness of facts, drawing particular attention to the relationships between that factualness and the verbal and numerical inscription of the fact.[36] Metrology is autonomous of neither social nor natural forces; it is an activity carried out by metrologists with some institutional authority backing them up. The discourse over technical standards, their claimed rationality and objectivity, rests in large part on their claim to a precision and accuracy which is independent of the measurer. The use of standard instruments allows facts both to be de-localized and commodified.[37] In a penetrating discussion, Patrick Carroll-Burke coins the term "epistemic engines" for the tools of metrology,

---

[32] Ibid. See also James Hull, "Technical Standards and the Integration of the U.S. and Canadian Economies," *The American Review of Canadian Studies* 32, no. 1 (Spring 2002): 123-42.

[33] Hydro One Networks Inc., Archives, GSI Collection, Accession #91-209, Bin #3-11, Box 931, W.P.Dobson (Hydro's Chief Testing Engineer and later Director of Research) to A.E. Davison (engineer in the Transmission Section), 20 December 1939.

[34] The literature is voluminous and growing. Good staring points are Jed Z. Buchwald, ed., *Scientific Credibility and Technical Standards* (Dordrecht: Kluwer, 1996); Donald MacKenzie, *Inventing Accuracy* (Cambridge: MIT Press, 1989); Andrew Barry, "The History of Measurement and the Engineers," *The British Journal for the History of Science* 26 (1993): 459-68; Jan Golinski, *Making Natural Knowledge* (Cambridge: Cambridge University Press, 1998); Ken Alder, "Making Things the Same," *Social Studies of Science* 28 (1998): 499-545; Witold Kula, *Measures and Men* (Princeton: Princeton University Press, 1986); and Theodore Porter, *Trust in Numbers* (Princeton: Princeton University Press, 1995).

[35] Simon Schaffer, "Accurate Measurement as English Science" in M. Norton Wise, ed., *The Values of Precision* (Princeton: Princeton University Press, 1995), 135-72.

[36] Mary Poovey, *A History of the Modern Fact* (Chicago: University of Chicago Press, 1998).

[37] Arne Hessenbruch, "Calibration and Work in the X-Ray Economy, 1896-1928," *Social Studies of Science* 30 (2000): 397-420.

calling them "crucial boundary objects in ... standardization."[38] The famous "thickness of a shilling" was a good enough standard for James Watt and could be judged in a way that any could grasp. The new industrial science required not just new instrumentation but acceptance that their numerical readings should be privileged over qualitative, sensory observation. In the end though it is the readers of the instruments and not the instruments themselves who are and who demand to be exercising judgement.

A traditional measure was something bargained face-to-face; in industrial society not so.[39] Engineers learnt in the classroom concepts and techniques of measurement and their meaning. They then carried this technical result into industry, making of it a social practice. Sometimes, however, it did not work. Many physical qualities which could be tested and which industry engineers would have like to have quantified proved recalcitrant. We can see different methodologies of testing and thus different epistemologies of production coexisting. The specifications for steel transmission towers used by Ontario Hydro included not just chemical tests of some sophistication but also what was dignified as a "Hammer Test" for galvanizing, essentially hitting a sample of material with a hammer to see if the coating flaked off.[40] Sensory observation of the simplest sort continued to be recommended even in specialized texts well into the twentieth century. One text included fifty pages on chemical methods for testing volatile oils but only after the author discussed the usefulness and limitations of the nose as a testing device.[41] Gelatines could be tested in an apparatus that applied increasing weight until penetrating the surface. But the preferred method simply involved poking the sample and comparing its resistance to that of standard samples.[42] Varnish film could be tested by thumbnail and thumb pressure for "tackiness" in drying or a device known as a Filometer could do the same. However, one technical expert insisted "an indifferent operator with an elaborate instrument [may] give a less true opinion of a varnish film than a true expert with his thumb and thumbnail."[43] This would seem to present a lingering victory for rule of thumb over the micrometers and pyrometers but in a deeper sense even that is not true. When reading even the most exact of instruments the readers used their bodies making the act of reading and the cognitive and cultural dimensions of perception crucial aspects of even the most hardware intensive mensuration.[44]

---

[38] Patrick Carroll-Burke, "Tools, Instruments and Engines: Getting a Handle on the Specificity of Engine Science," *Social Studies of Science* 31 (2001): 593-626.
[39] These issues are explored in James P. Hull, "Working With Figures: Industrial Measurement as Hegemonic Discourse," *Left History* 9 (2003): 62-78.
[40] Hydro One Networks Inc., Archives, GSI Collection, Accession #91-209, Bin #3-11, Box 93, General Specifications for Steel Transmission Towers, S.T.-010327.
[41] E. Gildemeister, *The Volatile Oils* (New York: Wiley, 1913), 553-617.
[42] R. Livingston Fernbach, *Glues and Gelatine* (New York: Van Nostrand, 1907), 20-48.
[43] McIntosh, *Varnishes*, 422.
[44] H. Otto Sibum, "Les gestes de la mesure. Joule, les pratiques de la brasserie et la science," *Annales: Histoire, Science Sociales* 53 (1998): 745-74; Graeme Gooday, "Spot-watching, Bodily Postures and the 'Practised Eye': The Material Practice of Instrument Reading in Late Victorian Electrical Life," in Iwan Rhys Morus, ed., *Bodies/Machines* (New York: BERG, 2002), 165-95.

Nonetheless, and crucially, having acknowledged the superiority of their approach to measurement, in which standards played so large a role, was vital to engineers' professional aspirations. Rooted in Enlightenment ideals of scientific rationality, this mathematized discourse of measurement came to be broadly regarded in society as having an especial validity. This implicitly privileged the actions of those controlling the discourse. This desire to measure and quantify was however a desire to impose not a natural order but a very human one.[45] University trained engineers saw standards as a key part of their vision of the profession and their vision of themselves in society. Standards at the work site are part of engineers' exercise of intellectual as well as managerial authority.[46] Standards redistributed power away from skilled workers to laboratory engineers who established and oversaw testing methodologies. Those who developed the standards were sometimes quite explicit about the power relationships being established. During the construction of its Niagara Falls generating station, Ontario Hydro developed what were probably the most technically sophisticated concrete standards in the world. Hydro's Toronto laboratory would be the centre for testing. A field lab for testing and inspection would be established and testing done at the cement mills was integrated into the purchasing and delivery process. The suppliers would use dedicated cement bins for Hydro which Hydro inspectors would test and oversee. Inspectors would test samples hourly using an on-site lab with later tests to check and record at the Toronto laboratory. The scheme placed control in the hands of the central lab over the inspection forces and ultimately suppliers since, as the architects of this scheme asserted, the "laboratory is better fitted to supervise inspection work than an inspector is to supervise laboratory work." The claimed pay-off for granting the technical authority of that lab would be "proper quality and an uninterrupted supply." [47]

Many of these issues can be explored in the context of a case study, one introduced by the example at the beginning of this paper - the City of Toronto Building Code. As the city of Toronto re-built from a disastrous 1904 fire which destroyed much of the downtown,[48] the municipal building code strained to keep up both with the commercial demands of builders and the evolution of reinforced concrete construction. These strains resulted in a public

---

[45] See J. L. Heilbron's "Introductory Essay" in Frängsmyr et al., *Quantifying Spirit*, 1-23.

[46] Yehouda Shenhav, *Manufacturing Rationality* (Oxford: Oxford University Press, 1999); Burton Bledstein, *The Culture of Professionalism* (New York: Norton, 1976); Amy Slaton, *Reinforced Concrete and the Modernization of American Building, 1900-1930* (Baltimore: Johns Hopkins University Press, 2001); Stuart Shapiro, "Degrees of Freedom: The Interaction of Standards of Practice and Engineering Judgment," *Science, Technology & Human Values* 22 (1997): 286-316; Amy Slaton, "'As Near as Practicable': Precision, Ambiguity, and the Social Features of Industrial Quality Control," *Technology and Culture* 42 (2001): 51-80.

[47] Hydro One Networks Inc., Archives, ORR 842.2, "Report on Cement and Concrete Tests and Specifications." See also Benjamin Sims, "Concrete Practices: Testing in an Earthquake-Engineering Laboratory," *Social Studies of Science* 29 (1999): 483-518, and James Hull, "'A Gigantic Engineering Organization': Ontario Hydro and Technical Standards for Canadian Industry, 1917-1958," *Ontario History,* 93 (2001): 179-200.

[48] Frederick H. Armstrong, *A City in the Making* (Toronto: Dundurn Press, 1988), 296-327.

inquiry, reorganization of the City Architect's office, appointment of a new, more professionally qualified, City Architect and a revised building code. Commentators at the time, including members of City Council, lauded the outcome as one which brought scientific rationality in the form of up-to-date technical practice to the overseeing and facilitation of the city's growth.

Most obviously this story sounds familiar to historians of North American urbanization and technology. It is a story of the rise of administrative expertise in municipal governance and a story of new engineering techniques based on laboratory investigation and university level programs of training. In both cases these stories have been told in terms of rational practice winning out over the customary. While occasionally still told this way, historians have for some time problematized such a view. The triumph of appointed administrators over grasping ward-healers seems much less obviously a victory of the good guys over the bad guys but rather a much more subtle dynamic as various groups contended for authority and advantage in expanding turn-of-the-century cities. Engineers wielded their new knowledge as much to their own benefit as for a claimed social good and that knowledge could be and was used to gain commercial advantage. In fact, the harder we probe, the more the claims of a victory of rationality break down. This is true if we criticize a naïve sociology of knowledge which reifies "facts" as things other than contested claims. It is true also if we simply ask *cui bono*.

The construction industry began pressing the City Architect and City Council in 1911 for changes in the municipal building by-law. Critics added defects with the code to a growing bill of particulars being advanced against the City Architect. By the late summer some Aldermen were proposing an inquiry into the Architect's office. A number of local engineers helped draw the daggers. In particular, University of Toronto Civil Engineering Professor C.R. Young labelled some regulations "unreasonable and unpractical," called an investigation "desirable," and insisted that the objections being voiced against the by-laws and the Architect's office were "made from a scientific standpoint."[49] The resulting inquiry under Judge Herbert Denton heard from 170 witnesses and resulted in a 2,500-page report. In it Denton urged that the "City Architect's Department should be completely reorganized under a new name and with increased jurisdiction and powers." The city's building inspection system was singled out for criticism, the Judge noting that "[t]he majority of the present inspectors are either bricklayers or carpenters." Denton recommended higher qualifications for the City Architect, as professional witnesses had urged. The Building By-law was characterized as excessively long and conservative and in need of revision for clarity and to reduce the cost of building. In coming to his conclusions, Judge Denton had relied heavily on a report produced by Professor Young, a rising star in the Canadian engineering profession. At the University of Toronto, where he would one day become Dean of Engineering, he taught engineering students the best new ideas in the use of standards and specifications in contract writing. Shortly after submitting his report to Denton, Young published an article based on it in which he offered scathing criticism of the existing by-law as much too strict, conservative, and

---

[49]*Toronto Evening Telegram*, 16 August 1912, 13-15.

adding materially to the cost of buildings especially by requiring too much steel in reinforced concrete construction.[50]

All of this is in the public record, indeed prominently reported in daily newspapers in Toronto. It is in Young's private papers however that we find a missing piece of the puzzle. In addition to his public role Young had been the key member of a committee developing a standard building regulation for the Canadian Cement and Concrete Association (CCCA). The Association had as its central purpose the promotion of concrete as a building material, and numbered among its members some of the City Architect's bitterest enemies.[51] The differences between its standard and the existing Building By-law informed the technical criticism of the latter in the summer of 1912.[52] During the Denton inquiry *The Canadian Engineer* recalled that changes in the Toronto building code in 1912 removed "a little of the undue severity ... towards reinforced concrete construction" but that much of the revision recommended to the City in 1911, based on the CCCA standard, had not been adopted.[53] In effect, Young was using both the technical press and his role as a paid expert witness to criticise the Toronto City Architect for not using a standard which he had played a principal role in developing. Moreover, it was one developed for a building material trade association with its own interests very much at heart. This alone demystifies some of the aura of scientific rationality surrounding this particular technical standard.

Standards are an important, literally a defining, part of material culture and the industrial order. The discourse around them is a specialized one but one which is accessible at a number of points. In the first place standards are by their very nature public or at least open. They are published and easy to find. As well as in sources which formally promulgate standards, they can be encountered in contracts, laws, and regulations. On rare occasions they were the subject of open debate, either in the general press or more specialized technical publications. Digging more deeply in engineers' papers and the papers of public and private bodies using technical standards can produce a wealth of information on how standards were developed and used. These documents may be read at a number of levels. The first is the surface level where we can treat them as part of the history of technology narrowly considered. That surface reading should not be ignored lest we forget that standards actually do, physically and economically, what they claim to do. They can also be read for what they say about social as well as technical and economic considerations. We can then go further and attempt to deconstruct these standards. In addition to their own analytic and forensic skills, historians

---

[50] C.R. Young, "The Structural Requirements of the Toronto Building By-Law of 1913," *The Canadian Engineer*, 26 February 1914, 383-88.

[51] *Programme of the 1st Annual Meeting of the Canadian Cement and Concrete Association* (Toronto, 1909).

[52] The CCCA code is given in *Canadian Cement and Concrete Association Proceedings* (1911), 86-95. Young's correspondence regarding the code is in University of Toronto Archives, Department of Civil Engineering papers, C.R. Young correspondence, A66-0011, Box 05.

[53] "Defects in the Toronto Building By-Law," *The Canadian Engineer*, 26 February 1914, 381.

can borrow techniques from the sociology of knowledge and ideas about language. Engineers' commitment to standards did not derive merely from an analysis of their economic efficiency. As well, an ideology of progress, a commitment to a "rational factory," sped the adoption of the new technology.[54] Engineers' ideology of rationality informed a hegemonic discourse. Integral to its success was the veiling of such a purpose. But with both theory and more traditional historical detective work we can lift the veil and see the manner and purposes of the construction of these standards.

---

[54] I am borrowing the term from Lindy Biggs, *The Rational Factory* (Baltimore: Johns Hopkins University Press, 1997).

– 3 –

Model Behaviour
A Material Culture Approach to the History of Anatomy Models

Susan Lamb

The anatomical model - a re-creation of normal or pathological anatomy created in various material - is usually regarded as simply a teaching aid for those studying to be physicians, and although the historical discourse surrounding anatomy often testifies to that purpose alone, a diversity in its function emerges if the researcher looks beyond the written text. The artistic choices made by creators of anatomical models reinforce messages about how a society views its own corporality, and by examining the way in which anatomy models are fabricated and decorated, cultural attitudes about the body in a given time period can be analysed and better understood. This study will consider both an eighteenth century and a twentieth century anatomy model, and will show that groups outside the world of medicine were encouraged to view, examine, and interact with anatomical models. In each instance, the visual details of the reproduction provide historical insight into the social and cultural messages their use was intended to reinforce.

The challenge for the historian then, becomes accessing the historical evidence that is not written down. By taking an approach that includes the methodologies and techniques used by material culture studies, the intricate historical narrative can be more thoroughly interpreted. Material culture methods rely upon material evidence like consumer goods, architecture, clothing, landscape, photography, and museum pieces to inform historical inquiry. As Anne Smart Martin noted, "Material objects matter because they are complex, symbolic bundles of social, cultural and individual meanings fused onto something we can see, touch and own."[1] Each thing forged by humankind is produced for a reason and in each instance, the maker has in his or her mind the reason as to why the item should exist and why it should look the way it does. Jules Prown asserts that by taking a material culture approach, the researcher can exploit the "empathic link" which exists between the material world of the object and the perceiver's world of existence and experience. In other words, the observer can reflect upon what it would be like to use or interact with the object, and be "transported into the depicted world."[2] This concept of the "empathic link" will be utilised in this investigation of two very different anatomical representations.

The cultural history of the body and its representations continues to generate a vast number of works, spanning a diverse range of themes from

---

[1] Ann Smart Martin, "Makers, Buyers, and Users: Consumerism as a Material Culture Framework," *Winterthur Portfolio* 28, nos. 2/3 (1993): 141-57.
[2] Jules Prown, "Mind in Matter: An Introduction to Material Culture Theory and Method," *Winterthur Portfolio* 17, no. 1 (1982): 1-19.

autopsy to art, and from metaphor to the Madonna. Much of the literature on anatomical modeling has been focused on the genealogy, use, and influence of those anatomy models created in wax.[3] This is not surprising given that the advent of wax anatomical modeling coincided with, and according to some scholars, reified other sweeping political, philosophical, religious, and social transformations happening in Europe in the eighteenth century.[4] One is hard-pressed, however, to find academic investigations devoted to the more recent manufacture and use of anatomy models made from materials other than wax. The aim of this paper is to add further insight to the existing body of literature on wax anatomical models, and to begin to explore the relatively new domain of twentieth century models and their social meanings.

As is well known, the eighteenth century saw great change in Western and European intellectual thought. A new model of natural knowledge emerged that was based on dualistic, atomistic, and mechanistic assumptions. A rigid distinction between mind and body had been posited by philosophers like René Descartes and John Locke[5] in the century before, and their ideas, along with those of many others, were used as the basis for experimental activity over the eighteenth century.[6] Experimentation prompted new accounts of vitality and the relationship of body and soul, and discussion flourished

---

[3] See Rebecca Messbarger, "Waxing Poetic: Anna Morandi Manzolini's Anatomical Sculptures," *Configurations* 9, no.1 (2001): 65-97; Thomas Schnalke, *Diseases In Wax: The History of the Medical Moulage*, Kathy Spatschek, trans. (Zurich: Quintessence Publishing, 1995); Jonathan Simon, "The Theater of Anatomy: The Anatomical Preparations of Honore Fragonard," *Eighteenth-Century Studies* 36, no.1 (2002): 63-79.

[4] Michel Lemire, "Representations of the Human Body: The Colored Wax Anatomical Models of the 18th and 19th Centuries in the Revival of Medical Instruction," *Surgical and Radiological Anatomy* 14 (1992) 283-91; Rebecca Messbarger, "Waxing Poetic," 65-97.

[5] For Descartes, mind and matter were incommensurable: matter was quantifiable and the mind or soul was insubstantial and immortal, and the two could (almost) never meet. This philosophy is expanded upon in his *Discourse On Method*. In his *Essay Concerning Human Understanding*, Locke proposed the notion of the *tabula rasa*, stating that prior to the acquisition of knowledge the mind was a blank sheet of paper, after which it was shaped by experience. Summary taken from Roy Porter, *The Greatest Benefit to Mankind: A Medical History of Humanity* (New York: W.W. Norton and Company, 1997), 217, 243.

[6] The literature on both the Enlightenment and the Scientific Revolution is vast, including the literature as to the legitimacy of those very terms. For an introductory, but comprehensive and critical, survey of the former, see Thomas Munck, *The Enlightenment: A Comparative Social History* (London: Arnold, 2000) or Dorinda Outram, *The Enlightenment* (Cambridge: Cambridge University Press, 1995. For the latter, see A. Cunningham and P. Williams, "De-centring the Big Picture," *British Journal for the History of Science* 26 (1993): 407-32 or Steven Shapin and Simon Schaffer, *Leviathan and the Air-pump: Hobbes, Boyle, and the Experimental Life* (Princeton: Princeton University Press, 1985). For historiography see David C. Lindberg, "Conceptions of the Scientific Revolution from Bacon to Butterfield: A Preliminary Sketch," in David C. Lindberg and Robert S. Westman, eds., *Reappraisals of the Scientific Revolution* (Cambridge: Cambridge University Press, 1990), 1-26.

within the republic of letters[7] in an attempt to re-examine the laws of health and sickness.[8]

These new ideas challenged a centuries-old medical canon that had been formulated and practiced according to the texts of the Greek physician Galen. Often referred to as humoral medicine,[9] this complex set of beliefs decreed that the body and the cosmic realm were closely connected, and that sickness and ill-health were visible on the exterior of the body.[10] Renaissance anatomical studies, however, had begun to reveal that the structures of the body were not exactly as Galen had described, and William Harvey's discovery of the circulation of the blood in the 1620s further called into question the wisdom of ancient medical belief.[11] Harvey's account of the heart and circulation found favour with Descartes who used it to promote a mechanical philosophy. Descartes regarded medicine as one of the keys to understanding the natural world and often dissected animals, producing several works on what would now be called the life sciences. Overall, the Cartesian view of the body would revolutionize the study of medicine; Descartes regarded the body exactly as he viewed the world as a mechanism and he dismissed the Aristotelian-Galenic idea of the relation of body and cosmos.[12] Thus, by the middle of the seventeenth century, traditional medical knowledge was being challenged, and opening up dead bodies or live animals had become one of the places to locate new truths.[13] All of this makes clear the important point that what we understand as "science" was not yet a separate discipline with practitioners of its own, nor was it disparate from the study of philosophy. It was practiced

---

[7] The so-called "republic of letters" was an informal and international network of contacts and correspondence which was essential to the world of learning in the dissemination of new Enlightenment ideas. See Munck, *Enlightenment* or Outram, *Enlightenment*.

[8] Harold J. Cook, "The New Philosophy and Medicine in Seventeenth-century England," in Lindberg and Westman, *Reappraisals of the Scientific Revolution*, 400; Andrew Wear, *Knowledge and Practice in English Medicine, 1550-1680* (Cambridge: Cambridge University Press, 2000), 365.

[9] "The doctrine of the four humors was not Galenic; it was Hippocratic. But the emphasis on these four humors as *the* Hippocratic humors, the linking of them with the Aristotelian qualities and with the tissues in the body was largely Galenic." From Owsei Temkin, *Galenism: Rise and Decline of a Medical Philosophy* (London: Cornell University Press, 1973), 103.

[10] Mary Lindemann, *Medicine and Society in Early Modern Europe* (Cambridge: University of Cambridge Press, 1999), 9-17; Katherine Young, "Management of the Grotesque Body in Medicine," in Katherine Young, ed., *Bodylore* (Knoxville: Tennessee University Press, 1993), 126.

[11] Harvey's innovation was one important factor that contributed to the decline of Galenic theory. For a comprehensive and careful treatment of Galenic medicine, including the impact of Harvey, consult Temkin, *Galenism*. For Harvey in a broad context, and a critical historiography, see Lindemann, *Medicine and Society in Early Modern Europe*, 67-85. For a detailed account of Harvey's discovery see Jerome J. Bylebyl, "William Harvey, A Conventional Medical Revolutionary," *JAMA* 239, no. 13 (March 27, 1978): 1295-98.

[12] Andrew Wear, "Early Modern Europe, 1500-1700," in Lawrence I. Conrad, et al., eds., *The Western Medical Tradition* (Cambridge: Cambridge University Press, 1995), 339-40.

[13] Ibid., 349-50. For a fuller account of the history of dissection see Temkin, *Galenism*, 135-38.

within other disciplines under the general term "natural philosophy."[14] As Cunningham and Williams noted, "the whole point of natural philosophy was to look at nature and the world as created by God, and thus as capable of being understood as embodying God's powers and purposes."[15] To that end, many men, along with some women, began to seek out an understanding of nature through a multitude of means.

By the mid-eighteenth century, natural knowledge was seen as an appropriately genteel pursuit for members of aristocratic society.[16] Science gradually became visible and accessible to the broader public with an expanding publications market that included books on popular science; in urban centres there were public lectures and scientific demonstrations, along with the creation of scientific societies.[17] Diderot and D'Alembert published their *Encyclopédie* and Parisians especially indulged themselves in a passion for natural history which included an anatomy craze. Lectures and anatomical demonstrations were held in the drawing rooms of Paris, and aristocratic women went so far as to carry with them dried specimens prepared by famous anatomists.[18] The pursuit of both scientific understanding and amusement included visits to newly-opened anatomical collections.

The vogue for artificial anatomy in Europe was largely due to the prestige conferred upon the Specola Museum, the first great collection of anatomic wax models, which belonged to the Grand Duke of Tuscany, brother of Joseph II of Austria. It was a collection formed by the naturalist Felice Fontana in 1775, with the intent of both augmenting the natural knowledge of anatomy and honouring his sovereign and patron. Fontana's aim was to establish a collection that would demonstrate all knowledge of the human body in order to teach anatomy without having to directly observe a cadaver[19] and without the need of a demonstrator or guide.[20] The collection was three-faceted in that each example consisted of a wax model, a tempera drawing, and a written explanation.[21]

---

[14] Lindemann, *Medicine and Society in Early Modern Europe*, 66-67; Outram, *Enlightenment*, 48.

[15] A. Cunningham and P. Williams, "De-centring the Big Picture," 407-32.

[16] Arnold Thackray, "Natural Knowledge in Cultural Context," *American Historical Review* 79 (1974): 675-98.

[17] Outram, *Enlightenment*, 47-62.

[18] Lemire, "Representation of the Human Body," 286.

[19] Web site of the Natural History Museum of the University of Florence, Zoological Section, "La Specola"1999, Marta Poggesi: text, Saulo Bambi: photos, Daniele Parpagnoli: web design, http://www.specola.unifi.it/cere/history.htm.

[20] Lemire, "Representation of the Human Body," 288.

[21] The Specola collection still exists today, with some models on permanent display at the Natural History Museum of the University of Florence, Italy. The entire collection was exhibited to the public in 1999. The permanent display consists of rooms of various themes, designed to move the visitor from the outside of the body to its inner-most structures, with the configuration of the rooms having been in existence since the collection's formation in the eighteenth century. The Specola collection includes portrayals of skinned or flayed figures, partial and full representation of dissection, and replicas of specific anatomical structures and organs. See Annette Burfoot, "Surprising

Guided by Fontana, talented wax modelers worked under anatomists who dissected cadavers obtained from the Santa Maria Nuova hospital and who exposed the part to be modeled. The element was reproduced in clay from which a plaster cast was made. Into this the wax, or rather, a mixture of waxes, resins and dyes, of which the exact composition is unknown, was poured. Finally, the model was assembled and artistic elements refined.[22]

The models and figures that make up the Specola collection are numerous and varied. There are the so-called "muscle men" who are full-sized, upright figures with certain organic systems as their focal point; several portray the nervous system, tissue composition, or the organization of muscle masses. Some sculptures depict the various stages of decomposition, while others illustrate views that can otherwise only be achieved with the dissection blade, like a cross-section of an organ or limb. For many observers, the centre-piece of this large assemblage is a full-size female figure known as the Medical Venus (Figure 1).

The model lies flat on a velvet cushion and under a glass case, both of which are replicas of the Venus' original accoutrements.[23] A breast plate is removable, as are four subsequent layers, to reveal the anatomical structures inside the female body, including a fetus in the uterus (Figure 2). Upon first encountering the wax figure, either in person or in a photograph, witnesses become immediately aware of the painstaking efforts that would be necessary to achieve such an intensely realistic re-creation. The delicate features - hands, feet, and face - and the far-away gaze are unnerving and enticing. When the visual details of the Medical Venus are examined, they render a greater understanding of the messages conveyed to an eighteenth century public.

While better facilitating the instruction of anatomy was certainly an important goal of the collection, the Specola was also open to all classes of the public from its inception, as long as visitors were clean and presentable.[24] This exemplifies nicely the increased consumption of popular science, but fashionable entertainment and mere curiosity are only part of the narrative. The museum was installed in an annex of the royal palace of the Grand Duke Peter-Leopold of Tuscany, very much at his behest.[25] Peter-Leopold is considered by many eighteenth century historians to be the quintessential "enlightened" monarch because of his deliberate efforts to implement in Tuscany the new ideas being discussed in Italy, France, England, and the Holy Roman Empire. Although many monarchs across Europe participated and contributed to the intellectual trends of the movement broadly known as the Enlightenment, Peter-Leopold actually changed policies to reflect his enlightened stance - social welfare programs were introduced, ties to the papacy cut, and a constitution calling for elected representation was drawn

---

Origins: Florentine Eighteenth-Century Wax Anatomical Models as Inspiration for Italian Horror," *Kinoeye* 9 (2002): 1-9.
[22] http://www.specola.unifi.it/cere/history.htm.
[23] Saulo Bambi, *Encyclopaedia Anatomica* (Koln: B. Taschen, 1999), 77.
[24] Burfoot, "Surprising Origins," 4.
[25] http://www.specola.unifi.it/cere/history.htm.

up.[26] The anatomical wax models on public display beside the royal palace were for the Grand Duke another way of promoting the new philosophy, and eradicating superstitious ideas about the connection of body and soul. The artistic choices made by the modeler reflect that goal of educating the observer.

The wax figures of the Specola collection are incredibly realistic, with some scholars insisting that they are, in fact, more than simply realistic. Ludmilla Jordanova asserts that "lashes, head and pubic hair were added painstakingly and serve no other function than to make the body as lifelike as possible. They add nothing to the anatomical detail of the model ... we have more than realism; a verisimilitude so relentless that it becomes hyper-realism."[27] Remarkable similarities are found between accounts of seeing the wax models of the Specola for the first time, and the reminiscences of physicians today about their initial encounter with a cadaver as a young medical student. Psychiatrist and anthropologist Simon Sinclair notes the "sacredness of the Dissection Room" as reported by medical students upon entering it for the first time. Students are often greatly unnerved, some fainting and some dropping out of med-school entirely after seeing the cadavers. Sinclair relates an introductory address by a medical school professor explaining to new students that the work done in the dissection room is about "doing things that may frighten you so the next time you have to do something frightening, you won't be frightened."[28] Emotional response and educational objectives are connected to create a physician who can overcome uneasiness and in turn become blasé about the grotesque realities of the human body. Annette Burfoot, a scholar currently studying the wax figures at the Specola, noted that the experience of entering the museum is not to be under-estimated. "Nearly everyone walking into the first room of models recoils at the hyper-realism ... a sense of edging towards the abyss and the horrific is heightened as you move into the next room ..."[29] Again, an emotional response is a desired effect intentionally solicited by the modelers for educational purposes.

---

[26] George Rudé, *Europe in the Eighteenth Century: Aristocracy and the Bourgeois Challenge* (London: Phoenix Press, 1972), 99.

[27] Ludmilla Jordanova, *Sexual Visions: Images of Gender in Science and Medicine between the Eighteenth and Twentieth Centuries* (New York: Harvester Wheatsheaf, 1989), 43-65. Although it is not the focus of this study, it is hardly possible to undertake an analysis of the Specola waxworks without pausing to consider its implications for gender studies. In her book *Sexual Visions*, historian Ludmilla Jordanova analyzes the cultural impact of biological and medical science from the eighteenth to the twentieth century with respect to gender. The anatomical wax models of the eighteenth century feature prominently in her study as a way of exploring the relationships between body image and sex roles, as well as cultural assumptions about gender that are imbedded in the models. The recumbent female figures are, according to Jordanova, presented as objects and not subjects, and are designed to invoke sexual thoughts. The research probes what Jordanova calls "centuries of dichotomous thought," contrasting the recumbent, female models to the upright, male figures as passive/active, nerves/muscles, experience/action, and passion/reason. Overall, Jordanova's study is an important one for those grappling with the significance of eighteenth century anatomical waxes.

[28] Simon Sinclair, *Making Doctors: An Institutional Apprenticeship* (Oxford: Berg, 1997), 170-95.

[29] Burfoot, "Surprising Origins," 1-9.

Stark realism is a hallmark of the eighteenth century Specola waxworks, and it is evident that the spectator is meant to have an affective, perhaps even emotional, experience. Some historians struggle with the "dangerous territory" of speculation arguing that just because such objects elicit powerful reactions today, it in no way tells us that they did so in the past.[30] I argue that it is very likely that the use of hyper-realism was intended by the modeler to elicit a powerful response, and that speculation and empathic reasoning are valuable tools for the historian. As discussed, material culture analysis allows the researcher to exploit the "empathic link" between the world of the artifact and the world of the observer.

The string of pearls around the neck of the Medical Venus always draws comment from those to whom I have shown its photograph. It gives pause because, from a twenty-first century perspective, the intersection of art and science is unsettling and unfamiliar (Figure 3). French scholar Michel Lemire goes so far as to say that "these (eighteenth century) models rather evidenced the esthetic contamination of scientific progress, the overtaking of science by art."[31] Lemire's interpretation has a positivistic bent; as discussed, science was not yet a separate discipline in the eighteenth century, and the exploration of natural philosophy included what today would be considered both artistic and scientific endeavor. The pearls are a fine example of the fusion of art and science in this period, but this detail offers us even more than that.

The model was constructed so that the pearl necklace hides the crevice created between the body and the removable plate when the model is fully assembled and complete. In fact, the long, flowing locks of hair (that nearly every commentator of the Medical Venus remarks upon) cover the cracks just below the shoulders. Moreover, by examining a variety of sources in which the artifact appears, it is apparent that when the model is photographed today the hair is re-adjusted to mask the lines created by the breast plate when it is in place.[32] If the Medical Venus was created primarily for the teaching of anatomy, why all of this seemingly superfluous detail? In a word - perfection.

Both the model's creator and twentieth century photographers recognize the utility of the necklace and the hair for masking imperfections. Anatomical artists laboured to construct an example of the faultlessness of the human form. Some scholars attribute this quest for perfection to the re-discovery by Renaissance artists of the ancient canons of classical Greece and the new aesthetic criteria of realism that followed, pointing out the regular dissections by Michelangelo, da Vinci, and Rubens.[33] However, attempts by the maker to eliminate flaws on the model stretch beyond trends in art (as

---

[30] Jordanova, *Sexual Visions*, 49.

[31] Lemire, "Representations of the Human Body," 286.

[32] Notably, although not surprisingly, the photograph of a recumbent, female wax model appearing in Jordanova's *Sexual Visions*, shows the cracks around the breast plate clearly, and the velvet cushion has either been removed or airbrushed out of the image. No effort is made to mask imperfections or enhance the object.

[33] Lemire, "Representations of the Human Body," 284.

influential and sweeping as they might be), and even beyond artistic ego or creative gratification. We must return to the implications of Cartesian dualism.

The separation of mind and body and the view that all life forms were mechanistic challenged long and closely held beliefs about humanity, and the anatomical exhibitions of Europe helped to facilitate an understanding and acceptance of these new concepts.[34] The Specola models forced observers to question their own mortality and corporality. New discoveries were seen to bolster religion, not dispel it, and consumers of popular science who stood in front of the Medical Venus were given the opportunity to realise and internalise the majesty of God's handiwork. Empiricists and philosophers argued that the supremacy of God was demonstrated in the perfection of the mechanics of the human body. This idea propelled the reception of dualistic reasoning, and by the twentieth century, the separation of mind and body would become an indisputable tenet of modern medicine.

Scientific medicine came to possess a monopoly over medical knowledge in the twentieth century and the public became distanced from the material of anatomy.[35] In every medical interaction there exists a contract - usually verbal, but often unacknowledged altogether - in which the patient assumes of the healer an expert knowledge and anticipates the fulfillment of his or her expectations. Quite simply, as Jacalyn Duffin has stated, doctors can only be doctors when someone else agrees.[36] As diagnoses came to rely less on patient report and more on the results of diagnostic technology, the patient was required to contribute less actively to the doctor-patient encounter. Once diagnostic innovations like the stethoscope and the X-ray appeared, doctors had access to what was going on inside the living body, without relying on the subjective report of the patient. Moreover, with technology like X-ray and radiological imaging, doctors began to diagnose in the complete absence of the

---

[34] By no means was any new philosophy embraced immediately or categorically, nor did it go unchallenged. New ideas were considered and adopted gradually over the eighteenth century. Further, I do not intend to suggest that the average person in the eighteenth century was reading Descartes, Locke, Kant, or Voltaire as a deliberate means of seeking out a new and different way of seeing the world. The Enlightenment was lived and experienced by the people of the western world, and through increased cultural consumerism and the creation of a market for knowledge discussed above, new conceptions of the universe were slowly disseminated and considered. See Lindemann, *Medicine and Society in Early Modern Europe;* Munck, *Enlightenment;* or Outram, *Enlightenment.*

[35] A well-known and influential study of this phenomenon is Eliot Freidson, *Profession of Medicine: A Study of the Sociology of Applied Knowledge* (New York: Harper, 1970). See also R.D. Gidney and W.P.J. Miller, *Professional Gentlemen: The Professions in Nineteenth-Century Ontario* (Toronto: University of Toronto Press, 1994); Terrie Romano, "Professional Identity and the Nineteenth-Century Medical Profession," *Histoire sociale / Social History* 28, no. 55 (1995); S.E.D. Shortt, "Physicians, Science and Status: Issues in the Professionalization of Anglo-American Medicine in the Nineteenth-Century," *Medical History* 27 (1983).

[36] Jacalyn Duffin, *History of Medicine: A Scandalously Short Introduction* (Toronto: University of Toronto Press, 1999), 115.

patient.[37] It is essential to remember, however, that both physician *and* patient would come to rely on pieces of diagnostic equipment for answers to their medical questions. Over time, the doctor-patient relationship became less of a collaborative effort.

Biomedical discovery also transformed the doctor-patient interaction as the public began to experience successive positive outcomes after specific interactions with scientific medicine. Subsequently, expectations of what medical practitioners could provide in *all* areas of illness increased substantially. With the major discoveries of anesthesia and antisepsis,[38] diseases and ailments that had once been considered fatal could now be painlessly treated and post-surgical infection staved off in many cases. Each individual positive encounter with scientific methods like the use of anesthesia and antisepsis demonstrated to the patient and his or her family the value and promise of scientific medicine. Even if someone had not had a personal experience with the new successes of surgery, reports were available from the highest source; in 1902, King Edward owed his life to the surgical treatment of his appendicitis.[39] As a new and positive perception of surgical outcome gradually supplanted the great fear that had once been associated with surgery, patients came to expect a "technical fix" for every ailment. Consequently, by demanding more and more from scientific medical expertise, patients willingly raised the profession to new heights.[40] Moreover, the public did not simply acquiesce to a medical monopoly over healthcare, it began to demand one.

The gradual acceptance of culturally constructed notions of "science" by the public permitted the establishment and recognition of a homogeneous medical profession by the community at large. Growing public trust in an abstract vision of the "Man of Science" helped to raise the physician to a place of reverence and respectability in the community, indeed, onto so high a

---

[37] Stanley Joel Reiser, *Medicine and the Reign of Technology* (Cambridge: Cambridge University Press, 1978), 121.

[38] Anesthesia was a term coined to indicate the effects of ether, which eventually made surgical trauma bearable. There had always been pain-deadening agents called analgesics, but the first operation performed under ether in 1846 was a milestone. Gradually thereafter, new surgical procedures of all kinds became possible. Alone, however, anesthesia would not have been enough to revolutionize surgery because post-operative infection brought about the highest number of surgical fatalities. Antisepsis involves killing infective agents already present in a wound and its discovery and application reduced post-operative sepsis. From Roy Porter, ed., *Cambridge Illustrated History of Medicine* (Cambridge: Cambridge University Press, 1996), 226-33. For more detailed analyses see Lindsay Granshaw, "The Rise of the Modern Hospital in Britain," in Andrew Wear, ed., *Medicine in Society* (Cambridge: Cambridge University Press, 1998); Charles Rosenberg, *The Care of Strangers: The Rise of America's Hospital System* (Baltimore: The Johns Hopkins University Press, 1987), 143-47; and Paul Starr, *The Social Transformation of American Medicine* (New York: Basic Books, 1982).

[39] Porter, *Greatest Benefit to Mankind*, 600.

[40] Duffin, *History of Medicine,* 123.

pedestal, that by the middle of the twentieth century, scientific medicine had a relatively unchallenged dominance over healthcare.[41]

By examining a twentieth century anatomical model, the transition of the balance of medical power and subsequent adaptations of the doctor-patient paradigm, can be better understood and analyzed. An anatomical model of a female torso manufactured in the 1930s substantiates these changes. The model is called the 2000 "Durable" Life Size Female Torso and appears in a 1938 mail-order catalogue issued by the Clay-Adams Company with an accompanying price of $180.00[42] (Figure 4). The exterior of the model and the removable organs are made of papier-mâché, which have then been hand-painted and heavily lacquered for structural fortification and durability. The torso is relatively solid throughout, perhaps built over a frame, while the removable parts are hollow, light, and would crack if moderate force were applied. An oval-shaped breast plate can be lifted to expose over forty detachable anatomical structures that mount together in a precise and intricate puzzle, with some components fitted with tiny hook and eye fasteners to ensure their placement within the body cavity.[43]

The delicate nature of the Clay-Adams model would seem to indicate that it was designed for use by a small number of careful persons, rather than numerous casual users, for example, a new swarm of medical students year after year. This initially was corroborated by the curator who first acquired the model for a now dispersed collection, who indicated to me that it had belonged to a physician and had sat in his office for many years.[44] The 1938 Clay-Adams catalogue, however, advertised that "this model is now in use in leading universities, nurses' training schools, and other institutions teaching anatomy, physiology, hygiene and physical education."[45] But despite the catalogue's claims of durability, including the promise that the model could be washed with soap and water, the model's fragility is patent, and doubts about its intended usage linger.

This created a quandary for me the historian: the catalogue advertises the figure for use in educational settings, yet its fragility seems to belie that kind of usage. Something is possible (indeed probable) however, when I consider usage and consumption behaviours: the potential for cultural bias. Material culture methodology requires that careful attention be paid to the researcher's preconceptions about a given artifact. My own lifelong knowledge of, and interaction with, durable plastic objects like Fisher Price toys and Tupperware may facilitate a predisposition to regarding papier-mâché, by

---

[41] Rosenberg, *Care of Strangers*, 150; Starr, *Social Transformation of American Medicine*, 17-21; Edward Shorter, *Doctors and Their Patients: A Social History* (London: Transaction Publishers, 1991), 126-27.

[42] Clay-Adams Co., Inc., *Manufacturer's Mail Order Catalogue* (New York: 1938), 6.

[43] This artifact is owned by the Canada Science and Technology Museum in Ottawa, Ontario, and I am grateful to the museum for allowing me the opportunity to examine the model.

[44] Personal communication via e-mail from Kathryn Voss, former curator of the University Healthcare Network History of Medicine Collection, Toronto, Canada (dispersed in 2001), to the author, 24 February 2003.

[45] Clay-Adams Co., Inc., *Manufacturer's Mail Order Catalogue*, 6.

comparison, as exceptionally delicate. Before the early twentieth century, the other materials used in the manufacture of anatomy figures had been primarily ivory and wax. Ivory, of course, was expensive and heavy, and did not allow for much detail. Wax models were delicate and onerous, and had to be kept below a certain temperature so they would not melt. Thus, it is entirely possible that the heavily lacquered papier-mâché model *was* more resilient and better suited to casual, regular handling than models previously available, and was welcomed as a new alternative for the fabrication of anatomical teaching aids for use in institutions. Nevertheless, we know that this particular artifact was a fixture in a physician's office who had a general medical practice.

The 1930s Clay-Adams model belonged to a Dr. Yankoff, who practiced in the Leaside area of Toronto, Ontario. Other sources of information about his practice have not been found, and so we must rely on the artifact to generate both questions and answers. Medical training in the first decades of the twentieth century included plenty of time dissecting cadavers and memorizing the patterns of both healthy and diseased tissue as they appear under a microscope. During the hospital internship and residency, new doctors would witness and interact with the human body in almost every imaginable way. From delivering babies to assisting autopsies, from attending emergency room tragedies to performing hundreds of manual internal examinations, medical doctors had an extensive and *tactile* knowledge of the body and its components.[46] Indeed, many returned home from a tour of duty in the Medical Corps having witnessed the utter devastation that could be inflicted upon the human body. In sum, the doctor's experience with the biological reality of the body was comprehensive, even if more extreme instances of anatomical contact became less frequent once one was established in general office practice. With this kind of experience behind him, why did Dr. Yankoff have need of an anatomy model that was so unrealistic?

The Clay-Adams model is viewed like an impressionistic painting; from a distance, its organs and tissue look fairly realistic and well-formed, but studied up close, they are barely identifiable. Both the interior removable elements and the exterior skin and tissue of the model are painted by hand. Various techniques are used to achieve the look of a particular organ. Scenic painters and interior decorators call these techniques "treatments" and regularly use them to create a three-dimensional look on a flat surface. For instance, a technique where different colours of thin, wet paint are applied to the object, allowed to mix erratically and then blotted with a rag are used on the lungs to create a mottled, marbled effect. Spackling, or freckling, is used on the spleen to create a textured, porous look.[47] In fact, some structures are painted simply to imply their biological reality, and seem quite decorative; the component representing the interior of the breast looks more like the decoration

---

[46] Richard Peschel and Enid Rhodes Peschel, *When a Doctor Hates a Patient, and Other Chapters in a Young Physician's Life* (Berkley: University of California Press, 1986), 67.

[47] My undergraduate degree was in the Fine Arts where I majored in Theatre. I was trained and worked as a set designer, scenic painter and prop builder, and regularly used these same techniques.

embroidered on the hem of a traditional folk costume than fatty, mammary tissue (Figure 5).

Thus, unlike the Medical Venus, the Clay-Adams figure does not provoke an extreme reaction from viewers, but it does arouse curiosity and interest. As I was examining the Clay-Adams model at the Science and Technology Museum in Ottawa, and placing her forty some odd parts around her on the table, a member of the maintenance staff took an interest in what it was I was researching and approached me. I asked her what she would think if she saw this in her doctor's office, and she exclaimed, "I would think she just had an operation! She's all chopped up!" The woman pointed to the model's missing arm and laughed. Interaction with the twentieth century papier-mâché model is fairly straightforward and even blasé. But recall the hyper-realism of the eighteenth century wax figures and the kind of affective, intense experience they can elicit in spectators. Now imagine the Clay-Adams figure just as realistically formed and confronting the patient in Dr. Yankoff's office - skinned, amputated, and eviscerated. An uneasy, terrified patient is not what the doctor ordered! Once again, the visual design of the object reveals the intentions of the maker and the kind of reaction expected from users.

The medical sphere of the twentieth century emerged from its nineteenth century professionalization process as separate and insulated, its knowledge and expertise completely detached from the public realm. Many historians of medical professionalization have laid the responsibility for this marked separation squarely at the feet of the medical elite, claiming physicians agitated for a monopoly over medical knowledge merely to enhance their income and prestige.[48] This narrow view of the monopolization of medicine is misguided, and other scholars have explored the broader social and cultural attitudes that attest to the willingness of the laity to have scientific medicine control and facilitate the delivery of its healthcare.[49] Rapid urbanization during the Victorian era focused public attention on new social issues like crime, prostitution, mental hygiene, and public sanitation. A faith in scientific management and professional expertise saturated politics, criminal justice, and extended to medicine and public health as well.[50] Victorian middle-class concerns about public health[51] provided an intellectual environment in which science held the answers for grave social problems. Whether for pleasure,

---

[48] Ronald Hamowy, *Canadian Medicine: A Study in Restricted Entry* (Vancouver: The Fraser Institute, 1984); Bernard Bledstein, *The Culture of Professionalism: The Middle Class and the Development of Higher Education in America* (New York: W.W. Norton, 1976).
[49] S.E.D. Shortt, "Physicians, Science and Status," *Medical History* 27 (1983), 51-68; Mark Weatherall, "Making Medicine Scientific: Empiricism, Rationality, and Quackery in mid-Victorian Britain," *Social History of Medicine* 9, no. 2 (1996): 175-94.
[50] Colin D. Howell, "Medical Science and Social Criticism," in David Naylor, ed., *Canadian Healthcare and the State: A Century of Evolution* (Montreal and Kingston: McGill-Queen's University Press, 1992), 16.
[51] Bruce Haley, *The Healthy Body and Victorian Culture* (Cambridge: Harvard University Press, 1978), 11; Heather MacDougall, "Public Health and the 'Sanitary Idea' in Toronto: 1866-1890," in Wendy Mitchison and Janice Dickin McGinnis, eds., *Essays in the History of Canadian Medicine* (Toronto: McClelland and Stewart, 1988), 63.

prevention or reform, scientistic thought permeated the public sphere, and by the turn of the twentieth century, a new trust in scientific medicine became almost absolute.

In the post-war medical paradigm, it is the responsibility of the medical professional to shoulder the reality of the biological body and mediate the complexities and sometimes the horrors of medical knowledge into more acceptable and less threatening terms for the patient. The physician comes to understand his or her role in this relationship during medical school - recall the professor who told his students that dissection would help them not to be "frightened" when next confronted with "frightening" things. This division of the medical world and the "normal" world is reified by another item that appears in the Clay-Adams catalogue. A steel display cabinet was available for order which would accommodate not only small anatomical preparations on two shelves, but also the 2000 "Durable" Life Size Female Torso[52] (Figure 6). Let us return to the scene in Dr. Yankoff's office. The doctor wishes to convey some medical information to the patient. He walks to the cabinet containing the anatomy model, perhaps unlocking it, and he removes the needed organ or points out the region in question. The cabinet becomes a metaphor for the new doctor-patient relationship. Dr. Yankoff possesses medical knowledge which is inaccessible to the patient. Both are aware that this is part of their unspoken doctor-patient contract and his monopoly over this knowledge meets the expectations of the patient. He then uses the model as a vehicle for mediating and expressing medical knowledge in a language the patient is comfortable with.

But if the public not only accepts but demands that medical knowledge remains marshaled by the medical sphere alone, why does the patient need to receive any medical knowledge whatsoever? Why not simply follow the doctor's orders and graciously accept his or her authority? Stated in a different way, if the diagnosis is cancer of the liver, why does the patient need to see a representation of a liver and understand the pathological changes happening to it? These are complicated questions about a complex relationship between society and medical culture. Thomas Kuhn, of course, began to explore the artificial nature of a scientistic society,[53] and other historians continue to examine the impact of scientific thought on our social interactions and conventions,[54] but more research must be done in investigating how the emerging culture of science changed the doctor-patient relationship.

The steady amassing of medical triumphs in the early twentieth century caused patient expectations of what medicine could and should provide to soar, and as Roy Porter notes, "as those expectations become unlimited, they are unfulfillable."[55] What must still be explored by historians of medicine then, are the details surrounding why, in the era after World War II, it came to be a

---

[52] Clay-Adams Co., Inc., *Manufacturer's Mail Order Catalogue*, 68.
[53] Thomas Kuhn, *The Structure of Scientific Revolutions* (Chicago: University of Chicago Press, 1962).
[54] See Stanley Joel Reiser, *Medicine and the Reign of Technology* (Cambridge: Cambridge University Press, 1978); Shortt, "Physicians, Science and Status," 51-68; Weatherall, "Making Medicine Scientific," 175-94.
[55] Porter, *Greatest Benefit to Mankind*, 718.

fundamental desire of patients to understand in scientific terms the biological happenings inside their bodies, while at the same time, continue to seek protection from the grotesque and frightening aspects of anatomical reality.

When the Clay-Adams model and the Medical Venus are examined side by side, the observer is struck by the virtually identical features of the internal anatomical structures - the relative consistency of human anatomy over time if you will. The years that separate their manufacture are not immediately apparent when examining the viscera alone. When the eye travels to the exterior representations, however, all similarities are forgotten - one is an object and the other a person; one sparks curiosity and invites interaction, the other creates unease and cautious observation. It is evident that the artistic qualities of anatomical models help to convey not only information about human anatomy but also that of abstract social meaning. As seen in the eighteenth century design of anatomy models, hyper-realism was employed to provoke an affective experience in observers and to encourage a particular philosophy or reform. As medical knowledge came increasingly under the guardianship of scientific medicine, the anatomy model became impressionistic, a tool used to gently convey medical ideas while continuing to shield the patient from the more grotesque nature of the human body. When material culture methodologies are used to analyse the artistic elements of these artifacts, there is seen deliberation and intention beyond, and in addition to, the primary aim of teaching anatomy.

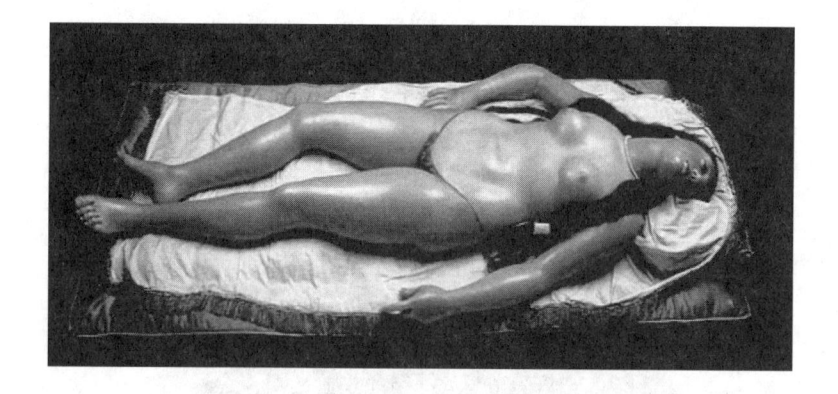

Figure 1 *Eighteenth century wax anatomical model known as the "Medical Venus" (Natural History Museum, Florence University, Italy)*

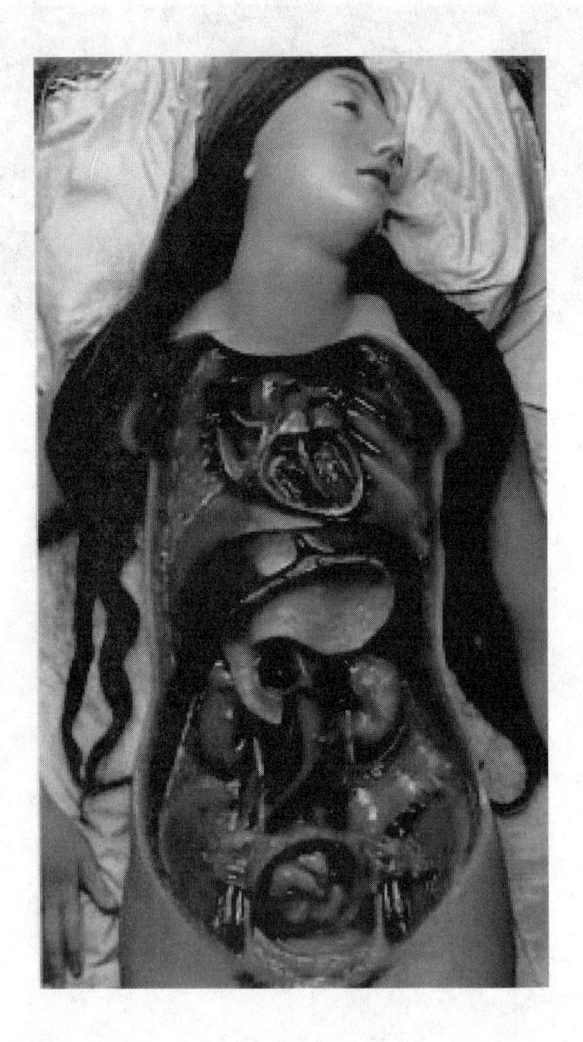

Figure 2 *Medical Venus with breast plate removed to reveal inner anatomical structures including a fetus in the uterus (Natural History Museum, Florence University, Italy)*

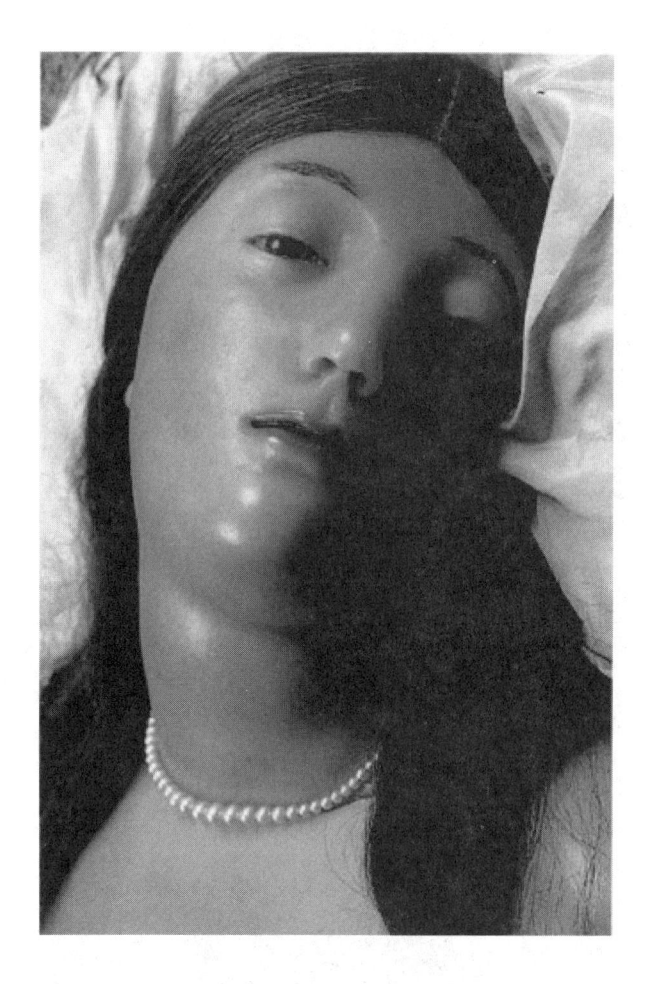

Figure 3 *A string of pearls masks the crevice of the removable breast plate (Natural History Museum, Florence University, Italy)*

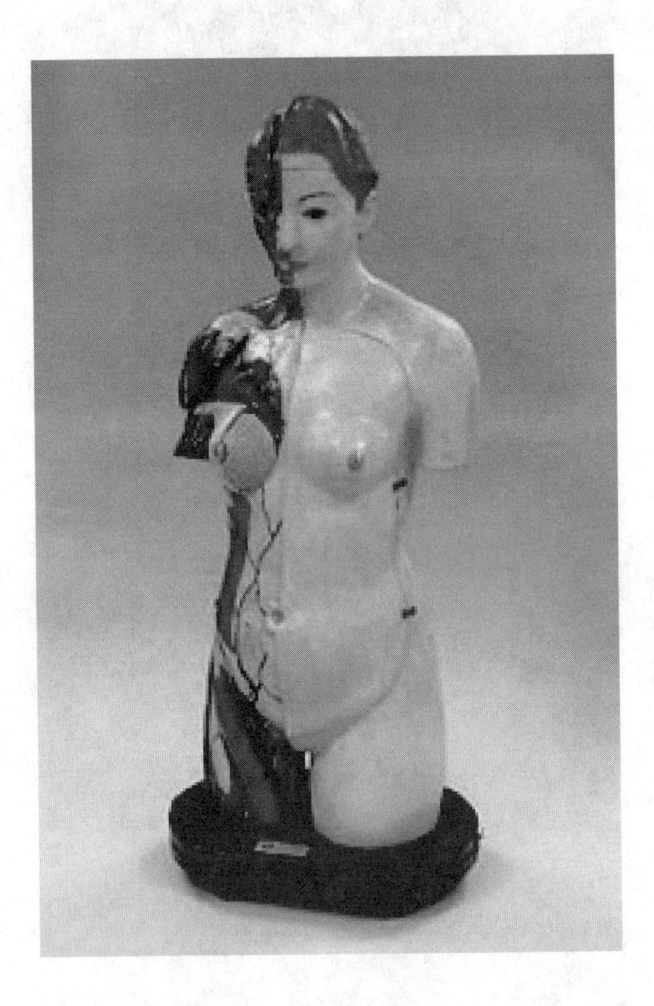

Figure 4 *Early twentieth century anatomy model called the 2000 "Durable" Life Size Female Torso (Canada Science and Technology Museum, UHN 1980.26.2)*

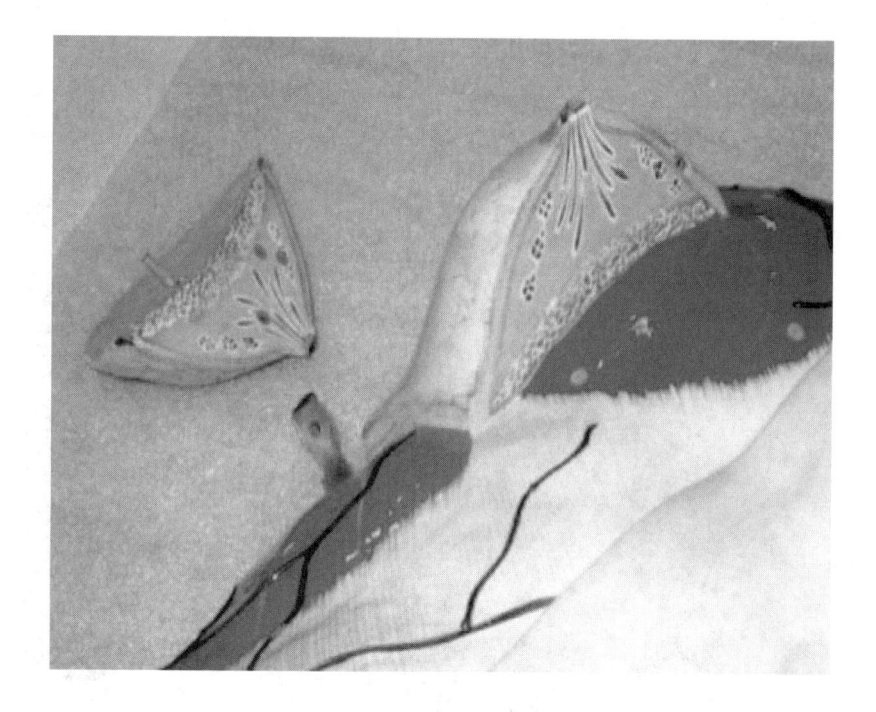

Figure 5 *Impressionistic representation of breast tissue on the Clay-Adams model (Canada Science and Technology Museum, UHN 1980.26.2)*

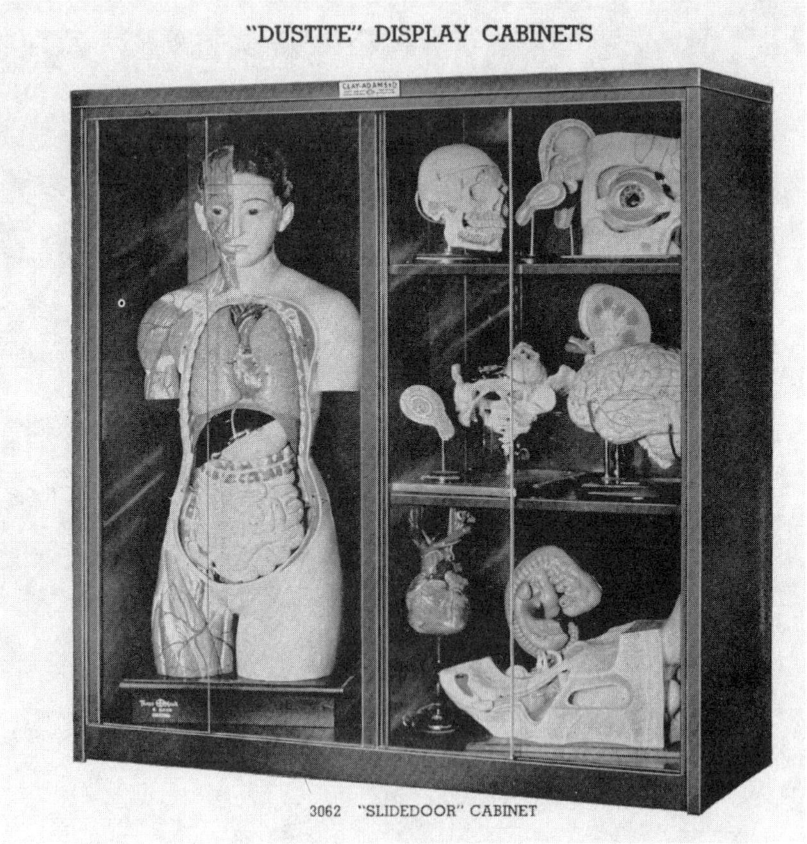

Figure 6 *Display cabinet available in 1938 Clay-Adams catalogue designed to house the 2000 "Durable" Life Size Female Torso anatomy model (Canada Science and Technology Museum, UHN 1980.26.2)*

– 4 –

Re-disciplining the Body

Lisa Helps

Despite the "veritable flood of books, conferences, and panels on body history, or bodies in history," why, historian Kathleen Canning asks, has the body remained a largely "unexplicated and undertheorised *historical* concept."[1] I would add that this lack of historical theorization is particularly surprising in light of the veritable torrent of literature on the body over the last fifteen years in areas as diverse as geography, philosophy, anthropology, cultural studies, and biology, to name only a few. In addressing this disparate body of work, medieval historian Caroline Bynum has argued that "despite the enthusiasm for the topic, discussions of the body are almost completely incommensurate – and often incomprehensible – across the disciplines ... *Body* can refer to the organ on which a physician operates or the assumptions about race and gender implicit in a medical textbook, to the particular trajectory of one person's desire or to inheritance patterns and family structures." Bynum points out that "there is no clear set of structures, behaviours, events, objects, experiences, words, and moments to which *body* currently refers."[2] What then of the body in history?

Historians of the body, gender, and medicine as well as philosophers, literary theorists, psychologists, and others whose work is examined here, not surprisingly, approach the body (in history) from a multiplicity of perspectives, and have a variety of empirical and epistemological projects and goals. What is evident from a review of these studies is that there is no such thing as body history. Other than Barbara Duden, Ivan Illich, and perhaps Roy Porter, no scholars self-consciously identify themselves as practitioners of a sub-discipline known as "body history." However, many of them do argue, to varying degrees, for the necessity of historicizing the body, for examining the myriad of ways in which the post-Cartesian, iatrogenic, disembodied body is not the body that has always been. In so doing, many formulate their arguments on the basis of dichotomies which, for the most part, tend to privilege the "material" body and to shy away from, or implicitly deny, the "discursive." After reviewing these calls for historicization and investigating the most prominent dichotomy expressed by many of these scholars, that of "experience versus representation," I propose a theoretical framework, which posits bodies (in history) as historically contingent and as *simultaneously* material-discursive, experience-representations constituted through relations of power. I argue that, using this framework, *all* history might indeed be "body

---

[1] Kathleen Canning, "The Body as Method? Reflections on the Place of the Body in Gender History," *Gender and History* 11, no. 3 (1999): 499.
[2] Caroline Bynum, "Why All This Fuss About the Body? A Medievalists' Perspective," *Critical Inquiry* 22 (1995): 5.

history" for as Leslie Adelson asserts, "What is history if not the accounts of human bodies in and over time? History without bodies is unimaginable."[3]

The Corporeal Turn – Historicizing the Body
> The body is so many things all at the same time. Sometimes the victim of history, it is always the object of historical construction, the site of historical experience, the arbiter of all cognition, and the material ground of freedom. It is a thing and a sign, an inside and an outside, a boundary constantly crossing itself.[4]

If, as Adelson suggests above, the body is indeed all of these things, what precisely are those who advocate an historicist approach to the body calling for? What exactly is it that must be historicized? The material body? Bodily experience? Representations of the body? What is this "body" to which scholars so assuredly refer? An examination of the work of Roy Porter, Barbara Duden, and Robert Romanyshyn will reveal the complexity of attempting to answer any of these questions.

Historians of medicine, and/or those who use medical records as sources, have been at the forefront of interrogating the propensity of historians to view the body as a "natural fact" or a "biological given." These scholars tend to examine the physical, material body, "one's very flesh and blood."[5] Roy Porter, the most eminent of these, argues in "The History of the Body," that scholars must not assume that the "human body has timelessly existed as an unproblematic natural object with universal needs and wants."[6] He draws attention to the 1960s and 1970s; in his view, the emergence of the sexual revolution, consumer capitalism, and critiques from both the counter-culture and feminists culminated in a "cultural revolution," the outcome of which "demolish[ed] old cultural hierarchies of mind over body." As a result, scholarly attention has shifted from "well-established sub-disciplines such as the history of ideas, and towards the exploration of 'material culture', one limb of which is the history of the body."[7] Both Porter's claim, and the embodied (limb-like) metaphor through which he makes it, clearly point to the material body as his preeminent object of historicization. Ardently empiricist, Porter argues that the most effective way to approach different bodies in different times and places is through empirical research rather than general theorizing. Thus, he praises Barbara Duden's work, which is concerned with how "real people felt pain" and which investigates the (actual) "sickness experiences" of women in early eighteenth-century Germany and dismisses Elaine Scarry's philosophical and literary analysis in *The Body in Pain: The Making and*

---

[3] Leslie Adelson, *Making Bodies, Making History: Feminism and German Identity* (Lincoln: University of Nebraska Press, 1993), 1.
[4] Ibid., 34.
[5] Barbara Duden, "History Beneath the Skin," *Michigan Quarterly Review* 30 (1991): 174.
[6] Roy Porter, "The History of the Body," in Peter Burke, ed., *New Perspectives on Historical Writing* (Cambridge: Polity Press, 1991), 208.
[7] Ibid., 207.

Unmaking of the World which argues that pain is often "inexpressible." Contrary to Scarry's claim, he maintains that "actual accounts of pain ... are often expressed with exactitude and eloquence." Re-asserting his materialist/empiricist leanings, he remarks in the conclusion to his discussion of Scarry's work that "of course, to someone aspiring to the higher intellectual exegesis, empirical research may, like the body itself, seem gross and banausic."[8]

It is through Porter's condemnation of Scarry, however, that a strictly empiricist/materialist approach to historicizing the body can be called into question. In making a declaration about "the body itself," Porter appears to do precisely what he cautions scholars against, that is, taking the body for granted. *The body* is *itself* constituted through history and thus must be understood and investigated as such. On one level, Porter does recognize this. He notes, for example, that "pursuing the history of the body is ... not merely a matter of crunching vital statistics or decoding representation. Rather it is a call to make sense of the interplay between the two." Yet he does not offer any theoretical or methodological guidelines as to *how* historians might go about accessing and examining this interplay. Finally, in his list of seven agenda items for exploring the history of the body, the material body (which is clearly his "body itself") is centred and privileged. In "3. *The Anatomy of the Body*" he asks: "What did people mean when they talked, literally and figuratively, of their blood, their head or their heart, their bowels? How did people think of their bodies, their aches and pains when they fell sick?"[9] Continuing with his relatively anti-discursive stance, Porter does not consider that the ways in which people thought about and explained their sickness (and their health), for example, depended on the discourses of illness and health available to them in a given time and place, nor does he examine how their experiences in turn might have shaped those discourses. Indeed to subsume the blood, the head, the heart, the bowels under the heading "anatomy" suggests that these are (only) material and somehow separate from the wider symbolic world in and through which they were experienced historically.

Barbara Duden, like Porter, uses the paradigm of modern medicine to historicize the body. As she points out in her article, "History Beneath the Skin," to render the body historical involves an examination of the ways in which the body of experience, the body that one *is,* has become objectified by and through modern medicine. She argues that there is a "gulf between diagnostic vocabulary and the experience of the sick" and that this gulf has a history: "This history has two sides. On one side is the sociogenesis of the clinical, modern body, which is linked to the development of medical terminology; on the other side are the sick who have been silenced, and then trained to experience the body they are told 'have'." In Duden's conceptualization, the historicized body is the muted material body. When the eighteenth-century women patients she examines using physicians' records complained "about the anguish of their heart, how it is hard and burdened, and

---
[8] Ibid., 209.
[9] Ibid., 211, 224.

when they seek relief from a heart that is grudging and biting, or a heart that is eaten up ... They speak about something that is 'real' is 'body'."[10] The body for Duden, then, as investigated through a medical paradigm was once "real" and is now metaphor and object. To make this argument overlooks the critical point that the body must be conceived as inextricably and simultaneously real and metaphorical, material and discursive, that is, when a woman said her heart was hard, she represented her body in the metaphorical language of suffering in order to make sense of her life and to obtain relief from her physician. Furthermore, to assert that the sick have been silenced and trained to experience their bodies as objects which they "have," Duden, like Porter, fails to consider how the making of modern medicine and the making of the modern body were constitutive *of each other*.

In stark contrast to the material and experiential approaches of Porter, Duden and others,[11] in "The Human Body as Historical Matter and Cultural Symptom," psychologist Robert Romanyshyn seeks to historicize the body by examining the history of its representation. Like the scholars discussed above, he argues that "the body as anatomical object ... is *not* so much a natural fact as it is a cultural-historical matter." He further asserts that "the history of the flesh has taken two distinct but related paths, there's the history of the corpse, the abandoned body which is a kind of official history ... And there is an unofficial history, a kind of shadow history, which remembers the body of living flesh disguised, forgotten, or otherwise ignored in that official history." Romanyshyn traces the beginning point of these two notions of the body (and the two sides of history), as well as the nascence of modern consciousness, to Renaissance Florence[12] and the advent of linear perspective drawing, which prescribed the geometrical rules for representing the illusion of three-dimensional space on flat two-dimensional surfaces. He maintains that this mode of representation "is a prescription for vision which invites the viewer to look upon the world as if he or she were fixed and immobile on this side of a window." This window-effect creates a boundary between the onlooker and the world and is an "invitation not only to keep an eye upon the world, but to lose touch with it." In his estimation, linear perspective drawing created a three dimensional representational space through which the self abandoned the body (as the self was cast out of the picture as "viewer") and simultaneously, the

---

[10] Duden, "History Beneath the Skin," 175, 181.

[11] For other material and experiential approaches to historicizing the body, see Ivan Illich, "A Plea for Body History," *Michigan Quarterly Review* 26 (1987): 342-48, and Joy Parr, "Notes for a More Sensuous History of Twentieth-Century Canada: The Timely, The Tacit, and the Material Body," *Canadian Historical Review* 84, no. 2 (2001): 720-45.

[12] Robert Romanyshyn, "The Human Body as Historical Matter and Cultural Symptom," in Maxine Sheets-Johnstone, ed., *Giving the Body its Due* (New York: State University of New York Press, 1992), 161,168-69. Also see Sylvana Tomaselli, "The First Person, Descartes, Locke and the Mind-Body Dualism," *History of Science*, 22, no. 2 (1984): 185-205, for a discussion of pre-Cartesian and Cartesian perspectives. Tomaselli outlines arguments made by scholars in which Descartes is credited for merely encoding what was already in thought-practice regarding the mind/body. Thus, Romanyshyn is not radical in situating the so-called mind/body split before Descartes.

abandoned body, the specimen, the corpse was born. It is the abandoned corpse-like body which functions as Romanyshyn's metaphor for official history and the shadow of the corpse that of unofficial or repressed history. He makes the important argument that "each age in the span of ... history has missed how its shadow body is the other side of the body it invented."[13] He illustrates this point by arguing that in the age of industrialization, for example, "the madman and madwoman in their cells are the shadows of the workers in their factories, factories are the social counterpart of the asylum."[14]

What can we make of Romanyshyn's historicized body? First, and significantly, he traces the origins of the modern body and the origins of modern consciousness to the same time and place. According to him, modern consciousness, represented in, by, and through linear perspective drawing, created the modern body by a process of abandonment. In this sense, body and mind remained linked at the point of constitution in a way they did not in Cartesian thought, to which is attributed the creation of the modern thinking self but not of modern (dis)embodiment. Second, though he appeals to the "flesh" and the "corpse," it is evident that his analysis functions at the level of theoretical generalization for which Porter condemned Elaine Scarry and her *Bodies in Pain*. For example, in the last section of Romanyshyn's article entitled "The Astronaut and the Anorexic," he does not examine the "actual experiences" of the (actual) bodies of astronauts or anorexics, but uses these as yet another metaphor of the abandoned body, and its shadow, respectively. Although primarily working in the realm of discourse/representation, he does not ardently deny the material. In fact, he asserts that the shadow history, the unofficial history, is "a history of the repressed living flesh."[15] This seems, curiously, to echo Porter's claim that the body in history is a "suppressed presence."[16] Although situated differently in their approaches to historicizing the body, both these authors argue that what has not received attention from scholars is a history of the flesh, of the senses. Yet significantly, neither draws explicit attention to the importance – in terms of historicizing the body and in doing "body history" – of examining what it might have meant to *make sense* of oneself/the world in a given time and place, through epoch-specific discourses and particular relations of power.

Making Sense – Representing the Experienced Body

The question of how to access historical experience has been a central focus of recent historiographical debate, particularly in post-linguistic-turn feminist history/historiography. Certain women's and feminist historians

---

[13] Romanyshyn, "Human Body," 162, 171.

[14] Ibid., 172. In *Discipline and Punish: The Birth of the Prison* (New York: Random House, 1995), Michel Foucault makes a similar argument. However, Foucault is concerned with the factory, the asylum, the school, the hospital, and, of course, the prison, as surveying and discipline-enforcing institutions. While Foucault argues that all of these institutions were interested in disciplining the body, Romanyshyn importantly distinguishes between the *different bodies* contained in different institutions.

[15] Romanyshyn, "Human Body," 169.

[16] Porter, "History of the Body," 226.

cling to experience as an unproblematized category of analysis,[17] whereas others concede the usefulness of experience as a site of investigation but claim that it must be understood as constituted through discourse.[18] Joy Parr argues that to historicize experience is to examine historical systems of meaning, that is the ways in which people have made experience meaningful through discourse.[19] Any attempt to study the body in history necessarily complexifies this debate – the dyad of experience-discourse becomes the triad of experience-body-representation. Perhaps unable to think trialectically, or on all of these levels simultaneously, the question for most historians of the body seems to be whether it is more useful to examine historical experience *or* representation. In most instances, historians concerned with the body tend to privilege the first two terms of the triad and to eschew representation as something other than the body. Such an approach is limited in that it fails to take seriously the complex material-discursive, experience-representations of the bodies of historical subjects and the worlds in which they moved or the possibility that the body, conceived in this way, might alter the way we do history.

One of the ways in which historians have endeavoured to deal with this tension of experience-body-representation is by attempting to tease this triad apart. In his "Plea for Body History," Ivan Illich notes that he "began to see that there was a distinct awareness of the body as the primary *locus* of experience. *This* body, specific to one period, but subject to profound transformations, sometimes occurring within relatively short spans of time, was parallel to but clearly distant from the body that was painted, sculpted, and described in that historical moment."[20] Michel Feher, in his introduction to the dense three-volume, *Fragments for a History of the Human Body,* expresses a similar sentiment. He argues that,

> the history of the human body is not so much about the history of its representations as of its modes of construction ... the history of its representations always refers to a real body considered to be 'without history' – whether this be the organism observed by the natural sciences, the body proper as perceived by phenomenology, or the instinctual, repressed body on which psychoanalysis is based – whereas the history of its modes of construction can, since it avoids the overly massive oppositions of science and ideology or of

---

[17] See Joan Hoff, "Gender as a Postmodern Category of Paralysis," *Women's Studies International Forum* 17, no. 4 (1994): 443-47, and Joan Sangster, "Re-Assessing Gender History and Women's History in Canada," *Left History* 3, no. 1 (1995): 109-121.

[18] See Joy Parr, "Gender History and Historical Practice," *Canadian Historical Review,* 76, no. 3 (1995): 354-76, and Joan Scott, "The Evidence of Experience," in Henry Abelove, Michele Aina Barale, and David M. Halperin, eds., *The Lesbian and Gay Studies Reader* (New York: Routledge, 1993), 397-415.

[19] Parr, "Gender History," 365.

[20] Illich, "Plea for Body History," 345. Emphasis in original.

authenticity and alienation, turn the body into a thoroughly historicized and completely problematic issue.[21]

For both Illich and Feher, analyzing the history of the body through its representations is problematic. Illich's assumption is that representation and experience are parallel but not interwoven. Therefore, if historians were to study representations of the body, they might not attend to the body as a "*locus* of experience," and hence there is a danger of "missing" the body and its experience altogether. Feher's wariness of representation is somewhat different. His fear is that representations of the body often purport to be representations of the *real*, which in his implicit definition seems to connote fixity, stasis, and ahistoricity. Both authors seem to be addressing representations of the body in dominant discourse and both appear to assume that a body's "experience" and "modes of construction" might somehow be probed historically without attention to these representations. However, does (bodily) experience have meaning outside its representations? How can historians examine body-experience as *made* in specific times and places without examining how the body was represented in these same times and places? The body is made, in part, through its representation; representation is one of the body's modes of construction.

Equally challenging for historians as sorting out the relationships among bodies, experiences, and dominant representations is the issue of how to study the sensing body of experience. In a recent article calling for a more sensuous history of twentieth-century Canada, Joy Parr argues that "neither the ahistorical [physical] body nor the physical body trussed up as a discursive construct alone is going to take us far along the path towards a more sensuous history." Parr posits that there "is a material, non-discursive body that sensuously perceives space and place and other bodies." The problem here, of course, is that if a pre-discursive sensing body exists, how can historians access this body/these bodies historically without examining what they tell us they sense. While conceding that there are two elements, the "sensation itself and the way of making sense of it," Parr advocates that "researching this subject means asking questions about the particular matrix of relationships among the senses of those whose past we seek to know." For example, she argues that the "gnawing undertone in a village whose factory has ceased production during a strike" makes, in part, "the historical bodies whose actions we watch and whose records we read." If Parr is asking scholars to expand their own sensuous historical imaginings, taking these "keynotes" – as she calls these types of sounds (and silences) – into consideration is useful.[22] However, the only way historians can access the impact this "gnawing undertone" might have had on the experiences-bodies of the villagers is if these were *represented* in the

---

[21] Michel Feher, "Introduction," in Michel Feher, ed., *Fragments for a History of the Human Body* (New York: Zone, 1989), 12.

[22] Parr, "Notes for a More Sensuous History," 729, 735-37. She gets this concept from the "experimenting contemporary Canadian composer" Murray Schafer. She argues that "historical bodies live in the presence of keynotes, the tonalities of their place and their time created by climate, geography and changing technology."

"records we read." Parr seems to privilege a pre-discursive sensing body without providing adequate suggestions as to how the historian might come within reach of this body. In terms of doing sensuous body history, then, the critical question is: how can we examine the sense that people made of their sensing bodies and the ways in which they made this sense?

Barbara Duden is able to answer this question, in part, by attempting to access the "voiced body of experience." In order to do so she intentionally shifted her attention "from the history of the organism and its perceived shape to the history of the art of telling one's own story about suffering." Although she claims to be analyzing the experiences of eighteenth-century women patients, what Duden undertakes is a discourse analysis of their stories as recorded in a doctor's diary between 1721 and 1742. She asserts that "more than a report of sensations, the women provide the story of connected feelings and experiences." These stories are "bio-logies," she argues, "spoken self-revelation[s]," "discoursing about one's life." By using this definition of biology she is able to cleverly weave self-representation in language and women's bodily experiences inextricably together. She seems to understand, although does not explicitly address, that analyzing the ways in which the women spoke – their self-representations – does not obscure their bodies of experience. Such an analysis may in fact bring historians "closer" to them, right in/on/through them, as discourse on the body cannot be separated from the body itself. What is problematic about Duden's approach, however, is her assertion that, unlike the bodies of her eighteenth-century patients, the experiences of modern bodies have become "disembodied"; "the body ... has been removed from experience" through modern medical science. In the end, she privileges experience-body over experience-body-representation as she assumes that when the *representations* change - for example when blood is described as "circulating" rather than "urging, raging and gushing"[23]- experience-body no longer exists. Representations are thus clearly not integral to Duden's body of experience.

Finally, there are some scholars who do point to the importance of examining experience-body-representation and who see the body as the site in/on/through which this triad is constituted. In *Making Bodies Making History: Feminism and German Identity,* Leslie Adelson deals explicitly with the relationship among bodies, experiences, representation and history. Drawing on the work of German social theorists Oskar Negt and Alexander Kluge and their approach to bodies and history, she argues that "their concept of an economy of experience [*Erfahrungsokonomie*] allows for the body as the site of cognition, the organ of historical experience, and the field onto and on which multiple, sometimes contradictory social antagonisms are projected and enacted." Quite simply, Adelson conceives the body as a site of both representation *and* experience where the body and the world – if such a distinction can be made for the moment – are both active and are mutually constituted/constituting. While she cautions that "the discursive representation of the body must not be mistaken for the body of experience, however

---

[23] Duden, "History Beneath the Skin," 175, 176, 180, 183, 185, 187.

intricately imbricated the two may be,"[24] she does not address how historians might make this mistake nor does she consider that it might be impossible to separate the two.

Considering that neither experience nor representation are possible without the body and that the body is the site where these are filtered through each other, discursive representation cannot help but be "mistaken" for the body of experience. The site of production of both are the same, and simultaneous. The question, then, is how to examine the dissonances and tensions of representations and experiences, discourses and materialities? What might such an examination reveal? And what are the implications of such an investigation for Adelson's assertion, posited at the outset, that "history without bodies is unimaginable," and my own initial claim that all history might indeed be "body history?"

Framing Bodies of History/Histories of the Body

One of the key limitations in current work on the history of the body, as alluded to above, is that scholars have yet to provide a theoretical framework with which to approach the bodies of history and all history as embodied. In an effort to develop such a framework, I turn from historical scholarship to recent writing on the body in geography, anthropology, feminist philosophy, literary theory, and cultural studies. My purpose is not to engage in a sustained critique of these works, but to consider how they might be theoretically useful to the practice of "body history" and historical practice in general. Drawing on these studies, my proposed framework includes four key points. First, it conceives "the body" as simultaneously and always material and discursive, experienced, and represented. Second, it relies on embodiment as the mode through which bodies are in the world. Third, it situates the body in space where spaces-bodies are not separate, but are constitutive of each other. Fourth, it sees power as productive.

1. Material-discursive Bodies

In considering the lives of chronically ill women, feminist geographers Pamela Moss and Isabel Dyck have refused to theorize the "chronically ill body." Rather, they look at the ways in which women with chronic illnesses are both well and ill, able and disabled as they "exist through corporeal sensations and meanings of bodies ascribed by discourses." Their focus is on the "entwinement, to the point of simultaneity rather than unity, of the discursive body – through inscription, signification, complicity – and the material body – through activity, sensation, modification."[25] Through these recursive constitutive processes, there can be no general body; rather, they demonstrate that the body is always becoming specific through interactions with other bodies in lived corporeal spaces. English scholar Samira Kawash's important work on "the homeless body" pushes Moss and Dyck's analysis

---

[24] Adelson, *Making Bodies*, 20.
[25] Pamela Moss and Isabel Dyck, *Women, Body, Illness: Space and Identity in the Everyday Lives of Women with Chronic Illness* (New York: Rowman & Littlefield Publishers, 2002), 34, 37.

further. In tracing the "homeless body" as a "product" of the struggle for control of so-called public space, she argues that "the homeless body emerges as the corporeal mark of the constitutive outside of the realm of the public, a product of the same spatial and economic processes that work to secure a place for the public. The body is therefore simultaneously material and emergent."[26] To illustrate this claim, she points out the association between "filth and stench" and homeless bodies and argues that this mode of embodiment/the homeless body emerges through discourses and practices of power.

How are these concepts useful for history? These works are important to approaching the body historically, first, because they posit that there is no such thing as the body in general. Historically speaking, then, these theoretical insights are useful in problematizing, for example, the notion that a medieval body and a twenty-first century body can be conceived and approached by historians as one and in the same. Second, they posit that the body is something which *becomes specific,* emerging through material practice and representational discourse. In these conceptions the body is not a preconceived object to be sought out in history but is to be understood by historians as *made,* both within time and over time, through recursive experiential and representational constitutive processes.

2. Embodiment

In "The Body as Method?" Kathleen Canning suggests that the notion of embodiment, "a far less fixed and idealised concept than body," might be useful for studying the body in history, in that it "encompasses moments of encounter and interpretation, agency and resistance."[27] Similarly, philosopher N. Katherine Hayles argues that "embodiment is contextual, enwebbed within the specifics of place, time, physiology and culture that together comprise enactment. Embodiment never coincides exactly with the 'body'... Embodiment is the specific instantiation generated by the noise of difference."[28] Echoing this definition, and clarifying the ways in which embodiment does not coincide exactly with the body, Moss and Dyck define embodiment as "those lived spaces where bodies are located conceptually and corporeally, metaphorically and concretely, discursively and materially, being simultaneously part of bodily forms and their social constructions." They argue that embodiment is about being connected – temporally and historically – to other discursive and material entities – other bodies – in concrete practices, politically, culturally, socially, economically and spatially.[29] Simply put, embodiment is the mode through which bodies are in the world.

A slightly different, but equally significant perspective on embodiment is put forth by feminist cultural studies theorists Abigail Bray and Claire Colebrook who argue that "if the body is not a prediscursive matter that is then organized by representation, one might see the body as an event of

---

[26] Samira Kawash, "The Homeless Body," *Public Culture* 10, no. 2 (1998): 329.
[27] Canning, "Body as Method?," 505.
[28] N. Katherine Hayles, "The Materiality of Informatics," *Configurations* 1, no. 1 (1993): 154-55.
[29] Moss and Dyck, *Women, Body, Illness,* 55.

expression ... The body would be understood in terms of what [Gilles] Deleuze calls its becomings, connections, events and activities ... Action is productive rather than representational. Accordingly one should ask what an action does rather than what it means."[30] The notions of embodiment and the body as an event of expression are almost but not quite synonymous. When held in tension these concepts can be helpful in studying "the body" in history. By employing "embodiment" and "the body as an event" it is possible to see bodies as actions and processes and to ask and explore what they *do* and what they *did* in the past. Rather than merely examining and ascribing meaning to the relatively fixed body, as Canning sees it, analyzing embodiment as a process of negotiation and constitution between the self and the world, and bodies as productive events whose "doings" might be scrutinized, is a far more dynamic and fruitful mode of historical investigation.

3. Space

On a material level, Duden's work contains an important conception of space. She asserts that the idea of body and space as separate is itself a historical construction: "The body and its environment have been consigned to opposing realms: on one side are the body, nature, and biology, stable and unchanging phenomena; on the other side are the social environment and history, realms of life subject to constant change. With the drawing of this boundary, the body was expelled from history."[31] Emphasizing the importance of conceptualizing bodies and spaces as one and the same, Moss and Dyck use the theoretical concept of "corporeal space," which they define as "an interim state within spatiality, constitutive of the discursive and the material. Corporeal space comprises the living spaces of 'bodies in context,' claiming both the temporal and spatial specificity of bodies, giving rise to specific bodies and specific environments."[32] In their conception, bodies and spaces are made specific through their relationships in specific arrangements of the deployment of power. Illustrating this claim materially, Kawash notes that the "homeless body" emerges within the continuous negotiation between the functions and needs of the body (sleeping, eating, excreting, warmth, rest, safety) and the places the body can function. She argues that "the specificities of its functioning, its contours, and its conditions, are produced in and by its contingent and continuously contested emplacements."[33]

Feminist philosopher Elizabeth Grosz articulates a different, yet equally important, conceptualization of space. According to Grosz, French sociologist Roger Callois has argued that "for a subject to take up a position as subject, he must be able to situate himself as being located in the space

---

[30] Abigail Bray and Claire Colebrook, "The Haunted Flesh: Corporeal Feminism and the Politics of (Dis)Embodiment," *Signs: Journal of Women in Culture and Society* 24, no.1 (1998): 36, 57.
[31] Barbara Duden, *The Woman Beneath the Skin* (Cambridge: Harvard University Press, 1991), vi.
[32] Moss and Dyck, *Women, Body, Illness*, 54.
[33] Kawash, "Homeless Body," 334.

occupied by his body."³⁴ This might appear straightforward and it could potentially be argued that *all* bodies are located in the spaces which they occupy. Kawash, however, illuminates that this is not always so. For her, the relationship between bodies and spaces is a relationship of power: "the closure of society that is the aim of securing the public requires that a public space for the homeless body be denied." She highlights the contradiction which results between the material body that certainly does occupy space and the denial of any place for such a body. The resolution to this contradiction, as Kawash notes, is enacted through "violent processes of containment, constriction and compression that seek not simply to exclude or control the homeless but rather to efface their presence altogether."³⁵

As bodies in history certainly existed in space, and space shaped bodies, historians can use the work of these scholars to ask a series of significant historical questions. First, how did specific spaces – for example, the trenches of World War I, the nineteenth-century Canadian hospital, the early twentieth-century American college football field, the 1950s North American suburbs - "give rise to specific bodies?" How did bodies shape these environments? What new historical insights might emerge from undertaking such an analysis? Second, in what times and spaces have certain people – for example "slaves" in the early nineteenth century American South, First Nations peoples in colonial British Columbia, people charged as vagrants and vagabonds in seventeenth-century Europe - been dislocated from certain spaces? What were the implications of this dislocation? How were these bodies contained and constricted? What might this spatial and embodied examination reveal to the historian about larger historical processes such as slavery, colonialism, state formation, and the maintenance of social order?

4. Power

In order to understand the workings of power in shaping, enabling, and producing specific bodies in specific "pasts," Judith Butler's reading of Michel Foucault is indispensable. Drawing on his work, Butler asserts that relations of power are always productive. Importantly, she does not locate power as an external force that "acts on," but argues "there is no power that acts, but only a reiterated acting that is power in its persistence and instability." She sees power as a constitutive restraint which does not foreclose the possibility of agency. However, if agency is to be conceptualized within the relations of productive power, then power must also be viewed as a constitutive possibility for in every instant that something is restrained, something else is also made possible. If productive power is thus conceived, Butler's notion of "agency as a reiterative or rearticulative practice, immanent to power, and not a

---

[34] Elizabeth Grosz, *Space, Time and Perversion* (New York: Routledge, 1995), 89. She justifies her use of "he" by stating that she uses it "advisedly; the relevance of the question of sexual difference to Callois's account needs careful consideration if it is to be taken as relevant for women as well." This is clearly an important question; however, due to space constraints, I will not address it here.

[35] Kawash, "Homeless Body," 330.

relation of external opposition to power"[36] is useful in attempting to access bodies in history and (their) modes of embodiment as always embedded within particular deployments of power through which they are constituted, and through which power is resisted, contested and thus is also constituted.

What is (Body) History?
> History does not happen *to* people; it is a function of the relationships among bodies, which are themselves historically constituted, and the concretized structures of social organization in which they interact.[37]

Thus conceived history is undeniably a history of bodies and the ways in which they moved in the world, shaping it, and being shaped, as they went. History is the study of the relationships among bodies, their experiences and their representations. It is an examination of how people negotiated embodiment – the relationships between themselves, their bodies, and the world. It is an analysis of what bodies did and an interrogation of the implications, consequences, and products of these "doings." History is the exploration of the ways in which bodies and spaces were made specific in particular times and places; it is an investigation of the violent exclusion of certain bodies from certain spaces and the processes and bodies through and by which this exclusion was executed. Finally, and critically, history is an examination of the workings of power and agency, acting on, and enacted by, historical subjects within and against institutions, political, social and economic forces, dominant discourse and practice, that is, within and against other historical bodies.

---

[36] Judith Butler, *Bodies that Matter: On the Discursive Limits of "Sex"* (New York: Routledge, 1993), 9, 15, 109.
[37] Adelson, *Making Bodies*, 23.

–5–

The Uncooperative Primary Source
Literary Recovery versus Historical Fact in the Strange Production of *Cogewea*

Robert Strong

As the first novel written by a Native American woman, *Cogewea: The Half-Blood* holds a position of historical and symbolic importance for American literature. Prepared in manuscript form as early as 1914, but not published until 1927, *Cogewea* is a fascinating read that blends tropes from romance, Western, autoethnography, captivity narrative, and realism. In its confusions, earnestness, and collaborative minglings, Mourning Dove's novel is uniquely North American; it could not have been written by anyone but a North American. The excitement and tension of its contents, its multi-voicings, and the necessary frustrations of its narrative sutures comprise a consummate artistic enactment of the American West in the nineteenth century.

Unfortunately, the bulk of criticism on Mourning Dove's novel is stuck on two things: the fact of its collaborative nature with Lucullus Virgil McWhorter and the "recovery" impulse in current literary scholarship. The latter may seem an odd predicament for a text that was never "lost." But the impulse toward this gesture is so strong that as late as 1999, in an article that otherwise takes some preliminary steps toward a progressive criticism, Alicia Kent feels compelled to proclaim, "My endeavor is an attempt to 'recover' a forgotten Native American writer" (41). Granted, Kent makes this statement in the same spirit of this paper - to expand the readership and understanding of an important text - but her use of "recovery" terminology reveals the framework in place.

This sort of "revisionist reclaiming," as Kent calls her mission, stands implicitly and firmly in a certain relation to the American canon. This vision, like our history, is tangled up with issues of power, race, and gender. The arguments here are familiar to all. In the case of *Cogewea*, however, the fact that Mourning Dove created the book we know in collaboration with a white male anthropologist sets the novel in a diametric symbiosis with the "recovery" trend. In a sense, for a critical mode engaging and re-visioning the white patriarchy's hold on literature, *Cogewea* is almost too perfect. Current critical impulses lock in a closed-circuit with the fact of the book's composition; the two circle in an endless loop.

The irony is large. *Cogewea* provides the source text for so many fertile issues in our literature, yet the critics cannot proceed. In my investigation of the relevant scholarship, its repeating nature became clear immediately. Take this passage describing Mourning Dove from Dexter Fisher's introduction to the novel:

> Always encouraged by McWhorter to share the knowledge with a wider audience, she began to give public lectures on the traditions

of her tribe and was invited back east to speak, but her appearances were infrequent because she was uncomfortable before strange audiences and could not afford the money to cover her travel expenses. The one accolade she did eventually achieve, and the one that meant the most to her, was her election as an honorary member of the Eastern Washington State Historical Society (ix).

And here, from a completely different author, is a passage from the *Heath Anthology*'s introduction to Mourning Dove:

> Occasionally she traveled to lecture in the East, but she was uncomfortable before strange audiences and could hardly afford the travel expenses. The single honor bestowed on her was her election as an honorary member of the Eastern Washington State Historical Society (1813).

The *Heath* is perhaps the most important institution for the spirit of "recovery" in American Literature and, as such, we owe it a great debt. But these mirrored passages serve as a high profile example of the shallow loop which exists in *Cogewea* scholarship.

As we will see later, a central problem with this mode of scholarship is that, while it claims to recover texts, it often ghettoizes them in the process. This may be, I am willing to concede, a necessary step on the road to a fuller, healthier, reading; but it's not a step we should linger on any longer than necessary. The *Heath* claims that Mourning Dove's introduction to *Coyote Stories* (a collection of native tales encouraged by McWhorter) "gives *authenticity* to her collection by describing her family heritage and the tribal setting in which these stories were passed on" (1813, my emphasis). The barest investigation, however, reveals that Mourning Dove was actively working *against* authenticity. Her twin reasons for this effort were a desire to make "literature," as she understood it, in the White/Western tradition and the knowledge that such a thing was very different from her native oral tradition. Mourning Dove removed

> morals and "just-so" explanations from some of the stories so they could not be ridiculed by whites. The accounts of how things came to be as they are and episodes likely to suggest superstition to a white audience were deleted, though such alterations made the stories unrecognizable to her own family and other Colville elders (Miller xxiii).

In pursuing her desire to create a literature that would be accepted by literary society, Mourning Dove "removed scatological and sexual elements of the Coyote stories in order to avoid reinforcing mainstream audience's stereotypes of Native American peoples" (Bernardin 508). Her "fear that McWhorter's revisions might alienate a white audience suggests that her western romance was designed to draw in readers otherwise indifferent to Native American perspective" (Ibid., 492). Mourning Dove was aware that her culture and literary culture were separate, so, quite simply, she set out to synthesize them - a very different approach than the *Heath*'s recycling of dull stereotypes of Native Americans in its assessment that *Coyote Stories* provides "aboriginal insight into the subtle connections between physical and psychological vitality and their grounding in cosmological mystery" (1813).

Critical recourse to Mourning Dove's letters and commentary is shockingly limited. The fascinating thing about this writer and her work/correspondence with McWhorter is that they enacted the opposite positions we would expect of them. Mourning Dove is the aspiring novelist of fictional romantic realism and McWhorter the politically motivated supporter of native rights. For critics invested in the framework of "recovery," it seems the documentation of the collaboration will tell this story - the "wrong" story. The most referenced letter (perhaps simply because the novel's introduction makes part of it available) is Mourning Dove's 4 June 1928 response upon finally receiving a copy of her published novel. Nowhere have I discovered the entire text of the letter put to use. Here is the section which appears in Fisher's introduction ("Big Foot" was the name given McWhorter by the Colville Salishan):

> Dear Big Foot,
>
> I have just got through going over the book *Cogewea*, and am surprised at the changes that you made. I think they are fine, and you made a tasty dressing like a cook would do with a fine meal. I sure was interested in the book, and hubby read it over and also all the rest of the family neglected their housework till they read it cover to cover. I felt like it was some one else[']s book and not mine at all. In fact the finishing touches are put there by you, and I have never seen it (xv).

In an article in *American Literature* in 1995, Susan K. Bernardin is content to quote from the letter thus:

> I have just got through going over the book *Cogewea* and am surprised at the changes that you made ... I felt like it was some one else[']s book and not mine at all. In fact the finishing touches are put there by you, and I have never seen it ... Oh my Big Foot, you surely roasted the Shoapees [whites] strong. I think a little too strong to get their sympathy. I wish we had not gone too strong now. That is the only thing I am afraid of (492).

Most articles are content to boil the letter down to the single sentence "I felt like it was some one else[']s book and not mine at all." Such elliptical citations hint at the correspondence's untapped potential for *Cogewea* scholarship. The gaps we are allowed to "see" here are suggestive. Bernardin erases Mourning Dove's praise for the book (the novelist elsewhere admits to McWhorter it never would have been published without him) while revealing what Fisher omits - Mourning Dove's complaint concerned with her desired white audience. In the diametric structure of "recovery vs. canon," the book is too politically "native" for the author's taste. (As her caution in editing the subsequent *Coyote Stories* shows, Mourning Dove learned her lesson on this issue.)

It is the strength of this diametric structure, I believe, that lends itself to a misreading of *Cogewea*. "Recovery" demands an "outsider" text suppressed or manipulated by the dominant structure to serve its own ends. The Mourning Dove/McWhorter dynamic is not such an easy fit. The critical framework currently at play, entangled as it is with racial history, contemporary identity politics, and corrective gestures from the academy, ironically forces the players into the "proper" positions opposite from the ones they actually inhabited. Thus we have Charles Larson, in what Alicia Kent labels the "seminal study on American Indian Fiction" declaring that it is "regrettable for the student of Indian fiction that Mourning Dove relied on others for help in writing the book, since it is impossible to determine the extent of the editor's coloring of her story with his own interpretations and judgments. Although the novel might have been less polished if she had written it herself, the author's stance toward her Indian subject (and toward white culture) might not have been so ambivalent" (Kent 46). Quite to the contrary, as my cursory gloss shows above, Mourning Dove was actually worried about McWhorter's changes making the text more *un-ambivalent.* Such concern reveals the author's understanding, over and above her editor's, that literature's mettle is tested by the complexity of its ambivalences.

I wish to show that the very things which the critics have been shying away from (because they don't fit into the "recovery" model) are, in fact, the issues that will simultaneously break the critical feedback loop, confirm the issues that have been unproductively pursued, and free *Cogewea* to give it its full contribution to American reading. Our literature is inextricably bound with issues of politics, power, and race; I suggest no political shifts here. Recovery is, indeed, an essential tool for our scholarship. I am, however, deeply disturbed by the results: a ghettoization of certain literatures inevitably bound within the terms which were meant to set them "free." This dynamic is beginning to extend off the page, having the horrific and ironic effect of insisting that literary content is inextricably bound to skin color and ethnicity. We want our students of American Literature (who, where I teach, are overwhelmingly white and upper class) to experience all its voices as relevant to them. The critical framework which keeps insisting on Mourning Dove's "nativeness" in the face of all the evidence that she struggled for a less native effect, makes the same demand of its professors. Ironically, the unedited text of her correspondence, in voice and grammar, *would* apparently reveal the "native" writer - just not in the correct terms.

Allowing the recovery framework to dictate the "position" of minority writers reinforces stereotypes; it makes them, first, "minority" writers. My goal here is to offer a corrective extension to that framework which will allow us to continue "recognizing" past injustices and facts-of-literature while using them as a positive tool to continue our critical evolution - both in scholarship and in teaching.

***

> It is all wrong, this saying that Indians do not feel as deeply as whites. We do feel, and by and by some of us are going to be able to make our feelings appreciated... Mourning Dove in a 1916 interview (Miller xxi).
>
> McWhorter was concerned that Indian themes and concerns be highlighted, whereas Mourning Dove wanted to express her knowledge and literary talents (Ibid., xxiii).
>
> When Nature, as self-proximity, comes to be forbidden or interrupted, when speech fails to protect presence, writing becomes necessary. It must be *added* to the word urgently. Derrida, "That Dangerous Supplement," *Of Grammatology* (144).

Derrida's concept of "That Dangerous Supplement" of writing is where I begin my reassessment. Mourning Dove, as we see in the first two quotes here, understood the necessity of engaging with the Dangerous Supplement. Indeed, this is the dilemma for any oral culture when confronted with "civilization." The "danger" of writing becomes a necessary one for a group of people who suddenly have nothing (or everything) to lose. Derrida, perhaps, is considering only a "monocultural" context when he describes the supplemental "act of writing [as] essentially ... the greatest sacrifice aiming at the greatest symbolic reappropriation of presence" (Ibid., 142). We can certainly speak of "sacrifice" in Native American writing; indeed, there are issues of cross-cultural translation, power dynamics, and absolute physical survival not included in Derrida's sense of the word. As the fictional character, Cogewea herself is aware the natives "had suffered as much from the pen as from the bayonet of conquest; wherein the annals had always been chronicled by their most deadly foes and partisan writers" (Mourning Dove 92). If the reality of one's "presence" is the bayonet, then the "danger" that writing intrinsically "dislocates the subject that it constructs, prevents it from being present to its signs, torments its language with a complete writing," is less a loss than a positive gesture of adaptive self-preservation (Derrida 141). This fact, at least, is not completely lost on critics:

> Mourning Dove's response to the forced assimilation was to adapt to [make] the transition from oral to written expression. She was thus able to engage in modernity, literally by adopting the modern mode of expression in writing ... For many Native Americans, the transition from tribal languages to English and from oral to written meant a loss of culture and tribal identity. But, as another response to the modern period, some American Indians turned to writing literature as a way of surviving and preserving in the face of the dramatic upheaval and forced assimilation at the turn of the century. As Dexter Fisher points out, "Writing became a means to perpetuate tradition in the face of cultural disintegration." Through

the written text, Native American writers attempt to reclaim textually what has been taken from them geographically. American Indian texts aim to right (write) the wrongs of the past and preserve in writing the oral stories for the future (Kent 44).

I must note, however, how Kent diverges from Mourning Dove in the last sentence. As we have seen, Mourning Dove's intent was much more complicated than simply to "preserve in writing the oral stories for the future." This critical slippage is symptomatic (and I will note the shallow critical cycle, again, indicated by the reference to Dexter Fisher). The evidence suggests, actually, that Mourning Dove knew such preservation was impossible. Her goal was to help the white audience realize the humanity of Native Americans by presenting trans-cultural communications of their culture.

In her conscious appropriation of the Supplement, Mourning Dove necessarily chose Realism, the genre which is closest to the spirit of Derrida's "Dangerous Supplement" and its "straining toward the reconstruction of presence" (Derrida 141). Mourning Dove, I argue, was conscious of her use of the Supplement in some very sophisticated ways. She was using it to prove her people felt "as deeply as whites." At the same time, she was aware of the Supplement's oppositions to the natural structures of her culture, as her letter of 12 February 1930 on the editing of *Coyote Stories* shows: "You will see in my recasting I have purposely omitted a lot of things, that is an objection to printing and editing, but an Indian that knows the story can read between the line[s]" (Mourning Dove, Letters).

This is a writer who realizes the Supplement is double-edged, but is confident that she can wield this dagger both ways. I propose a critical approach to American Ethnic Realism that is as brave and headstrong as Mourning Dove's creative approach. And it is with the Dangerous Supplement that our instincts for "recovery" can be renewed in a way that refuses easy stereotypes and the unintended hypocrisy of institutional ghettoization of the literature.

If there is one thing in need of (and indeed available to) "recovery" in Mourning Dove's *oeuvre*, it is her correspondence with McWhorter. Why, if their collaboration is so central to the existing scholarship on the novel, has it *not* been recovered? The entire collection is sitting in the Washington State University Library; I have been communicating with the librarians there, and they know of no scholar ever making a full transcription. Why not? I believe that the introduction of the full text of the letters would greatly interfere with current readings of *Cogewea* - and, yet, I contend that it need do so only to move us forward to a more productive analysis. The recovery gesture makes the necessary move of claiming antitheses to a stifling canon while refusing to move toward a synthesis. In fact, taken together with Derrida's ideas, Mourning Dove's technique can become proactive in its own fully synthesized recovery. As we have seen from her statements, this was, indeed, her goal - to bring a native literature to a middle ground to meet a white audience.

It is perhaps not surprising that the most honest assessment of Mourning Dove's writing and biography comes, not from a literary scholar, but rather from an expert in native history: the editor of her autobiography, Jay

Miller. (He also did the research necessary to establish that Mourning Dove was not, as she claimed, a "half-breed," but actually a full-blooded Native American.) In detailing his difficulties in preparing the manuscript of her autobiography, he explains that Mourning Dove was "[u]nsure about spelling and usage, she was never comfortable with English, and some of her phrasings can be difficult to understand unless one is familiar with Colville English idiom" (Miller xxxiii). While I disagree with this analysis, Miller is helpful in pointing out how the unique grammatical structures of Salishan and its lack of gendered pronouns influenced Mourning Dove's English writing. He provides us with this wonderful writing sample from her manuscript:

> The clothing of the family is usually made of deer skins tanned, or furs of small animals like the rabbit skin is used for babies in winter months to keep them snug and warm. Coyote skins make the jackets of the older people when tanned with the fur on by tying the rear end around the neck and tying it under the arms and down in front to keep their shoulders warm (Ibid., xxxvi).

If the scholars I have cited have actually been to the letters, the only reason for keeping such writing from the audience is that it suggests a massive amount of editing done by McWhorter to produce the book's final form (there are no extant working manuscripts of the collaboration). For critics invested in an uncritical mode of recovery, such an admission might represent a step backward, returning to the previous (and incorrect) critical stance: that Mourning Dove should not be considered the *Cogewea* full author.

However, rather than allowing the inclusive gestures which were essential to Mourning Dove's project as we can now understand it, leaving such writing "unrecovered" has the same effect as McWhorter's editorial interference (such as his use of epigraphs to frame each chapter): preventing Mourning Dove from writing the synthesis that is the American voice, the voice of the "half-breed." (And here it is significant that, as we now know, Mourning Dove had to invent her half-breed status.) Both McWhorter's editorializing and critics' avoidance of the true nature of the writing it affected is a denial of the possibility of a *half-breed language*. Just as Mourning Dove was able to draw on all her resources (including McWhorter) to approach the reality of her American existence, we, the scholars of today, should recognize the *positive* reification of her dilemmas in the odd text that became *Cogewea*. The facts of its production informs a fertile tension with Derrida's concept that

> the person writing is inscribed in a determined textual system. Even if there is never a pure signified, there are different relationships as to that which, from the signifier, is presented as the irreducible stratum of the signified. For example, the philosophical text, although it is in fact always written, includes, precisely as its philosophical specificity, the project of effacing itself in the face of the signified content which it transports and in general teaches. Reading should be aware of this project, even if, in the last analysis, it intends to expose the project's failure. The entire

history of texts, and within it the history of literary forms in the West, should be studied from this point of view. With the exception of a thrust or point of resistance which has only been very lately recognized as such, literary writing has, almost always and almost everywhere, according to some fashions and across very diverse ages, lent itself to this transcendent reading, in that search for the signified which were here put in question, not to annul it but to understand it within a system to which such a reading is blind [sic] (Derrida 160).

Cogewea, of course, is subject to this analysis, but the text also accomplishes the opposite. Rather than attempting to "efface itself of the content it transports," Mourning Dove's writing tries desperately to enter into that content. And she is able to attempt this because she is *not* "inscribed in a determined textual system" but, rather, attempting to co-opt and invent a truly American system. (As McWhorter simultaneously encourages her to co-opt her orality *into* the system.) Mourning Dove operates, therefore, outside (or, if not strictly "outside," further than any of her contemporary writers toward the "edge of") the "entire history of texts." Given her unique cultural relationship to writing, Mourning Dove's goal is pre-"*transcendent.*" She wants to enter and then, rather than transcend, to *transform* the "immense series of structures, of historical totalities of all orders ... organized, enveloped, and blended" into the Supplement she is stepping into (Ibid., 161).

***

In classical ethnographies the voice of the author was always manifest, but the conventions of textual representation and reading forbade too close a connection between authorial style and the reality represented ... The subjectivity of the author is separated from the objective referent of the text. At best, the author's personal voice is seen as a style in the weak sense: a tone, or embellishment of facts (Clifford 13).

This passage from a collection of essays on the politics of writing ethnography helps elucidate the unique position of Mourning Dove's novel. Above, the author *is* the ethnographer. In *Cogewea*, that position of authority is split in two: becoming Mourning Dove *and* McWhorter. The close connection between authorial style and reality represented is therefore collapsed (in that the single author-as-ethnographer conflict of interest which "forbade" the connection does not exist). But this very fact also serves to complicate the connection and complicate our reading. For Derrida, however, it is with the *reader* that the Supplement moves from dangerous to productive:

[T]he writer writes *in* a language and *in* a logic whose proper system, laws and [her] life discourse by definition cannot dominate absolutely. [She] uses them only by letting [her]self, after a fashion and up to a point, be governed by the system. And the reading must always aim at a certain relationship, unperceived by the writer, between what [**she**] commands and what **he** does not command of the patterns of the language that [**she**] uses. This relationship is not a certain quantitative distribution of shadow and light, of weakness and force, but a signifying structure that critical reading should *produce* (Derrida 158, my emphasis).

I manipulate Derrida's pronouns here to highlight how his thinking cannot quite embrace Mourning Dove's unique situation and to reveal how, on the contrary, the Dove/McWhorter collaboration is a lively enactment of the drama of the Supplement. I argue that the bulk of scholarship is blinded by its need, inherent to the current ideas of recovery, to map "a certain quantitative distribution of ... weakness and force." Rather, it should move forward with critical readings that can "produce" everything that *Cogewea* makes possible. The critic Brian Massumi, in his recent calls for a more "productivist" criticism, echoes my concern when he claims that critical thinking "disavows its own inventiveness as much as possible ... [b]ecause it sees itself as uncovering something it claims was hidden or as debunking something it desires to subtract from the world" (Massumi 12).

The idea that a critical reading should "produce" is tempered by Derrida's warning that this mode can also "risk developing in any direction at all and authorize itself to say almost anything." He reminds us that while a "reading must not be content with doubling the text," there is also "nothing outside the text" (Derrida 158). This is, indeed, the fertile dilemma provided by *Cogewea*. It is a text that comes to the reader already "doubled" - doubled in authors, cultures, agendas, and productions. It comes to the reader indicating a multitude of forces outside the text, or, perhaps we should say, the novel tells us that its text extends to the correspondence, to the "source" novel *The Brand* (which Mourning Dove inserts into her own text), and to the ethnography detailed in *Cogewea*'s notes (appended by McWhorter). If a critical reading is to produce anything that is truly in the spirit of this text, it will be the very synthesis it desires. Mourning Dove did not write to further delineate her American world, but to show it melting together (romantically) in some more humane and just way. The complications of the text's production and presentation are a raw enactment of that possibility.

The world depicted in *Cogewea* represents the American melting pot just as the heat is rising. Today, the metaphor of the melting pot is often derided as a metaphor of hierarchical homogenization. But, as Mourning Dove knew, every ingredient changes the final flavor; the destiny of America is to be a land of "half-breeds." America may never again produce a novel that so perfectly reveals and enacts the country's bizarre origins and growth pains. In this sequence of supplements, Derrida writes,

> a necessity is announced: that of an infinite chain, ineluctably multiplying the supplementary mediations that produce the sense of the very thing they defer: the mirage of the thing itself, of immediate presence, of originary perception. Immediacy is

derived. That all begins through the intermediary is what is indeed "inconceivable [to reason]" (157, Derrida's brackets).

America is derived; the intermediary is a collaborative contact zone of cultures, each taking on the opposite project the critics want them to have. For a culture and its literature created in the melting of many cultures, there is no original presence - all creation meets and begins within the Supplement. It is dangerous and productive, and a necessary synthesis.

References

Bernardin, Susan K, "Mixed Messages: Authority and Authorship in Mourning Dove's *Cogewea, The Half-Blood: A Depiction of the Great Montana Cattle Range.*" *American Literature* 67, no. 3 (1995): 487-509.

Clifford, James and George E. Marcus, eds., *Writing Culture: The Poetics and Politics of Ethnography*. Berkeley: University of California Press, 1986.

Derrida, Jacques, *Of Grammatology*. Baltimore: The Johns Hopkins University Press, 1977.

Kent, Alicia, "Mourning Dove's *Cogewea*: Writing Her Way into Modernity." *MELUS* 24, no. 3 (1999): 39-67.

Lauter, Paul, ed., *The Heath Anthology of American Literature*, 4th ed Boston: Houghton Mifflin, 2002.

Massumi, Brian, *Parable for the Virtual*. Durham: Duke University Press, 2002.

Miller, Jay, ed., *Mourning Dove: A Salishan Autobiography*. Lincoln: Nebraska University Press, 1990.

Mourning Dove, *Cogewea: The Half-Blood*. Lincoln: Nebraska University Press, 1991.

Washington State University Library, Lucullus Virgil McWhorter papers, Mourning Dove Letters.

– 6 –

Reading Books/Reading Lives
Culture, Language and Power in Nineteenth-Century School Readers

Barbara Lorenzkowski

Written in pencil, the letters on the page are fading, yet still convey a boyish exuberance. "Today," Louis Breithaupt scribbled into his diary on March 21, 1867, "I received a beautiful picture from Mr. Wittig (the German teacher at school) because I read from page 120 to 215 in the German reader. I'm good." In deciphering the Gothic print of his German reader, the twelve-year heir of one of Berlin's premier families enjoyed a distinct advantage. Louis was growing up in Waterloo County, the heartland of German settlement in nineteenth century Ontario, whose residents lived their lives in both German and English. His diary is a humbling reminder that learning depends more on a child's social world than it does on textbooks, teachers, and curricula.[1]

When Louis immersed himself into the pages of his "German reader," his reading of religious verses, moral tales, and edifying fables was filtered through the lenses of his ethnicity, class, and gender. To the classroom, the twelve-year old brought not only a ready command of oral and written German, but also a familiarity with German culture and lore that helped him unravel the cultural connotations of the lessons. The values of thrift, hard work, piety, character, and obedience, in turn, which mid-nineteenth century school readers sought to inculcate, resonated with the expectations of Louis's family that was bourgeois in its ownership of a leather tannery, but essentially middle class in its outlook.[2] Because of his gender, finally, Louis spent far fewer hours in the classroom than his younger sisters. Readily, Liborious and Katharina Breithaupt pulled their eldest sons out of school to work at the leather tannery, run errands, buy staples, help on the farm, and tend to pigs, cows, and horses. The demands of the family economy valued children's labour over regular school attendance, thus teaching lessons in living more varied, and perhaps more colourful, than those learned at the school bench. While Louis' comments on his schoolwork were brief and perfunctory, he meticulously chronicled his father's business-trips, negotiations, and investments, growing into a world of work that gradually began to overshadow his life as a pupil. In the fabric of Louis' life schooling is represented but one

---

[1] University of Waterloo, Doris Lewis Rate Book Room, Breithaupt Hewetson Clerk Collection, "Diaries of Louis Jacob Breithaupt," March 21, 1867, and Neil Sutherland, "The Urban Child," *History of Education Quarterly* 9, No. 3 (Fall 1969): 305.

[2] As Mary P. Ryan has observed in her analysis of Victorian child-rearing practices, the "sly manipulations of maternal socialization" were intended to implant "the usual array of petit bourgeois traits - honesty, industry, frugality, temperance, and, pre-eminently, self control." See *Cradle of the Middle Class: The Family in Oneida County, New York, 1790-1865* (Cambridge: Cambridge University Press, 1984), 161.

thread that was tightly interwoven with many others.³

In providing a privileged inroad into a world of childhood where family, work, school, and church were inseparably intertwined, the diary of Louis Breithaupt suggests new ways of thinking about school readers as an historical source. By shifting attention from the *texts* of the readers to actual *reading practices,* Louis' diary reveals, in tantalising glimpses, how the world beyond the classroom translated into classroom understandings and gave meaning to letters deciphered and stories read, much as Elsie Rockwell has observed in her perceptive study of reading practices at rural Mexican schools. "Local cultures," Rockwell writes, "moulded the actual everyday life in schools" and thus mediated the cultural messages of textbook lessons.⁴ As such, they deserve as much attention as the discursive universe constructed within the readers themselves.

This paper seeks to uncover reading practices in Waterloo County's public schools by blending two approaches that often remain quite separate. It is interested both in the textbooks' cultural narratives that constitute a fascinating repository of cultural values and a purported instrument of social control, and the social history of the classroom. How did the county's schoolchildren, who poured over German and English textbooks, learn to read in the decades between 1850 and 1914? Which books were assigned for classroom use? Upon which educational theories did their teachers draw when instructing their young charges? What were the "protocols for reading," to quote Roger Chartier, that were "encoded" in the textbooks themselves and helped determine the manner of reading?⁵ In which ways, finally, did the local world of Waterloo County, with its unique patterns of language use, shape the use of textbooks in the classroom?

To situate the text of school readers into a specific local world is a challenging undertaking since it means examining cultural practices that have left few traces on the historical record. It is a quest largely ignored by the international literature on textbooks that has probed the construction of social identities instead, offering richly textured accounts of the cultural meanings of virtue, class, gender, race, empire, and national belonging, as they were both reflected in and shaped by school readers.⁶ Other scholars still, Bruce Curtis foremost among them, have characterized school readers as instruments of governance that replaced local knowledge with state-sanctioned lessons in morality and citizenship and drew local communities ever closer into a system

---

³ "Diaries of Louis Jacob Breithaupt," March 5, 6, and 19, 1867; April 1, 1867; May 13, 1867; July 12, 1867; October 17, 1867; June 22, 1868; October 7, 1868; and November 13, 1868.
⁴ Elsie Rockwell, "Learning for Life or Learning from Books: Reading Practices in Mexican Rural Schools (1900 to 1935)," *Paedagogica Historica* 38, no. 1 (2002): 134.
⁵ Quoted in Ibid., 113.
⁶ Linda Clark, *Schooling the Daughters of Marianne: Textbooks and the Socialization of Girls in Modern French Primary Schools* (Albany: State University of New York Press, 1984); Cynthia M. Koch, "The Virtuous Curriculum: Schools and American Culture, 1785-1830" (PhD diss., University of Pennsylvania, 1991); and Stephen Heathorn, *For Home, Country, and Race: Constructing Gender, Class, and Englishness in the Elementary School, 1880-1914* (Toronto: University of Toronto Press, 2000).

of state education.[7] What has escaped the attention of both cultural and socio-political historians is the everyday reality of the classroom - the proverbial "black box" of educational history, as Marc Depaepe and Frank Simon have called it.[8]

This paper pieces together the disparate clues on reading practices and reading protocols that can be gleaned from children's diaries, teaching manuals, German and English school readers, inspectors' reports, visitors' books, private correspondence, government records, and school board minutes. As we shall see, the inter-cultural setting of Waterloo County that was home to a predominantly German-origin population, and yet shared many characteristics of the surrounding "British" counties, not only brought to the fore conversations on reading practices, but also infused these conversations with an added passion; for at stake seemed both the "Canadianness" of the school system and the "Germanness" of Waterloo County. That these debates unfolded in often unexpected social constellations - it was the German settlers of Waterloo County, for example, who lobbied vigorously for a more "Canadian" series of school readers - is vivid testimony to the agency of local society in moulding the province's emergent public school system. And neither was reading a passive process that saw children simply absorbing the moral tales of authorized textbooks. Rather, local authorities re-fashioned teaching tools and pedagogical discourses to suit the changing language patterns of Waterloo County, while readers imbued the German- and English-language lessons with a meaning all of their own.

Whose Textbooks?

In 1865, the Board of Public Instruction of the County of Waterloo published a scathing critique of the Irish readers that had served the county's schools ever since Egerton Ryerson, the superintendent of public schools, had made their adoption all but mandatory in 1846.[9] "In what respect," the board asked, "can these School [sic] books be fairly defined as the 'National Series' when the name Canada is scarcely mentioned in their pages, or only obtains a passing and contemptuous reference?" The defects of the readers were many, the board held. "Canada is invariably treated as a foreign, a wild and uncultivated country; as being barren, covered with dreadful forests (some

---

[7] Bruce Curtis, "Schoolbooks and the Myth of Curricular Republicanism: The State and the Curriculum in Canada West, 1820-1850," *Histoire sociale / Social History* 16, no. 32 (November 1983): 305-29. See also Oisin Patrick Rafferty, "Balancing the Books: Brokerage Politics and the *Ontario Readers* Question," *Historical Studies in Education / Revue d'histoire de l'éducation* 4, no. 1 (1992): 84, 92.

[8] Marc Depaepe and Frank Simon, "Is there any Place for the History of 'Education' in the History of Education?: A Plea for the History of Everyday Educational Reality in and outside Schools," *Paedagogica Historica* 31, no. 1 (1995): 10. See also Harold Silver, "Knowing and not Knowing in the History of Education?" *History of Education* 21, no. 1 (1992): 104-105.

[9] *Report of the Minister of Education for the Years 1880 and 1881* (Toronto: C. Blackett Robinson, 1882), 222. Although school trustees retained the right to choose books of their own liking, they did risk "losing the government grant if they persisted with unauthorized texts." Susan E. Houston and Alison Prentice, *Schooling and Scholars in Nineteenth-Century Ontario* (Toronto: University of Toronto Press, 1988), 238.

books have 'frosts') and hideous marches, as once offensive to the senses and injurious to the human constitution." In embracing the language of progress, so characteristic of nineteenth century boosterism, the elected officials of Waterloo County pointed to the fact that "Not a word is said about the industry and intelligence of the people of Canada ... nor indeed of anything which the reader can treasure in his young mind, and which shall foster the love of country and the pride of citizenship." In moral values, too, the board alleged, the Irish readers were sadly lacking, for they employed "such words as 'debauchery', 'licentiousness', 'concubine', 'pregnancy," that offended Victorian sensibilities and were "only calculated to call up unchaste images."[10]

Egerton Ryerson responded with a passionate defence of the Irish readers and an indignation that was, perhaps, predictable. For him, a graded series of textbooks which carried the stamp of official approval had long constituted the cornerstone of a more uniform and effective school system. Eventually, however, he had to bow to mounting public pressure. In 1868, the Canadian Readers replaced the Irish series of National Readers as Ontario's authorized textbooks, only to be superseded by the Ontario Readers in 1884.[11]

The politics of the textbook is a familiar tale that is commonly viewed through the lenses of state formation. As Oisin Patrick Rafferty has argued, the introduction of a new series of readers "signalled a tightening of the central authority's control over the educational machinery of the province" and led to "diminishing local autonomy."[12] But as the example of Waterloo County vividly illustrates, local society, too, could appropriate the language of nationalism to lobby for a series of readers it regarded as appropriate.[13] These local school promoters, for one, did not reject the policy of standardization as it was symbolized in the state-sanctioned textbooks, but they insisted on shaping its overall thrust. To this end, they entered a conversation with educational authorities that featured co-operation, persuasion, and compromise, and was not above cheerful evasion, whenever the politics of the provincial government clashed with local educational wisdom.[14]

---

[10] *Memorial to the Council of Public Instruction of Upper Canada from the Board of Public Instruction of the County of Waterloo* (Galt: Jaffrat Bros., 1865), 6-8.

[11] See Egerton Ryerson's rebuttal in the *Annual Report of the Normal, Model, Grammar and Common Schools in Upper Canada for the Year 1865* (Ottawa: Hunter, Rose & Co., 1866), 9-11; Houston and Prentice, *Schooling and Scholars*, 237-46; and Curtis, "Schoolbooks and the Myth of Curricular Republicanism," 305-29. For the authorization of the Canadian and Ontario Readers see *Report of the Minister of Education for the Years 1880 and 1881* (Toronto: C. Blackett Robinson, 1882), 222.

[12] Rafferty, "Balancing the Books," 82, 84, and Bruce Curtis, *Building the Educational State: Canada West, 1836-1871* (London: The Althouse Press, 1988).

[13] In calling for a greater Canadian sentiment in school readers, Waterloo County's school promoters coached their criticism in the language of nationalism: "Should not every leaf of these little volumes while conveying the seeds of elementary knowledge to the children of the land, stimulate their youthful patriotism and exalt their love of country?" See *Memorial to the Council of Public Instruction*.

[14] The classic formulation of the influence of local society in shaping the emergent public school system is D. A. Lawr and R. D. Gidney, "Who Ran the Schools?: Local Influence on Education Policy in Nineteenth-century Ontario," *Ontario History* 72, no. 3 (September 1980): 131-43.

And nor should we assume that the world of literacy to which Waterloo County's schoolchildren were introduced between the mid-nineteenth century and the Great War consisted of authorized English-language textbooks alone. In the early 1870s, fifty to seventy-five per cent of the county's schoolchildren - "yes, in some sections, even 100 per cent" - made their first attempt to speak English when they entered school. By 1874, sixteen per cent of the county's schoolchildren attended German-language classes that offered up to twelve hours of weekly instruction in reading, writing, and grammar.[15] The strongholds of German-instruction were located in towns and incorporated villages - Berlin, Preston, New Hamburg, and Waterloo Village - that enrolled roughly equal percentages of German- and English-speaking children in the late 1880s.[16] In the absence of authorized German readers, the county's teachers and trustees introduced a variety of German-language textbooks into the classroom that had been published both locally and in the United States. Unbeknownst to the Department of Education in Toronto, a chorus of different German voices thus joined the approved English-language reading fare.

The choice of German readers reflected the changing cultural mentalities of Waterloo County's residents. Settled by Pennsylvania Mennonites in the early nineteenth century, the area later attracted Catholics from Germany and Alsace, who worked as day labourers on Mennonite farms until they could afford their own parcels of land. As the historian Kenneth McLaughlin has suggested, the relationship between Mennonite settlers and subsequent Catholic and Protestant arrivals was characterized not by conflict, but manifold interactions and cultural exchanges - a fluidity that hardened only later in the nineteenth century.[17] The pan-Christian spirit that imbued these early encounters is captured in the first locally-published German primer, the *Neues Buchstabir-und Lesebuch* (1839) by Mennonite Bishop Benjamin Eby. Infused with religious imagery, the primer's tone is one of inclusion and tolerance. "All Christian denominations," young readers learned, "enjoy equal rights and unlimited freedom of conscience in Upper Canada." The "Church of Christ," the lesson continues, includes "Episcopalians, Lutherans, Reformed, Presbyterians, Catholics, Methodists, Baptists, Mennonites, Quakers, Tunker, Evangelicals, Congregationalists, and others."[18]

Drawing heavily of the conduct manuals of the late eighteenth and

---

[15] Kitchener Public Library (KPL), Waterloo Historical Society (WHS), WAT C-87, "Report on the Public Schools of the County of Waterloo, for the Year 1875, by the County Inspector Thomas Pearce" (Berlin: Telegraph Office, 1876), 6.

[16] *Regulations and Correspondence relating to French and German schools in the Province of Ontario* (Toronto: Warwick & Sons, 1889), 110-14.

[17] Kenneth McLaughlin, "Waterloo County: A Pennsylvania-German Homeland - Revised and Revisited," Paper presented to the Canadian Historical Association, Sherbrooke (Quebec), June 1999. See also Hans Lehmann, *The German Canadians, 1750-1937: Immigration, Settlement & Culture* (St. John's, Newfoundland: Jesperson Press, 1986), 66-79 and Elizabeth Bloomfield, "City-Building Processes in Berlin/Kitchener and Waterloo, 1870-1930" (PhD diss., University of Guelph, 1983), 50-52.

[18] Benjamin Eby, *Neues Buchstabir- und Lesebuch, besonders bearbeitet und eingerichtet zum Gebrauch Deutscher Schulen, enthaltend das ABC, und vielerlei Buchstabir- und Leseübungen* (Berlin: Heinrich Wilhelm Peterson, 1839).

early nineteenth centuries, Benjamin Eby's reading lessons spelled out the rewards of virtue, obedience, diligence, religious devotion, and hard work. Instruction was firmly centred on the nuclear family and the classroom, with frequent admonitions to learn cheerfully, guard against indolence, and honour parents, elders, and teachers, the latter of which were invariably God-fearing, learned, and beloved.[19] While this idealized world of the classroom may have borne little resemblance to the informal and haphazard nature of schooling in early nineteenth century Waterloo County, whose teachers were mostly "mechanics who during the winter months would engage to teach" and commonly restricted their lessons to "very elementary reading, writing and arithmetic," the ritual use of the German language likely resonated with the county's schoolchildren, as did the omnipresence of God in the school lessons.[20]

In the early 1850s, Jacob Teuscher published a German primer that was less overt in its religious imagery and more firmly "embedded in the oral discourse of the community," to borrow Elsie Rockwell's succinct phrase.[21] It went through six editions between 1855 and 1866. Although cultivating a heavily moralistic tone and peopling his lessons with angelic boys and girls, Teuscher broadened the social setting of his stories to include villages, towns, fields, woods, and rivers. His was a child-centred world anchored not in abstract spirituality, but in pastoral landscapes, German folk songs, family, school, and agricultural work. Where Bishop Eby had sought to teach reading through spelling exercises, which were recited in unison and later memorized, Jacob Teuscher embraced the phonic method (*Lautiermethode*) as it had been pioneered by Pestalozzi. By breaking down the units of instruction into their simplest elements - be they letters or syllabi - children were introduced to the sounds and patterns of language in systematic fashion. The language in the early lessons was simple and direct, whereas later lessons introduce more complex and challenging word and sentence structures.[22]

To this was added in 1867 a German handbook by Otto Klotz, Waterloo County's longest-serving school trustee, that promised a concise introduction to the grammatical rules which governed the German language. If the Table of Contents dryly lists the subjects under discussion - among them adjectives, articles, verbs, and punctuation - the six-page introduction offers a fascinating tribute to the science of language as it had been formulated by

---

[19] Ibid, 131: "Good children are attentive, obedient, peaceful, God-fearing and as orderly in the presence of their elders, teachers, and superiors as they are in their absence." See also Michael V. Belok, "The Courtesy Tradition and Early Schoolbooks," *History of Education Quarterly* 8, no. 3 (Fall 1968): 316.

[20] For the early school history of Waterloo County see National Archives of Canada, MG 30, B13, vol. 9, "Statistics and history of the Preston School compiled and written by Otto Klotz for the use of his family," 58; Tomas Pearce, "School History, Waterloo County and Berlin," *Waterloo Historical Society* 2 (1914): 33; KPL, WHS, Manuscript Collection 53, "Rev. A. B. Sherk," 23-25; KPL, WHS, Manuscript Collection 71, Isaac Moyer, Biography and Reminiscences, January 1st, 1915," 11-13.

[21] Rockwell, "Learning for Life or Learning from Books," 124.

[22] Jacob Teuscher, *ABC Buchstabir und Lesebüchlein mit Rücksicht auf die Lautiermethode, für die Elementar-Schulen in Canada* (Waterloo Village: Bödecker and Stübing, 1866).

German philosophers in the late eighteenth and early nineteenth centuries, foremost among them Johann Gottfried von Herder (1744-1803) and Johann Gottlieb Fichte (1762-1814).[23] Not only did Otto Klotz endorse Herder's contention that languages embodied a nation's soul, he also followed the lead of Fichte in declaring the German language superior to all others.[24] In an age of national movements, Klotz upheld the German language as a badge of honour, rather than a medium of communication, as Eby and Teuscher had done in earlier decades. In this, he was not alone. As a reading of the local German-language press reveals, German ethnic leaders in Waterloo County began to embrace the language of cultural nationalism in the latter half of the nineteenth century, in the process ascribing a new symbolic significance to the German mother tongue.[25]

In later decades, these local German primers would be supplanted by readers published in the United States, where German-American communities sustained elaborate German-language programs at both public and private schools, and German-American pedagogues debated teaching strategies with passion. Although these pedagogical discourses rarely crossed the border into Canada, they were "encoded" in the textbooks used in Waterloo County's classrooms, among them the Milwaukee Readers and the readers by Schatz, Resselt, and Ahn. It was precisely this diversity of German-language textbooks that produced a provincial commission in 1889, which was charged with investigating the conditions of minority-language schooling in Ontario. Professing itself delighted with the fact that the "learning of German does not seem to have interfered with the progress of the pupils in English or in other subjects," the commission nonetheless recommended the authorization of just a single series of German readers.[26]

A rationale for standardization was furnished not by the commission itself but by the Ontario Education Department that would authorize the "Steiger German Series of Readers" (more commonly known as the Ahn's Readers) in the following year, stating concerns over the denominational content of other German-language textbooks and suggesting that the "considerable diversity in the German text-books used ... is found to be inconvenient and expensive."[27] These objections, to be sure, had never once surfaced in local school records, nor had they unduly concerned the commissioners. More likely, uniformity was pursued for the sake of uniformity alone, making German-language readers conform to the precedent set by a

---

[23] Vicki Spencer, "Herder and Nationalism: Reclaiming the Principle of Cultural Respect," *Australian Journal of Politics and History* 43, no. 1 (1997): 13; F. W. Barnard, *Herder's Social and Political Thought: From Enlightenment to Nationalism* (Oxford: Clarendon Press, 1965), 57; Elie Kedourie, *Nationalism* (Oxford: Blackwell, 1993), 58-62.
[24] Otto Klotz, *Leitfaden der deutschen Sprache oder kurzgefasstest Lehrbuch der deutschen Sprache in Fragen & Antworten* (Preston: Im Selbstverlag des Verfassers, 1867), 1-6.
[25] Barbara Lorenzkowski, "Border Crossings: The Making of German Identities in the New World, 1850-1914" (PhD diss., University of Ottawa, 2002), 20-57.
[26] *Regulations and Correspondence*, 110.
[27] *Annual Report of the Minister of Education for the Province of Ontario (Canada), 1890* (Toronto: Warwick & Sons, 1891), 65.

single series of English-language textbooks. If the educational bureaucracy in Toronto had been able to read the German textbooks it so heartily endorsed, it might have reconsidered its decision; for the Ahn's Readers presented a radical departure not only from the "Canadian" world which the Canadian and Ontario Readers sought to construct, but also the pedagogical assumptions that underlay reading lessons in authorized English-language readers.

"Protocols for Reading"

The "Canadian Series of School Books" which Egerton Ryerson had reluctantly launched in 1868 embodied a new approach to teaching reading. In strong terms, it discarded the alphabetical method of reading instruction that saw students mechanically reciting the letters of the alphabet or spelling isolated words pointed out by the teacher. Instead, teachers were encouraged to print entire sentences on the blackboard, pronounce each word distinctly and lead the class in recitation "until the children can read the sentence as a whole." Assimilation of reading materials through the recognition of "word-forms" was meant to promote understanding, where the alphabetic method had provided for mere mechanical competency. Teachers were called upon to explain the meaning of new words in familiar terms and to use words "*from the lessons*" (as the Canadian Readers took pains to emphasize) in new combinations on the blackboard. Creativity was encouraged only within tightly drawn boundaries, lest individual teachers subvert the pedagogical wisdom of the textbook. In adopting the phonic method, the Canadian Readers organized lessons around the "*letter-sounds* of the language," proceeding from "monosyllables" ("which are commonly met with, and more easily pronounced by, children") to "easy words of two syllables." If spelling was attempted at all in the classroom, the textbook advised teachers "to give the words in short connected phrases, and to call upon each pupil to spell all the words of a phrase." Reading was a means to an end, with each word being embedded in larger sentence structures and webs of meaning that connected pupils with the world beyond their classroom.[28]

Although the Canadian Readers endorsed a new approach to reading instruction, their discursive universe was firmly rooted in an earlier time period.[29] For children still struggling with "Is it an ox?," the moral injunction "If we are bad, God will not love us; and we can not go to Him when we die" just four pages later, must have proved challenging indeed. Whenever pupils strayed from the rules of acceptable behaviour, judgment in the Canadian Readers was swift and harsh: "Harry Badd is a sad dunce, and so he cannot get his sums right. I think he does not try much, for one can see at a glance that he

---

[28] Emphasis in the original. See *Canadian Series of School Books: First Book of Reading Lessons, Part I* (Toronto: James Campbell and Son, 1867), 13-14, and *Canadian Series of School Books: First Book of Reading Lessons, Part II* (Toronto: William Warwick & Son, 1867), Preface.

[29] For a stimulating discussion of narratives of gender, virtue, national identity, and empire see Harro von Brummeleen, "Shifting Perspectives: Early British Columbia Textbooks from 1872 to 1925," *BC Studies* 60 (Winter 1983-84): 3-27, and Lauren Jeffs, "'Snips and Snail' and 'Sugar and Spice': Constructing Gender in Ontario Schools, 1846-1909" (Master's research paper, University of Ottawa, 1998).

does not give his mind to work."[30] Yet perhaps the starkest difference between the Canadian Readers and the Ontario Readers, which superseded them in 1884, was what the literary scholar Peter Hunt has called the "implied reader." "In any text," Hunt writes, "the tone of features of the narrative voice imply what kind of reader - in terms of knowledge or attitude - is addressed." In his analysis of nineteenth century children's literature, Hunt observes a shift from a "directive narrative relationship" with children to an "empathetic" one that seeks to engage children on their own terms and values entertainment over "didactic intent."[31]

While the Ontario Readers, too, sought to impart moral lessons, they did so by telling stories that viewed the world through a child's eyes, displayed touches of humour, and allowed for transgressions that were gently corrected by wise mothers and grandmothers. When playing truant or disobeying elders, children were portrayed not as innately bad ("a sad dunce") but merely misguided.[32] In the narrative world of the Ontario Readers, the literary protagonists soon internalized their lessons, making obsolete the omnipresent narrator of the Canadian Readers who had praised virtue and denounced disobedience.[33] Only in fables was deviant behaviour punished promptly, as in the tale of "The Lazy Frog" which was killed unceremoniously by the "butcher-bird," whereupon the sparrow flew home and told her children "that it was of no use to be able to hop well, or to be a fine swimmer, if one only sat all day on a bank; that dinners didn't drop into people's mouths, however wide open they might be; and that the sooner they could manage to fetch their own worms the better she should be pleased."[34] Fables allowed for the stern warnings and admonitions that had characterized an earlier generation of textbooks, yet softened their impact on young readers' minds. Their inclusion in the Ontario Readers reflected the rise of the new education in the late nineteenth century.

The new "principles of pedagogy," wrote the Minister of Education, George Ross, in 1887 in his annual report, "led to more scientific methods of teaching, and ... forced educationalists everywhere to consider the

---

[30] *Canadian Series of School Books, First Book, Part I*, 20 and *Canadian Series of School Books, First Book, Part II*, 73.

[31] Peter Hunt, *An Introduction to Children's Literature* (New York: Oxford University Press, 1994), 12, 30, 59.

[32] *The Ontario Readers: Second Reader, Authorized for Use in the Public Schools of Ontario by the Minister of Education* (Toronto: Canada Publishing Company, 1884), "The Idle Boy," 12-14, "The Little Girl That Was Always 'Going To'," 34-36, "No Crown for Me," 47-51, and "Tommy and the Crow," 76-82.

[33] *Canadian Series of School Books, First Book, Part II*, 98 ("George and Charles are both good boys ... These boys do not waste their time at school. They try to learn fast, so that, when they grow up they may be of some use to those whom they love. They know that they cannot go to school, when they grow to be men, for all men have to work for their food; so they try to learn, and their papa is pleased to see them so good.") and 66 ("Ah, Carrie, it would have been well, had you done what mamma thought was best, and left your sweet doll at home.").

[34] *The Ontario Readers: Second Reader*, "The Lazy Frog," 132-33 and "The Fox and the Crow," 15-17.

preparation of text-books in conformity with these principles."[35] These principles were spelled out at length in the preface of the Ontario Readers. In seeking to make the lessons more child-centred, the textbook advised teachers to engage children in an on-going conversation on the meanings of words, phrases, and lessons, thereby leading them "to observe, compare and judge, and state in words the results of their observations, comparisons, and judgments." Illustrations, as well, were to develop the "power of imagination" by becoming a focal point of discussion between teachers and pupils and reinforcing "the ideas involved in the lessons."[36] The authors of the Ontario Readers recommended object lessons and field trips as a supplement to the botanical lessons they provided in the Second Reader. Their scientific ambition was reflected in lessons on "natural objects" that introduced children to black bears and polar bears, lions, tigers, elephants, and ostriches, thus offering education and enjoyment in equal measures (or so the authors hoped).[37] Later textbooks included lessons in history and physical science, integrating reading instruction into the larger curriculum and building bridges between core subjects.[38] In a marked departure from the Canadian Readers, teachers were encouraged to use their own judgment in preparing exercises, introducing new words and concepts, and teaching their students to think independently.[39]

The scientific tone of the readers notwithstanding, they reflected and reinforced notions of gender and race that were widely shared in white, middle-class, Anglo-Saxon Ontario. In textbook tales, fathers and uncles served as guides to the natural world by recalling reindeer drives in Lapland, describing whale hunts in the Arctic, and examining the shape of snow-flakes with their children, while mothers and grandmothers provided emotional warmth and moral guidance. Not coincidentally, the latter appeared in poetry, the language of the heart, while the former spoke in prose, as befit matters of the mind.[40] Just as the gendered precepts of Victorian Canada entered the Ontario Readers, so, too, did the rhetoric of white supremacy.[41] Illustrations

---

[35] *Report of the Minister of Education for the Year 1887* (Toronto: Warwick & Sons, 1888), xxxvii.

[36] Much like other textbooks of the time, the *Ontario Readers* self-consciously sought to construct an ideal reader by giving detailed instruction on how to read.

[37] *The Ontario Readers: Second Reader*, 5-6 and *The Ontario Readers: Third Reader, Authorized for Use in the Public Schools of Ontario by the Minister of Education* (Toronto: W. J. Gage Company, 1885), 3-4. For botanical lessons, see *The Ontario Readers: Second Reader*, "The Root," 154-56, "The Leaf," 160-63, "The Flower," 166-71, "The Fruit," 175-79, "The Seed," 182-83. For discussions of the natural world see "The Black Bear," 19-21, "The Boy and the Chipmunk," 23-27, "The White Bear," 31-32, "The Lion," 72-74, "The Tiger," 89-93, "Elephants," 106-110, and "The Ostrich," 110-13.

[38] *The Ontario Readers: Third Reader*, "Egypt and Its Ruins," 143-48, "The Thermometer," 182-86, and "Heat: Conduction and Radiation," 194-99.

[39] *The Ontario Readers: Second Reader*, 6 and *The Ontario Readers: Third Reader*, 4.

[40] *The Ontario Readers: Second Reader*, "A Reindeer Drive," 38-41," "The Whale," 63-66, "Shapes of Snow-Flakes," 125-27, "My Mother," 46-47, and "Grandmamma," 114-16.

[41] For a discussion of representations of race, ethnicity, and the nation in school readers see Timothy J. Stanley, "White Supremacy and the Rhetoric of Educational

featured black sharecroppers in a romanticized plantation setting. Dressed in the rough cloth worn by the slaves of ante-bellum America, they harvested coffee, sugar, and cotton. More graphic, still, was the characterization of Chinese farmers picking tea leaves. The "busy Chinaman, with his small, funny-looking black eyes, and long pigtail hanging down his back" was denied even the quiet dignity of labour that characterized illustrations of African-Americans. Exotic and different, "the Chinaman" was "the other" against which an imagined "white" nation of Canada defined itself.[42] Not for him was the Dominion of Canada that the Ontario Readers celebrated in references to Canadian artisans, Canadian folklore, and an increasingly Canadianized landscape of lakes and "Canadian" trees.[43]

The Canada that Waterloo County's schoolchildren encountered in the newly authorized "Steiger German Series of Readers" - the Ahn's Readers - was markedly different. At a time when George Ross, the Minister of Education, called for a greater "Canadian sentiment" of textbooks that "could be recognized as our own, without looking to the title page," the mental map of the German-American readers was firmly centred on the United States.[44] The lessons' protagonists resided in New York, Philadelphia, New Orleans, Chicago, Baltimore, and Brooklyn; they strolled down Broadway and visited Central Park; they celebrated George Washington's birthday and sang "The Star-Spangled Banner."[45] In the Ahn's Readers, it was Canada that represented "the other." It was a nation defined by its climate (the proverbial "long cold winters and short hot summers"), characterized as colonial ("Canada belongs to the British"), and renowned only as a convenient way-station for steamships travelling from Boston to England via Halifax.[46] This, ironically, was the very image of Canada that Waterloo County educators had so vigorously attacked in their criticism of the Irish Readers in 1865.

Yet even more so than in their content, the Ahn's Readers differed from their English-language counterpart in the way they sought to instil knowledge. Their pedagogical principles dated back to the mid-nineteenth century, when modern languages had first "won inclusion in the liberal curriculum by capitalizing on their similarity to the classics as subjects with complex linguistic textures and rich literatures." In an academic culture that

---

Indoctrination: A Canadian Case Study," in Jean Barman and Mona Gleason eds., *Children, Teachers and Schools in the History of British Columbia* (Calgary: Detselig Enterprise, 2003), 113-31, and Stuart J. Foster, "The Struggle for American Identity: Treatment of Ethnic Groups in United States History Textbooks," *History of Education*, 28, 3 (1999), 251-78.

[42] *The Ontario Readers: Second Reader*, "Tea," 43-45, "Coffee," 68-70, "Sugar," 84-86, and "Cotton," 96-99.

[43] Jeffs, "'Snips and Snails' and 'Sugar and Spice'," 56, and *The Ontario Readers: Third Reader*, "A Canadian Boat Song," 73, "Canadian Trees, First Reading," 202-206, "Canadian Trees, Second Reading," 210-14.

[44] *Report of the Minister of Education for the Year 1887*, xliii.

[45] P. Henn, *Ahn's First German Book* (New York: E. Steiger & Co., 1873), 36, 37, 51, 52; P. Henn, *Ahn's Second German Book* (New York: E. Steiger & Co., 1873), 103, 123; P. Henn, *Ahn's Third German Book* (New York: E. Steiger & Co., 1875), 58; P. Henn, *Ahn's Fourth German Book* (New York: E. Steiger & Co., 1876), 128, 146, 164, 168.

[46] *Ahn's Third German Book*, 78, 83.

regarded conversational skills as a "trifling accomplishment," modern languages were cherished not as a medium of communication but as a means to

"Cotton": Illustrations in the Ontario Readers upheld the notion of white supremacy. They depicted African Americans in subservient roles: as sharecroppers in a romanticized plantation setting. Source: *The Ontario Readers: Second Reader*, 44.

"Tea": A story on the origins of tea featured this stereotypical portrayal of the Chinese. The accompanying text introduced pupils to the "busy Chinaman, with his small, funny-looking black eyes, and long pigtail hanging down his back." Source: *The Ontario Readers: Second Reader*, 98.

sharpen the intellect.[47] Self-consciously, the Ahn's Readers embraced the "grammar-translation" method, as it had been pioneered in the teaching of Latin and Greek. Each lesson opened with the discussion of a grammatical principle that was reinforced through a series of fifteen to twenty sentences. The result was a collection of disjointed phrases, whose only commonality lay in the illumination of grammatical rules:

> Your forks are too large and too heavy. Where are your sisters now, Miss Lee? They are in New Orleans. Oysters are nutritious. These needles are very good. Your pens are too soft. These flowers are for Lizzy ... Do you believe the lessons are too long? No, Sir, I believe they are not long enough. These roses are splendid.[48]

Conversational exercises were relegated to the readers' closing pages, where they sought to engage children in conversations about the everyday world and matters of history, geography, and science. Even here, however, the structure of conversational exercises mirrored the question-answer scheme of religious catechisms that did allow for just one correct answer, rather than the more emphatic, storytelling tone of the Ontario Readers.[49]

It was translation, not conversation, that represented the organizing principle of the Ahn's Readers. The early lessons of *Ahn's First German Book* provided word-by-word translations into the English, with English words being dwarfed by the far larger Gothic print of their German equivalents. Small figures reminded pupils that the word order in German sentences differed from that in English ones. Parentheses, in turn, indicated words "not to be read, but translated," whereas "words within brackets [] are to be read, but not translated."[50] In alternating paragraphs between the German and the English, the Ahn's Readers created a bilingual world that, never once, allowed children to immerse themselves into the sound and sight of the German language alone. In so doing, the readers violated the cardinal rules of German-language teaching as they had been formulated by the National German-American Teachers' Association in the early 1870s.

In discarding the conventional grammar-translation method, the association had stipulated that language lessons ought to teach children how to *speak* the German language fluently, correctly, and clearly. Hearing and

---

[47] Susan Bayley, "The Direct Method and Modern Language Teaching in England, 1880-1918," *History of Education* 27, no. 1 (1998): 39, 42.

[48] *Ahn's Second German Book*, 84.

[49] *Ahn's Second German Book*, "On objects seen at school," "On objects seen at home," "On parts of the human body," "On clothing and food," 188-92; *Ahn's Third German Book*, "The Seasons: Winter and Spring," "Geographical Topics," "Historical Topics," 82-84; and *Ahn's Fourth German Book*, "The Atmosphere, Rain," "Flax, Linen," "From General History," 178-80.

[50] These examples are taken from the entire "Steiger German Series of Readers." For the explanation of the system of brackets and parentheses used, see, for example, *Ahn's First German Book*, 37.

speaking, its members urged, were the foundations of all language teaching. Instead of submitting children to a torturous course of grammatical rules, conjugation, and declension, they were to learn grammar inductively. Conversational exercises and a systematic course in *oral* instruction were to supplant formal lessons in grammar and translation. In heeding Pestalozzi's advice to see the world through the child's eyes, teachers should proceed from the simple to the difficult, from the concrete to the abstract, from the known to the unknown. Instruction in reading and writing should be postponed until the children had immersed themselves into the sounds of the German language, able both to understand the teacher (who, of course, spoke German only) and formulate simple thoughts of their own.[51] It was not before the turn of the century that the suggestions of the National German-American Teachers' Association were embraced by Anglo-Americans. Yet given the association's role in shaping national debates on modern-language teaching, it is startling to find not even an echo of its recommendations resonating in the Ahn's Readers.[52]

Little wonder that the readers were rejected as "unsuitable for our primary German classes" by the New Hamburg school trustees in November 1890. In asking the Minster of Education for "his sanction for the use of Resselt's 1st Lesebuch," this local school board, for one, opted for a reader that introduced children to the German language through stories, proverbs, and folk songs, rather than dreary grammatical treatises.[53] In the two decades to come, Waterloo County's residents would continue to shape the use of authorized textbooks in the classroom by translating their cultural messages into a language of their own.

Reading Practices

The annual reports of County School Inspector Thomas Pearce provide glimpses into the reading practices at Waterloo County public schools. Finding "reading and spelling ... very much neglected" in the county's rural township schools when he began his annual rounds in 1872, Thomas Pearce soon noted improvements "beyond my expectations."[54] And yet, he encountered a source of constant frustration in the children's English that,

---

[51] This discussion is based on an examination of the association's journal that appeared under the titles *Amerikanische Schulzeitung, Erziehungs-Blätter für Schule und Haus, Pädagogische Monatshefte/Pedagogical Monthly: Zeitschrift für das deutschamerikanische Schulwesen,* and *Monatshefte für deutsche Sprache und Pädagogik.* See Lorenzkowski, "Border Crossings," 311-56.

[52] For the impact of the "natural method" and "direct method," as it was advocated by German-American pedagogues, see E. W. Bagster-Collins, *Studies in Modern Language Teaching - Report Prepared for the Modern Foreign Language Study and the Canadian Committee on Modern Languages* (New York: Macmillan Company, 1930), 88-91.

[53] Waterloo County Board of Education, Wilmot Township, S.S. 2 (New Hamburg), School Board Minutes, 1875-1896, November 3, 1890, and Herman Resselt, *Das Erste Lese- und Lehrbuch für Deutsche Schulen oder Erste Übungen im Lesen, Schreiben und Zeichnen verbunden mit Denk- und Sprachübungen* (New York: E. Steiger, n.d.).

[54] Archives of Ontario, RG 2-109-130, Box 2, Misc. School Records, "Report on the Public Schools of the County of Waterloo by the County Inspector Thomas Pearce (for 1872)" (Galt: Hutchinson, 1873), 5.

although competent, was heavily accented. With more than a note of exasperation he remarked upon a visit to St. Jacobs in March 1880 where the "pupils did fairly in the subjects in which I examined them, except in reading, which is, apparently, very difficult to teach in this place." When visiting the county's Roman Catholic Separate School in 1876, he found "room for improvement, perhaps, in the subjects of reading and arithmetic" in an otherwise glowing report. Two years later, having paid a courtesy visit to the school once again, he declared "Reading on the whole good - making allowance of course for the strong German accent of many of the pupils." In 1894, he reported rather regretfully that still "distinct articulation, good inflection and naturalness of expression are heard in few schools."[55]

The repeated references to children's German-accented English revealed Inspector Pearce's deep-seated reservations against enrolling "very young children" in German language classes. This practice, he charged, led "to such confusion of sounds of letters and pronunciation of words in the minds of the little ones as greatly to retard their progress in both languages." In attributing the low standing of several rural schools to the attempt "to lead children to this bewildering maze," Pearce recommended to reserve German-language instruction exclusively for the higher grades.[56] Written by a man who would later send his own daughter Harriet to the German Department at Berlin's Central School, this was a criticism not of German language instruction per se, but of bilingual instruction in the children's early years.[57] Seemingly unaware of the success of bilingual school programs in the United States that enrolled elementary schoolchildren as young as five years, Pearce reasoned that children could not simultaneously assimilate the sounds and structures of two different languages.[58] But his suggestion went unheeded.

In introducing their young flock to the English language, Waterloo County's teachers likely met with greater success than Thomas Pearce's exhortations. At a meeting of the *Berlin Teachers' Association* in May 1895, "Miss Scully" presented a step-by-step manual on how to teach composition to "Junior Pupils, especially German Children." Rather than relying on the rehearsal of grammatical rules, she regarded oral lessons - the hearing and speaking of English - as the key to learning. She granted her pupils the time to assimilate the structures of the English language inductively before moving on to written exercises. Gentle coercion, as well, played an important role in Miss

---

[55] Waterloo County Board of Education, Woolwich Township, S.S. 8 (St. Jacobs), Visitors' Book, 1861-1912, March 26, 1880. See also earlier entries on reading on April 29, 1875 and August 31, 1875; KPL, WHS, KIT 6, "Visitors' Book: Roman Catholic Separate School," June 2, 1876 and February 6, 1878; KPL, WHS, WAT C-67, "Twenty-Third Annual Report of the Inspector of Public Schools of the County of Waterloo, for the Year ending 31st December, 1894."

[56] "Report on the Public Schools of the County of Waterloo, for the Year 1875," 7.

[57] Manuscript Census of Canada, 1901, and *Berliner Journal*, May 6, 1880 and June 3, 1884.

[58] See Steven L. Schlossman, "'Is There an American Tradition of Bilingual Education': German in the Public Elementary Schools, 1840-1919," *American Journal of Education* 91, no. 2 (February 1983): 139-86, and L. Viereck, *Zwei Jahrhunderte Deutschen Unterrichts in den Vereinigten Staaten* (Braunschweig: Friedrich Viereck und Sohn, 1903).

Scully's teaching arsenal. She confined the use of German to the German-language classroom and insisted that children spoke English even on the playground. In practising the children's writing skills, she favoured the writing of simple stories ("Going to School" "What I would do if I had $ 10?") over having the children copy English-language lessons at their desks.[59] Intuitively - by drawing on her experiences in the classroom - she had arrived at much the same pedagogical principles that the National German-American Teachers' Association was advocating south of the border. In her classroom, the textbook constituted just one teaching tool among many.

It was rare that teachers lavished such care and attention on reading instruction. In the annual school examinations in turn-of-the-century Berlin, reading ranked lowest on the list, which provided teachers with little incentive to correct the children's accented English or invest time in reading lessons. Given the "crowded curriculum" at Berlin's public schools and the "large amount of German spoken at School and at home" reading skills remained uneven, as High School Inspector Seath observed in February 1900. The *Berlin News Record* could not agree more: "That the Queen's English is murdered on every hand is admitted," the editors wrote and were quick to point out the reasons why. "Oral reading will not reach the highest standards in North Waterloo for several generations, owing to the difficulties that pupils of German descent have to surmount in mastering the English tongue."[60] Always striving for excellence in schooling, the Berlin Public School Board instructed Inspector Pearce to submit "a report on the situation," which the latter promptly delivered. "I was more than surprised to find children of British parentage reading and speaking fully as 'broken' as those of German parentage," he wrote. The reason, Thomas Pearce reiterated, was simple. By allowing young children to study German and English simultaneously, their minds were "confused with the sounds of letters and the pronunciation of words of two languages in many respects so very different." Was it not a matter of common sense to limit German-language instruction to the upper grades?[61]

Thomas Pearce was unaware that he had stirred up a hornet's nest. At a time of heightened ethnic nationalism, the outcry in the community was almost immediate. It was the craftsmen of the singing society *Concordia*, supported by the German-language weekly *Berliner Journal*, who organized an indignation meeting on 22 June 1900 to discuss "the better development of German instruction in our public schools." Confronted with the determined campaign for German-language schooling that united Berlin's political, economic, religious, and intellectual elites, Inspector Pearce made one feeble attempt to clear up the matter and then fell silent. In future years, he seemed determined to avoid any further controversies by describing the reading ability of Berlin's pupils as "generally speaking, good."[62] He evidently had

---

[59] Waterloo County Board of Education, "Minute Book of Berlin Teachers' Association, October 1891 to November 8, 1912; May 10, 1895.
[60] Ibid., May 11, 1900. See also *Berliner Journal*, June 7, 1900 and *Berlin News Record*, April 27, 1900.
[61] Quoted in the *Berliner Journal*, July 4, 1900.
[62] Ibid., June 29, 1900 and June 27, 1901.

misjudged the quiet, but powerful, current of ethnic identity that he had so successfully navigated for over three decades. As an object of cultural heritage, German continued to command powerful loyalties even as enrolment in the county's German-language classrooms was steadily declining.[63]

The German School Association (*Schulverein*), formally founded in August 1900, suggested substituting the provincially authorized German readers for a new series of textbooks. In January 1904, the children in Berlin's German-language classrooms opened their new German readers, which had been sanctioned by the *Schulverein*, local trustees, and provincial authorities alike.[64] The association continued to create a climate conducive to German-language learning. It subsidized the children's school readers, organized school picnics, and awarded prizes to outstanding students.[65] Honourary German school inspectors helped develop a curriculum of German-language schooling, examined the language and teaching abilities of German-language teachers, and alerted school trustees to weaknesses in the present system of instruction.[66] The number of school children enrolled in the German-language program subsequently increased from twelve per cent in 1900 to sixty-seven per cent in 1912, among them many British-origin children whose work garnered praise from German school inspectors. In November 1911, the Berlin School Board went further still. It instructed the German teachers in its employ "to make more use of conversational exercises and not to lay so much stress as heretofore on reading and writing."[67] The pedagogical principles of the Ahn's Readers, which Berlin's schools had abandoned in 1903, officially belonged to the past.

The teaching of German, once intimately linked to the textbook, now lay in the hands of individual teachers who created exercises of their own imagination. The newly re-discovered orality of instruction allowed language lessons to be shaped by local values and experiences, rather than by distant textbook authors. As the dependence on German textbooks lessened, so, too, did the reliance on the Ontario Readers. By the early twentieth century, the intensive reading of a single series of authorized textbooks was giving way to extensive reading practices. Berlin's school libraries expanded as they acquired books for "supplementary reading" in 1905 and purchased the "Young Folks' Library" in 1908. Although the textbook would remain a mainstay of instruction in Waterloo County, proving its resilience well into

---

[63] For a point of comparison see Herbert J. Gans, "Symbolic Ethnicity: The Future of Ethnic Groups and Cultures in America," *Ethnic and Racial Studies* 2, no. 1 (1979): 1-19, and Jeffrey Shandler, "Beyond the Mother Tongue: Learning the Meaning of Yiddish in America," *Jewish Social Studies* 6, no. 3 (2000): 97-99.

[64] Waterloo County Board of Education, "Berlin Board Minutes, 1898-1908," September 1, 1903 and December 31, 1903. Eight years later, these textbooks would, once again, be substituted by Wilhelm Gelbach's *Erstes Deutsche Lesebuch für Schule und Haus* (New York: E. Steiger & Co., 1906). See Ibid., "Berlin Public School Board Minutes, 1908-1915," August 18, 1911.

[65] *Berliner Journal*, February 12, 1903; June 25, 1903; July 23, 1903; June 21, 1905; and December 5, 1906.

[66] Ibid., December 27, 1900; January 4, 1905; December 5, 1906; April 8, 1908; January 6, 1909; and June 28, 1911.

[67] "Berlin Public School Board Minutes, 1908-1915," November 17, 1911.

the twenty-first century, it no longer demanded its students' exclusive attention, if, indeed, it ever had.

Drawing Conclusions

This study, then, is a cautionary tale of the role of textbooks in Canadian classrooms. History's linguistic turn has encouraged historians to probe the discursive universe that unfolded between the covers of these slim volumes. Less often do they reflect on the pedagogical principles that shaped the content and form of reading lessons, and more rarely still on the way local societies responded to the authorized readers by rejecting, embracing, or ignoring them. While Bruce Curtis has portrayed textbooks as instruments of state governance, this study has found local school promoters who viewed the officially sanctioned reading lessons through the prism of their own values and needs. From their actions and negotiations emerges a picture of education more colourful than that of a uniform, centralized school system: the diversity of (German-language) readers was far greater than provincial authorities ever expected; the pedagogical assumptions and cultural messages of the Ahn's readers ran counter the policies of the Department of Education; Waterloo County's teachers devised their own program of literacy instruction that relied heavily on conversational exercises; and local trustees substituted authorized readers with books of their own choosing, after having secured the approval of Toronto authorities. Not content to replace the Ahn's Readers with another series of textbooks, Berlin's community leaders launched an elaborate program of German-language instruction that fostered reading skills through extra-curricular activities and a new curriculum, supervised by local German School Inspectors. Little did it matter that, by 1913, even the president of the German School Association, Louis Jacob Breithaupt, was writing to his children in English, not German, thus revealing a language shift in the most "German" of families.[68] As a symbol of ethnic identity, and a medium of oral conversation, the German language continued to exist independent of the reflections it cast into the school readers of the time.

---

[68] University of Waterloo, Doris Lewis Rare Book Room, Breithaupt Hewetson Clark Collection, Box #8, "Catherine Olive, née Breithaupt (1896-1977), Letter by Louis Breithaupt, September 3, 1913."

– 7 –

Rigueur et sensibilité dans un parcours historien

Hubert Watelet

L'exposé comprend deux parties. La première traite d'exigences de rigueur dans une thèse sur la révolution industrielle dans un bassin houiller belge. Conçue dans les années 1950-1970, elle s'inscrit dans le contexte des belles thèses françaises d'histoire économique régionale de l'époque. Cependant c'est aussi une étude de *business history*, qui relevait plutôt d'historiens britanniques ou de Harvard. À cet égard, elle se différencie de l'historiographie française. Le titre du livre signale cette originalité en annonçant la spécificité de la région étudiée et l'approfondissement d'une entreprise[1]. La recherche fut pensée très tôt selon les thèses d'État encore en cours en France à l'époque; ou les « grandes thèses », comme on les qualifiait parfois en milieu anglo-saxon. Mais on l'a dit, on se limitera ici à certaines exigences de rigueur – et d'interdisciplinarité – caractéristiques du travail.

La seconde partie évoquera un tout autre domaine, qui fait partie de mes intérêts actuels : celui du rôle du sentiment en histoire et dans le métier d'historien. N'étant pas suffisamment formés pour traiter de l'affectif, nous évitons d'ordinaire d'en parler, ce qui ne signifie nullement que cet aspect de la vie humaine soit négligeable. Mais du point de départ qui fut le mien, je dirais que si l'histoire des entreprises peut profiter d'une science économique relativement avancée, on aborde ici un champ en défrichement. On le verra en évoquant deux essais touchant à l'affectif. Néanmoins, ceux-ci tentent de tirer parti de l'acquis au plan de la rigueur, plutôt que d'y renoncer.

I

Revenons à la première partie. Dès le deuxième cycle, je voulais faire une histoire d'entreprise, ce qui posait la question des sources. À l'époque, en France ou en Belgique, les archives d'entreprises étaient rarement confiées aux dépôts d'État. C'est auprès d'institutions financières ou de responsables de firmes qu'il fallait obtenir l'autorisation de consulter les archives de celles-ci. L'accès au fond très considérable de la mine du Grand-Hornu, dans le bassin de Mons, détermina finalement le sujet. L'essentiel était sur place : actes notariés, titres de propriété, documents de l'assemblée des sociétaires et de la direction, correspondance et comptabilité, documents du service géologique, etc. Ayant fait entrer ce fond aux Archives de l'État à Mons au début des années 1960 pour l'inventorier, il fallut un camion de dix tonnes pour le transporter[2]. C'est

---

[1] Hubert Watelet, *Une industrialisation sans développement. Le bassin de Mons et le charbonnage du Grand-Hornu du milieu du XVIIIe au milieu du XIXe siècle,* Ottawa, Éd. de l'Université d'Ottawa et Louvain-la-Neuve, Faculté de Philosophie et Lettres, 1980 (ci-après *ISD*).
[2] Hubert Watelet, *Inventaire des Archives des sociétaires et de la Société civile des usines et mines de houille du Grand-Hornu*, Bruxelles, Archives générales du Royaume, 1964.

dire son importance, mais aussi pourquoi je n'ai pas envisagé toute l'histoire de la société, de la fin du XVIIIe siècle à l'arrêt des activités en 1953-1954. Ayant choisi la période de la Révolution industrielle, le sujet se précisait : il s'agissait de comprendre le « comment » de cette transformation au Grand-Hornu.

Mon promoteur, Léopold Genicot, me prêta alors l'ouvrage de Pierre Lebrun, d'ampleur comparable aux thèses françaises prises comme exemples, sur l'industrie de la laine à Verviers, près de Liège[3]. C'était déjà un livre d'histoire régionale et de *business history*, dont je me suis inspiré.

Il fallait cependant faire œuvre originale pour trois raisons. Premièrement, il était essentiel d'avoir une bonne connaissance géologique en histoire minière. Ensuite le Grand-Hornu posait un problème particulier : cette mine faisait l'admiration des observateurs au début du XIXe siècle, à l'échelle européenne comme au plan régional, avec ses étonnants bâtiments en forme d'ellipse, sa cité ouvrière, son atelier de construction de machines à vapeur, son petit chemin de fer, etc.[4]. Du point de vue d'une thèse, c'était un fort beau sujet, mais au-delà du récit, il importait de comprendre le caractère exceptionnel de cette industrialisation. La troisième raison tenait à la spécificité du bassin minier : ce Grand-Hornu qui s'était développé de façon si remarquable, se trouvait au coeur d'une région qui n'avait guère diversifié ses activités. Les bassins voisins du Nord de la France et en Belgique du Centre – entre Mons et Charleroi – et surtout de Charleroi, au contraire, avaient su tous trois attirer de la sidérurgie notamment, dès la première moitié du XIXe siècle. Pourtant les quatre bassins allaient peu ou prou alimenter un même marché franco-belge. Pourquoi pareil contraste? Cette originalité ou cette faiblesse montoise, il s'agirait aussi de la comprendre.

Pour bien caractériser cette exception dans une exception en somme, de l'entreprise dans sa région minière, je m'orientais vers un approfondissement comparatif, en élargissant le sujet; notamment grâce aux archives de l'Administration des mines. Outre l'effort statistique des ingénieurs des mines, leurs rapports étaient plus précis, plus soucieux des conditions d'exploitation des entreprises que la correspondance et les procès-verbaux des chambres de commerce par exemple. Le fond de l'Administration des mines des Archives du Royaume à Bruxelles venait d'être inventorié quand j'ai commencé à y travailler. Ce double élargissement comparatif Grand-Hornu / autres exploitations minières du bassin, et bassin de Mons / bassins voisins a joué bien entendu dans la continuation du travail au troisième cycle.

Voici maintenant quelques exemples d'exigences de rigueur de la démarche. À mes yeux celle-ci impliquait un triple effort d'interdisciplinarité –

---

[3] Pierre Lebrun, *L'industrie de la laine à Verviers pendant le XVIIIe et le début du XIXe siècle*, Liège, Faculté de Philosophie et Lettres, 1948.

[4] Voir notamment Jean-Jacques Baude, « Hornu », *Revue encyclopédique* (Paris), t. 35, 1827, p. 787-790; Philippe Vandermaelen, *Dictionnaire géographique de la province de Hainaut*, Bruxelles, Établissement géographique, 1833, p. 254-55 (réimpression Bruxelles, Culture et civilisation, 1970); ou plus récemment Hubert Watelet, « Un site exceptionnel d'archéologie industrielle en Belgique : Les établissements et la cité ouvrière du Grand-Hornu, 1820-1835 », *Journal of The Canadian Historical Association / Revue de la Société historique du Canada*, Vancouver, 1990, vol. 1, Ottawa, Société historique du Canada, s.d., p. 273-292.

conçue comme appropriation de concepts, de façon de raisonner, de techniques, de procédés graphiques ou cartographiques –, en géologie, en économie et en statistique. L'objectif était d'intégrer dans le travail les acquis de ces trois disciplines jugés nécessaires pour la maîtrise ou une exposition adéquate des problèmes étudiés. S'approprier des connaissances dans une autre discipline, c'est un peu comme apprendre à nager. Après un certain temps, brusquement on flotte et on s'étonne! J'évoquerai seulement ici l'exemple de la géologie. Quand j'ai pu faire la critique d'une coupe verticale du gisement que l'on venait de réviser au Service géologique de Belgique, et informer celui-ci d'une erreur graphique subsistante; ou enrichir des plans ou des coupes partielles selon mes besoins; concevoir mes propres cartes du gisement en fonction de mes analyses – non seulement comme illustration mais pour étayer une argumentation[5] –, l'essentiel de l'effort paraissait atteint. Sans illusion cependant, car je n'étais pas devenu géologue pour autant : acquérir certaines connaissances dans une discipline ne signifie pas que l'on puisse contribuer comme chercheur de cette discipline à son avancement.

Ce travail d'interdisciplinarité contribue beaucoup à l'originalité et à la solidité du livre, comme à la compréhension de l'évolution du Grand-Hornu et du bassin minier. On a ainsi pu montrer que dans le cas de la mine, les difficultés des années 1778-1810 et la transformation spectaculaire des années 1814-1832, ne tiennent pas seulement au rôle des entrepreneurs. Elles s'expliquent tout autant par les conditions d'exploitation du gisement[6]. Et dans le cas du bassin, la connaissance de celui-ci a permis de confronter les affirmations d'exploitants ou les avis d'ingénieurs des mines concernant certaines situations, avec la documentation géologique[7]. On ne s'est donc pas contenté d'un cadre géo-lithologique initial comme ces « introductions géographiques à l'histoire » ... « de tant de livres », déplorait Braudel, sans utilité puisqu'ensuite « il n'[en] est plus jamais question[8] ». L'index onomastique montrerait cela clairement.

Par ailleurs, le chapitre sur le gisement fait voir qu'au milieu du XIXe siècle, près de 70 p. cent des quantités de houilles produites à Mons sont du « flénu », qualité absente dans les bassins voisins du Nord, du Centre et de Charleroi[9]. Si cette houille montoise fut excellente au début de la Révolution industrielle pour une série d'entreprises dont les compagnies de gaz d'éclairage, et pour les machines à vapeur, elle ne convenait ni pour les forges ni pour la cokéfaction. Certes, les planches du livre et l'analyse montrent ensuite la portée de cette spécificité du *bassin du flénu* pour la période étudiée, mais dès l'entrée en matière, le lecteur pouvait entrevoir l'importance des houilles produites dans la faiblesse de diversification des activités, de développement de la région.

Le quantitatif ne suscite plus en histoire l'enthousiasme des années 1960-1970. On en avait trop attendu. Je ne vais pas ici accumuler des chiffres,

---

[5] Par exemple Planche 4, « Le vieux Borinage », *ISD*, p. 75.
[6] Ibid., p. 313, 362-63.
[7] Ibid., p. 144, 146, 177-79, 189, 266-67, 303-04, 312-18.
[8] Fernand Braudel, *La Méditerranée et le monde méditerranéen à l'époque de Philippe II*, t. 1, 2e éd. revue, Paris, A. Colin, 1966, p. 16.
[9] *ISD*, Tableau II, p. 61.

mais montrer comment j'ai dû travailler pour les obtenir. *L'industrialisation sans développement* n'est d'ailleurs pas à proprement parler un ouvrage d'histoire quantitative. On chercha plutôt à y confronter documentation qualitative et données quantitatives; plus précisément à se donner des garde-fous quantitatifs autant que possible, pour les analyses qualitatives. Mais pour comprendre la transformation du Grand-Hornu, l'obtention de données sur la production, les prix de vente et les profits et pertes était essentiel. Une histoire d'entreprise sérieuse paraissait impensable sans ce genre d'informations, à moins de s'en tenir à bien des suppositions ou à des à peu près. Pour les quantités vendues et les prix de la mine, ce fut pourtant un travail long et difficile. Si ce fut beaucoup plus simple, apparemment, dans le cas du bassin, on verra qu'au niveau d'une compagnie, les données de l'Administration des mines sur la production risquaient d'être fort contestables à l'époque étudiée.

Commençons par ce qui fut le plus difficile. On dispose de très peu de données chiffrées dans les archives du Grand-Hornu avant 1810. La description des débuts de l'affaire est donc restée qualitative. En revanche, étudiant l'entreprise jusqu'au début des années 1840 pour couvrir suffisamment sa transformation industrielle et sa mécanisation, et disposant de sa comptabilité à partir de 1810, on devait obtenir des séries de prix et de production, de même que les profits et pertes correspondant à une phase essentielle de son évolution. On y est arrivé effectivement, mais pour les prix et la production de cette époque, le Grand-Hornu n'avait pas conservé de résultats annuels. Il a fallu noter les ventes semaine par semaine ou vente par vente, d'après les journaux des comptabilités, pour les reconstituer.

À partir des années 1820 en effet, l'entreprise innova en installant des rivages le long du canal de Mons à l'Escaut, non loin du siège de l'exploitation. Elle vendit ainsi directement à la clientèle par affrètement de bateaux, plutôt que de recourir, selon l'usage, à des marchands de charbon. Elle tint alors une seconde comptabilité, dite « du commerce des rivages », en plus de celle « de l'exploitation ». Celle-ci donnait notamment les transactions locales. C'est celle des rivages qui permettait de connaître les ventes à la clientèle des Flandres belges, du Nord de la France et de la région parisienne. Mais c'est elle aussi qui enregistrait les opérations vente par vente.

On a donc établi des fiches de client sur lesquelles on a noté pour chacun d'eux, au fur et à mesure des transactions et pour chaque catégorie de charbon – les plus courantes étaient les gaillettes, les gailleteries et les fines –, les quantités, prix unitaires, prix totaux, destinations. Ce travail fut comparable en un sens aux fiches de famille d'un Pierre Goubert, en démographie historique[10]. Après quoi on a pu envisager d'établir des mouvements annuels par exemple, en termes de prix et de production.

Ce fichier était terminé quand, au milieu des années 1960, le Centre de calcul de l'Université d'Ottawa créa un programme d'incitation du personnel à recourir à l'ordinateur central pour fins de recherche. J'ai donc pu bénéficier de ce programme et disposer assez rapidement d'une série de totaux

---

[10] Voir notamment Jacques Dupâquier, « Démographie historique », dans André Burguière (dir.), *Dictionnaire des sciences historiques*, Paris, Presses Universitaires de France, 1986, p. 187.

mensuels et annuels pour chaque catégorie de charbon vendue, avec prix moyens correspondants, etc., selon les questions posées[11].

Cependant il restait une difficulté de taille, car on ne connaissait pas suffisamment les unités de mesure en usage dans l'entreprise. C'étaient des mesures de capacité – des mannes ou des muids, par exemple – dont il fallait évidemment déceler la valeur et la convertir en unités de poids, donc en kilogrammes et en tonnes métriques. Or, non seulement les mesures des ventes par bateau différaient de celles des ventes locales, mais à plusieurs reprises il y eut des changements de mesure à des moments qui pouvaient varier selon qu'il s'agissait des ventes locales ou par bateau, ou selon la grosseur des houilles. Si la France avait adopté le système métrique en 1795, peu avant d'annexer la Belgique, son application se fit lentement, particulièrement dans les mines. En France même, le système métrique ne devint vraiment obligatoire qu'en 1840. Pour l'informatisation des données, les mesures de capacité des fiches de client des ventes par bateau avaient simplement été codées[12].

Sans entrer dans le détail de ces problèmes de mesure, disons que c'est en partant des unités de capacité les plus connues qu'on a pu déterminer les équivalences en kilogrammes de l'ensemble des mesures en usage. C'est pour les ventes par bateau, exprimées en mesures des rivages, qu'on avait le plus d'informations, grâce à la correspondance du Grand-Hornu avec sa clientèle. Mais les deux comptabilités avaient permis de rassembler les données de deux autres mouvements, exprimées en mesures mal connues du carreau de la mine, donc des ventes locales : celui de la sortie de la mine vers les rivages et celui des entrées aux rivages. On a comparé, pour les gaillettes, les gailleteries et les fines notamment, les progressions annuelles cumulatives des ventes par bateau, avec celles des deux autres mouvements. Cette comparaison a été faite en tenant compte des rares équivalences en kilogrammes dont on disposait pour le carreau de la mine. Ce travail a fini par faire connaître les ventes locales en kilogrammes et en tonnes métriques.

Après avoir déterminé la correspondance des unités de capacité en unités de poids, on a aussi pu établir les mouvements des prix. Ils étaient très importants, car les prix du flénu pouvaient révéler la conjoncture de l'ensemble des houillères qui produisaient cette qualité dans la région minière.

Au début de son *Introduction* de 1865, Claude Bernard compare les sciences d'observation aux sciences expérimentales. À la différence de l'observateur, écrit-il, l'expérimentateur « provoque à son profit l'apparition de phénomènes »; l'expérience est « une observation provoquée »[13]. Sans doute faudrait-il distinguer : bien que la reconstitution des courbes démographiques d'Ancien Régime et des courbes des ventes et des prix du Grand-Hornu soient des formes d'observation provoquée, ces opérations ne semblent que partiellement expérimentales.

---

[11] *ISD*, p. 368.
[12] Voir par exemple, Nicole Caulier-Mathy, « La métrologie du charbon à Liège au XIXe siècle », *Revue belge d'histoire contemporaine*, t. 1, 1969, p. 207-215.
[13] Claude Bernard, *Introduction à l'étude de la médecine expérimentale*, Paris, Garnier-Flammarion, 1966, p. 48-49.

Il restait une autre question. Les mines payaient des redevances pour le service des administrations des mines, et les ingénieurs s'efforçaient d'évaluer le « produit net » des exploitations minières (les bénéfices moins les dépenses ordinaires), en tenant compte des déclarations des exploitants, mais aussi, le cas échéant, des plans d'extraction. Comment s'assurer que les comptabilités de l'entreprise n'avaient pas falsifié certaines opérations, afin de réduire le montant des redevances? J'ai donc reconstitué moi aussi le mouvement annuel de l'extraction, à partir des plans de la mine, pour le comparer à celui des ventes totales. Sans être aussi complexe que la conversion des mesures de capacité employées, l'évaluation de l'extraction en tonnes ne fut pas non plus des plus faciles. Disons simplement que dans l'ensemble, la comparaison de l'extraction et des ventes totales annuelles fut intéressante et fructueuse : elle ne permettait pas de conclure qu'il y avait eu fraude dans la tenue des comptabilités, mais au contraire que les mouvements qu'on en avait tirés étaient vraisemblables.

Par contre, cette comparaison a montré combien, à l'échelle d'une entreprise, les données annuelles sur la production retenues par les administrations des mines risquaient d'être fragiles à l'époque. Tantôt elles pouvaient révéler l'habileté de certains exploitants à réduire leurs redevances, tantôt au contraire elles pouvaient traduire un certain durcissement des ingénieurs dans la vérification de certaines déclarations. Ainsi, par rapport aux mouvements annuels des ventes totales et de l'extraction du Grand-Hornu, celui de sa production selon l'Administration des mines de Mons était le moins homogène[14]. C'était important du point de vue critique.

Au terme de cet aperçu sur la rigueur, vous pensez peut-être : un tel travail valait-il la peine? Bien que ce ne soit pas à moi à répondre à cette question, voici deux propositions : la première fait le lien entre le travail exigé et certains résultats. Si l'on savait, par les milieux d'affaires notamment, qu'il y avait une crise de surproduction et de baisse des prix pour les mines de flénu du bassin montois, entre 1825 et 1830, les prix du Grand-Hornu ont précisé l'ampleur et la durée de la crise, en particulier pour les gaillettes dont la vente aurait dû être la plus profitable pour les exploitants. Or c'est pendant la crise que Henri De Gorge, l'entrepreneur de l'entreprise, déploie sa cité de plus de 400 maisons autour du siège de l'exploitation et construit son atelier de machines en l'équipant chez John Cockerill, le fournisseur le plus réputé du pays. Et tout cela par autofinancement. Au même moment pourtant, d'autres exploitations importantes de flénu de la région, qui construisent comme le Grand-Hornu des machines à vapeur, s'endettent et finissent par dépendre du capitalisme financier. Voici donc deux éléments importants de l'explication : la connaissance du gisement montrait que la mine exploitait à l'époque des veines très régulières et relativement peu profondes. Il en résulta une production nettement plus riche en gaillettes qu'ailleurs. Ayant dû travailler par grosseur pour connaître le poids des unités mesure employées, on pouvait montrer cela très facilement[15]. Et puis, l'entreprise exploitant des veines régulières et riches en gaillettes à faible profondeur, ses coûts de production étaient moindres

---

[14] *ISD*, Graphique 20, p. 388.
[15] Ibid., Graphique 22, p. 394, et p. 398.

qu'ailleurs également. Un entrepreneur comme De Gorge sut en profiter. L'une des deux interrogations initiales : comment comprendre le développement exceptionnel du Grand-Hornu, économiquement parlant, trouvait sa solution.

La seconde proposition est une incitation à réfléchir d'Henri Marrou : quand j'ai entrepris ce travail, je ne pensais pas à son conseil au jeune historien : « Tu n'es qu'un homme, non un dieu, apprends à bien compter tes jours, à ne pas gaspiller tes efforts[16] ». La suite de cette remarque suggère que Marrou ne l'aurait probablement pas trouvée plus applicable aux reconstitutions des mouvements du Grand-Hornu qu'à celles de la démographie historique des années 1960.

II

C'est par l'enseignement que j'ai abordé ensuite l'histoire des sentiments. Mon cours de prédilection devenait un séminaire d'histoire des mentalités et de la vie affective dans la famille, en France, du XVIIe siècle à nos jours. Il était frappant de voir combien l'affectivité, cette dimension essentielle de la vie humaine, restait en friche dans nos préoccupations d'historiens. Avec raison certes, nous avons développé un grand intérêt pour les sources, les méthodes de recherches ou l'interdisciplinarité, mais combien d'historiens risquent de se spécialiser, comme un Alain Corbin en France, en histoire des sentiments? Deux mots d'historiographie française pour que l'on se comprenne bien : c'est ici à Ottawa, en 1973, que Robert Mandrou rappelait l'observation de Lucien Febvre, de 1941 : « Nous n'avons pas d'histoire de la peur, nous n'avons pas d'histoire de l'amour ». Et Mandrou estimait devoir ajouter : « Après un si long temps, nous ne les avons toujours pas[17] ». Dix ans plus tard – c'était à Vancouver en 1983 –, Jean-Louis Flandrin, dont l'apport reste si précieux, constatait : « qu'il y a des historiens qui refusent toute histoire des sentiments, convaincus qu'ils sont que les sentiments humains sont les mêmes chez tous les peuples et qu'ils n'ont pas changé depuis trois millions d'années ». Et Flandrin précisa : « J'ai entendu l'un des plus grands historiens français le proclamer avec force, lors d'une soutenance de thèse sous les applaudissements de ses collègues[18] ».

Les choses changent heureusement : recherches et jugements sur les sentiments deviennent plus sérieux. *La peur en Occident*, par exemple, de Jean Delumeau, date de 1978[19]. André Burguière écrit de son côté, quelques années plus tard : « Il serait absurde de prétendre que personne ne s'est marié par amour ni qu'aucun couple ne s'est aimé véritablement avant le XVIIIe siècle. Mais une telle disposition affective ne constituait ni un idéal ni une nécessité[20] ». Et Jacques Gélis, au même moment :

---

[16] Henri-Irénée Marrou, *De la connaissance historique*, 7e édition, Paris, Seuil, 1975, p. 78.
[17] Robert Mandrou, « Sentiments et sensibilités dans l'Europe des XVIe et XVIIe siècles », *Histoire sociale / Social History*, t. X, n° 20, 1977, p. 228.
[18] André Burguière, « Histoire de la famille et histoire des mentalités », *Historical Papers / Communications historiques, 1983*, Ottawa, Société historique du Canada, s.d., p. 141.
[19] Jean Delumeau, *La peur en Occident (XIVe-XVIIIe siècles)*, Paris, Fayard, 1978.
[20] André Burguière, « La formation du couple », dans André Burguière et al. (dir.), *Histoire de la famille*, t. 2, *Le choc des modernités*, Paris, A. Colin, 1986, p. 134.

l'intérêt ou l'indifférence à l'égard de l'enfant ne sont pas vraiment la caractéristique de telle ou telle période de l'histoire. Les deux attitudes coexistent au sein d'une même société, l'une l'emportant sur l'autre à un moment donné pour des raisons culturelles et sociales qu'il n'est pas toujours aisé de démêler. L'indifférence médiévale face à l'enfance est une fable[21].

Cette fois, les approches de la vie affective dans la famille devenaient plus réfléchies. Les problèmes commençaient d'être bien posés. Mais par rapport à l'histoire économique et sociale, par exemple, il est clair qu'on en était encore à l'abc.

Passons maintenant aux deux essais mentionnés en introduction : le premier concerne notre réticence à réfléchir au rôle du sentiment dans notre métier de chercheur; l'autre tente de rejoindre par une enquête orale, la part du sentiment dans la vie professionnelle de la dernière génération des mineurs du même bassin de Mons d'abord étudié du point de vue de l'industrialisation. Côté sujet et côté objet donc : ce sont les deux faces d'un même champ.

L'essentiel de la première étude est un exercice d'autocritique sur l'objectivité : combien d'entre nous ont noté que les idées courantes sur l'objectivité selon Ranke et Seignobos étaient mythiques, et qu'elles ont longtemps déformé notre pensée? Sans doute commence-t-on à savoir que le *wie es eigentlich gewesen*, constamment cité hors contexte, ne signifiait pas pour l'historien allemand qu'il convenait de dire les choses «*as it really happened*», comme elles s'étaient réellement passées. Ce qu'on sait moins par contre, c'est qu'à ses yeux, l'une des grandes qualités du bon historien, c'est sa capacité d'avoir une réelle affection pour les humains *quels qu'ils soient*, sans oublier qu'il fait lui-même partie de la même humanité, pour le meilleur et pour le pire. En écrivant cela, Ranke se situait dans la tradition historique allemande. Tout en se donnant des garde-fous pour éviter d'être partial, il soulignait nettement l'importance du sentiment dans le métier des historiens. Pourtant, c'est le *wie es eigentlich gewesen* qui fit fortune chez eux, en langue latine et surtout anglo-saxonne : la formule correspondait si bien au rêve d'objectivité qu'elle persista en gros de la fin du XIXe siècle aux années 1960[22].

Le procédé fut comparable dans le cas de Seignobos. De la formule : « L'histoire se fait avec des documents », qu'on trouve effectivement dans son *Introduction aux études historiques* (1899), on lui imputa en France l'idée que l'historien s'efface devant les documents; que ce sont eux qui fondent le travail

---

[21] Jacques Gélis, « L'individualisation de l'enfant », dans Philippe Ariès et Georges Duby, *Histoire de la vie privée*, t. 3, *De la Renaissance aux Lumières*, Paris, Seuil, 1986, p. 328.

[22] Voir Hubert Watelet, « Illusions et sous-estimation du rôle du sentiment dans la démarche historienne », dans Carlos Barros (dir.), *Historia a Debate. Actas del II Congreso Internacional celebrado del 14 al 18 de Julio de 1999 en Santiago de Compostela,* t. 1, *Cambio de Siglo*, A Coruña (España), Historia a Debate, 2000, p. 235-36, 245. Trad. angl. « Illusions About and Underestimation of the Role of Sentiment in the Historian's Work », dans Carlos Barros et Lawrence J. McCrank (dir.), *History Under Debate. International Reflection on the Discipline*, New York, The Haworth Press, 2004, p. 219-220, 232-33.

historique. Or Seignobos écrivait tout le contraire : « on ne fait pas la construction historique avec des documents », peut-on lire dans cet ouvrage, mais avec un questionnaire et de l'imagination. La lecture des sources, ajoutait-il, amène l'historien à se donner des images à partir d'autres images, ce qui implique nécessairement « une forte part de fantaisie ». Ainsi « L'histoire est forcément une science subjective[23] ». Mais à l'époque où l'on rêvait d'objectivité dans le sens d'une neutralité faisant abstraction de tout sentiment et de toute idéologie, on préféra déformer, ridiculiser le réalisme de Seignobos à partir d'une formule, plutôt que de discuter sa pensée. Les conséquences de cette attitude eurent toutefois moins d'ampleur que dans le cas de Ranke, au plan international.

C'est en 1952-1954 que Paul Ricoeur et Henri Marrou en sont arrivés, indépendamment l'un de l'autre, à une réflexion nettement plus élevée sur le métier d'historien. Quelle que soit l'importance du travail fourni aux niveaux de l'érudition, des méthodes ou des procédés techniques, estime Marrou; ou encore aux plans de l'interdisciplinarité ou de la quantification le cas échéant, etc., on ne peut qu'approcher sans rejoindre « l'essence même de la connaissance historique », c'est-à-dire « la richesse de la réalité humaine ». L'ampleur de la recherche peut accroître les « motifs de crédibilité », mais en son fond, ce cœur de la connaissance reste « seulement une connaissance de foi[24] ». Dans sa présentation, cet essentiel reste donc subjectif, même si l'œuvre bénéficie par la suite de l'éloge des pairs.

Que devient alors la nature de l'objectivité historienne? La réponse est venue de Ricoeur : au plan de ce même essentiel qui, selon les termes du philosophe, sont le vécu, « les valeurs de vie des hommes [et des femmes] d'autrefois », l'objectivité du chercheur implique l'intervention de sa subjectivité par un transport dans d'autres subjectivités. Car il distingue une subjectivité de recherche, faite de sympathie et de distanciation, ce dont il s'agit ici, de ce qu'il appelle la subjectivité passionnelle. Ainsi, dans le projet d'objectivité historienne, précise-t-il, la rationalité traverse le « cœur même du sentiment et de l'imagination » en s'efforçant d'écarter toute subjectivité passionnelle de la subjectivité de recherche[25].

Il est dommage que ces réflexions pénétrantes de Marrou et de Ricoeur sur le travail de l'historien, quand il touche à l'essentiel, aient été trop négligées. Mais lorsqu'elles furent formulées la première fois, on approchait du tournant des années 1960. Quand on n'a plus admis cette sorte de neutralité olympienne qui n'était pas de Ranke, la tendance fut de passer à l'autre extrême : de devenir subjectiviste ou d'affirmer que tous les jugements historiques, toutes les interprétations se valent[26]. De toute façon les deux attitudes, celles du mouvement positiviste et des débuts du postmodernisme, témoignent de nos frilosités d'historien.

En sciences dures en effet, il n'est pas rare de rencontrer – parmi ceux qui réfléchissent à leur métier de chercheur ici aussi bien entendu – des

---

[23] Ibid. (2000), p. 232, 243; (2004), p. 214, 230.
[24] Ibid. (2000), p. 243 ; (2004), p. 229.
[25] Ibid. (2000), p. 244; (2004), p. 232.
[26] Ibid. (2000), p. 233, 235; (2004), p. 216, 219.

savants qui soulignent aisément la part du sentiment ou de la subjectivité dans leurs activités. Citons ici le physiologiste Claude Bernard, mais dans la recherche effectuée, on signale aussi ce réalisme chez un spécialiste de pathologie animale comme William I. B. Beveridge, ou un physicien comme William H. George, et chez les deux prix Nobel de chimie Ilya Prigogine (1977) et John Polanyi (1986). Les publications de ces chercheurs s'échelonnent de 1938 à 1995[27]. Tous quatre attirent l'attention sur la part de l'art, du savoir-faire, du jugement personnel, de la subjectivité du scientifique dans la démarche expérimentale.

Mais c'est Bernard qui affirme le plus nettement, dès 1865, dans l'*Introduction à l'étude de la médecine expérimentale*, le rôle du sentiment dans ce qu'il caractérise comme « l'art de l'investigation scientifique » :

> La méthode expérimentale, écrit-il notamment, [...] s'appuie successivement sur les trois branches de ce trépied immuable : le sentiment, la raison et l'expérience. Dans la recherche de la vérité, au moyen de cette méthode, le sentiment a toujours l'initiative, il engendre l'idée a priori ou l'intuition [...].

Puis il précise :

> le sentiment engendre l'idée ou l'hypothèse expérimentale [...]. Toute l'initiative expérimentale est dans l'idée, car c'est elle qui provoque l'expérience. La raison ou le raisonnement ne servent qu'à déduire les conséquences de cette idée et à les soumettre à l'expérience[28].

Le plus remarquable, c'est que le physiologiste écrit cela à l'époque du positivisme. En 1913, Henri Bergson déclare que l'*Introduction* de Bernard est une œuvre majeure, comparable en importance au *Discours de la Méthode* de Descartes[29]. Plus récemment pourtant, un philosophe des sciences comme Georges Canguilhem semble partager la gêne des historiens, lorsqu'il s'agit de l'affectif : la première partie de l'*Introduction*, où l'on trouve les extraits cités, constitue, avance-t-il, « une somme de généralités, sinon de banalités, en cours dans les laboratoires [...][30] ». Dommage. C'est ainsi qu'on entretient l'illusion que le travail scientifique n'est que rationalité et rigueur, alors qu'il est d'abord d'ordre affectif et intuitif, quand il se veut novateur. La rigueur vient ensuite.

De l'enquête orale chez des mineurs retraités du bassin de Mons devenu inactif vingt ans auparavant, on s'en tiendra ici à l'essentiel de la démarche. J'ai voulu rencontrer de vrais mineurs, des mineurs de fond, en 1996-1997, pour tenter de découvrir une perception du vécu de ce milieu. Et puisque celui-ci était devenu pluriethnique, de voir comment les 27 anciens mineurs que j'ai pu visiter avaient vécu leurs relations interethniques. En choisissant de rencontrer des Belges, des Polonais et des Italiens, je voulais rejoindre trois groupes principaux d'anciens mineurs de la région.

---

[27] Ibid. (2000), p. 239-240 ; (2004), p. 225-26.
[28] Repris dans Ibid. (2000), p. 238 ; (2004), p. 223-24.
[29] Ibid. (2000), p. 238 ; (2004), p. 223.
[30] Georges Canguilhem, *La connaissance de la vie*, Paris, Hachette, 1952, p. 16.

Le choix d'une enquête orale répondait au désir d'approcher l'affectif par échanges directs[31], plutôt que par le biais de documents écrits comme dans l'article sur le métier d'historien. Je me suis donc présenté chez les retraités ayant accepté de me recevoir avec une disposition d'esprit d'écoute de l'autre, de sympathie et d'admiration : je devinais trop ce qu'avait dû être leur vie de travail et ce que continuait d'être leur vie de retraité, à cause de la silicose, cette maladie progressive des mineurs, qui les affectait si souvent avec plus ou moins de gravité. Et quand le courant passe, suggère Philippe Joutard, on peut tenter d'aller plus loin que la sympathie. J'avais été frappé par le témoignage de Pierre Perreault, le cinéaste d'*Un pays sans bon sens!* (1970), à qui j'avais eu l'occasion de demander comment il s'y prenait pour faire parler les Québécois ou les Acadiens de ses documentaires, de façon si simple et si vraie. « Il faut être complice », me dit-il. Ce qu'il y avait entre Perreault et les milieux modestes de ses films, c'était une connivence de sensibilités[32]. Complicité, connivence de sensibilités peuvent paraître à l'opposé des dispositions que requiert la critique historique classique. Pourtant Marrou soutient que l'attitude de l'historien devrait d'abord être d'amitié pour l'autre qui « se révèle à travers le document » qu'il examine. Chez Marrou le travail critique intervient ensuite, comme dans l'amitié, quand vient le doute[33]. De toute façon, l'historien doit jouer constamment de deux registres : celui de la sensibilité à « l'autre » et celui de la rigueur critique. Mais on ne peut en dire plus ici. Ajoutons simplement que l'article cité précise les relations et la manière d'aborder les retraités, qui ont permis de réussir ces rencontres. Il donne aussi deux fragments d'entretien où l'on rejoignit l'affectif : l'un sur le regret éventuel d'avoir été mineur, l'autre sur l'empreinte de la peur de la mine pendant la retraite[34].

Un dernier mot : aujourd'hui, je dirais qu'il y a une lacune dans ces approches du sentiment. Quand on a entrepris les recherches d'histoire minière, l'effort d'interdisciplinarité parut vite indispensable. Mais en histoire des sentiments, on a simplement travaillé dans le cadre disciplinaire. Tout au plus a-t-on recouru dans l'enseignement à un philosophe comme Erich Fromm ou à un neurobiologiste comme Jean-Didier Vincent. Il est vrai que c'est depuis quelques années que les travaux de différentes disciplines qui tentent d'éclairer le champ de l'affectif se multiplient. Mais justement, un Clifford Geertz montre combien les anthropologues notamment sont partie prenante dans cette pluridisciplinarité, alors que les historiens semblent absents. Comme si dans l'ensemble, ceux-ci restaient marqués, en ce qui touche aux sentiments, par de vieilles réticences [35].

---

[31] Hubert Watelet, « La dernière génération des mineurs du Borinage », dans Véronique Fillieux et al. (dir.), *Angles d'approches. Histoire économique et sociale de l'espace wallon (XVe-XXe siècles)*, Louvain-la-Neuve, Bruylant-Academia, 2003, p. 213-229.
[32] Ibid., p. 221.
[33] H.-I. Marrou, *De la connaissance*, p. 92-93.
[34] Hubert Watelet, « La dernière génération », p. 218-19 et 224-26.
[35] Clifford Geertz, « Culture, Esprit, Cerveau », dans François Rastier et Simon Bouquet (dir.), *Introduction aux sciences de la culture*, Paris, Presses Universitaires de France, 2002, p. 229-241.

– 8 –

Inside Out
The Use and Inadvertent Misuse of Oral Histories

Laura E. Ettinger

In the space of a few years, I did two very different kinds of research projects. One involved interviewing Jews, who, as children, had attended a social settlement house in early twentieth century Rochester, New York, while the other entailed interviewing nuns, who had gone to nurse-midwifery school at Catholic Maternity Institute in Santa Fe, New Mexico, in the 1950s and 1960s.[1] This article focuses on oral histories and interviewers' complex relationships with their subjects by comparing the interviews I conducted for these two projects. In one case, I shared the cultural background of the people I interviewed - that is, I had insider status. My place as a member of the reference group - a Jew - tended to put the subjects and me at ease, but it also discouraged them from defining more precisely their comments or terms. In addition, my own complex feelings about my Jewish identity affected my interpretations of what the subjects said and even the questions I asked. In the other project, I did not share the cultural background of the people whom I interviewed - that is, I had outsider status. As a non-Catholic, I had preconceived notions of nuns, and when interviewing these women, my prejudices, both positive and negative, shaped my questions and my understanding of their responses. When I found them to be adventurous risk-takers, was it because I had assumed them to be women with uneventful lives? When I found one of the nuns to be irreverent, was it because I had assumed nuns to be unquestioning? Because researchers cannot disassociate from their own backgrounds when interviewing and assessing subjects, oral history may present as many problems and questions as answers. This article explores the ways in which interviewers' biases shape history. I argue that there is no clear advantage to being an insider or an outsider - that both positions have advantages and disadvantages and both create biases. I also argue that the historian is never fully insider or outsider, but has multiple and changing identities vis-à-vis his or her subjects. In addition, oral history, as a dynamic process with living subjects, demonstrates in exaggerated form what goes on in all historical research and interpretation, and thus all historians need to think carefully about their relationships with their subjects.

Ironically, although this article argues that it is essential for historians to analyze and share their own stories in order to understand the oral histories they create, I had never done this publicly until I presented the conference

---

[1] A paper based on the second project was published as Laura E. Ettinger, "Mission to Mothers: Nuns, Latino Families, and the Founding of Santa Fe's Catholic Maternity Institute," in Georgina Feldberg, Molly Ladd-Taylor, Alison Li, and Kathryn McPherson, eds., *Women, Health, and Nation: Canada and the United States Since 1945* (Kingston and Montreal: McGill-Queen's University Press, 2003), 144-160.

paper on which this article is based. I had learned what the discipline of history teaches its students: serious historians do not make their own stories central to the histories they write. Historian Leslie Reagan explains that her hands shook as she departed from this disciplinary convention at an international meeting of historians. As Reagan argues, "plac[ing] the author visibly in the forefront ... goes against the grain of being an historian: too personal, too vested, too presentist," and "those who do not conform to the scholarly and social rules of their own discipline may be seen as unprofessional or weak scholars."[2] In fact, even as I wrote the conference paper, I had those unwritten rules in my head and was concerned that the paper was not professional enough. I was excited when during the lively question and answer period at the conference session, audience members of many different backgrounds - Italian-Canadian, Jewish-Canadian, Mexican-American - indicated that they could relate to what I was saying. My story, just like the stories of my subjects, provides a window into understanding bigger, broader issues because my story, about the interviewer's relationship to and with her subjects, is not unique. It connects to an evolving approach to oral history.

Professional oral history was first developed in the 1930s by Columbia University's Allan Nevins and Louis Starr, who saw it as a way to collect valuable information about important individuals.[3] In the 1960s and 1970s, it changed its focus to various groups, like women, immigrants, people of color, and the working class, who up until that time had been ignored. As part of the growth of social history, which called for a broadening of history to include these groups, oral history became much more popular. Because social historians sought information about people who had left few written records, they tapped into a wider and more diverse set of sources: gravestones, census data, probate records, and oral histories.[4] With few exceptions, oral historians in the 1970s did not talk about the complex relationships between interviewers and interviewees. They tended to see oral histories as simply a form of data, just like any other, to be collected. Like other historians, oral historians argued that they were objective. In fact, more than other historians, oral historians were "on the defensive" because they used "the testimony of living witnesses, [and] wanted to show that [their] ... method was a rigorous, disinterested pursuit of truth and therefore respectable."[5] However, in the 1980s, historians began questioning the notion of scientific objectivity. Influenced by anthropologists, sociologists, biographers, and feminist theorists, some oral historians now openly discussed their place in the histories they created. They commented on the reasons they chose their project, their feelings about it, the

---

[2] Leslie J. Reagan, "From Hazard to Blessing to Tragedy: Representations of Miscarriage in Twentieth-Century America," *Feminist Studies* 29, no. 2 (Summer 2003): 371- 72.
[3] David K. Dunaway, "The Interdisciplinarity of Oral History," in David K. Dunaway, and Willam K. Baum, eds., *Oral History: An Interdisciplinary Anthology*, 2d ed. (Walnut Creek, CA: Alta Mira Press, 1996), 8.
[4] Valerie Matsumoto, "Reflections on Oral History: Research in a Japanese American Community," in Diane L. Wolf, ed., *Feminist Dilemmas in Fieldwork* (Boulder: Westview Press, 1996), 161.
[5] Valerie Yow, "'Do I Like Them Too Much?': Effects of the Oral History Interview on the Interviewer and Vice-Versa," *Oral History Review* 24, no. 1 (Summer 1997): 56-60.

ways their gender, class, race, ethnicity, and age affected their questions and interpretations of the interviewees' answers, as well as the collaborative nature of the interview.[6] Following this trend, by the late 1980s, a number of scholars, especially anthropologists and sociologists, began to write about the advantages and disadvantages of sharing or not sharing the same cultural background as the people they interviewed. However, this kind of analysis has not been done enough, especially by historians. In addition, few scholars have discussed their experiences as both insiders and outsiders.

When I went to interview the Jews who had gone to the social settlement house as children, my background as a Jew shaped every aspect of the interview. It affected my choice of subject, access to interviewees, the assumptions I made, the questions I asked, the interactions that took place in the interview, and the way I interpreted the interviewees' comments.

My Jewish heritage helped my subjects and me to feel comfortable during the interviews. When I interviewed Eva Goldberg, she was 85 years old, and I was 25 years old. As a child, she had attended the social settlement house located in a poor Jewish immigrant neighbourhood in Rochester. Born in 1908 and the daughter of recent immigrants from Odessa, Eva met her friends at "the Home," as the settlement house was called, every day after school from the time she was eight or nine until she was thirteen and left school to work in a clothing factory. At age 85, Eva lived in a nicely appointed home in Brighton, the suburb to which many of Rochester's Jews had moved.

So much about being with Eva in her home was familiar to me. My grandparents and great-grandparents were born in Eastern Europe. Eva was the exact same age as my beloved grandmother, who had died two years before. I also had extensive experience with elderly Jews who were not my relatives. For two years, I had been the program coordinator for an adult day services program at Jewish Family Service in Buffalo. I had enjoyed hearing about the lives of those women and men, and I liked the playful banter I often had with them. I even took pleasure in the rhythm of their speech and intonation in their voices, particular to eastern European Jewish immigrants and their children. I was comfortable, in both my personal and professional life, spending time with older Jews.

So, when I sat down to interview Eva Goldberg for an academic project, I felt at ease, and I suspect that Eva may have as well. I had told Eva that I was Jewish when we talked on the telephone for our exploratory interview. The comfort level we shared probably helped her to talk, but it might have discouraged both of us from talking about certain difficult subjects, especially given the enormous age difference between us. I found myself in a granddaughter role, similar to the "daughter role" that anthropologist Micaela di Leonardo describes regarding her interviews.[7] Invited into the living room, I

---

[6] Ibid., 60-70.

[7] Micaela di Leonardo, *The Varieties of Ethnic Experience: Kinship, Class, and Gender Among California Italian-Americans* (Ithaca: Cornell University Press, 1984), 37. Di Leonardo discussed something similar in the complications inherent in what she called the "daughter role" she had in her interviews with fellow California Italian-Americans. Di Leonardo explained that this "already established role" created an easy rapport between her and her informants, but it had its limits, as the informants put her into a

was given a delicious pastry, told that I should have "a little more, dear, because it's good for you," and primed to listen to stories about the "olden days." Although my role as a surrogate granddaughter gave me an immediate entrée into Eva's life and made her eager to tell me her life story, she may have wanted to leave out some of the "messy" parts so as not to damage my naïve ears. Plus in my respectful "granddaughter role," I may have prevented Eva from telling me certain things, offering what sociologists Sherryl Kleinman and Martha A. Copp call "instant sympathy," "where we offer sympathy before we understand what the action or event meant to the participant."[8] For example, when Eva told me that she felt terrible for trying to use what she had learned in the settlement to teach, and improve, her mother, I quickly jumped in. "But that's what you were taught to do. I mean, I'm sure you were taught to go home and tell your parents."[9] I discouraged Eva from revealing more because our warm, comfortable connection caused me to empathize with her, and because I was deeply *un*comfortable with my elder exposing herself so I gave her an opportunity to save face.

My cultural background affected my ability to gain access to interview subjects in the first place. I learned about former settlement house attendees by using connections of connections. Although I was not well connected within the Rochester Jewish community and did not belong to a synagogue in Rochester, I knew from personal experience how Jewish communities worked. I knew to contact the synagogues, the synagogue sisterhoods, Jewish Family Service, the Jewish Federation, the Jewish newspaper, and the Jewish nursing home. Personal contacts within the Jewish community had also given me access to interviewees. I suspect my Jewish identity probably helped to give me easier access to interviewees once I called them or visited them. My interviewees may have made erroneous assumptions about my Jewish background, assuming that I grew up in a much more culturally Jewish household than I did. I let these assumptions stand, sometimes even finding myself dropping true references to my Jewish upbringing that resulted in my gaining access. However, I felt somewhat uncomfortable using my Jewishness; in many ways, I felt that while I was assumed to have "insider" status, I really had "outsider" status. I was not religious, and I did not feel myself to be very culturally Jewish. I grew up in a predominantly Christian area, and I was the only Jew I knew outside of my immediate family and my Hebrew tutor until I went to college. I married a Catholic man, although a Catholic who did not identify as such. In a sense, I felt myself almost to be an outsider peering in at these Jewish immigrants, eager to learn about this culture that was, and yet was not, mine. My ambivalent relationship with Judaism helped me to choose this project, and it dramatically affected my feelings about it.

---

certain position and judged her actions and comments based on their assumptions about that position. She did not like, for example, being scolded by one interviewee who said: "You mean Mommy and Daddy *allowed* you to have Thanksgiving away from home?"

[8] Sherryl Kleinman and Martha A. Copp, *Emotions and Fieldwork* (Newbury Park, CA: Sage Publications, 1993), 47.

[9] Interview by the author with Eva Goldberg, Rochester, New York, 29 March 1993.

Even while feeling like an "outsider" to Judaism in some ways, my Jewish heritage could not help but influence the way I understood what my interviewees said. My interviewees were eastern European Orthodox Jewish immigrants. The directors of the settlement, on the other hand, were German Reform Jewish women who had lived in Rochester for decades, and had assimilated into American life. The eastern European immigrants' customs, dress, manners, and behaviour embarrassed the German Jews; they were seen as strange and unacceptable in this new American setting. When huge waves of eastern European Jewish immigrants arrived in Rochester from the 1880s through the 1910s, the German Jewish women felt that something had to be done to help their coreligionists and to make them less conspicuous in their new homeland.[10] The settlement house enabled these German Jews to accelerate their coreligionists' assimilation while emphasizing their own status as Americans. My own background mirrored, in many ways, both the experiences of the German *and* eastern European Jews. My ancestors came to the United States from Poland and Russia between 1880 and 1920. I spent my childhood years hearing from my mother about how German Jews looked down upon her parents and grandparents. Yet I grew up as a third and fourth generation Jew in a Christian suburb of Baltimore, who sometimes felt embarrassed by distinctively Jewish Jews. In fact, I am embarrassed to admit that I probably had some of the same feelings about my coreligionists that the German Jews had in the early twentieth century.[11] Did my own eastern European heritage make me too quick to find fault with the German Jews running this settlement house? Or perhaps did my embarrassment with Jews who enjoyed, expressed, and sometimes advertised their Jewish identity lead me to sympathize too quickly with the German Jews?

My Jewish background also discouraged the interviewees from defining more precisely their comments or terms because they assumed that I would understand. Although as mentioned earlier I had a Hebrew tutor, and although I probably know a few more Yiddish words than the average American, I do not speak Hebrew or Yiddish. Yet many of the interviewees used Yiddish in conversation. In particular, Eva and a few former immigrant children referred to the founders, directors, and teachers of the settlement as *Deutscheshe Yehudim*. I did not understand the meaning behind this phrase. I learned later that *Deutscheshe* is Yiddish for German-like, and *Yehudim* is Hebrew for Jews. Eastern European Jews used the term *Yehudim*, the formal Hebrew rather than the familiar Yiddish, to mock the German Jews' airs to social superiority.[12] Looking back, I cannot believe that I did not ask my interviewees exactly what they meant when they used the phrase, *Deutscheshe*

---

[10] Gerald Sorin, *A Time for Building: The Third Migration, 1880-1920*, The Jewish People in America, Vol. 3 (Baltimore: The Johns Hopkins University Press, 1995).

[11] John L. Aguilar explains that acculturated "ethnic scholars" may have negative biases as they "may reject or feel ambivalence toward their group and its customs." John L. Aguilar, "Insider Research: An Ethnography of a Debate," in Donald A. Messerschmidt, ed., *Anthropologists at Home in North America: Methods and Issues in the Study of One's Own Society* (New York: Cambridge University Press, 1981), 22.

[12] Charlotte Baum, Paula Hyman, and Sonya Michel, *The Jewish Woman in America* (New York: The Dial Press, 1976), 180.

Yehudim, but I was embarrassed to admit that I did not completely understand what they meant - as though this might call attention to something Jewish that I somehow should have known.

Less than three years after I interviewed the elderly Jews about the social settlement house, I interviewed people who did not share my cultural background. These people were nuns who lived at the Motherhouse of the Medical Mission Sisters in a suburb of Philadelphia. Prior to my trip to the Motherhouse, I had never met any nuns. As a result, I felt very free to ask naïve and very basic questions because I did not think that the nuns would assume that I had extensive knowledge of their world. I had assumed nuns were universally dowdy, formal, strict, and boring. I had mostly heard about nuns from the many people my parents' age who had gone to Catholic school and talked about being afraid of various nuns, their rules, and their rulers. When I went to interview the sisters, I tried to be conscious of my assumptions. I may have tried too hard to think positive thoughts about them because I feared that my biases would get in the way, or that at the very least I did not really understand the sisters. My first meetings with the nuns eased my fears, and caused me to re-think my assumptions. Seventy-one-year-old Sister Anne Cauzillo, in particular, challenged my preconceptions. Sister Anne had graduated from Santa Fe's nurse-midwifery school - the institution I was researching - in 1961. I liked her instantly. She was smart, critical, analytical, and playful, and more than that, she was irreverent and had an almost wicked sense of humour. Because I liked her, I was hesitant to delve into subjects about which I suspected we did not share the same view or which I thought might be offensive; for example, I asked her very little about birth control. I also felt as though I was betraying her when I left our interview in my car with a pro-choice sticker, parked next to the Motherhouse. Like the other Medical Mission Sisters, Sister Anne had spent much of her life in medical missions in developing countries. She lived in Ghana from 1953 until 1967, except for her brief time in Santa Fe. Sister Anne explained that while working in maternal health care in Ghana, she and the other nuns were against herbal medicine. They saw themselves as the "GGG girls - God's Gift to Ghana," replacing superstition and herbal folk remedies with scientific medicine. As she commented wryly, "The drug companies loved us. We saw problems after women had taken herbal medicine. Now we like herbal medicine."[13] After leaving Ghana, Sister Anne returned to the United States to get a bachelor's degree in nursing at St. Louis University, and then went to work once again in maternal health care in an isolated village in Nigeria for four years. Sister Anne called those four years "fun" and "very hard." She said that there was "something very earthy" about the experience, where she lived far into the bush - 12 miles from the main road, and 60 miles from a city. I wonder looking back if I was too quick to be impressed by her self-reflectivity, by her dry humour, and by the adventures she had while helping poor people throughout the world. When I saw her as an extraordinarily adventurous and rough-and-

---

[13] Interview by the author with Sister Anne Cauzillo, Philadelphia, Pennsylvania, 7 September 1995.

ready kind of woman, was it because I was comparing her to the strict schoolmarm vision of nuns that I had in my head?

Sister Anne and I did not share age, religion, or ethnic background. While I had purposely revealed my Jewish heritage to my elderly Jewish interviewees, I had no special desire to reveal my Judaism to the nuns. One found out about our religious differences when she explicitly asked about my "church affiliation"; even though I was interviewing her, she understandably was assessing me.[14] But in some ways, I was not completely an outsider with the nuns. We were all women who were interested in maternal health care, and we were all women who carved out a place and space in our lives that gave us independence. I knew, though, that when these nuns came of age, the barriers facing women were much greater than the ones I had faced. And the nuns I interviewed were, in many ways, much more independent than I was, living in developing countries for extended periods of time, moving around frequently, and devoting their lives to helping the poor. I admired the way their lives contrasted with mid-twentieth century expectations for women, and the way their commitments reflected their passions. The high regard that I developed for these women provided me with a comfort level that I had feared I would not have, but it also may have led me to see them through rose-coloured glasses.

These two sets of interviews - one where I had insider status, and the other where I had outsider status - graphically demonstrate the extent to which biases pervade all oral history work. Insider status offers some advantages; outsider status provides others; but both present problems. On the plus side, the insider status gave me a way to find and gain access to subjects, and once I was with them, it provided me and probably my subjects with familiarity and a sense of ease. On the minus side, insider status can lead to a quickly defined, familiar role, such as the granddaughter role, with all of the assumptions and barriers accompanying that. Also, being an insider discouraged interviewees from explaining their language and meaning because they assumed that I would understand them, and made me reluctant to ask questions. Finally, my ambivalent relationship with the part of the identity that I shared with the interviewees shaped my interpretations of what the interviewees said. On the other hand, the outsider status gave me freedom to ask basic questions because I was not concerned that the elderly nuns would think that I should be an expert on nuns, Catholicism, or sister-nurse-midwives. However, because my ill-conceived assumptions and ignorance about nuns may have led me to overcompensate by being too positive, ultimately I may have measured them against an inaccurate yardstick.

While insider and outsider status convey advantages and disadvantages, the truth is that oral historians are never fully insiders or outsiders. Often they identify with some aspects of their subjects, and not with others. Sometimes an oral historian is what one researcher called a "halfie," that is, someone with two very different identities, or even multiple identities.[15]

---

[14] Telephone interview by the author with Sister Catherine Shean, 18 August 2000.
[15] Diane L. Wolf, "Situating Feminist Dilemmas in Fieldwork," in Wolf, ed., *Feminist Dilemmas in Fieldwork*, 16-17.

Interviewers' multiple identities constantly affect the oral history they create. By definition, oral history is an interaction, a kind of dance where the interviewer and interviewee affect one another. Oral historians need to understand the ways their multiple identities might affect that dance, rather than pretending that they bring nothing to it. Of course, knowing the ways that one might affect the dance requires a fairly deep self-knowledge. It is not simply navel-gazing, but necessary for oral historians to engage in self-reflection to understand the way they shape the research they do, the questions they ask, and the history they write.

While recognizing that it is impossible to eradicate bias, how can oral historians avoid the more egregious problems caused by their biases? Historians need to do more than just idly speculate about their insider or outsider or multiple statuses after a project is completed. As Valerie Yow explains, "although this matter of researcher influence on the research is often mentioned now in oral history literature, it is not often dealt with in any detail." Yow argues that oral historians need to move the relationship between interviewer and interviewee from "corridor talk" or "the side show" to centre stage.[16] They need to ask themselves questions to understand their relationship to the interviewee, the interview process, and the project they are doing, such as: "What am I feeling about this narrator?" "What similarities and what differences [between the narrator and me] impinge on this interpersonal situation?" "In selecting topics and questions, what alternatives might I have taken? Why didn't I choose these?"[17] One way to direct this introspection is to keep diaries, like ethnographers do, of interviewers' feelings and reactions before, during, and after their interviews.[18] By raising self-awareness, such diaries would help to prevent oral historians from approaching their subjects and interpreting their subjects' words in unintentional ways.

Another way to mitigate the biases inherent in the insider or outsider status of the interviewer is to learn - *really* learn - how to be a good listener and how to pay attention to all aspects of the interview process while it is happening. Dana Jack explained that her training as a therapist helped her when conducting oral histories because she had learned how simultaneously to listen to others and pay attention to her own responses.[19] I would argue that all oral historians would benefit from that kind of training. It would help oral historians to ask more effective questions, as well as to understand better the subjects' understanding of their experiences, their feelings, and what the subjects are not saying. In addition, therapeutic training would help oral historians to listen to themselves, paying careful attention to their own feelings, responses, confusion, certainty, comfort, and discomfort.[20]

---

[16] Yow, "'Do I Like Them Too Much?'" 56, 71.
[17] Ibid., 79.
[18] Margaret D. LeCompte, "Researcher Roles," in Margaret D. LeCompte et al., eds., *Researcher Roles and Research Partnerships*, Vol. 6 in *Ethnographer's Toolkit* (Altamira Press: Walnut Creek, CA, 1999), 66-69.
[19] Kathryn Anderson and Dana C. Jack, "Learning to Listen: Interview Techniques and Analyses," in Sherna Berger Gluck and Daphne Patai, eds, *Women's Words: The Feminist Practice of Oral History* (New York: Routledge, 1991), 19.
[20] Ibid., 11-26.

But I would go further than encouraging oral historians to ask self-reflective questions and get training in good listening. I think that publishing information about interviewers' complex relationships with their subjects is important because it does away with the pretension of objectivity and it provides context for the author's ideas and interpretations. It is becoming more common for anthropologists and feminist scholars to put this kind of information in the introduction or afterward of an article or book, although few historians do this. It would be more radical to include the self-reflective information throughout the article or book. But then how does one keep this from being too intrusive and perhaps too narcissistic? To include this material in the body of the work might shift the focus inappropriately to the writer. However, current practice has not yet found fully effective or honest ways to reveal this important information.

Not only is it important for scholars to analyze and write about their relationship to their research. Teachers must develop their students' ability to recognize and question their biases. They could require students writing research papers, using oral histories or any historical sources, to include a section on "My relationship to this research project," or "How who I am has shaped this paper." I suspect such a requirement would lead to better student papers because students would be forced to reflect on the process of understanding history. I want my undergraduates to know about historical issues, to do good research, and most important, to understand how bias shapes the collection, creation, and presentation of historical information, and for that matter, any information.

Finally, I would argue that these insider/outsider issues exist not only in oral history, but in all kinds of history. The interaction between interviewer and interviewee in oral history simply makes explicit what goes on in all historical projects. All of history is an interaction between historian and subject. All historians come to a project with insider, or outsider, or multiple statuses and these statuses change as a project continues.[21]

While writing a book that used mostly sources other than oral histories, I have experienced the impact of changes in status first-hand.[22] When I started the project, a history of nurse-midwives in the United States, I identified as an outsider because I am not a nurse-midwife, and sometimes that created wariness ("You don't understand because you're not one of us"), and sometimes respect. However, in the nearly ten years that I have been doing research on nurse-midwives, my relationship to the project has changed. I have spent much more time with nurse-midwives, both for this project and for my

---

[21] Sociologist Nancy A. Naples argues that the insider/outsider division is a false divide because "we negotiate and renegotiate our relationship" to the "people whom we are interviewing through particular and ongoing everyday interactions." Nancy A. Naples, "A Feminist Revisiting of the Insider/Outsider Debate: The 'Outsider Phenomenon' in Rural Iowa," *Qualitative Sociology* 19, no. 1 (Spring 1996): 103. Anthropologist Renato Rosaldo argues that ethnographers (and social critics, his focus) often belong to many different, shifting, and overlapping communities. Renato Rosaldo, *Culture and Truth: The Remaking of Social Analysis* (Boston: Beacon Press, 1989), 168-95.
[22] Laura E. Ettinger, *Modern Midwives: The Birth of Nurse-Midwifery in America* (Columbus, OH: The Ohio State University Press, forthcoming 2005).

own health care, than I had previously. In particular, I went through pregnancy and childbirth with two wonderful nurse-midwives. At the same time, through my historical research, I have come to see nurse-midwifery as an underutilized solution to many maternal health care problems in the United States. Thus, personally, politically, and professionally, I am more invested in nurse-midwives than ever before. I feel as though I have a relationship with what I have often called "my" nurse-midwives, the ones I have written about, even though I have met few of them and most are long since dead. I suspect that the process I just described happens to many historians.[23] The changes in my relationship with specific nurse-midwives and to my research project mean that I ask different questions now than I did eight or nine years ago. These changes also mean that I interpret and present the information differently. I do not cover up things about nurse-midwives that might be perceived as negative, but my greater investment in them leads sometimes to greater disappointment in the negatives, although even this changes. When I wrote my dissertation, the precursor to the book, I was very disappointed in nurse-midwives for not being able to buck the American health care establishment. Now, I have more empathy for the difficult choices they faced, even though I am still sometimes disappointed in them. I use the example of my own ongoing work to show the ways in which all historians, not just oral historians, can have complicated relationships with their subjects. I began with outsider status, and although I still have that, I now have a bit of an insider perspective, at least personally and politically.

Oral historians, whether insiders, or outsiders, or both, need to reflect critically on their own personal histories as well as on the ways their insider/outsider status has affected the creation of oral history. That self-knowledge helps oral historians to understand the ways they identify and do not identify with their interviewees, and more generally what they bring to the interview exchange as well as how they affect and respond to it. In addition, the lens of insider/outsider status helps us to understand not only the exchanges that occur in oral history, but in all history. The more we understand our complicated relationships with our subject matter, the better historians we will be.

---

[23] For one well-known historian who describes this experience, see Kathryn Kish Sklar, "Coming to Terms with Florence Kelly: The Tale of a Reluctant Biographer," in Sara Alpern et al., eds., *The Challenge of Feminist Biography: Writing the Lives of Modern American Women* (Urbana, IL: University of Illinois Press, 1992), 17-33.

– 9 –

Les sources juridiques au service de l'histoire socio-culturelle de la France médiévale et moderne

Kouky Fianu/Sylvie Perrier

Depuis quelques décennies, l'histoire sociale, médiévale aussi bien que moderne, exploite ce matériau de choix que sont les archives judiciaires pour étudier le fait social dans toute sa complexité : travail, migrations, pratiques matrimoniales, marginalité, criminalité, etc. Depuis peu cependant, le questionnement s'est porté sur la nature et la signification des actes juridiques et sur les pratiques qu'ils révèlent. Le renouveau de l'histoire du notariat, en particulier, a amené les historiens à s'intéresser à la pratique notariale autant qu'au contenu des actes, redonnant ainsi sa juste place au contexte juridico-professionnel qui a produit à ces sources incontournables de l'histoire sociale[1].

De son côté, l'histoire du droit s'est traditionnellement intéressée aux sources normatives (lois, coutumes) et a mis en évidence les évolutions des institutions juridiques (organes de législation, tribunaux, notariat, etc.) comme de la procédure. L'apport de l'anthropologie a récemment ouvert de nouveaux horizons en plaçant les utilisateurs et les agents de cette justice au centre du questionnement. L'anthropologie historique a également favorisé la comparaison des systèmes juridiques avec les sociétés non-occidentales et à travers le temps[2]. Une histoire des pratiques juridiques et de leur impact social est donc désormais possible.

Nos recherches respectives s'inspirent de ces approches pluridisciplinaires et cette parenté intellectuelle nous est vite apparue comme une invitation au dialogue. Au fil de nos conversations informelles, nous avons constaté que nous traitions des sources similaires, juridiques et para-juridiques, et que nous étions toutes deux sensibles à l'utilisation qui était faite de ces documents par les acteurs sociaux. Nous avons toutefois réalisé que nos démarches étaient distinctes, puisque nos questions de départ nous amenaient à explorer des univers tout à fait différents. Fortes de ce constat, nous avons décidé de tenter une expérience formelle et de nous engager dans un exercice comparatif. Quels résultats deux démarches différentes, mais basées sur des sources et une approche similaires peuvent-elles produire? Nous avons donc entrepris de décortiquer notre pratique historienne en comparant les diverses étapes de nos méthodes respectives ainsi que les résultats qui en sont issus.

Nous explorerons dans ce texte des pratiques sociales liées à la justice : d'une part, le rôle de l'écrit dans la société médiévale et, d'autre part,

---

[1] Jean L. Laffont, « Introduction », dans *Notaires, notariat et société sous l'Ancien Régime*, Toulouse, Presses universitaires du Mirail, 1990, p. 13 à 17.
[2] Voir en particulier Norbert Roulant, *Anthropologie juridique*, Paris, PUF, coll. « Droit fondamental », 1988; Louis Assier-Andrieu, « L'anthropologie et la modernité du droit », *Anthropologie et Société*, vol. 13, n° 1, 1989, p. 21 à 34.

les recompositions familiales dans la société d'Ancien Régime. Ce faisant, nous chercherons à tracer des liens entre nos deux démarches pour souligner en quoi ce questionnement comparatif peut nous mener à une meilleure compréhension des rapports entre les individus et la justice aux époques qui nous intéressent. De plus, nous tenterons également de montrer en quoi cette expérience méthodologique a influencé nos deux recherches en cours.

L'utilisation de la justice d'après des sources juridiques médiévales

À partir du XIIe siècle, les établissements juridiques s'organisèrent et se multiplièrent dans le royaume de France : grands seigneurs, rois, villes, guildes, etc. se dotèrent d'institutions judiciaires, administratives et fiscales[3]. Cette évolution s'accompagna d'un écrit « conquérant », l'administration du pouvoir (fiscalité, justice, etc.) reposant sur la production d'écrits authentiques, sur la constitution d'archives, et la justice exigeant de manière croissante des preuves écrites[4]. Dans la partie nord du royaume, où s'exerçait un droit coutumier, l'authentification des actes se traduisit le plus souvent par l'apposition du sceau d'une autorité, laïque ou cléricale, chargée d'attester la véracité et la légitimité des transactions inscrites dans les actes[5]. Dès la fin du XIIe siècle apparurent donc en France du Nord de nouvelles formes d'authentification des actes et de nouvelles pratiques de l'écrit, des pratiques qui se précisèrent avec le temps et que partagea à long terme l'ensemble de la population.

C'est dans ce contexte que s'insèrent les deux questions qui nous retiendront ici : comment se manifestèrent ces nouvelles pratiques? Comment et pour quelles raisons les individus faisaient-ils appel aux diverses instances responsables de la production d'un écrit authentique? L'étude qui suit repose essentiellement sur l'examen d'actes privés (ventes, donations, ententes, attestations, testaments, contrats d'apprentissage, etc.) émanant de juridictions gracieuses (tribunaux qui entérinent les transactions volontaires, non contentieuses) d'Orléans entre les XIIIe et XVe siècles. À ce corpus de base s'ajoute un fonds d'inventaires après décès parisiens du XVe siècle qui mentionnent les actes détenus par des chanoines de Notre-Dame au moment de leur trépas.

---

[3] Olivier Guillot, Albert Rigaudière et Yves Sassier, *Pouvoirs et institutions dans la France médiévale, tome II : Des temps féodaux aux temps de l'État*, Paris, Armand Colin, 1994.

[4] Raoul C. van Caenegem, « La preuve dans le droit du moyen âge occidental – Rapport de synthèse », dans *La preuve*, Bruxelles, Éditions de la librairie encyclopédique, 1965 (Recueils de la Société Jean Bodin pour l'histoire comparative des institutions, t. XVII), p. 691-753, plus particulièrement p. 742 et suivantes. Voir aussi Kouky Fianu et DeLloyd J. Guth (éd.), *Écrit et pouvoir dans les chancelleries médiévales : espace français, espace anglais*, Louvain-la-Neuve, FIDEM, 1997.

[5] Robert-Henri Bautier, « L'authentification des actes privés dans la France médiévale : notariat public et juridiction gracieuse », dans *Notariado público y documento privado, de los orígenes al siglo XIV. Actas del VII Congreso international de diplomatica - Valencia 1986*, Valencia 1989, vol. II, p. 701-772 (Repris dans R.-H. Bautier, *Chartes, sceaux et chancelleries. Études de diplomatique et de sigillographie médiévales*, Paris, École des chartes, 1990, vol. I, p. 269-340).

Les nouvelles pratiques de l'écrit juridique

Dès la fin du XIIe siècle, la justice ecclésiastique était la plus étendue et la mieux organisée du royaume, surpassant les autres cours, seigneuriales ou princières. Son apogée eut lieu au XIIIe siècle : les laïcs recouraient aux tribunaux épiscopaux (officialités) pour des actions entre laïcs, en raison de la faiblesse des pouvoirs temporels et de l'efficacité d'une procédure ecclésiastique plus rationnelle[6]. Parallèlement, chaque diocèse développa un service d'écritures authentiques, munies du sceau de l'évêque ou de son juge délégué, l'official. À partir des années 1250, des contestations, en nombre croissant, s'élevèrent de la part des pouvoirs seigneuriaux et royaux du Nord contre la main-mise des officialités sur la juridiction gracieuse[7] et les juges royaux n'acceptèrent plus ce type de lettres que comme des demies-preuves dans leurs tribunaux. La raison de ces attaques est liée aux ambitions de pouvoirs de mieux en mieux organisés : le droit leur servait en effet à affirmer autorité et légitimité, mais également à capter une importante source de revenus, celle de la taxe du sceau en particulier et de la justice en général. Tout au long du XIIIe siècle, le pouvoir royal s'affirmait. En 1280, le roi Philippe III le Hardi, ordonna l'instauration d'un tabellionnage (bureau d'écritures) dans toutes les prévôtés du royaume : ainsi naquit la lettre de baillie ou de prévôté, dont le succès fut immédiat car elle avait force exécutoire dans tout le royaume et dans toute cour laïque (contrairement à la lettre d'officialité)[8]. Ces bureaux d'écritures reposaient sur le travail de notaires royaux (aussi appelés tabellions) chargés d'entendre les parties et de mettre leur transaction en forme dans un acte, avant qu'il ne fût scellé par un garde du sceau. À Orléans, comme dans les rares régions du Nord qui ont été étudiées[9], on assiste à un basculement du recours aux juridictions gracieuses entre 1280 et 1300 : les officialités furent délaissées au profit des prévôtés et de leurs tabellions, chargés d'authentifier les actes privés. Comment expliquer ce phénomène? Les informations sont très minces, mais la réponse réside sans doute dans la procédure juridique : plus les tribunaux royaux accroissaient leur compétence au détriment de l'officialité et privilégiaient la lettre de prévôté sur toute autre, plus les justiciables étaient amenés à s'en munir en cas de procès. Cette réponse logique doit toutefois être

---

[6] Paul Fournier, *Les officialités au Moyen Âge (1180-1328)*, Paris, Plon, 1880, p. 94-97. La question de la rationalité de la procédure inquisitoire adoptée par l'Église au XIIIe siècle est remise en question depuis plusieurs années, comme le résume Bruno Lemesle, « Premiers jalons et mise en place d'une procédure d'enquête dans la région angevine (XIe-XIIIe siècle) », dans B. Lemesle (dir.), *La preuve en justice de l'Antiquité à nos jours*, Rennes, PUR, 2003, p. 69-93, plus particulièrement p. 70-71.

[7] P. Fournier, op. cit., p. 188 : l'auteur cite le cas de porteurs de lettres d'officialités qui, à Tours en 1294, furent attaqués et forcés à les manger...

[8] Louis Carolus-Barré, « L'ordonnance de Philippe le Hardi et l'organisation de la juridiction gracieuse », *Bibliothèque de l'École des Chartes*, vol. 96 (1935), p. 5-48. R.-H. Bautier, op. cit., p. 765-767.

[9] L. Carolus-Barré, op. cit. et « L'ordonnance de Philippe le Hardi sur la juridiction gracieuse et son application en Champagne, dès 1280 », *Revue historique de droit français et étranger*, vol. 39 (1961), p. 296-303. Robert-Henri Bautier, « L'exercice de la juridiction gracieuse en Champagne, du milieu du XIIIe siècle à la fin du XVe siècle », *Bibliothèque de l'École des Chartes*, vol. 116 (1958), p. 29-106.

nuancée : la prévention ne semble pas être la seule raison du recours à une juridiction gracieuse.

Le recours aux justices volontaires

Il convient en premier lieu de rappeler qu'au Moyen Âge rien ne forçait un individu à solliciter un acte authentique. En cour, la preuve écrite était de force égale à la preuve par témoins, ce qui se conçoit aisément dans la mesure où tout acte public était par sa nature même un témoignage attesté par un tabellion ou un notaire; jusqu'au XVIe siècle, elle pouvait d'ailleurs être renversée par le témoignage oral puisque, comme l'affirment les juristes médiévaux, « témoins passent lettres[10] ». L'utilisation d'une juridiction gracieuse (ou volontaire) répondait donc à la volonté d'y recourir. Volonté des deux parties ou de la plus puissante seulement? En tout cas le geste révèle un choix qui témoigne de préoccupations précises.

Puisque jusqu'au XVe siècle les juridictions gracieuses royales du Nord ne conservaient généralement pas trace des transactions, chaque partie était responsable de garder ses lettres précieusement en cas d'un recours ultérieur en justice. La sensibilité à l'écrit dans un tel contexte semble extrême : par exemple, l'inventaire après décès d'un chanoine parisien de 1468 révèle qu'il avait plus de 500 lettres dans plusieurs coffres au moment de son décès, certaines d'entre-elles remontant des décennies en arrière[11]. Les justiciables accumulaient donc les preuves de leurs transactions chez eux. Ces sources, on le devine, n'ont pas traversé les siècles : les médiévistes, contrairement hélas à leurs collègues modernistes, n'ont que très peu de chance de trouver le contenu de ces « trésors » personnels ou familiaux. Les rares cas qui subsistent laissent cependant deviner le caractère préventif d'une telle accumulation. En obtenant un acte, les parties venues devant le juge d'un tribunal volontaire s'assuraient de pouvoir démontrer leurs droits même lorsque les témoins ne seraient plus là pour témoigner. L'écrit, vecteur de mémoire, pouvait ainsi dire le droit et la propriété si jamais s'élevaient des contestations futures.

Un autre facteur susceptible d'expliquer l'utilisation des justices gracieuses est la réaction, rapide, des justiciables face à la procédure et à ses changements. Par exemple, la contestation seigneuriale contre la compétence de l'officialité, qui se manifeste dès le milieu du XIIIe siècle, se traduit exactement à la même époque par l'apparition de lettres de prévôté à Orléans, quelque trente ans avant l'ordonnance créant les tabellionnages royaux. Dans le cartulaire inédit de la Commanderie Saint-Marc d'Orléans qui couvre la période 1148 à 1434, la première lettre de prévôté date de 1259 : il s'agit d'un acte, en français, passé devant deux prévôts et scellé du sceau de la prévôté[12]. L'année suivante, une quittance entre particuliers est produite en latin sous le

---

[10] Jean-Philippe Lévy, « Le problème de la preuve dans les droits savants du Moyen Âge », dans *La preuve*, Bruxelles, Éditions de la librairie encyclopédique, 1965 (Recueils de la Société Jean Bodin pour l'histoire comparative des institutions, t. XVII), p. 137-167, plus particulièrement p. 153-156.
[11] Archives nationales (France) [ci-après AN], S 851B, n° 21, f. 16-44.
[12] AN, S 1010^1, f. 22, don de terres et de meubles de Jehanne la Paillarde à Saint-Marc (1259).

sceau de la prévôté[13] et, en 1264, un acte de vente en latin est également produit par deux prévôts sous le sceau de la prévôté[14]. Les pratiques juridiques des particuliers s'ajustaient donc à la procédure en vigueur au moment de la transaction. C'est ainsi que l'on peut interpréter l'utilisation successive de plusieurs cours dans le cas de l'authentification d'une transaction entre les Templiers et le seigneur de Beaugency : garantie une première fois par le sceau du seigneur lui-même en 1233, la transaction fut authentifiée (sous forme de *vidimus*) en 1295 par les prévôts de Beaugency et scellée du sceau de la prévôté[15], puis authentifiée à nouveau en 1427 par la prévôté d'Orléans[16].

Les particuliers étaient conscients du poids et de la valeur des sceaux : ils pouvaient recourir, pour une même transaction, à plus d'un bureau d'écriture, comme s'ils s'assuraient, en période de changements juridiques, d'avoir en main tous les instruments possibles de la preuve. En sollicitant une juridiction plutôt qu'une autre, les parties demandaient à être placées sous l'autorité d'un juge particulier : plus favorable, plus clément, plus efficace, incontournable, etc. L'élément économique ne doit pas être négligé non plus : les frais de sceau, variables d'une juridiction à une autre, pouvaient jouer un rôle déterminant dans le choix d'une institution plutôt que d'une autre. Les caractéristiques personnelles pouvaient également entrer en compte dans le choix effectué : certains individus avaient des actes pour la moindre transaction, tandis que d'autres se contentaient d'ententes verbales, comme le montre la comparaison des inventaires après décès d'Étienne de Montdidier et de Jean Oche, deux chanoines parisiens[17]. Enfin, les parties acceptaient de prendre plus ou moins de risque en optant pour une opération verbale ou un acte écrit.

Au-delà de ces aspects pragmatiques, de prévention, réaction et créativité, on voit également dans le recours à la juridiction gracieuse une dimension plus symbolique. On pouvait affirmer son statut juridique en imposant un tribunal à l'autre partie contractante (par exemple un clerc exigeant une lettre d'officialité pour une transaction avec un laïc). On pouvait également confirmer son statut social et signaler par l'usage que l'on faisait des tribunaux le type de relation que l'on entretenait avec la partie associée[18], par exemple en obtenant une reconnaissance de dettes pour des montants infimes ou en n'en demandant pas pour des montants importants[19]. Enfin, affirmer la

---

[13] AN, S 1010[1], f. 67v, quittance pour la vente entre particuliers d'une pièce (avril 1260).
[14] AN, S 1010[1], f. 68 (août 1264).
[15] AN, S 1010[1], f. 54v (décembre 1295).
[16] AN, S 1010[1], f. 55 (novembre 1427).
[17] Étude effectuée dans Kouky Fianu, « Enregistrer la dette : le témoignage des sources de la justice gracieuse à Orléans (XIIIe - XVe siècle) », à paraître dans Julie Mayade-Claustre (dir.), *Endettement privé et justice au Moyen Âge*, Paris, Publications de la Sorbonne.
[18] Craig Muldrew, *The Economy of Obligation. The Culture of Credit and Social Relations in Early Modern England*, Palgrave, 1998, chap. 8 et 9 en particulier, où l'auteur montre la place occupée par les tribunaux dans les relations sociales tournant autour du crédit et la réticence des justiciables à y recourir.
[19] K. Fianu, « Enregistrer la dette », op. cit.

hiérarchie (la plus puissante des parties imposant son choix de juridiction[20]) ou l'appartenance (les universitaires forçant le recours au prévôt, gardien de leurs privilèges[21]) pouvait se traduire par le recours à l'une ou à l'autre des juridictions gracieuses. En somme, l'utilisation de l'écrit authentique permettait d'exprimer des normes juridiques mais également des normes sociales. Aller chez le notaire revêtait aussi un aspect rituel, créateur de liens sociaux.

La famille recomposée et la justice à l'époque moderne

C'est dans le contexte du renforcement du pouvoir monarchique et de la mise en place de l'État moderne que s'est développée la structure documentaire désormais à la disposition de l'historien de la France prérévolutionnaire. La masse des sources juridiques dont disposent les modernistes n'est pas tant le produit d'innovations institutionnelles dans la France d'Ancien Régime que de l'effort du pouvoir royal pour uniformiser les procédures judiciaires et pour assurer un meilleur enregistrement des actes de la pratique ainsi que leur conservation. C'est tout d'abord par le biais des grandes ordonnances, dont les plus marquantes sont celle de Villers-Cotterêt (1539), le Code Louis (1667) et l'Ordonnance criminelle (1670), que les souverains et leurs principaux ministres ont mieux défini les compétences juridictionnelles et établi des procédures judiciaires valides pour l'ensemble du royaume[22]. Cette oeuvre législative fut complétée par les juristes qui ont expliqué toutes les finesses du système dans leurs nombreux traités de procédure[23]. Par ailleurs, la nécessité d'assurer la publicité des actes privés et les impératifs fiscaux ont amené le pouvoir royal à mettre en place des bureaux d'enregistrement des actes, insinuations laïques et contrôle des actes, et à produire des outils de recherche (tables de mariages, de tutelles, de testaments, de ventes, etc.) pour localiser rapidement les documents recherchés[24].

---

[20] Bien qu'il n'ait pas étudié la question du rôle des justiciables dans le choix d'une juridiction ou d'une autre, R.-H. Bautier signale la forte compétition qui eut lieu en Champagne entre les pouvoirs ecclésiastiques et les autorités royales lorsque les « lettres de baillie » firent leur apparition. Voir R.-H. Bautier, « L'exercice de la juridiction gracieuse en Champagne », op. cit., p. 37.

[21] Serge Lusignan, *« Vérité garde le roi » - La construction d'une identité universitaire en France (XIIIe-XVe siècle)*, Paris, Publications de la Sorbonne, 1999, p. 122-123.

[22] Jean-Marie Carbasse, *Manuel d'introduction historique au droit*, 2e éd., Paris, PUF, 2003, p. 202-205; Bernard Barbiche, *Les institutions de la monarchie française à l'époque moderne*, 2e éd., Paris, PUF, 2001, p. 64-67.

[23] Claude de Ferrière, *Le nouveau praticien contenant l'art de procéder dans les matières civiles, criminelles, et bénéficiales, suivant les nouvelles ordonnances*, Paris, Denys Thierry et Jean Cochart, 1681; Jacques-Antoine Sallé, *L'esprit des ordonnances de Louis XIV*, Paris, Veuve Rouy/Knapen, 1755; Eustache Nicolas Pigeau, *La procédure civile du Châtelet de Paris et de toutes les juridictions ordinaires du royaume*, Paris, Veuve Desaint, 1779, 2 vol. Il existe également des « styles », sorte de guides de procédure à l'usage des praticiens.

[24] Marie-Françoise Limon, articles « Contrôle des actes » et « Insinuations laïques », dans Lucien Bély (dir.), *Dictionnaire de l'Ancien Régime*, Paris, PUF, 1996, p. 332-333 et 665-666; voir également Françoise Hildesheimer, « Insinuation, contrôle des actes et absolutisme », *Bibliothèque de l'école des Chartes*, vol. 143, p. 163-164 et Gabrielle

Cette mentalité procédurière se reflète dans les documents judiciaires produits par les institutions de la France d'Ancien Régime. L'exemple des comptes de tutelle des orphelins mineurs est particulièrement éloquent[25]. On y retrouve la transcription intégrale des actes relatifs à la tutelle (nomination du tuteur, avis de parents, décisions judiciaires) ainsi que des références précises à d'autres pièces utiles à la compréhension du compte (contrats de mariage, testaments, inventaires, etc.). Avec un peu de flair et beaucoup de patience, le chercheur peut retrouver ces documents parmi les milliers de mètres linéaires de sources juridiques conservées dans les divers dépôts d'archives français. Cela permet donc d'envisager une autre méthode que celle de ma collègue médiéviste, une approche qui place les acteurs sociaux au centre du projet.

Ce projet de recherche porte sur le remariage et les recompositions familiales dans la région de Toulouse au XVIIIe siècle. Pour mener à bien cette enquête, il a d'abord fallu constituer un échantillon de familles, tant urbaines que rurales, à partir d'un ensemble de contrats de mariage passés chez quatre notaires entre 1761 et 1770[26]. La seconde étape a consisté à rassembler les actes juridiques (actes notariés et procédures au civil) qui permettaient de baliser la trajectoire familiale pour mieux comprendre l'incidence du remariage dans l'expérience des familles de la France d'Ancien Régime. En se plaçant dans la perspective de ces familles toulousaines du XVIIIe siècle, on peut reproduire un questionnement similaire à celui employé par ma collègue médiéviste : comment et pourquoi les familles utilisaient-elles la justice sous l'Ancien Régime?

De nombreux motifs poussaient alors les familles à avoir recours à des procédures juridiques. Ce choix n'était pas toujours libre, puisque les dispositions royales imposaient plusieurs démarches, notamment quand des mineurs, ou leur patrimoine, risquaient d'être mis en péril par une situation familiale instable. Ainsi, Anne Cornus, veuve de Jean Poux, dut-elle d'abord abandonner la tutelle de son fils Philippe, faire procéder à la nomination d'un nouveau tuteur et rendre son compte de tutelle en justice avant de pouvoir contracter une nouvelle union avec Jean-Antoine Ayrolle[27]. Les procédures requises étaient plus lourdes pour les femmes qui passaient en secondes noces

---

Vilar-Berrogain, *Guide des recherches dans les fonds d'enregistrement sous l'Ancien Régime*, Paris, Imprimerie nationale, 1958, introduction.

[25] Sylvie Perrier, *Des enfances protégées. La tutelle des mineurs en France (XVIIe-XVIIIe siècles)*, Saint-Denis, Presses Universitaires de Vincennes, 1998, p. 41-46.

[26] Corpus global de 596 contrats de mariage passés entre 1761 et 1770 chez deux notaires de Toulouse (Archives départementales de la Haute-Garonne [ci-après ADHG], 3E26494 à 3E26498, minutes du notaire Jean-Pierre Richard; 3E7631 à 3E7640, notaire Jean Vidal) et chez deux notaires du village de St-Jory (ADHG, 3E20907 à 3E20909, notaire Jean Claverie Rapas; 3E20916 à 3E20919, notaire Jean-Blaise Marmond). Des sous-ensembles ont ensuite été constitués pour regrouper les contrats où l'un des conjoints avait été précédemment marié et les contrats où l'un des conjoints était issu d'une famille recomposée.

[27] ADHG, B Sénéchal/Audience (1761-1765) : sentence sur compte de tutelle présenté par Anne Cornus, 1er juin 1764; 3E 7634 : contrat de mariage de Jean-Antoine Ayrolle et Anne Cornus, 19 juin 1764, notaire Jean Vidal. Après la mort de son premier mari, Anne Cornus avait aussi fait faire un inventaire puisque son fils héritier était alors mineur (3E 11939 : inventaire des biens de Jean Poux, 2 septembre 1763).

que pour les veufs dans la même situation, la puissance paternelle n'étant pas troublée par le remariage du père, qui conservait la gestion du patrimoine familial quel que fût son état matrimonial.

Le contrat de mariage était la pierre angulaire du système matrimonial toulousain au XVIIIe siècle et même les conjoints les plus pauvres y avaient recours[28]. Répondant au besoin d'établir et/ou de spécifier les intérêts économiques des deux conjoints dans le futur ménage, le contrat de mariage était un acte complexe qui pouvait comporter de nombreuses clauses (composition et paiement de la dot, donation, gains de survie, institution d'héritier, etc.). Il avait un caractère préventif, puisque l'accord des deux familles sur certaines dispositions et le respect général des contrats de mariage dans la société toulousaine constituaient une garantie pour l'avenir. Mais il s'agissait également d'un acte juridique où les parties pouvaient se montrer très créatives, soit en s'écartant de la coutume locale, soit en ajoutant des dispositions particulières. Le contrat qui a uni le jeune Jean Bouisson, un garçon charron toujours mineur, et Jeanne Gauté, veuve d'un charron, illustre très bien comment les parties pouvaient s'écarter du modèle familial de préférence de leur société et établir leur propre pacte familial[29]. Normalement, selon la coutume de Toulouse, la fiancée apportait une dot que recevait le futur époux, qui devait par la suite en garantir l'intégrité sur ses propres biens (hypothèque légale). Dans le cas de l'union Bouisson-Gauté, le contrat stipule que les époux habiteront chez la veuve et que la dot de celle-ci sera constituée par les meubles qui se trouvent dans la maison. D'autre part, la mère et le frère de l'époux ont fait une donation à ce dernier, aussitôt remise entre les mains de la veuve Gauté qui a hypothéqué ses biens en garantie de la somme. Le contrat respectait donc la coutume puisqu'il contenait une constitution dotale en bonne et due forme, mais la véritable dot était la donation des parents de l'époux : les rôles étaient ainsi inversés et c'est Jean Bouisson qui entrait en position d'épouse dans la maison!

Les recompositions familiales donnaient aussi lieu à des situations où les membres non-apparentés de la famille reconstituée désiraient renforcer leurs liens de belle-parenté par des dispositions juridiques stabilisatrices. Ainsi, Pierre Roques, second époux de Jeanne Lassage, auparavant veuve de Jean Fagès, a choisi une solution originale pour resserrer les liens avec ses beaux-fils François et Jean Fagès. En effet, ils sont passés tous ensemble chez le notaire de St-Jory, en zone rurale près de Toulouse, pour faire écrire un acte de société les unissant à même pot et à même feu, pour profits et pertes[30]. Actes assez courants chez les métayers qui s'unissaient pour exploiter de vastes terres, de telles sociétés étaient très rares au sein des familles. Les Roques-Fagès ont

---

[28] Germain Sicard, « Comportements juridiques et société : les contrats de mariage avant et après la Révolution (Toulouse et pays toulousain) », dans G. Sicard (dir.), *Notaires, mariages, fortunes dans le Midi toulousain*, Toulouse, Université des Sciences sociales de Toulouse, 1997, p. 89-153.

[29] ADHG 3E 7637 : contrat de mariage entre Jean Bouisson et Jeanne Gauté, 7 février 1767 (notaire Jean Vidal).

[30] ADHG 3E 20918 : acte de société entre Pierre Roques et Marguerite Lassage d'une part, et François et Jean Fagès d'autre part, 10 septembre 1767 (notaire Jean Blaise Marmond).

poussé la logique jusqu'au bout puisqu'ils ont effectivement signé des baux de métairie ensemble et que les dots des filles du second lit ont été versées par la société et non pas par le père seul[31].

Dans toutes les familles, et plus particulièrement dans les familles recomposées, vouloir prévenir d'éventuels conflits ou en régler certains qui existaient déjà étaient des motifs puissants pour avoir recours aux services des notaires et de la justice civile[32]. Les actes d'accord/transaction sont nombreux dans les minutes des notaires. C'est la voie choisie par certaines veuves pour régler leurs créances avec la famille de leur conjoint défunt pour pouvoir se reconstituer une dot afin de passer en secondes noces. C'est aussi le moyen emprunté par des cohéritiers, souvent de lits différents, pour régler les questions patrimoniales après le décès du père commun. Toutefois, ces querelles ne trouvaient pas toujours leur solution dans la discrétion de l'étude du notaire et les parties devaient alors recourir aux tribunaux civils pour régler leurs différends. Souvent utilisées stratégiquement pour faire pression sur l'adversaire, les procédures civiles n'arrivaient pas toujours à l'étape de la sentence définitive.

D'autres procédures juridiques avaient un caractère moins contentieux et si elles avaient une raison d'être très concrète, souvent dictée par les lois, elles comportaient également une part symbolique qu'il ne faut pas négliger. Ainsi, les pères, ou à leur défaut les mères, qui ne pouvaient être présents à la signature du contrat de mariage de leur enfant devaient se faire représenter par un procureur qui attestait de leur consentement à l'union. Cette situation était plus fréquente pour les mariages urbains, ce qui témoigne du fait que l'éloignement ne mettait pas fin à la puissance paternelle : tant les familles que les pouvoirs publics tenaient à ce que le consentement parental fût respecté. Autre procédure liée à la puissance paternelle, l'émancipation (qui à Toulouse pouvait être officialisée devant notaire contrairement aux autres régions du sud où celle-ci devait être faite en justice) avait une dimension économique et pratique, puisqu'elle permettait au fils de gérer ses biens et de faire des transactions publiques sous son propre nom. Mais elle avait également une importante dimension rituelle, les notaires décrivant la cérémonie où le fils agenouillé plaçait ses mains entre celles de son père et lui assurait respect et obéissance, malgré l'indépendance que le père lui concédait par acte juridique[33].

Les familles recomposées de la France pré-révolutionnaire offrent donc une perspective intéressante pour étudier les pratiques sociales de la

---

[31] ADHG 3E20918 : contrat de mariage entre Geraud Ferail et Marie Roques, 27 juin 1767 (Marmond); contrat de mariage entre Pierre Blanc et Jeanne Roques, 4 juin 1769.
[32] Isabelle Carrier a montré récemment que les familles pouvaient également se servir de la justice civile pour entretenir, voire provoquer, des querelles et non pas seulement dans la perspective d'une résolution de conflit. I. Carrier, *Virtuosité procédurière. Pratiques judiciaires à Montpellier au Grand Siècle*, thèse de doctorat, Université McGill, 2003.
[33] Ainsi, devant le notaire Jean Vidal, François Touigne, domestique, émancipe-t-il son fils Jacques : « Et pour marquer ladite emancipation ledit Touigne pere a dejoint les mains et donné sa benediction a sondit fils », ADHG, 3E7631 : contrat de mariage entre Jacques Touigne et Marie Roche, 21 novembre 1761. Les formules d'émancipation contiennent parfois aussi des références au droit civil et au droit divin.

justice. Ces familles devaient souvent recourir à tout le potentiel que leur offraient les institutions judiciaires pour aplanir les difficultés créées par l'enchevêtrement des patrimoines à transmettre, pour assurer le bon fonctionnement de la cellule familiale malgré les intérêt divergeants des individus qui la composaient et pour protéger les plus faibles d'entre eux.

En guise de conclusion

Les résultats de l'expérience que nous avons tentée n'ont, bien entendu, pas la prétention d'offrir des conclusions générales aux innombrables questions que l'on peut se poser sur la justice médiévale ou d'Ancien régime. Mais ils reflètent un exercice méthodologique fort enrichissant à maints égards. Le tableau page suivante résume les deux projets, leurs similarités et leurs différences.

Les deux projets ont pour point de départ deux démarches différentes : dans un cas il s'agit de pister des actes privés pour comprendre des pratiques sociales de l'écrit juridique; dans l'autre, d'identifier des familles pour saisir des pratiques familiales d'utilisation de la justice. Chaque recherche est donc menée de façon totalement indépendante et s'articule dans un contexte historiographique qui lui est propre. Cependant, une approche méthodologique commune est rapidement venue bâtir des ponts entre ces projets. À une même méthode historique de base (constitution d'un corpus, mise en contexte et critique documentaire) s'ajoute un intérêt commun pour la norme juridique (institutions, juristes, etc.). Un questionnement similaire, portant sur les acteurs et les pratiques juridiques, nous rassemble finalement autour de la question de l'utilisation de la justice, dans une perspective d'anthropologie du droit.

Tableau 1 : Comparaisons des démarches de recherche

	K. FIANU	S. PERRIER
DÉMARCHES	à partir d'actes privés	à partir de familles
RÉSULTATS	⇒ normalisation • de l'official au tabellion royal	• de la famille en crise à la famille « normale »
	➔ la justice est utilisée pour intégrer des codes sociaux, normaliser des rapports	
	⇒ résolution de conflit • ententes (ex. : épuration de comptes, contrats d'apprentissages)	• accords (ex. : transactions entre une veuve et sa belle-famille)
	➔ la justice est utilisée pour apaiser à l'avance des relations potentiellement conflictuelles	
	⇒ protection • garantie de privilèges (ex. : vidimus)	• protection des veuves et orphelins (ex. : tutelle)
	➔ la justice est utilisée pour rappeler et conserver des prérogatives légales	
	⇒ rituel • affirmer la hiérarchie ou l'appartenance	• soutenir la puissance paternelle (ex. : émancipation)
	➔ la justice est utilisée pour son pouvoir symbolique	

La principale observation à laquelle nous sommes parvenues au terme de l'exercice confirme que l'utilisation de la justice répond, dans les deux cas étudiés, à des besoins sociaux. Ce qui peut sembler ici une évidence mérite cependant d'être rappelé, dans la mesure où l'historiographie s'est longtemps attaché à comprendre les institutions judiciaires plutôt que leur interaction avec la société dans laquelle elles s'insèrent. La volonté de placer l'acteur social au cœur de cette justice est un phénomène assez récent et tributaire de la démarche inter-disciplinaire : l'anthropologie juridique associée à la discipline historique a permis d'éclairer le rôle des individus et des communautés dans la mise en place et le fonctionnement des institutions judiciaires.

Notre expérience a également mis en valeur la continuité pluriséculaire des phénomènes étudiés, nous permettant ainsi de mieux évaluer nos résultats respectifs, de donner à nos observations des interprétations plus nuancées, d'aller au-delà du cadre temporel qui nous est propre. Elle a permis de déborder des pratiques historiographiques parfois trop étroites et surtout de faire éclater la frontière si insidieuse qui malheureusement persiste entre l'étude du Moyen Âge et celle des Temps modernes. Si l'interdisciplinarité favorise l'enrichissement des approches et du questionnement, l'intradisciplinarité est sans aucun doute pour l'historien le meilleur moyen de préciser la validité de ses hypothèses.

Nous sommes cependant conscientes des pièges que peut présenter une telle démarche : elle est par définition construite sur un terrain d'enquête commun et tend à faire valoir des similitudes, au détriment des spécificités temporelles. Par exemple, le recours à des catégories contemporaines (donc communes) pour expliquer le passé peut entraîner des anachronismes si l'on n'y prête pas attention. Un regard critique permanent est donc de rigueur, tout comme il l'est dans la démarche interdisciplinaire ou, en tout état de cause, dans la démarche historique elle-même.

Les avantages de l'approche intradisciplinaire l'emportent nettement sur ses inconvénients. Outre l'apport personnel incontestable, nous avons voulu ici faire partager aux étudiants et aux collègues une expérience qui, en dépit de sa rareté dans le milieu académique, peut offrir de précieuses avenues méthodologiques à la recherche future.

– 10 –

Revisiting Quantitative Methods in Immigration History
Immigrant Files in the Archives of the Russian Consulates in Canada

Vadim Kukushkin

In the last two decades, quantitative methods of analyzing historical sources seem to have lost much of their appeal in Canadian and American immigration historiography, reflecting a trend common to social historians in general. Historians on both sides of the border have largely abandoned analyzing international population movements from a macrohistorical perspective in favour of studying local immigrant neighbourhoods through the prism of ethnicity/race, class, and gender.[1] Influenced by the postmodernist critique of historical objectivity and the knowability of the past, academic scholars are becoming increasingly sceptical of seeing population statistics and other serial datasets as windows on past reality. It seems, however, too early to pronounce quantitative analysis dead for the purposes of immigration history. While the post-structuralist critique has raised our awareness of the problems and pitfalls behind the study of serial data, it can hardly be said to have rendered them hopelessly obsolete or redundant.[2] One does not need to be a hard-core quantifier to recognize the fact that as long as immigration history remains (as it should) interested in broader patterns of population mobility, it will not be able to do without resorting to statistical data generated by both donor and recipient societies.

Obviously, not all sources used by immigration historians can or should be analyzed using large computerized databases. Census forms, shipping manifests, or border entry records lend themselves to the use of quantitative methods more easily - one could say, "naturally" - than other types of records. Over the last three decades, Canadian historians have successfully probed many of these serial sources, though quantitative analysis has been practised primarily by students of

---

[1] For good, albeit now somewhat dated, overviews of the achievements of the "new social history" in the areas of Canadian immigration and ethnicity studies, see Franca Iacovetta, "Manly Militants, Cohesive Communities and Defiant Domestics: Writing about Immigrants in Canadian Historical Scholarship," *Labour / Le travail* 36 (1995): 217-52, and Anthony W. Rasporich, "Ethnicity in Canadian Historical Writing 1970-1990," in J.W. Berry and J.A. Laponce, eds.., *Ethnicity and Culture in Canada: The Research Landscape* (Toronto: University of Toronto Press, 1994), 153-78.

[2] A thoughtful discussion of the merits of statistical analysis can be found in Eric Sager, "Employment Contracts in Merchant Shipping: An Argument for Social Science History," in Franca Iacovetta and Wendy Mitchinson, eds., *On the Case: Explorations in Social History* (Toronto: University of Toronto Press, 1998), 49-64. See also Kris Inwood, "The Promise and Problems of Quantitative Evidence in Canadian History," *Histoire sociale / Social History* 27, no. 53 (1994): 139-46.

eighteenth and nineteenth century immigration.³ Eric Sager's recent work on the 1901 Canadian census and the excellent study of emigration from Canada to the United States by Bruno Ramirez, however, show us how statistical analysis can be made to work for historians of Canada's twentieth century.⁴ That historians of ethnic groups that came to Canada in more recent times have remained less interested in the use of quantifiable serial records is, of course, not wholly their fault: the battle for public access to the post-1901 federal census records - the most complete source of demographic and other data on twentieth century immigrants - is still not over. However, the choice of sources and methods by a historian is also a matter of his or her conceptual preferences. In this respect, the historiography of twentieth century immigration stands as a notable contrast to the work of those scholars who study earlier (primarily Anglo-Saxon and Irish) immigrant populations and who have been the primary compilers and users of serial data. For reasons too complex to discuss here, most of the recent work on twentieth century Canadian immigrants has been written within the matrix of *ethnic* (not *migration*) history, which aims primarily at reconstructing the lived experiences of its subjects (usually after the migratory move has been completed) and studying societal discourses surrounding ethnicity and race - things that are obviously difficult to measure in numerical terms.⁵ While the contribution of these studies to our understanding of immigrant *culture* is indisputable, they seldom pay much attention to what may be termed the *structure* or "anatomy" of migration - the geography and chronology of the migration process, the demographic, social and occupational profiles of the immigrants, and migration trajectories and chains. In these studies, chapters on the Old-World backgrounds of the immigrants often serve as mere prefaces to the Canadian part of the story.

The history of any immigrant group, however, must begin by answering the basic questions, first posed over sixty years ago by Marcus Hansen: who emigrated and why, what routes did the migrants take, and where did they settle in the new country?⁶ Contrary to what one may think based on the quantity of academic literature on immigration and ethnicity produced in the last several decades, we have made surprisingly few advances in producing detailed answers to these questions, especially as far as urban immigrants are concerned. While oral accounts, the ethnic press, memoirs and autobiographies can give us glimpses of

---

³ For a historiographical exploration of recent Canadian and American immigration scholarship using large datasets see Bruce S. Elliott, "The Genealogist and the Migration Historian," *Families* 39, no. 3 (2000): 131-45.
⁴ Eric Sager, "Immigrants, Ethnicity and Earnings in 1901: Revisiting Canada's Vertical Mosaic," *Canadian Historical Review* 83, no. 2 (2002): 196-229; Bruno Ramirez, *Crossing the 49th Parallel: Migration from Canada to the United States, 1900-1930* (Ithaca: Cornell University Press, 2001).
⁵ See, for instance, Franca Iacovetta, *Such Hardworking People: Italian Immigrants in Postwar Toronto* (Montreal and Kingston: McGill-Queen's University Press, 1992); Ruth A. Frager, *Sweatshop Strife: Class, Ethnicity and Gender in the Jewish Labour Movement of Toronto, 1900-1939* (Toronto: University of Toronto Press, 1992); John Zucchi, *Italians in Toronto: Development of a National Identity, 1875-1935* (Montreal and Kingston: McGill-Queen's University Press, 1988); and Lillian Petroff, *Sojourners and Settlers: The Macedonian Community in Toronto to 1940* (Toronto: Multicultural History Society of Ontario, 1995).
⁶ Marcus Hansen, *The Atlantic Migration, 1607-1860: A History of the Continuing Settlement of the United States* (Cambridge: Harvard University Press, 1940).

this information, they alone cannot reveal the broader patterns of a migration movement. For this we need to turn to serial sources, including those that have been available to historians for years but nonetheless attracted little interest. Among such largely neglected sources are the records of the three Russian imperial consulates that functioned in Canada between 1899 and 1922, known as the Likatcheff-Ragosin-Mathers Collection (also, for the sake of simplicity, dubbed Li-Ra-Ma Collection).

The collection is a treasure trove for any historian interested in the background, ethnic and social composition, and patterns of early twentieth century Canadian immigration from the easternmost reaches of Europe, although its use requires an advanced knowledge of Russian, including an ability to decipher peasant handwriting. The history of these papers goes back to 1899, when the Russian imperial government first established its consular missions in this country, largely in response to the growing number of Russian subjects living within its borders. In 1900, Nikolai Struve, a career diplomat, was posted to Montreal to serve as the first Russian consul (later consul general) in Canada and Halifax businessman Henry Mathers, was hired as honorary Russian consul in that city. After Struve's departure from Canada in 1912, the position of consul general was held for various periods of time by three other men, including Sergei Likatcheff (Likhachev), an energetic and efficient diplomat, who ran the office from 1914 until late 1920. The establishment of a Russian consular service in Canada was completed in 1915, when Konstantin Ragosin was appointed as consul in Vancouver. After the Bolshevik coup of 1917, the consuls refused to serve the Soviet government, as did most Russian diplomats stationed abroad, and the consular missions were forced to close in 1921-1922.[7] Their archives eventually found their way to the United States and were amalgamated with the papers of other former Russian consulates in North America, which were subsequently deposited at the U.S. National Archives in Washington. In 1983, the then Public Archives of Canada obtained a full microfilm copy (89 reels) of the Canadian part of the collection.[8]

During the two decades of their operation, the consulates served thousands of Russian immigrants, generating a mass of administrative documentation in the process. In their present state, the consular papers are divided into two main parts: the operational records of the consulates and the so-called Passport/Identity series. The first part includes the correspondence between the consuls and their superiors in the

---

[7] See Vadim Kukushkin, "Protectors and Watchdogs: Tsarist Consular Supervision of Russian-Subject Immigrants in Canada, 1900-1922," *Canadian Slavonic Papers* XLIV, nos. 3-4 (2002): 209-32.

[8] Library and Archives of Canada (hereafter LAC}, MG 30 E406, Likatcheff-Ragosin-Mathers Collection. For a more detailed description of this collection see E.W. Laine, "On Documenting the Russian Presence in Canada," in Tamara Jeletzky, ed., *Russian Canadians: Their Past and Present* (Ottawa: Borealis Press, 1983), xvii – xxiii. A short story of these documents after the fall of tsarism is related in Bruce Franklin Ashkenas, comp., *Records of Imperial Russian Consulates in Canada, 1898-1922* (Washington, DC: National Archives and Records Administration, 1992). See also Finding Aid No. 1411 (prepared by George Bolotenko) at LAC.

Russian Ministry of Foreign Affairs, as well as the Canadian government and private agencies, on various issues including Russian immigration to Canada. Of particular interest is the correspondence with hundreds of individual immigrants who sought assistance in their dealings with Canadian officials, laid complaints against employment agents and contractors, asked permission to enlist in the Canadian military forces, applied for Russian identification documents, or had other business with the consulates. In bringing to us the voices of these immigrants, many of them transient labourers who left few other traces in historical records, this correspondence has few equivalents in Canada.

Our focus here will be on the second part of the Li-Ra-Ma records - the Passport-Identity series, which comprises some 11,400 case files created by the consulate general in Montreal and the consulate in Vancouver for Russian-subject individuals who contacted these offices for various identity documents. So far this series has been used primarily by genealogists searching for Russian family roots. What follows below is a discussion of the provenance and content of these files and their utility as a statistical source on early twentieth century immigration from Russia to Canada. The last part of the paper presents, in a concise form, selected results of a case study of about 750 Russian-subject immigrants in early twentieth century Montreal based on the data obtained from the files.

The majority of the files that constitute the series are dated 1917-1918, although there are smaller subsets created as early as 1916 and as late as 1921-1922. Depending on the purpose of their creation, they fall into two main categories. The first contains applications for Russian entry permits, submitted to the two consulates at various times, but mostly in late 1917 and early 1918, by individuals desiring to return to the homeland.[9] With some exceptions, all of these files owe their origin to the new passport regulations adopted by the Russian government on 25 October 1916 and put into effect in July 1917. These regulations annulled all passports and other travel documents then in possession of Russian subjects abroad and replaced them with a uniform entry permit *(prokhodnoe svidetel'stvo)*, which was issued by Russian consular missions. To apply for a permit, one was required to provide detailed personal information on a special "interrogatory form" *(oprosnyi list)*, which could be obtained by mail or in person from the nearest consulate, attach two recent photographs of oneself and one's accompanying dependents, and any documentary proof of Russian citizenship the applicant possessed. Such proof might include an old passport, an internal pass (issued by local Russian authorities to peasants wishing to travel beyond their parish), a certificate of military standing, a copy of a baptismal or marriage record or postmarked family letters from Russia. The "interrogatory form" contained twenty-one questions: given names; surname; rank *(zvanie)*; occupation; place of registry and social estate *(soslovie)*; date and place of birth; marital status, the number of children (if any) and their names; military standing; year of summons to military service; current place of residence (and number of years there); names of parents and their places of residence; all places of residence during the last five years; religion; nationality; citizenship; citizenship of parents; changes of citizenship (if any); return destination in Russia; purpose of return and a list of documents proving

---

[9] There are a limited number of files that do not quite fit this classification, either because they have no documents except a piece of correspondence, or because they hold both an "interrogatory form" and an affidavit.

identity; relatives in Russia and their places of residence; and journeys outside of Russia during the last three years and their purpose, including dates of departure and return. After it was completed, signed and dated, one copy of the form along with the attached documents was forwarded to the Second Section of the Russian Ministry of Foreign Affairs for verification of the applicant's identity. With minor modifications, the form remained in use until April 1919, though shortly after the Bolshevik coup the sending of the files to Russia came to an end. Along with completed "interrogatory forms" and photographs, most files also contain correspondence between the applicant and consular officials. A large portion also holds originals of passports and other documents submitted by the applicants as proof of citizenship.

The second group of the Passport/Identity files consists of applications for certificates of Russian citizenship. During the First World War, which made Canadians even more aware of the presence of a large "foreigner" population in their midst, such certificates were sought by hundreds of Russian-subject immigrants, especially after the introduction of conscription, when many Russian labourers who could not prove that they were not British subjects were forced to register and enlist in the Canadian Expeditionary Force. Any individual claiming to be a Russian national and wishing to obtain a certificate was required to produce a Russian passport, which was stamped and signed by the consul. When no passport could be produced (as was usually the case), the seeker of a certificate had to swear an affidavit on a special form, supplied by the consulate and containing the following items: name; religion; native province, district, parish, and town/village; marital status, names and address of wife and children; names and addresses of closest relatives in Russia; military standing; criminal convictions in Russia and the nature of the offence; identity documents in possession; time, place, and mode of crossing the Russian border; direct or indirect entry into Canada and port of entry; criminal convictions in Canada and the offence; occupation in Canada; and real estate ownership in Canada.

The extensive character of both documents - the "interrogatory form" and the affidavit - demonstrates that during World War I the Russian state became increasingly concerned with maintaining a record of its emigrant subjects and their movements.[10] The creation of the files should therefore be seen in the context of expanding supervisory functions of the modern state - a process greatly accelerated by the First World War. Outdated and inconsistent Russian passport regulations that were - contrary to a common stereotype - easily circumvented by the emigrants and led to a large amount of illegal traffic across the empire's borders, were to be replaced by a better organized system of record-keeping designed to prevent individuals whose Russian citizenship was in doubt from entering Russia and reduce the possible damage to Russian interests that might occur from Canadian residents of "enemy origin" posing as Russians. The fall of the Russian monarchy in February 1917 did not stop this process, for the new Provisional Government claimed no radical break with the external policies of its predecessor and left the Foreign Service bureaucracy of the Tsarist state largely intact. Even after Petrograd and much of the country fell to the Bolsheviks, the doggedly anti-Communist consuls, faithful to the letter of the law and hoping for the eventual establishment of legitimate authority in

---

[10] General information on Russia's passport system can be found in Mervyn Matthews, *The Passport Society: Controlling Movement in Russia and the USSR* (Boulder: Westview, 1993).

the home country, continued to enforce the 1916 regulations, trying to filter out illegitimate claimants of Russian citizenship despite the fact that all reliable channels of verifying the applicants' identity were lost.

The provenance of the Li-Ra-Ma files puts them in the large and diverse class of personal case records created by government or private institutions that served, supervised, or controlled large groups of people. In recent years, Canadian historians have uncovered and analyzed many types of such files both as textual documents and (less commonly) as sources of quantifiable data.[11] While similar in many ways to other institution-generated records, the Li-Ra-Ma files also have characteristics that make them stand out. Although they owe their origin to the operation of particular government agencies, the bulk of the documents they contain were not "physically" created by officers of these agencies. Information that appears in these documents is by and large unmediated by the voice of an interrogator, translator, professional expert or a government official (illiterate persons, who dictated their answers to a friend or had their forms completed by a clerk at the nearest steamship or labour agency are something of an exception). To be sure, the reporting of personal data occurred within officially prescribed parameters, but the consuls had neither the time nor the administrative resources to intervene in the completion of the forms in order to ensure full uniformity of the provided information or greater compliance with the letter of the instructions. A textual analysis of the files shows that, as long as the essential data were supplied, the applicants were allowed much freedom in the way they phrased their answers and the amount of detail they cared to report. This led to significant variations in the level of assiduousness with which "interrogatory forms" and affidavits were filled out. As a result, files rich in personal detail are interspersed with those containing a bare minimum of demographic and personal data and having only limited historical value.

Dealing with the Li-Ra-Ma files as a source of statistical information on Russian-subject immigrants presents the researcher with several methodological issues. Because the files were compiled neither by a systematic count (unlike censuses) nor by scientific sampling (unlike modern-day sociological surveys), the question of their statistical representativity inevitably comes to the fore. Even a perfunctory analysis of the series shows that it should not be used as a cross-section of Canada's entire immigrant population of Russian extraction. As might be expected, I found only a handful of files belonging to immigrants who had been naturalized in Canada purposely severed all connections to the Old Country or simply lived in Canada too long to feel any affinity with the Russian state or need for its protection. Therefore, the representation of certain ethnic, religious, and social groups in the files is inversely related to the likelihood of their falling into one of the above categories of individuals. There are, for instance, few cases of religious dissenters such as the Doukhobors, Mennonites, and Baptists or those of German and Jewish immigrants who came to Canada before 1900. Farmers are another underrepresented class of immigrants. Obtaining a title to land required naturalization, which usually

---

[11] See Iacovetta and Mitchinson, *On the Case* for an excellent collection of recent work using case files. It should be noted, however, that their definition of case files as representing primarily "individuals and groups deemed in some way deviants or victims" (p. 3) is restrictive, for it misses a large and important category of such files (of which the Li-Ra-Ma records are an example), like those created as a result of individuals applying for government services.

brought permanent settlement in Canada and the cutting of ties to the state of origin. While the files have less to offer to the student of what historians refer to as "permanent immigration," they are a priceless source for the analysis of temporary labour migration from Tsarist Russia to Canada (and, contrary to the well-entrenched stereotype, it was immigrant workers rather than farmers or religious dissenters that dominated the flow of population between the two countries after the mid-1900s). The vast majority of these labour migrants were sojourners - "birds of passage" who came to Canada without an intention to stay. If they became naturalized in Canada at all, it was usually after five, eight, or even ten years of residence in the country, normally after the last hopes of returning home had faded away. During all this time, these immigrants not only remained Russian nationals and continued to maintain close ties with the home country, but also held on mentally to the world they had left behind.

The reliability of personal information contained in the files is another important question. Can we be sure that some immigrants did not have a reason to conceal or misreport biographical data or perhaps tell the consuls what they presumably wanted to hear? While such a possibility cannot be totally excluded, the reasons that compelled the immigrants to seek out the consuls were far too important and the cost of being denied an entry permit or a citizenship certificate too high to justify the risk of lying. Moreover, distorting personal data brought no real advantages, for the bulk of the applications were submitted after the fall of the Tsarist monarchy, when the consuls' primary concern in processing them became to filter out persons falsely claiming Russian citizenship, not monitor the immigrants' political orientations or punish individuals who had past troubles with the Russian law (such as military deserters or illegal emigrants). Moreover, shortly after the revolution of February 1917, Russian consular missions around the world received instructions from the Provisional Government to provide assistance to any former political émigrés wishing to return to the homeland.[12] On the whole, there seems to be no reason to doubt the veracity of personal information found in the Li-Ra-Ma files more than one would question the reliability of such data in the census or other serial records commonly used by immigration historians.

The files include persons of virtually every nationality represented in the migrant stream, but it is difficult to determine whether they accurately represent the ethnic composition of Canada's large population of Russian-born labourers. Even if one examines the entire Passport-Identity series in an attempt to identify the ethnicity of every one of its subjects, there are no reliable statistics of the ethnic makeup of early twentieth century immigration from Russia with which these findings could be compared. The random sampling of the series shows that Ukrainians, Belarusans,[13] Poles, Lithuanians, Finns, Germans, and Jews constitute the majority of individuals represented in it. There are also some nationality groups very little known to historians - such as Ossetians and Georgians from the Black Sea littoral, who began to emigrate to Canada as labourers around 1909, heading primarily to British Columbia. One also comes across a significant number of ethnic Russians from the

---

[12] Li-Ra-Ma Collection, vol. 25, files 849-850.

[13] In using the spelling "Belarusan" rather than one of the other commonly used versions of the term (Belarusian, Belorussian etc.) I follow Paul R. Magocsi, ed., *The Encyclopedia of Canada's Peoples* (Toronto: University of Toronto Press, 1999), 253-57.

Volga region (the provinces of Saratov and Samara), who followed in the footsteps of the local German emigrants. The files show that, contrary to the established stereotype, many Volga Germans went to Canada not as agricultural settlers but as labourers and remained Russian subjects long after arrival.

In my own research I have been interested primarily in persons of Ukrainian and Belarusan origin, who constitute approximately half the total number of cases (about 5,700) and have the highest degree of representativeness among all the ethnic groups. According to my estimate (tentative at best, given the aforementioned unreliability of Canadian immigration and census statistics), the Passport/Identity series may encompass as many as 15-20 per cent of all Ukrainians and Belarusans that came from the Russian Empire before 1914. This conclusion is justified by the fact that *mass* emigration of Ukrainians and Belarusans from the Russian Empire to Canada began relatively late (around 1910) and consisted almost exclusively of labour migrants.

What can the files tell us about Ukrainian and Belarusan immigrant workers in early twentieth century Canada and what are some of the pitfalls the researcher should be aware of? They clearly are a priceless source on major emigration areas within the Russian Empire, migration routes, locally specific migration chains, the social and occupational status of the immigrants in Russia and Canada, and their religious affiliations and demographic profiles. Since most of the migrants' individual characteristics (place of birth, age, marital status, family size, literacy, occupation, etc.) had little or no relationship to the motives which brought them to the consulates, there is no reason to expect a significant over- or under-representation of persons sharing one or another of these characteristics. Some exceptions do apply, however. The collection may be somewhat less useful for analyzing the territorial distribution of the migrants in Canada because of the possible over-representation of persons who lived closer to the consulate sites, but it can still be used to determine major transatlantic migration chains. One should also be careful in using the files to establish the chronology of Slavic immigration from Russia, because the very likelihood of a person's appearance in the files may be inversely related to the number of years he or she lived in Canada. The use of the files to estimate the gender composition of the immigrant stream requires controls for the type of document. Because the ratio of women as primary applicants for entry permits or citizenship certificates is negligible (less than one per cent of the total), one has to search for them inside the files. The "interrogatory forms," however, have to be discounted as a source of data on the presence of women or children among the immigrants, for there is no way of establishing whether family members reported on these forms resided in Canada or remained in Russia (with the exception of those few cases when the male head of the family voluntarily gave such information). The extent of family migration for various groups of Li-Ra-Ma subjects can be estimated only from the affidavits, which required immigrants to report the current whereabouts of their immediate families.

Research Methodology

The research project that I have been engaged in for the last three years has involved an extensive use of the Li-Ra-Ma files with the goal of reconstructing the picture of pre-1914 migration of Ukrainians and Belarusans from the Russian Empire to Canada. Library and Archives Canada (LAC) provided me with an unfinished electronic database, which included file numbers, personal names, and sex of all individuals represented in the Passport-Identity series and in some cases also their date and place of birth, marital status, and religion. This database provided a good starting point for my research and gave me an overall (if very sketchy) picture of the series' contents.[14] My goal was to create a random sample of the series and then search the selected files for all remaining quantifiable information. In making the decision about the size of the sample, I was guided by two considerations: it had to be large enough to have a sufficient degree of representativeness but also manageable by one individual within a reasonable time frame.[15] I opted for a fifty per cent sample of the entire series, which was then further reduced by excluding individuals coming from places irrelevant to my study. I used the migrants' territory of origin, rather than ethnicity, as the main selection criterion, limiting the sample to cases originating in Ukraine and Belarus and leaving out persons that came from elsewhere in the empire (even if they might be of Ukrainian or Belarusan origin).

The next step was to identify and eliminate cases belonging to various non-East Slavic nationalities that populated Ukraine and Belarus. While Jews and Germans were easy to identify, Poles, Russians, and Lithuanians presented a greater problem. The complex ethno-political structure of Russia's western provinces, with their overlapping ethnic and administrative boundaries and the presence of minorities interspersed with the ethnically dominant population, made the creation of an ethnically "pure" Ukrainian and Belarusan sample impossible.[16] Furthermore, largely because of the similarity of Slavic surnames, there was sometimes not enough information that would allow me to identify precisely the ethnicity of the subjects. Although applicants for entry permits were required to indicate their nationality on the "interrogatory forms," their answers proved to be of little help, for the modern-day concept of ethnic identity was unknown to peasants in early twentieth century eastern Ukraine and Belarus, who, as we shall see below, routinely described themselves as "Russians" (just as Ukrainians in Austria-Hungary usually identified themselves as Ruthenians or Austrians). In most cases, a combination of surname, place of origin, and religion provided the needed clue, but it still could not wholly eliminate the problem of distinguishing between various nationality groups. The solution I finally adopted was to keep all Ukrainian- and Belarusan-born persons of Slavic and Lithuanian[17] origin in the sample, which, in its final version, included 2,743 cases.

Once the final sample was created, it was checked for duplicate cases, transliteration inconsistencies, spelling errors, and other technical flaws. The English

---

[14] I would like to thank Myron Momryk, a Project Archivist with the Social and Cultural Archives Division of the LAC, for his assistance with this project.

[15] For a good discussion of random sampling in historical research, see Konrad H. Jarausch and Kenneth A. Hardy, *Quantitative Methods for Historians: A Guide to Research, Data, and Statistics* (Chapel Hill: University of North Carolina Press, 1991), 68-74.

[16] For an insightful discussion of such ethnic intermixture, see Czeslaw Milosz, "Vilnius, Lithuania: An Ethnic Agglomerate," in George de Vos and Lola Romanucci-Ross, eds., *Ethnic Identities: Cultural Continuities and Change* (Palo Alto: Mayfield Publishing Company, 1975), 339-52.

[17] In some areas of Vilna (Vilnius) Province, Belarusans had long lived next to Lithuanians and shared many common cultural traits.

spelling of place names in Russia presented the greatest difficulty because the database compilers at the LAC had mechanically transliterated into English the Cyrillic spellings that appeared in the files. Due to multiple errors contained in the original renderings of these names (hardly a surprise given the migrants' low literacy), this method often resulted in multiple versions of the same geographical name, sometimes distorted almost beyond recognition. I did my best to correct these errors, adopting uniform English spellings for the same place names. I also filled in the missing names of Russian provinces, districts, and counties by cross-checking them against each other when possible (e.g., in many cases the missing province of birth could be easily established by the name of the district, if the latter was available).

At the next stage, the 2,743 case files that constituted the final sample were thoroughly examined for all information relating to the individuals they represented. The retrieved data were coded and added to the initial set of variables contained in the LAC database. I used a total of twenty-eight variables, most of them repeating questions contained in the "interrogatory form" and the affidavit.[18] Due to omissions in the original files, the amount of data for different cases, too, displays considerable variations; in fact, there are not many cases that have information in all twenty-eight variables.

The main sample is supplemented by a separate and smaller database, which I labelled the "Passport File." It includes 671 cases (including some of those that also appear in the main sample) which contain either a Russian passport or an internal pass attached as proof of citizenship, or both of the above. From these documents I retrieved data on the migrants' occupation in Russia, pre-emigration literacy, and points of Russian border passage.

In the way of a disclaimer, it needs to be emphasized that all statistical data calculated on the basis of the Li-Ra-Ma files should be treated as approximate. Even though I do believe that my findings are representative of the socio-demographic and geographic parameters of early twentieth century eastern Slav migration from Russia to Canada, obviously no sample, especially derived from an archival source that itself constitutes a kind of "sample" of the general migrant population, can be viewed as a mirror image of the social group(s) it is intended to represent.

A Case Study: Immigration to Montreal

The space limitations placed on this article does not allow me to provide full results of my Li-Ra-Ma-based study of labour immigration from the Russian Empire to Canada. Therefore, I thought it pertinent to illustrate the research possibilities of the Li-Ra-Ma Collection by choosing a particular group of immigrants from the sample: persons who resided in Montreal at the time when their files were created. The decision to focus on Montreal had a two-fold rationale. First, Montreal was by far the main destination point for Ukrainian and Belarusan peasant-workers arriving from Russia, and second, I felt the need to do justice to a city that, despite its

---

[18] For the list of variables and a more detailed discussion of research issues related to the Li-Ra-Ma Collection, see Vadim Kukushkin, "Peasants on the Move: Early Twentieth-Century Labour Migration from Russia's Western Frontier to Canada" (PhD diss., Carleton University, 2004), Chapter 1.

fascinating multi-ethnic mosaic, has never been given the attention it deserves by immigration historians.[19]

The Montreal sub-sample contains information on 752 Russian-subject individuals of Ukrainian and Belarusan origin who reported the city as their place of residence at the time of contact with the Russian consulate. This data allow us to explore the composite socio-demographic profile of these migrants, their geographic origins, and patterns of settlement in the city. I have omitted some of the less important information obtained from the files, focussing instead on the basic social and demographic parameters of the migrant population. Again, due to space constraints, the interpretation of the statistical data is kept to a minimum, with only brief remarks offered regarding each particular set of statistics.

As Table 1.1 demonstrates, more than three quarters of the migrants were natives of Ukraine and less than one quarter came from Belarus. The proportion of Ukrainians to Belarusans observed in the Montreal sub-sample was typical for Canada's entire population of Russian-born immigrants of eastern Slav origin. The preponderance of Ukrainians is due mostly to the fact that while Ukrainian peasants in Russia, like their neighbours in Austria-Hungary, migrated primarily to Canada, for Belarusans, who mainly headed south of the 49th parallel, Canada was a secondary destination.[20] The migrants came from the total of eleven Russian imperial provinces (seven in Ukraine and four in Belarus), primarily those west of the Dnieper River, which marked the geographic watershed between westward (trans-Atlantic) and eastward (Siberian) migration. Again, typical of the entire sample, the province of Podolia (Podillia) in the southwestern corner of Ukraine supplied by far the largest migrant cohort: every third Russian-born Slavic immigrant in early twentieth century Canada was likely a native of that province.

Figure 1.1 demonstrates that immigration of Ukrainians and Belarusans from Tsarist Russia reached its apex in the two years before the First World War; in fact, nearly half of the Montreal-bound Li-Ra-Ma migrants arrived in 1913. A comparison of the chronology of immigration by area of origin, however, reveals that Belarusans began to settle in Montreal earlier than Ukrainians. About twelve per cent of them already lived in the city by 1910, while among the Ukrainians the proportion of these

---

[19] The history of Montreal Italians is among the few significant exceptions. See Bruno Ramirez, *Le premiers Italiens de Montréal: l'origine de la Petite Italie du Québec* (Montréal: Boréal Express, 1984). A good, if too sketchy, historical survey of ethnic settlement in Montreal is Claire McNicoll, *Montréal, une société multiculturelle* (Paris: Belin, 1993). Two M.A. theses done over sixty years ago by McGill University sociologists Stephen Mamchur and Charles Bayley still remain the best source on Montreal Ukrainians. See Stephen W. Mamchur, "The Economic and Social Adjustment of Slavic Immigrants in Canada: With Special Reference to Ukrainians in Montreal" (Master's thesis, McGill University, 1934), and Charles M. Bayley, "The Social Structure of the Italian and Ukrainian Immigrant Communities in Montreal" (Master's thesis, McGill University, 1939).

[20] Virtually all published literature on Ukrainians in early twentieth century Canada deals with immigrants from the Austrian provinces of Galicia and Bukovyna (western Ukraine), ignoring the smaller community of Ukrainians from the Russian Empire. For general histories of Ukrainian-Canadian immigration to Canada see, Michael Marunchak, *Ukrainian Canadians* (Winnipeg: Ukrainian Free Academy of Sciences, 1970), and Jaroslav Petryshyn, *Peasants in the Promised Land: Canada and the Ukrainians, 1891-1914* (Toronto: Lorimer, 1985). For a short history of Belarusan immigration to Canada, see John Sadouski, *A History of the Byelorussians in Canada* (Belleville: Mika, 1981).

early comers was less than four per cent. Most left Russia illegally: persons who reported having government passports in their possession constitute less than a quarter of the entire Montreal sub-sample, the proportion being higher among immigrants from Ukraine.

One of the most important sets of data that can be extracted from the Li-Ra-Ma files is related to the social and demographic profiles of the immigrants. By subtracting an individual's year of birth from the year of his or her arrival in Canada, we can establish the age at which he or she immigrated. The results of this statistical operation are presented in Table 1.2, which breaks down the migrant population by five-year age cohort. The figures demonstrate that the Ukrainians had a considerably larger percentage of persons in each cohort 30 years of age and over. In other words, the average Ukrainian immigrant was slightly older than his Belarusan counterpart (the average age at arrival for the Ukrainians is 27.6 and for the Belarusans 25.4). The majority of immigrants from both regions were married men, usually with no more than one or two children (see Tables 1.3 and 1.4). The proportion of bachelors among the Belarusans was slightly higher and the average number of children lower than in the Ukrainian group - both facts doubtless related to the younger age of the Belarusan immigrants. Only twelve per cent of the persons in the Montreal sub-sample reported having families living with them; however, this exceeded by four per cent the proportion of men with families in the entire Li-Ra-Ma sample, highlighting the role of Montreal as the site of the oldest and most established "Russian colony" in Canada. Notably, most of the men were literate which we can establish from their ability to sign completed "interrogatory forms" and affidavits. In fact, my comparison of the Li-Ra-Ma data with 1897 Russian census statistics reveals that literates constituted a much larger (sometimes a double) proportion among the migrants than they did among the general population in the donor areas.[21] Some of the migrants seem to have mastered the basics of writing after they came to Canada, but it is possible that literates were also more likely to contact the consulates.

The church affiliations of the Li-Ra-Ma migrants by and large reflected the religious landscape of the territories of origin. Most of them belonged to the Russian Orthodox Church - the officially dominant religious denomination in Tsarist Russia. The higher percentage of Roman Catholics among the Belarusans than among the Ukrainians comes as no surprise. Catholics constituted up to a half of the Belarusan population in western Belarus (especially Vilna Province), which also had a substantial presence of Lithuanians, all adherents of the Roman Catholic Church.[22] Most of the Canada-bound Belarusan migration, however, occurred from territories with a predominance of Russian Orthodoxy (Grodno and Minsk provinces), which accounts for a relatively small proportion of Catholics among the Belarusans.

Particularly interesting for the immigration historian is the matter of ethnic self-identification. The analysis of data in line 14 of the "interrogatory form" ("Nationality") gives a picture of a virtually non-existent ethnic awareness of the eastern Slav respondents, about 90 per cent of whom put themselves down as Russians and only in rare cases as "Little Russians" (the official designation for Ukrainians in Tsarist Russia). Most of the Lithuanians and Poles, however, identified

---

[21] Kukushkin, "Peasants on the Move," 86-90.

[22] For more on the population structure of early-twentieth century Belarus, see Jan Zaprudnik, *Belarus: At a Crossroads of History* (Boulder: Westview Press, 1993).

themselves by their proper ethnic names, which points to a higher degree of ethnic awareness among these groups. Ukrainian and Belarusan peasants in Russia had not yet been exposed to nationalist agitation, which would lead them to question the official concept of a single Russian nation consisting of Great Russians, Little Russians, and White Russians. In this regard, "Russian" Ukrainians represented a marked contrast to their brethren from the Austrian provinces of Galicia and Bukovyna who were well on their way from "Ruthenians" to Ukrainians.[23]

Sifting through data on the migrants' places of residence within Montreal, one learns that after arriving in the city, Ukrainians and Belarusans gravitated to the same settlement areas, although not quite in the same proportions. Pointe St. Charles was the earliest enclave of Slavic and Eastern European settlement in Montreal. Here by the mid-1900s one could hear Ukrainian, Belarusan, Polish, Russian, and Lithuanian speech almost as often as French and English. Other major concentrations of Ukrainians and Belarusans emerged in the so-called St. Lawrence "immigrant corridor" (a downtown area east and west of St. Lawrence Boulevard, which also contained large numbers of Jews, Italians, and Chinese) and in the Hochelaga-Frontenac district at the eastern end of the city. Table 1.7, which shows the distribution of the Li-Ra-Ma migrants across the three main neighbourhoods, demonstrates that Belarusans were considerably more likely to settle in the Hochelaga-Frontenac area compared to Ukrainians, who preferred the downtown district and Pointe St. Charles. A minor concentration of eastern Slav immigrants from Russia existed in Côte St. Paul.[24]

Finally, the files have something to say about the occupational structure of the migrant population. Of 501 Montreal residents for whom occupational data is available, 417 (83.2 per cent) put themselves in the broad category of *chernorabochii,* translated from Russian as "one who performs black (i.e., unskilled or rough) labour." Carpenters, ironworkers, and mechanics constituted the majority among those who held jobs requiring some skill. The skilled worker category also included tailors, shoemakers, car drivers, bakers, cooks, firemen, machinists, and an electrician. There were also two musicians, one photographer, four small entrepreneurs (including a grocer and a restaurant owner), and a student. Interestingly, the proportion of workers who reported their jobs as other than "general labourers" was almost twice as high among Belarusans (26.6 per cent) as Ukrainians (13.5 per cent). The difference in occupational patterns between the two groups is probably due at least in part to the earlier beginnings of Belarusan immigration to the city. The analysis of the Li-Ra-Ma data also revealed a correlation between the year of arrival in Canada and the nature of employment held by the immigrant in 1917-18 - the time when most of the files were created. Among persons who came to the country before 1911, the proportion of "general labourers" was only 66.7 per cent

---

[23] On national identity and Russification see Theodore Weeks, *Nation and State in Late Imperial Russia: Nationalism and Russification on the Western Frontier, 1863-1914* (DeKalb: Northern Illinois University Press, 1996), and Paul Robert Magocsi, *A History of Ukraine* (Toronto: University of Toronto Press, 1996), 355.

[24] The satellite town of Lachine, officially beyond the city limits, also had a large Slavic immigrant population consisting mainly of Ukrainians.

compared to 85.3 per cent among those who arrived in later years.[25] A higher degree of socio-cultural adaptation and familiarity with the Canadian labour market that came with being an "old-timer" were likely to increase one's chances of breaking out of the endless cycle of exhausting low-end jobs and finding more skilled employment, which brought a higher income and greater economic stability. In many cases, it also heralded the beginning of transition from sojourning to permanent settlement. Not surprisingly, the percentage of individuals with resident families was significantly higher among skilled workers and artisans than "general labourers" (19.1 per cent compared to 11 per cent).

Conclusion

This paper has provided only a glimpse of the vast and barely tapped set of personal immigrant files preserved in the records of the three Russian imperial consulates that operated in Canada between 1900 and 1922. While I have focussed on immigrants of eastern Slav origin, similar opportunities for research also exist for at least three other major ethnic groups represented in the collection: Jews, Poles, and Finns. What draws the historian to these documents is not only the richness of biographic facts reported in the "interrogatory forms" and affidavits, but also the fact that, unlike most other sources used in immigration history, they bring together information from both ends of the migration chain. This unique combination allows the researcher to trace an individual or a group through their entire migration cycle - from their home villages to, say, a boarding-house in Montreal or miner's shack in Timmins. With due attention to the specific provenance of the collection - as resulting from voluntary contact between some Russian-subject immigrants and Russian consular posts - historians can continue using it to explore multiple aspects of early twentieth century immigration from Tsarist Russia that are difficult or impossible to analyze on the basis of other sources.

---

[25] This finding contrasts with the calculations of Eric Sager, who found no definitive correlation between the number of years spent by immigrants in Canada and their earnings (unless one assumes that more skilled jobs do not equate with higher wages). See Sager, "Immigrants, Ethnicity and Earnings in 1901," 217.

Table 1.1. Geographic Origins of Russian-Born Ukrainian and Belarusan Immigrants in Montreal
(*N* = 752)

Province of Origin	Per cent
Ukraine	
Bessarabia (Khotin District)	16.6
Chernigov	0.8
Kharkov	0.3
Kiev	11.7
Podolia	34.7
Poltava	0.1
Volhynia	14.1
Belarus	
Grodno	10.8
Minsk	6.3
Mogilev	0.7
Vilna	4.0
Total	100

Table 1.2 Age of the Immigrants at the Time of Arrival, by Origin (%) (*N* = 491)

Age cohorts	Belarus	Ukraine
Under 20	21.8	19.2
20 – 24	26.7	29.0
25 – 29	31.7	17.4
30 – 34	9.9	12.6
35 – 39	5.0	8.7
40 and over	5.0	13.1
Total	100	100

Table 1.3 Marital Status of the Immigrants (%) by Origin (N = 466)

Marital Status	Belarus	Ukraine
Married	55.3	61.4
Single	44.7	37.2
Total	100	100

Table 1.4 Number of Children in the Immigrant Families (%) by Origin (N = 369)

Number of children	Belarus	Ukraine
1	39.7	31.0
2	31.7	31.7
3	14.3	19.3
4	12.7	10.5
5 or over	1.6	7.4
Total	100	100

Table 1.5 Literacy of the Immigrants by Origin (%) (N = 724)

Literacy	Belarus	Ukraine
Literate	76.6	58.0
Illiterate	23.4	42.0
Total	100	100

Table 1.6 Religious Affiliations of the Immigrants by Origin ($N = 724$)

Religion	Belarus	Ukraine
Russian Orthodox	76.1	92.3
Roman Catholic	21.9	7.0
Other	2.0	0.7
Total	100	100

Table 1.7 Major Areas of Ukrainian and Belarusan Settlement in Montreal, ca. 1920 ($N = 471$)

Areas of settlement	Origins	
	Belarus	Ukraine
Centre	51.0	66.2
Hochelaga-Frontenac	26.0	14.4
Pointe St. Charles	14.4	16.1
Other	8.6	3.3

Fig1.1. Ukrainian and Belarusan Immigration to Montreal, 1903-1918

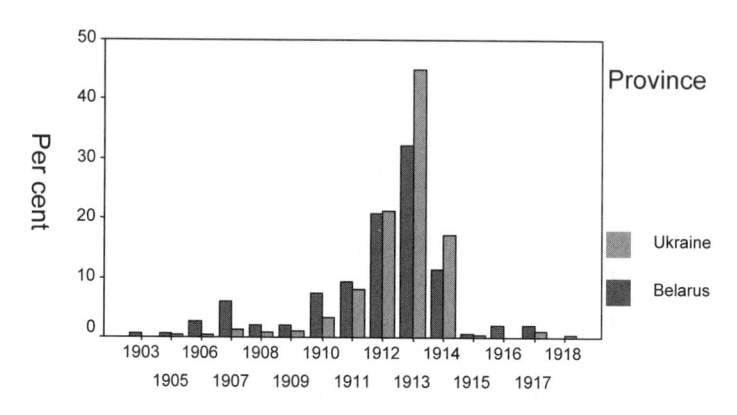

Year of Arrival in Canada

Source: Li-Ra-Ma Sample

– 11 –
Réflexions sur la question identitaire d'après les recensements informatisés
L'exemple des « Suisses » en Ontario (1871-1881)

Samy Khalid

En 1871, François Challet est fermier près du lac Huron, en Ontario. À l'occasion du recensement cette année-là, il explique qu'il est Suisse de naissance, mais Français de nationalité. Au même moment, à Toronto, l'apprenti Charles Sutter déclare au recenseur qu'il est né en Suisse et de nationalité suisse.

Dix ans plus tard, en 1881, François Challet confirme qu'il est né en Suisse, mais, cette fois, se décrit comme étant Suisse de nationalité. Quant à Charles Sutter, le recenseur le retrouve à Edmonton, où il se définit comme Allemand et affirme qu'il est né en Ontario.

Ces personnages n'ont rien d'extraordinaire à première vue, si ce n'est qu'ils font partie des rares immigrants recensés au Canada à la fin du XIXe siècle qui ont un lien direct avec la Suisse. En effet, sur une population totale de près de 3,7 millions, le gouvernement du Canada dénombre à peine 2 963 Suisses en 1871[1]. C'est donc dire que le pays compte environ un Suisse pour 1 250 habitants (0,0008 p.cent). Cette proportion augmentera légèrement au recensement suivant, pour s'établir à près de 0,001 p. cent selon les données de 1881 (un Suisse pour 923 habitants).

Des statistiques comme celles-là sont légion dans les livres d'histoire et les documents gouvernementaux, aux mains de spécialistes persuadés de leur utilité pour comprendre la composition de la société. L'intérêt de ces statistiques et des recensements est sans doute appréciable, mais leur manipulation est délicate et il faut s'y prêter avec prudence, si ce n'est circonspection, afin d'éviter les généralisations trompeuses. Les recensements, comme nous le verrons, ne sont pas le symbole de « vérité absolue » que l'on a pu croire. Ils représentent des constructions parfois abstraites qui donnent lieu à de nombreuses possibilités d'interprétations[2].

---

[1] Statistique Canada, « Population et composantes de la croissance démographique », http://www.statcan.ca/francais/Pgdb/demo03_f.htm. Notons que le Canada de 1871 n'englobe que le Québec, l'Ontario, la Nouvelle-Écosse et le Nouveau-Brunswick.

[2] Voir entre autres David Kertzer et Dominique Arel, *Census and Identity,* Cambridge, Cambridge University Press, 2002; Bruce Curtis, *The Politics of Population,* Toronto, University of Toronto Press, 2001; Chad Gaffield, « Linearity, Nonlinearity, and the Competing Constructions of Social Hierarchy in Early Twentieth-Century Canada », *Historical Methods*, vol. 33, n° 4, automne 2000, p. 255-260; Michael Wayne, « The Black Population of Canada West », *Histoire sociale / Social History*, vol. XXVIII, n° 56, novembre 1995, p. 465-485; Jean-Pierre Beaud et Jean-Guy Prévost, « Immigration, Eugenics and Statistics: Measuring Racial Origins in Canada (1921-1941) », *Canadian Ethnic Studies*, vol. XXVIII, n° 2, 1996, p. 1-24. Cette liste est loin d'être exhaustive, mais présente quelques

La présente recherche s'inscrit dans le cadre d'un effort visant à « bâtir de nouveaux ponts » en histoire, et notamment à explorer l'utilisation et le potentiel de sources récemment réorganisées dans des bases de données en ligne. Dans cet article, grâce à une étude de cas sur les recensements canadiens de 1871 et de 1881, nous évaluerons ainsi la façon dont certains ressortissants définis comme étant « Suisses » ont été recensés en Ontario au cours de la décennie. Nous tenterons notamment de faire ressortir certaines lacunes dont les statisticiens, et par ricochet les historiens, ne se sont pas méfiés pour établir leurs tableaux généraux de population et expliquer les tendances de l'immigration.

L'exercice en question se veut d'abord méthodologique. Vu les progrès sans précédent réalisés dans les dernières années au niveau de l'accès informatisé aux recensements, il nous a semblé intéressant de mettre à l'essai les fonctionnalités de ces bases de données. Pour ce faire, nous avons sélectionné un groupe de personnes habitant en Ontario et qui, au recensement de 1871, ont déclaré la Suisse comme lieu de naissance. Nous avons ensuite cherché à faire un jumelage manuel de ce groupe grâce au recensement de 1881 en vue d'en étudier l'évolution, et ce, non seulement du point de vue quantitatif, mais surtout identitaire. Une telle tentative de jumelage sert ici à évoquer une façon qui nous a semblé intéressante de souligner la richesse des bases de données pour mieux comprendre la question de l'identité chez une population qui, justement, est difficile à définir.

L'identité suisse

L'identité suisse est extrêmement complexe. En effet, malgré ses dimensions réduites, la Suisse est un pays composé de groupes linguistiques, religieux, socioculturels et politiques fort différents. Le pays, qui est bordé par quatre grands voisins (la France à l'ouest, les principautés allemandes au nord, l'empire d'Autriche à l'est et l'Italie au sud), compte quatre groupes linguistiques inégaux : les Romands (francophones) dans le quart ouest, les Suisses italiens vers le sud, les Suisses romanches, très minoritaires, dans certaines enclaves du sud-est, et les Suisses allemands ailleurs sur la majorité du territoire, notamment au centre, au nord et à l'est.

En plus de ces caractéristiques identitaires liées à la langue et à la géographie (la Suisse se trouvant entre des puissances parfois menaçantes, mais aussi blottie dans les montagnes), la configuration religieuse apporte une complication supplémentaire. La Suisse est divisée presque à moitié entre catholiques et protestants, mais en fonction de noyaux dispersés et irréguliers. Ainsi, certaines régions francophones sont protestantes depuis la Réforme, tandis que d'autres sont restées catholiques, et ce, parfois au sein d'un même canton ou d'une même zone culturelle.

Au fond, donc, la Suisse est depuis longtemps un pays multiculturel, multiethnique et multilingue. Comme le Canada, la Suisse s'est constituée au cours des siècles par la rencontre de peuples aux identités très variées. Pour cette

---

contributions marquantes à la recherche sur l'utilisation des recensements canadiens dans les dernières années.

raison, les migrants issus du territoire suisse sont extrêmement intéressants à étudier, peut-être surtout dans le contexte de l'histoire canadienne.

Les Suisses au Canada

En dépit de ces constatations, l'étude de l'immigration suisse au Canada a toujours été négligée par les historiens[3]. Au premier coup d'œil, l'apport des Suisses à notre pays peut effectivement passer inaperçu. Pourtant, leur impact est loin d'avoir été banal.

Malgré sa faiblesse endémique en termes absolus, la présence suisse au Canada est très ancienne, remontant aux origines même de la colonisation. Les annales relatent déjà la présence d'un petit contingent de soldats helvétiques en Acadie en 1604, avant même la fondation de la Nouvelle-France. Jusqu'au début du XIXe siècle, les habilités et la discipline des militaires suisses sont par ailleurs très recherchées, en entraînant certains, tels Frederick Haldimand et George Prevost, vers les plus hauts sommets de l'administration civile et militaire du Canada.

Au lendemain de la Révolution américaine, plusieurs vagues de mennonites déferlent sur le Haut-Canada. Plus tard, l'immigration directement depuis la Suisse augmente et s'organise. L'expédition de Lord Selkirk vers la rivière Rouge (Manitoba) en 1821[4], l'ouverture du « Huron Tract » à l'ouest de Guelph entre 1828 et 1856, la fondation de Zurich (Ontario) en 1856[5], attestent l'intérêt manifesté à la fois par les autorités canadiennes et par les migrants eux-mêmes de renforcer la présence suisse à l'ouest du Québec. Après la Confédération et l'adoption de la première loi fédérale sur l'immigration, le gouvernement du Canada confirme d'ailleurs son affinité pour les colons de l'Europe occidentale. Cette volonté politique donne lieu à la nomination en 1872 d'un agent fédéral d'immigration responsable de la Suisse, et par la suite à la publication de nombreux tracts pour promouvoir l'émigration française, belge et suisse vers le Canada[6]. En fait, la proximité linguistique et religieuse des Helvètes plaît aux autorités canadiennes parce qu'elle facilite leur intégration dans l'un ou l'autre des deux groupes majoritaires au Canada.

Les ressortissants suisses dont il est question dans la présente étude font en majorité partie de ces groupes de contestataires religieux, de grands aventuriers, mais aussi de victimes des disettes et de la pauvreté sur le Vieux Continent qui, au moment « de la révolution industrielle [...ont] conduit une masse d'environ

---

[3] Il n'existe qu'une poignée d'articles sur la question et deux livres, celui de Joan Magee, *The Swiss in Ontario* (1991), et celui de E. H. Bovay, *Le Canada et les Suisses* (1976). Les détails historiques de cette section proviennent de ce dernier ouvrage ainsi que de l'*Encyclopédie canadienne* (2000).

[4] Après la guerre de 1812, Lord Selkirk avait recruté quelques soldats du régiment suisse de Meuron pour peupler sa colonie de la rivière rouge. En 1821, d'anciens officiers font venir à leur tour des colons directement de Suisse.

[5] Zurich, dans le comté de Huron, a été fondée par un immigrant suisse, Frederick Knell.

[6] Mentionnons entre autres Stanislas Drapeau, *Canada : le guide du colon français, belge, suisse, etc.* (1887?) et Auguste Bodard, *En route pour le Canada : description du pays, ses avantages, la terre promise du cultivateur, les colonies françaises, belges et suisses* (1891?).

400 000 Suisses sur les routes d'Europe et du Nouveau Monde, de 1850 au déclenchement de la Première Guerre mondiale[7] ».

Mais alors comment évaluer le nombre de « Suisses » au Canada vers la fin du XIXe siècle? Et surtout, comment se définissait un « Suisse »?

Statistiques officielles

Selon le recensement de 1871, le Canada compte 2 963 ressortissants suisses, dont 950 en Ontario[8]. Ces statistiques officielles sont assez limitatives et somme toute inexpressives, comme nous le verrons plus loin, mais servent ici de point de repère utile.

De nos jours, les historiens ont la chance d'avoir à leur portée toute une panoplie de nouvelles technologies qui facilitent leur travail de recherche. Les organisations vouées à la généalogie, telles que la Société de généalogie de l'Ontario, Ontario GenWeb[9] et Census Online[10], sont des chefs de file dans le domaine de la transcription et de la diffusion des recensements et d'autres documents produits par les institutions politiques ou religieuses. Parallèlement, tout un réseau d'universitaires utilisent les recensements et les bases de données créées par les sociétés généalogiques pour étudier la composition de la société canadienne[11]. Les Archives nationales du Canada, elles, ont mis en ligne il y a quelques années l'index nominatif du recensement canadien de 1871 pour l'Ontario[12] et, plus récemment, la totalité du recensement canadien de 1901 sous forme d'images auxquelles renvoie un index géographique. Pour sa part, l'Église de Jésus-Christ des saints des derniers jours a informatisé les recensements américain de 1880, canadien de 1881 et britannique de 1881, qu'elle vend sur CD-ROM depuis mars 2002 et qu'elle a ouvert sur son site Web à la fin octobre 2002[13].

---

[7] Fabien Dunand, *Le modèle suisse*, Paris, Payot, 1991, p. 104.
[8] Statistique Canada, « Population et composantes », op. cit.
[9] Les bénévoles d'Ontario GenWeb (www.rootsweb.com/~ongenpro/census) procèdent depuis 1997 à la transcription des recensements disponibles pour l'Ontario (plus de 4 000 au total). À la fin juillet 2004, 172 recensements apparaissent en ligne, soit seulement une infime partie.
[10] Le site de Census Online (www.census-online.com/links/Canada/ON/All.html) répertorie 349 recensements en ligne pour l'Ontario, tous situés dans d'autres sites, notamment celui d'Ontario GenWeb et des bureaux régionaux de la Société de généalogie de l'Ontario.
[11] Par exemple, l'Institut d'études canadiennes, à l'Université d'Ottawa, est l'hôte de l'Infrastructure de recherche sur le siècle du Canada, qui établit entre autres une série de bases de données renfermant les résultats des recensements de la fin du XIXe siècle au milieu du XXe siècle. Également, le Département de démographie de l'Université de Montréal a mis au point le Programme de recherches en démographie historique et, plus récemment, une Infrastructure de recherche en démographie historique, qui vise l'intégration des données démographiques historiques longitudinales et transversales au niveau provincial et national.
[12] Archives nationales du Canada, *Index du Recensement du Canada pour l'Ontario (1871)*, www.archives.ca/02/02010803_f.html.
[13] Site Web des Mormons : www.familysearch.org. Dans la version Internet, il n'est possible de faire une recherche que par nom, prénom ou nom du chef de ménage.

En travaillant directement avec l'Index ontarien du recensement canadien de 1871 et le recensement canadien de 1881 sur CD-ROM, nous avons d'abord vérifié l'exactitude des données officielles du bureau de la statistique (voir tableau 1).

Tableau 1 : Nombre de « Suisses » recensés en Ontario en 1871 et en 1881 selon l'origine déclarée et le lieu de naissance

Année	Recensés d'origine suisse	Recensés nés en Suisse	Recensés d'origine suisse et nés en Suisse
1871	245 (chefs de ménage)	200 (chefs de ménage)	141 (chefs de ménage)
1881	2 315	644	487

Sources : Index ontarien du recensement canadien de 1871 et Recensement canadien de 1881 sur CD-ROM.

Pour 1871, précisons tout d'abord que la différence entre le nombre de Suisses notés dans les statistiques ($n = 950$) et celui de l'index ontarien ($n = 245$) tient à la façon dont l'information est présentée dans la base de données. En effet, celle-ci répertorie au premier titre le nom des chefs de famille qui résidaient en Ontario en avril 1871. Même si ce recensement a permis à l'État d'obtenir des données sur une variété de sujets, l'index informatisé ne donne un aperçu que d'une partie de la population (les chefs de ménage), et ce, sans précision sur leur état matrimonial, le nombre de cohabitants ni même leur lieu de résidence précis (outre le sous-district). Pour en savoir davantage, il est nécessaire de consulter les microfilms du recensement original.

Cet index, par ailleurs, est difficile à consulter parce qu'il n'autorise que six formes d'interrogation. Là encore, il faut la plupart du temps avoir une idée précise de ce que l'on cherche. Les clés de recherche sont le nom de famille, le prénom, l'occupation (c'est-à-dire la profession), l'origine ethnique (en fait la « nationalité » selon la terminologie employée dans le recensement), d'autres mots clés et enfin le district. Malgré la possibilité d'utiliser des caractères de substitution (le point d'interrogation pour remplacer une lettre ou le signe $ pour toutes les terminaisons possibles d'un nom ou d'un mot), le problème des variantes orthographiques reste entier. Par exemple, un nom comme Dufaut, dont les variantes orthographiques sont nombreuses en français (Dufault, Dufeau, Dufau, Dufaux, Dufaud, Duffaut, etc.), a très bien pu être épelé Defoe, Dafoe, Dussault au mieux des connaissances du recenseur ou du transcripteur ou selon leur bon vouloir.

Pourquoi cette difficulté de consultation? Pourquoi ces lacunes? Il faut rappeler que l'Index du recensement du Canada pour l'Ontario en 1871 a été conçu d'abord et avant tout comme un outil généalogique. Il s'agit au départ d'un projet de la Société de généalogie de l'Ontario, qui voulait aider les généalogistes à chercher certains patronymes en particulier. C'est pourquoi des centaines de bénévoles ont épluché les manuscrits du recensement et relevé uniquement les renseignements essentiels sur le chef de ménage, porteur du nom, ainsi que, dans de plus rares occasions, les noms des autres personnes (« strays » ou personnes égarées) dont le patronyme diffère de celui du chef de famille mais qui vivent sous le même toit; on peut penser par exemple à une belle-mère ou à un domestique. L'unité de base pour ce recensement n'était pas la famille, mais plutôt le ménage : ainsi, toutes les personnes qui habitaient à une même adresse étaient regroupées en un bloc.

En fait, donc, l'index ontarien de 1871 recense 304 chefs de ménage d'origine suisse ou nés en Suisse (voir graphique ci-dessous). Ce nombre est établi à partir des données du tableau 1, qui rappelle que 141 des 245 chefs de ménage s'étant déclarés d'origine suisse sont aussi natifs de ce pays; en procédant par élimination, il est facile d'en déduire que 104 personnes d'origine suisse ont dit être nées à l'étranger, tandis que 59 étrangers ont déclaré être nés en Suisse.

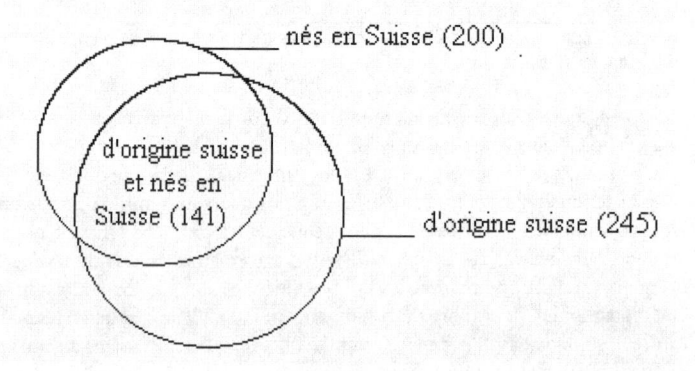

nés en Suisse (200)

d'origine suisse et nés en Suisse (141)

d'origine suisse (245)

En ce qui concerne le recensement de 1881, le même exercice permet de déceler la présence de 2 472 personnes d'origine suisse ou nées en Suisse (voir graphique ci-dessous). Ce résultat est étonnant, lui aussi, mais seulement parce qu'il révèle un plus grand nombre de « Suisses » que ce qui avait été annoncé par les statisticiens (2 382). On remarque ici qu'à peine 487 des 2 315 personnes ayant déclaré une origine suisse sont aussi nées en Suisse (21 %), ce qui peut laisser supposer un accroissement de la population grâce à des naissances récentes au sein des familles qui se considèrent suisses. Une nouvelle soustraction atteste que 1 828 personnes d'origine suisse seraient nées à l'étranger, tandis que 157 étrangers seraient nés en Suisse.

d'origine suisse (2 315)

d'origine suisse et nés en Suisse (487)

nés en Suisse (644)

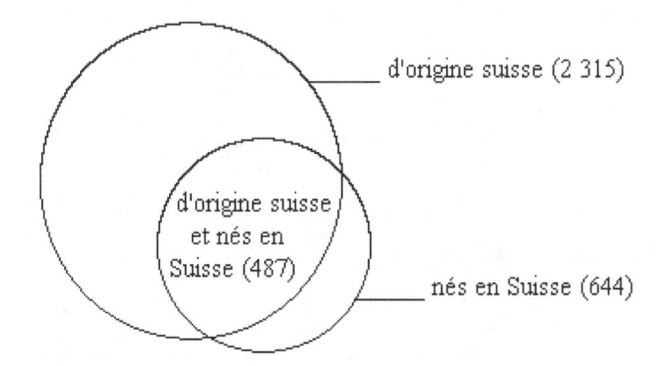

Méthodologie et résultats préliminaires (1871)

Pour les fins de cette recherche, il nous a paru bon de limiter notre corpus à une fraction clairement définie de ce groupe des « Suisses » en Ontario, ce que nous avons fait en ne retenant que les 200 chefs de ménage nés en Suisse (voir annexe), donc a priori immigrants de première génération.

Pour en arriver aux résultats de cette première recherche, rappelons que nous avons entré le terme « Switzerland » dans le champ des mots clés. Cette interrogation a donné 193 résultats. Les sept noms manquants (car nous en comptons 200 en tout) sont ceux de personnes dont le lieu de naissance a été indiqué par les recenseurs comme « swiss », « switerland », « switzd », etc.[14] La liste complète de ces orthographes divergentes figure au tableau 2.

---

[14] Il faut préciser que nous avons pu repérer ces mots clés mal orthographiés ou abrégés grâce à un autre instrument de recherche construit à partir du même index ontarien de 1871. L'outil « Searchable Database of Heads & Strays » (http://130.15.161.15/census/index.html) produit vraisemblablement par l'Université Queen's en 1994, est le même index que celui des Archives nationales, mais reconstruit dans une autre base de données qui présente deux grands avantages : il est possible d'y chercher d'après le lieu de naissance, et la fonction « Word Wheel » présente dans une liste facile et complète tous les termes relevés dans le recensement de 1871 pour chaque champ. On peut y voir, grâce à un clic de la souris, l'ensemble des noms de famille répertoriés (y compris les noms incomplets ou estropiés) ainsi que toutes les professions relevées dans le recensement (avec leurs multiples synonymes).

Tableau 2 : Descripteurs de lieu de naissance faisant référence à la Suisse dans les recensements

Mot clé utilisé	1871	1881
helvetic / helvetian	0	1
schwiss	0	2
suisse	0	1
swis	0	2
swiss	1	656
swit	1	1
switerland	2	0
switrld	0	1
switz	1	0
switzd	1	0
switzerd	1	0
switzerland	192	644
swizerland	1	0
autres orthographes erronées (swisse, switzerl, swz...)	0	0
lieux précis en Suisse (schweiz, bern, geneva, neuchatel, vaud...)	0	0
TOTAL	200*	644**

*Il s'agit de chefs de ménage uniquement en 1871.
**Le total est faussé par le fait que plusieurs des termes (notamment « swiss » et « switzerland ») se retrouvent à la fois dans les champs « origine » et « lieu de naissance ». Toutefois, la plupart des cas problématiques ont été épluchés par les éditeurs du recensement de 1881 et nous croyons donc pouvoir nous fier au nombre de 644 indiqué par le logiciel.

    Par la suite, l'extraction des noms recueillis dans un logiciel adéquat a nécessité un long travail de formatage, d'autant plus ardu qu'il a fallu vérifier manuellement chacune des 200 fiches pour y ajouter les données complémentaires sur l'origine déclarée, la religion, « l'occupation » (c'est-à-dire la profession) et toute autre note pertinente. Ces détails, en effet, n'apparaissent pas dans la page des résultats de recherche, mais doivent être obtenus en cliquant sur une icône à côté de chaque nom.
    Le tableau ainsi construit présente l'avantage de permettre le tri automatique des données (voir annexe).

Extraction des données pour 1871

Divers regroupements et recoupements sont possibles en réorganisant les dix colonnes correspondant aux dix types de données disponibles : nom et prénom, sexe, âge, lieu de naissance, district, sous-district, origine (« nationalité »), religion, occupation et notes diverses. Or, ces informations ne sont pas toutes utiles, surtout prises hors contexte. Qui plus est, elles sont très difficiles à mettre en rapport d'une année à l'autre. En effet, en 1871, les nombres portent sur les chefs de ménage et les « strays ». On se souviendra aussi qu'automatiquement à cette époque en Ontario, quand le père de famille se déclarait Suisse, tous ses enfants l'étaient également, peu importe l'origine de la mère[15].

Extraction des données pour 1881

En ce qui a trait au recensement de 1881, les données sont plus complètes, car c'est toute la population qui est comptée (et non seulement les chefs de famille). La version grand public offerte à partir du site Web des mormons depuis la fin 2002 est somme toute limitée. Il n'est possible d'y faire une recherche que par nom, prénom ou chef de ménage. Par contre, l'Église des saints des derniers jours a aussi produit une série de CD-ROM contenant une version informatisée un peu plus maniable du recensement canadien de 1881. En plus, pour les universitaires, les données complètes du recensement ont été mises en valeur par les collaborateurs du North Atlantic Population Project (dont font partie l'Université de Montréal et l'Institut d'études canadiennes à l'Université d'Ottawa) et on y a accès sur un serveur protégé depuis la fin décembre 2003[16].

Avant l'apparition de ces bases de données, les chercheurs devaient effectuer leurs travaux en passant en revue des bobines et des bobines de microfilms, et ils obtenaient des résultats plus ou moins satisfaisants. Maintenant, avec quelques touches du clavier, ils peuvent effectuer une recherche dans des millions de dossiers avec beaucoup plus de facilité. Comme pour l'index ontarien, ce sont des bénévoles qui ont transcrit pendant de nombreuses années les données du recensement à partir de microfilms ou de photocopies des formulaires originaux. Une fois ces données compilées, une équipe de généalogistes mormons, en partenariat avec l'Institut d'études canadiennes, a procédé à leur épuration. Grâce à cet outil, il est facile d'utiliser n'importe quelle clé de recherche pour trouver l'information souhaitée. Bien sûr, c'est en supposant que les détails voulus ne figuraient pas sur les pages manquantes ou illisibles du recensement.

L'annexe présente un exemple de notre tableau comparatif. Dans ce tableau, nous avons repris les données de 1871 auxquelles se sont ajoutées les données de 1881 lorsqu'il a été possible de faire un jumelage réussi. Cette première expérience, limitée ici à un groupe d'une cinquantaine de « Suisses » de

---

[15] Bruce Curtis, *The Politics of Population*, Toronto, University of Toronto Press, 2001, ch. 8. Au Québec, par contre, les enfants étaient forcément canadien-français si un parent l'était, peu importe que ce soit la mère ou le père.

[16] North Atlantic Population Project, « Beta release of coded Canadian 1881 census data », http://www.nappdata.org.

moins de 35 ans, nous a permis de retrouver environ 70 p. cent des personnes sélectionnées et de suivre leur trajet.

Sur les 49 Ontariens nés en Suisse et âgés de moins de 35 ans en 1871, nous avons pu en retrouver 32 hors de tout doute en 1881. La méthode de jumelage retenue a été basée sur le nom et les prénoms des individus en premier lieu, mais également sur toutes les autres variables[17]. Cet exercice s'est révélé beaucoup plus ardu que prévu en raison des énormes variations orthographiques dans les noms à consonance étrangère. Pour s'en convaincre, il n'y a qu'à penser au patronyme von Känel, qui a été épelé von Kumel en 1871 et von Kenel en 1881. Également, divers problèmes au niveau de l'âge et de l'origine ont complexifié la recherche. Dans le premier cas, prenons seulement l'exemple de Solomon Meier(s) qui, en 1881, a le même âge qu'en 1871 (34 ans) alors que son fils aîné en a 20. Dans le second cas, mentionnons Anthony Smith[18], d'origine allemande alors qu'il était qualifié d'Irlandais dix ans plus tôt, sans doute du fait que sa femme est Irlandaise.

Tableau 3 : Variation des données (1871-1881)

	Nombre absolu	%
Personnes retrouvées (avec ou sans variante orthographique)	32/49	65,3
Même orthographe	11/32	34,4
Variante orthographique mineure	23/32	71,9
Même date de naissance (à 1 an près)	14/32	43,7
Même lieu de naissance	20/32	62,5
Lieu de naissance devenu « Ontario »	7/32	21,9
Même district	23/32	71,9

---

[17] Contrairement à l'expérience de Raymond Roy, Christian Pouyez et François Martin au Saguenay (« Le jumelage des données nominatives dans les recensements : problèmes et méthodes », *Histoire sociale / Social History*, vol. XIII, n° 25, mai 1980, p. 173-193), ce ne sont pas les cas d'homonymie qui ont posé des difficultés, mais plutôt les mutations orthographiques majeures et, surtout, les variations au niveau des variables secondaires telles que l'origine déclarée, la religion et la profession (problème dont Roy, Pouyez et Martin n'ont pas eu à se soucier pour la population relativement homogène qu'ils ont choisie). Malheureusement, compte tenu des limites de l'index ontarien de 1871, il a été impossible de jumeler par couples. Nous nous exposons ainsi au risque non pas tellement de faire de faux jumelages (car les noms ne sont pas très communs), mais de sous-estimer le groupe des « Suisses ».

[18] Son nom est écrit Myne en 1871.

	Nombre absolu	%
Même origine	20/32	62,5
Origine devenue « German »	9/32	28,1
Même religion	18/32	56,2
Même profession	22/32	68,7

Somme toute, même si l'échantillon retenu n'est pas entièrement représentatif du groupe des « Suisses » en Ontario, certaines tendances se dégagent. Ainsi, en voyant que l'âge coïncide d'un recensement à l'autre dans 44 p. cent des cas (à un an près), nous aurions envie de postuler que près de la moitié des personnes ont reçu une forme d'éducation leur permettant de lire leurs papiers d'identité ou les rendant sensibles aux questions de l'âge et du passage du temps[19].

La question du lieu de naissance est à lier ici à l'origine ethnique et c'est elle qui renseigne le plus sur la rétention de l'identité suisse. Quelque 63 p. cent des moins de 35 ans nés en Suisse d'après le recensement de 1871 déclarent encore la Suisse comme lieu de naissance en 1881; le même pourcentage s'applique d'ailleurs à l'origine déclarée. Il faut donc y voir le fait qu'un peu moins du tiers des recensés conservent leur identité dix ans plus tard. Une nuance doit toutefois être apportée aux statistiques sur l'origine : neuf personnes (28 p. cent) sont devenues « allemandes », ce qui n'enlève peut-être rien à leurs origines suisses, mais confirme le flou entourant la définition de la question d'origine ethnique à la fin du XIXe siècle. Parmi les autres dont le lieu de naissance n'est plus la Suisse, 22 p. cent (surtout les plus jeunes) affirment être nés en Ontario, ce qui ne peut traduire qu'une volonté d'intégration à la société canadienne.

Ce qu'il faut retenir, par contre, c'est que le potentiel de ces deux bases de données est immense. Grâce à elles, nous sommes en mesure de faire relativement aisément sur une grande échelle ce que peu d'historiens ont eu les moyens de faire auparavant, c'est-à-dire de jumeler les données tirées de deux recensements différents. Cette perspective est particulièrement enthousiasmante pour ceux qui souhaitent étudier la façon dont l'identité est enregistrée et évolue dans le temps.

Challet et Sutter, prise 2

À présent, revenons-en aux deux « Suisses » du début, que nous avons cités en exemple pour tenter de donner un visage plus humain à ces statistiques.

Le premier personnage s'appelait François Challet. En 1871, il a 68 ans, est chef de ménage et habite dans le district de Huron Sud, où il pratique

---

[19] Grâce à la compilation d'une série de données complexes, Emmanuel Todd, dans *L'invention de l'Europe* (Paris, Seuil, 1990), classe la Suisse parmi les pays marqués par la Réforme dans lesquels le taux d'alphabétisation des hommes de 20 à 30 ans dépasse les 50 % avant l'an 1700. Selon lui, le franchissement de cette étape marque « l'entrée d'une société locale dans l'ère d'une culture écrite majoritaire « qui définit » une condition nécessaire de la modernité idéologique » (p. 142-144).

l'agriculture. Quand le recenseur vient l'interroger le 2 avril 1871, il indique la Suisse comme lieu de naissance, se déclare Français de nationalité et de religion protestante. Le recenseur note son nom « Francis » Challet, mais le fait qu'il se dise « Français » laisse entendre qu'il vient sans aucun doute de la Suisse romande[20].

Le second personnage se nommait Charles Sutter. En 1871, il n'a que 15 ans. C'est donc sans doute un « stray » plutôt qu'un chef de famille. Il vient d'Europe lui aussi, et est installé depuis peu en Ontario, à Toronto. Son emploi : apprenti. Quand le recenseur vient l'interroger au début avril 1871, il indique la Suisse comme lieu de naissance et se déclare Suisse de nationalité. Le code que le recenseur a utilisé pour noter sa religion n'est pas clair, mais il y a fort à parier que « LN » signifie « luthérien ». C'est sans doute un Charles ou un Karl Sut(t)er. Les Suter et Sutter sont des familles nombreuses en Suisse allemande.

À eux deux, ces hommes renvoient l'image classique de la Suisse. L'un est Romand, c'est-à-dire Suisse d'héritage français. L'autre est Suisse allemand. L'un est jeune, l'autre est plus âgé. L'un œuvre dans le domaine de l'agriculture, l'autre est citadin. Or, c'est à peu près tout ce qu'il est possible de savoir à leur sujet en se fondant sur les données de l'index ontarien de 1871.

En 1881, les recenseurs retrouvent François Challet dans la même région qu'auparavant. Il a 78 ans et est toujours fermier, mais le chef de ménage est maintenant son fils, Auguste, qui est marié avec une femme d'origine « française » née en Ontario, et qui a deux jeunes enfants. On apprend que François Challet, le grand-père, habite aussi avec son épouse, Antonine. Tous deux déclarent au recenseur qu'il sont nés en Suisse et se considèrent Suisses de nationalité. Seule variation notable par rapport au recensement de 1871, les membres de la maisonnée ne sont plus protestants, mais « Reformed Presbyterian » (variante nord-américaine de la doctrine presbytérienne écossaise).

Quant à Charles Sutter, en 1881 il a 25 ans, soit précisément dix ans de plus qu'au recensement précédent. Le recenseur le retrouve très loin d'où il était auparavant : à Edmonton (dans les Territoires du Nord-Ouest). Sa profession n'est pas indiquée, mais il habite seul avec un jeune Écossais de son âge qui est commerçant ou commis (« storekeeper »). Cette fois, il affirme qu'il est né en Ontario, qu'il est de nationalité allemande et qu'il est presbytérien, ce qui représente un net départ par rapport au recensement précédent.

Comme toutes les autres personnes recensées et peut-être encore plus les Suisses, ces deux citoyens tout à fait réels n'ont rien de typique. Parmi le groupe natif de Suisse que nous avons repéré dans l'index de 1871, quatre à peine viennent de Suisse romande, comme François Challet. La majorité vient de Suisse allemande. La majorité, aussi, pratique la religion protestante sous une forme ou une autre. Il y a bien quelques catholiques, mais aussi des anglicans, des méthodistes, etc., ainsi que des mennonites, que l'on retrouve concentrés dans une ou deux régions. Enfin, toutes ces personnes supposément nées en Suisse interprètent différemment la question de la nationalité ou de l'origine : beaucoup

---

[20] Selon le *Répertoire des noms de familles suisses* (Zurich, Schulthess, 1989), les Challet sont originaires de Genève, de Pleujouse ou de Cottens. Ces lieux se trouvent dans trois cantons de Suisse romande, respectivement ceux de Genève, du Jura et de Vaud.

se disent Suisses, mais certains sont Hollandais, Anglais ou Irlandais, Français, Allemands, même Suédois. Et cette origine déclarée peut varier d'un recensement à l'autre. Challet était Français, il devient Suisse dix ans plus tard. Sutter, lui, était Suisse, puis il devient Allemand. C'est comme s'il voulait se distancer de ses origines et s'intégrer à la société canadienne en se disant né en Ontario, ou s'il voulait s'intégrer à un quelconque groupe allemand ou germanophone en s'identifiant comme Allemand plutôt que Suisse.

Quoi qu'il en soit, ce qui est certain, c'est que jamais avant le présent exercice Challet ni Sutter n'ont été comptés comme Suisses dans les deux recensements à la fois. Est-il permis de parler de sous-dénombrement des Suisses? Cette constatation permet en tout cas de mettre le doigt sur un phénomène encore plus intéressant : celui du flou qui entoure la question de l'identité dans le cas des Canadiens d'origine étrangère à la fin du XIXe siècle.

Comme nous l'avons vu, les Suisses en général sont difficiles à distinguer. En fait, ils s'intègrent très rapidement dans la société d'accueil (ils deviennent Français ou Anglais, puis Canadiens français et Canadiens anglais) ou, parfois, ils sont pris pour des Allemands, des Français ou des Italiens en raison de leur langue ou de leur dialecte. La complexité de leur situation rend évidemment difficile la tâche d'étudier les populations qui composent le groupe des « Suisses », mais elle permet aussi de mettre en valeur à l'aide d'une stratégie de jumelage comme celle-ci diverses façons de manipuler les recensements informatisés pour en faire ressortir la richesse.

Conclusion

Les statistiques évoquent la présence de 3 000 à 4 500 Suisses au Canada dans les quinze ans suivant la Confédération. Selon nous, ces chiffres sont modestes, et cela tient à la façon d'une part dont les questions de recensement ont été conçues et d'autre part à la perception identitaire des recensés eux-mêmes.

À partir d'une expérience pratique comme celle décrite ci-dessus, nous avons voulu voir comment les prétendus Suisses se sont classés dans les deux recensements consécutifs de 1871 et de 1881. Cette réflexion nous a semblé utile pour cerner le groupe cible et commencer à comprendre les mécanismes d'intégration des immigrants à la société canadienne. Elle pourrait servir, nous l'espérons, de modèle à appliquer pour l'étude de tous les groupes amalgamés au Canada, car il faut bien se rendre compte que l'identité des groupes culturels a toujours été difficile à déterminer.

Il sera intéressant par la suite de dresser des liens avec le débat sur « l'origine » dans les recensements ultérieurs. Qu'est-ce qui définissait l'ethnie : le lieu de naissance, la religion, la langue? Par-dessus tout, comment les recensés comprenaient-ils les questions de recensement, et selon quels critères les recenseurs classaient-ils les données obtenues? Toutes ces questions permettront, à n'en point douter, de faire progresser les connaissances sur cette mystérieuse identité suisse, mais aussi sur la construction du Canada et les relations entre ses groupes sociaux.

Comme le rappelle Peter Baskerville, « [c]ensuses are constructions of the national population created by individuals and groups within the state. Censuses are surveys, reporting the voices of large numbers of people, speaking on behalf of their families or households to census enumerators, answering questions framed by census officers within the Canadian Department of Agriculture. The results should be understood as a dialogue, a long series of questions and answers in which class, race, gender, language, and other influences guide the conversations[21] ». Il reste au chercheur à comprendre ce dialogue.

---

[21] Peter Baskerville, « The Canadian Families Project », dans Patricia Kelly Hall et al. (dir.), *Handbook of International Historical Microdata for Population Research*, Minneapolis, Minnesota Population Center, 2000, p. 32.

Index ontarien du recensement canadien de 1871

Personnes nées en Suisse, par lieu d'origine déclaré (échantillon)

	NOM, PRÉNOM	SEXE	ÂGE	LIEU DE NAISSANCE	DISTRICT	SOUS-DISTRICT	ORIGINE	RELIGION	OCCUPATION	NOTES
137	MOSSER, CHRISTIAN	M	70	Switzerland	Waterloo South	Preston Village	-	GR	Cabinetmaker	Religion: (code inconnu) † avant le 2-4-1871
69	CHALLET, FRANCIS	M	68	Switzerland	Huron South	Stanley	French	Protestant	Farmer	
158	MYRES, ULRICK	M	42	Switzerland	York North	Georgina	Dutch	Anglican	Labourer	
181	STREET, JACOB	M	24	Switzerland	Hastings East	Thurlow	Swiss	Anglican	Labourer	
	SUTTER, CHARLES	M	15	Swiss	Toronto West	St. John's Ward	Swiss	LN	Apprentice	Religion: (code inconnu)

Recensement du Canada pour 1881 (Ontario)

Personnes nées en Suisse, de 0 à 35 ans (échantillon)
(les personnes mentionnées en 1871 qui ont été retrouvées en 1881 figurent en lettres italiques)

	NOM 1871	NOM 1881	DDN 1871	DDN 1881	LDN 1871	LDN 1881	DISTRICT 1871	DISTRICT 1881	ORIGINE 1871	ORIGINE 1881	RELIGION 1871	RELIGION 1881	OCCUP. 1871	OCCUP. 1881	NOTES
1	*SUTTER, CHARLES*	✓	1856	✓	Swiss	ON	Toronto W., St. John's Ward	NWT, Edmonton	Swiss		LN	Presbyterian	Apprentice	-	Habite avec Jhn Brown, storekeeper
2	MARNEW, MARIA		1851			CH		Hamilton, St. George's Ward		Swiss		Anglican		Servant	
4	*GUENTHER, JOHN*	GUENTHER, GUNTER	1850 1849	1841	CH	CH	Waterloo, Preston Village	Waterloo S., Renfrew S.	Swiss	German German	?	Catholic Lutheran	Watchmaker	Carpenter le bon?? Farmer	
5	MEYER, BALDAWIN		1850			CH		Waterloo S., Wilmot	-		Roman Catholic		-		
12	*STREET, JACOB*	✓	1847	1845	CH	✓	Hastings E., Thurlow		Swiss	✓	Anglican	Methodist	Labourer	✓	Marié, 3 enf. de +

157

– 12 –
The Politics of Sources and Definitions

Cristina Bradatan

Theory of Demographic Transition
Demographic transition is a well-known theory in demography, and it is still considered one that is "alive" (Hirschman, 1994). The ideas of a changing demographic pattern as societies modernize appeared sometime at the beginning of the nineteenth century. Among the first who gave a shape to this theory were Notenstein (1953) and Davis (1963). They observed that fertility and mortality decreased in most of the industrialized world and noted the relationships between these demographic phenomena and some other components of social life, such as modernization and economic development. The classical form of demographic transition states that industrialization and urbanization created the new ideal of the small family. An increasing level of women's education, a lower pressure for traditional behaviour, and a growing cost of rearing children were among the main factors which permitted the emergence of this new ideal of family. Another version of demographic transition theory - Davis' theory of change and response (Davis, 1963) - explains the change in fertility as an effect of population pressure that resulted from a decrease in mortality. The population can respond to this pressure through migration, by decreasing fertility, or by using both of these methods.

Demographic transition theory, with its various versions, initially created a lot of excitement among researchers, and for a number of years there were few voices criticizing it. That was a time when little empirical data was available so it was almost impossible to falsify it. However, during the 1960s, more data became available, and contradictory results appeared. Leasure, for example, found out that the decline of fertility in Spain was not a simple result of increasing levels of urbanization and education and changes in occupational structure (Coale, 1986: xx). Other researchers showed that countries at various economic levels shared a similar pattern of declining marital fertility: "They [Iskandar and Knodel] found a somewhat puzzling pattern in which the timing of the decline in marital fertility in England and in Hungary was only slightly different, despite the very different levels of education, mortality and stage of industrialization in the two countries. Another puzzling parallel in marital fertility occurred in Norway and Rumania" (Ibid).

In 1963, the Princeton Population Office, together with other research units from Western Europe, began to put together and analyze data regarding the fertility transition in Europe. The conclusions of this project showed that the decline in fertility cannot be related to economic development in a straightforward manner because the interaction level between people from different regions plays an important role. Regions that shared a common language tended to behave similarly with respect to fertility decline, and their behaviour was different from those who did not share the same languages (Watkins, 1991: 7). Some other factors, such as the economic circumstances and the moral milieus of the household, also had an influence on the pace of the fertility decline (Lesthaeghe and Wilson, 1986: 272).

The period prior to the Princeton Fertility Project was, probably, the highest point attained by the demographic transition theory. Then, the fall began: several researchers began to criticize the theory from various points of view. Some adjustments to, or replacements of, demographic transition theory appeared, and some of them were quite successful. Despite these critics, demographic transition theory is still a useful tool because it synthesizes well the demographic evolutions of the last hundreds of years. Hirschman (1994) argues that demographic transition theory needs to improve by getting more "flesh," that is, it has to be discussed more in particular contexts, taking into account the society's life in a certain period. Even if all regions did not evolve in a similar way, all modern societies decreased their fertility and mortality levels. Modernization may not have played the most important role. Maybe other factors are more important, but only studies done in particular cases can show which were relevant.

Eastern Europe from the Demographic Transition Perspective

There is a generally human, permanent need for grouping things together in order to understand them. It is a truism to say that this need manifests itself in the study of Eastern Europe, too. The 1990s political changes in the Communist Bloc ruled out the nicely packaged idea of a world divided into East and West, communist and capitalist, or centralized and free-market economies. There is no longer a clear-cut manner of grouping together the former communist countries; some of them are now rich and became part of the European Union, whereas others are still poor and hardly surviving the transition to a free-market system. So some other way of grouping these countries must be employed. This is one of the reasons why former "Eastern Europe" has been replaced by "Central Europe," "Balkan region," or "Southeastern Europe." The idea of Central Europe directly related to the former Habsburg Empire is relatively old, but was resurrected in the 1970s in an attempt to make people aware of the significant differences between Eastern Europe, on the one hand, and the USSR, on the other. The "Balkan" nations seemed to share only the fate of having been, for some 100 years, vassals of the Ottoman Empire, and renowned as a "barbarous" region especially during the Balkan War at the beginning of the twentieth century.

Although it is not always obvious which nations belong to which region, and many of the Balkan countries refuse to be considered Balkan, it is generally accepted that Albania, Yugoslavia, Bulgaria, Romania, and Greece belong to the Balkan region. Some studies have also included Hungary in the Balkans (Todorova, 1997), although in the case of Hungary there are good reasons to consider it as part of Central Europe. The inclusion of Greece in the same group with some former communist countries makes the discussion about the Balkans particularly interesting. Greece was never part of the Communist Bloc so its "likeness" to the other countries from the region could only be a result of having been part of the Ottoman Empire. On the other hand, it would be problematic to affirm that fifty years of completely different historical courses did not affect the alleged resemblance between Greece and the former communist countries from the Balkan Peninsula.

In the following, I will use Eastern Europe for countries that belonged during the Cold War to Warsaw Pact,[1] because this was the initial meaning of this term throughout much of the Cold War. Some statistics include the USSR, Yugoslavia, and Albania. In such cases, I was not able to distinguish between USSR and Eastern Europe, but I do note if both are included. Most of the statistics do not include Eastern Germany after reunification.

Generally speaking, Eastern Europe, and the Balkans in particular, are rather unstudied areas from the point of view of historical fertility changes. The focus of the Princeton Fertility Project was on Western Europe because fertility began to decline there. The statistics published by the Princeton Fertility Project on Eastern Europe are mainly results of computations using a model for a stable population (Coale, 1986: 170).

For Romania, for example, the Princeton Project used data for 1899, 1930, and 1956 and they were adjusted for under registration using the West model of stable population with life expectancy at birth equal to forty-five. (Ibid: 173) Definitions of the regions are missing from the conclusions of the Princeton Fertility Project, and this is very important because regions often changed their boundaries in this part of the world. Dobrogea, for example, a South Eastern region in Romania, had a different configuration before and after 1918 as a result of incorporating Cadrilater, a former part of Bulgaria inhabited mainly by Bulgarians and those of Turkish origin.

Graph 1.1 GDP* per capita, Eastern Europe** versus Western Europe

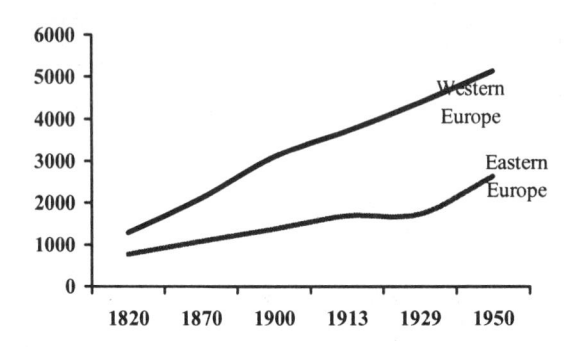

Source: Angus Madison, *Monitoring the World Economy, 1820-1992* (Paris: OECD, 1995), 56.
* GDP levels are measured using a standardized currency (Geary-Khamis dollars) which permits comparisons between countries.
** Eastern Europe includes Russia

---

[1] The following states were part of Warsaw Pact: Bulgaria, Czechoslovakia, East Germany, Hungary, Poland and Romania.

Fertility evolved very differently in Eastern than Western Europe (for instance, the fertility decline began later, but the decline was shaper). Moreover, the relationships between fertility decline and other population phenomena are not easily understandable.[2] As such, the studies done in Western Europe cannot be simply used for the eastern part of Europe.

Historically, Eastern Europe was poorer than the Western part of the continent, and the difference in wealth between the two regions increased during the first part of the twentieth century (Graph 1.1).

During the nineteenth and the first part of the twentieth centuries, population increased at a higher rate in Eastern than in Western Europe, mainly because of a higher rate of fertility in Eastern European countries. Although at the beginning of the 1800s, there were fewer people living in Eastern Europe than in Western Europe, by 1870 Eastern Europe was more populated than Western Europe (Graph 1.2).

Graph 1.2 Population in Eastern and Western Europe, 1820-1950*

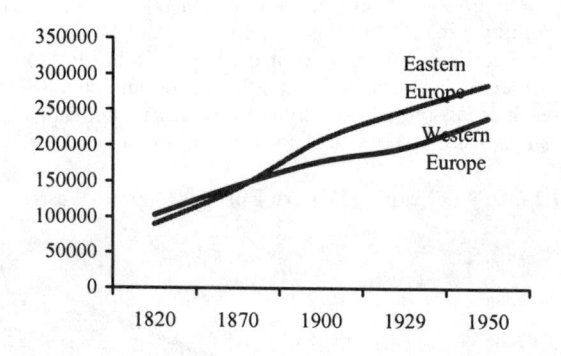

Source: Madison, *Monitoring the World Economy*, 56.
* Eastern Europe includes Russia

In comparison with Western Europe, Eastern Europe began to record a decrease in fertility relatively late, and several explanations were advanced for why this happened. One of them is related to poverty which resulted from lack of modernization; as Graph 1.1 shows, Western Europe was always richer than the eastern part of the continent. A second explanation refers to the different types of families in Eastern and Western Europe. Although demographers talk about the existence of a "European pattern of family," they always refer to Western Europe. Eastern Europeans seem to have historically a different type of family relationship, one similar to the Asian model.

Hajnal agues that the Western European pattern of household formation is a very particular case, completely different than that in all other

---

[2] For example, Șerbu (2000) showed the fertility decline in Romania was not a result of a decline in nuptiality, because nuptiality actually increased after 1900.

parts of the world. This pattern emerged earlier than the seventeenth century and it is characterized by late marriage for both sexes (over 26 for men and over 23 for women) and separate households for married couples (separate from the parents' household) (Hajnal, 1982: 452).Children from poor and landless families were sent, at a certain age, to be servants in another household; after they saved enough money they married and established households separate from their parents.

Eastern European populations are described as having a joint household system. Men and women married early (the mean age for men being around 26 and for women 21), started life in the household of an older couple and, after a while, a household with too many incorporated couples split into two or more households. This system of family helped fertility to remain at a high level, while the Western European system was an impediment to having many children. Hajnal uses data from the 1787 Hungarian census as proof of the existence of such a system (Table 1.1).

Table 1.1 Households in 1787

	Population (000s)	Persons per Household	Married Men per household
Hungary Proper	6,085	5.22	1.05
Transylvania	1,372	5.03	1.03
Croatia	617	8.33	1.7
61 "Free Royal Cities"	485	4.45	0.84

Source: John Hajnal, "Two Kinds of Preindustrial Household Formation Systems," *Population and Development Review* 8, no. 3 (1982): 469.

Although Hajnal's ideas are still very popular, other researchers presented different arguments. Sklar (1970) discusses some of the problems in establishing a "family pattern" for Eastern European countries. The geographic criterion is not a very good one for classifying and describing populations, especially in regions where the populations are very different with respect to history and culture. Eastern Europe, she says, does not seem to have been a coherent and homogeneous region from a demographic point of view. If we look only to the percentage of never-married women in various countries of Eastern Europe, it can be seen that heterogeneity rather than homogeneity characterizes the region. The percentage of never-married females is, for example, much higher in Poland than in other Eastern European populations (Table 1.2).

Age at marriage also varies between countries. As Table 1.3 shows, regions such as Estonia, Latvia, Lithuania and Poland had a high age at marriage for males as well as for females, and their pattern is more similar to Sweden and England than to Romania and Serbia, for example.

Table 1.2 Percentage of Never-Married Women in Selected Eastern European Countries

		Percentage Never Married	
Country	Year	20-29	40-49
Pre-war Poland	1900	36.3	7.8
Romania	1899	13.6	3
Bulgaria	1900	14	0.9
Bosnia	1910	11.3	1.6
Serbia	1900	9.4	0.7

Source: June Sklar, "The Role of Marriage Behavior in the Demographic Transition: The Case of Eastern Europe around 1900," *Population Studies* 28, no. 2 (1974): 234

Such data led Sklar to believe that the Eastern European countries did not have a single type of family system. At least two different types of families characterized this region. Balkan countries were characterized by the existence of *zadruga*, an "extended household of two or more nuclear families related by blood or adoption owning land, livestock, and tools in common, and sharing a common livelihood and residence" (Sklar, 1974: 235), while the other countries outside the Balkan peninsula had a more 'Western' type of family system.

Religion is considered an important factor in shaping households in Eastern European countries. Balkan countries are mostly Eastern Orthodox and Muslim, but Czechs and Poles are Catholic and Lutheran. For the Catholics, Sklar says, the church competes with kin authority because, by asking those who become priests and nuns to not marry, family and marriage are devalued. On the other hand, Islam and the Eastern Orthodox Church proved favourable to extended kinship because they do not have a separate or celibate clergy or a Church organization that can rival kinship (Sklar, 1974: 237). Czech, Baltic, and Polish regions were also characterized at the beginning of the century by high out-migration (about 130,000 between 1900 and 1914), which was much higher than Balkan countries' emigration (around 8,000). Sklar argues that this out-migration also has an important impact on the supply of mates for marriage. A rural woman who could not find a mate would go to work in the town, so she would often deliberately postpone marriage.

Botev (1990) focuses intensively on Sklar's arguments when he discusses characteristics of the family system and fertility evolution in Balkan countries during the twentieth century. He advanced another hypothesis for why fertility declined later in Eastern Europe (especially the Balkans) than in Western Europe. The most important feature of the fertility transition in the Balkan countries, he says, is a much faster decline in fertility than in Western Europe, despite the relatively low economic development of the Balkan countries.

Table 1.3 Age at Marriage for Regions of Eastern Europe

Later Becoming	Province or Country	Date	Age at marriage	
			Males	Females
Estonia, Latvia and Lithuania	Esland	1897	29.7	26.3
	Liftland	1897	30.2	26.6
	Kurland	1897	28.8	25.6
	Kovno	1897	29.7	25.4
Poland	Vistula	1897	25.8	23
	Vilna	1897	27.9	24.2
	Grodno	1897	26.3	22.8
	Volynia	1897	25.2	21.5
	West Prussia	1900	27.3	25.2
	Posen	1900	27	25.3
	Galicia	1900	26.9	23.3
Czechoslovakia	Bohemia	1900	27.9	25.4
	Moravia	1900	27.8	25.4
	Silesia	1900	27.7	25.2
	Slovakia	1891	24.6	21.3
Romania		1899	24.5	20.3
Bulgaria		1900	24.2	20.8
Bosnia		1910	25.5	20.5
Serbia		1900	23.0	20.1
Sweden		1900	29.5	27.5
England and Wales		1901	27.3	26.2
Finland		1900	27.9	25.6
Portugal		1900	27.4	24.9
Italy		1901	27.5	23.6

Source: Sklar, "The Role of Marriage Behavior in the Demographic Transition," 233.

The rhythm of fertility decline is somewhere between the pace of Western European countries and those of Asia. On the other hand, during the demographic transition, the Balkans had a high rate of population growth, much higher than in the rest of Europe (with the exception of Russia) - between 12-15 per 1,000, and sometimes over 20 per 1,000 (Botev, 1990: 121). Botev thinks that, after the liberation of Balkan countries from the Turks' domination, a lot of land began to become available to the native people (land which was previously owned by the Turks). This permitted them, for a while, to have many children without falling into poverty. However, land eventually grew scarce and in the absence of an out-migration tradition, people limited their births drastically. Although this explanation is interesting and very original, it is sustained only with data for Bulgaria, and it cannot be applied to other countries that did not have similar conditions (in Romania, for example, where Turks did not have land because it was only a vassal country).

On several points, Botev does not agree with Sklar's ideas. First, he is not convinced that *zadruga* was a frequently encountered type of family in the Balkans. He argues that *zadruga* was proven to exist only in a very limited territory of the former Yugoslavia and the western part of Bulgaria (Botev, 1990: 112) and, even there, nuclear families were not rare. Hammel shows that between 40 and 82 per cent of the families in different samples of the west Balkan population (regions where *zadruga* was considered to be predominant) were nuclear. Botev emphasizes that even if the people did not live in the same house, the proximity of the families made the familial relationships very strong. These strong kinship relations allowed people to marry young and have many children but did not require the existence of *zadruga*.

Sklar's arguments regarding religion (Muslim and Eastern Orthodox) as playing an important role in maintaining higher fertility levels in the Balkans in comparison with other European regions are also rejected by Botev. Using data on the average size of households in Bosnia-Herzegovina (Table 1.4), he shows it was larger for Catholics than for Muslims in all regions, thus suggesting that a higher percentage of Muslims in the Balkans cannot explain the higher fertility. However, he thinks that religion played an important role in the sharp decrease of fertility in the Balkans during the twentieth century. The Orthodox Church, Botev says, has a much more liberal ethical conception than the Roman Catholic Church by placing primary responsibility on the husband and wife for making conscientious decisions about birth control (Botev, 1990).

Table 1.4 Mean Household Size in the Provinces of Bosnia-Herzegovina, 1870

Province	Muslim	Orthodox	Catholic	Average
Banjaluka	10.6	14.8	12.1	13
Bihac	13.1	17.7	15.9	15.5
Herzegovina	10.5	12.5	12.1	11.1
Novi Pazar	10.2	15.3	-	12.3
Sarajevo	10.7	14.9	12.2	12.3
Travnik	11.5	16.6	14.5	13.9
Zvornik	4.7	13.1	13.9	8.9

Source: Nikolai Botev, "Nuptiality in the Course of the Demographic Transition: The Experience of the Balkan Countries," *Population Studies* 44, no. 1, (1990): 116.

In 1986, Jean Claude Chesnais published *The Demographic Transition* in which he tracked such change in sixty-seven countries from 1720-1984. He argues that in European countries there were several types of demographic transition. Romania, Bulgaria, and the former USSR are included in the same group, characterized by very high levels of pre-transitional growth, a rapid mortality decline, fairly high maximum levels of natural increase and a very short demographic transition of seventy years (Chesnas, 1986: 251).

Central Europe (including Czechoslovakia, Austria, Hungary, and Poland) experienced a plateau of growth which was: (1) later than in northern Europe; 2) centred around 1900; and 3) relatively brief (only ten to twenty years) (Ibid., 1992: 231). Chesnais' work is impressive because he provides an immense volume of data, but it is not always very clear what sources he uses. For example, he includes statistics about fertility in Romania during the Second World War, although during that time there were no demographic or economic statistics recorded in Romania.

Demographic Transition in Romanian Provinces

Data referring to the evolution of fertility in Romanian regions are mainly provided by the various censuses taken during the nineteenth and twentieth centuries. In Valachia and Moldavia, censuses were taken in 1860, 1899, 1912, and 1938. For Transylvania there are two censuses that are mostly used: 1910 and 1930. However, not all these censuses recorded the number of children in the household, and there are good reasons to believe the data is not very accurate (Chesnais, 1992).

Most of the studies argue that the fertility decline in Romania began after the First World War, and attained replacement level around 1950. The decline of fertility followed the decline of mortality that began around 1880. However, until around 1920, the decrease in the birth rate was less than ten per cent from the initial rate so, as also indicated in the Princeton Fertility Project, the fertility transition had not begun. Other authors (Ghetau, 1997) contend that the decline in fertility began around 1885, much earlier than is commonly believed.

The studies done on this area do not show how much heterogeneity existed in the Romanian territories. Romania, as all other countries from Eastern Europe, changed boundaries many times during 1850-1950. Actually, until 1859 there was no Romania, only separate regions where the majority of the population spoke Romanian: Wallachia, Moldavia, Transylvania, Besserabia and Bukovina. The first two regions were vassals of the Ottoman Empire; Transylvania, and Bukovina were Austro-Hungarian provinces; and Bessarabia was part of the Russian Empire. In 1859, Moldavia and Wallachia were unified and formed Romania (usually called the "Old Kingdom"). In 1918-1919, the other three regions joined the first two. A part of Bulgaria (Cadrilater) also became part of Romania. However, during the Second World War, Bukovina and Besserabia became parts of USSR; Besserabia remained part of USSR until 1990 when it became part of the Republic of Moldova.

Therefore, when one talks about fertility transition in Romania it is essential to be precise. Does this mean present-day Romanian territory? Romania at the beginning of the century? Some studies refer to nowadays Romania (Ghetau, 1997), while other authors use for each period whatever Romania meant at that time (Chesnais, 1992). Both methods have advantages and disadvantages. For the first method the most important disadvantage is the lack of appropriate data. The second method can give very biased results because the changes in territory added or took apart very heterogeneous populations. To give only one example, after 1918 four new territories were added to the "Old Kingdom" of Romania: Transylvania, Bukovina, Besserabia, and Cadrilater. The new territories added many minorities too, so that by 1930, nearly one-third of the population was Hungarian, German, and Jewish. Table 1.5 presents the composition of the Romanian population for "new" and "old" territories in 1930.

Table 1.5 Population by Ethnicity (Selected Ethnic Groups) in the New and Old Territories, 1930

	Region	Romanians	Hungarians	Germans	Bulgarians	Jewish
Old territories	Oltenia	97.5	0.2	0.2	*	0.2
	Muntenia	93.4	0.8	0.5	*	2.1
	Moldova	89.8	0.9	0.3	*	6.5
Mixed	Dobrogea	44.2	0.3	1.5	22.8	0.5
New territories	Besserabia	56.2	*	2.8	5.7	7.2
	Bucovina	44.5	1.4	8.9	*	10.8
	Transylvania	57.6	29.1	7.9	*	2.4

Source: *Romanian Yearbook*, 1935-1936: 38

The new territories had, in some cases, more than half of the population with a non-Romanian ethnicity. This is not a problem for studying changes in fertility if different ethnicities had a similar fertility behaviour. However, this was not the case for Romanian provinces. As Table 1.6 shows, the ethnic profile of a region shapes fertility behaviour. The average general fertility rate (the number of live births per 1,000 females between the ages of 15 and 44) for areas with a Romanian majority was, in 1932, 190.4 for old territories and 175.0 for new territories. The average for areas with a Hungarian majority was 142.8 and 112.7 for areas with a German majority.

Table 1.6 General Fertility Rate for Districts Where the Majority has a Certain Ethnicity, 1932

Districts where the majority are:	General Fertility Rate
Romanians	190.4
Germans	142.8
Hungarians	112.7
Ukrainians	132.4
Bulgarians	216.5
Turks	243.4

Source: D.C. Georgescu, *La fertilité différentielle en Roumanie* (Bucureşti: Institutul Central de Statistică, 1940), 16.

In conclusion, the Eastern European demographic transition had different characteristics for Balkan countries and Central European countries. Central European countries followed closely the Western European pattern of demographic transition (Chesnais, 1992: 231). However the Balkan countries began the transition later, and the decrease in fertility was sharper than in Western Europe. The demographic transition was also shorter in the Balkans than in Western Europe. As data for Romanian regions show, a deeper study of what happened in Eastern Europe has to take into account that various populations living in the same region have different demographic transition patterns, and that changes in regional boundaries that occurred several times during the nineteenth and the first part of the twentieth centuries strongly affect the viability of studies.

References

Botev, Nikolai. 1990. "Nuptiality in the Course of the Demographic Transition: The Experience of the Balkan Countries," *Population Studies* 44 no. 1, 107-26.

Bucur, M. 2002. *Eugenics and Moderniization in Interwar Romania*, Pittsburgh: University of Pittsburgh Press.

Carlson, Elwood, Meguni Omori. 1998. "Fertility Regulations in a Declining State Socialist Economy: Bulgaria, 1976-1995," *International Family Planning Perspectives* 24, no. 3, 184-87.

Chesnais, Jean Claude. 1992. *The Demographic Transition. Stages, Patterns, and Economic Implications. A Longitudinal Study of Sixty-Seven Countries Covering the Period 1720-1984.* Translated by Elisabeth and Philip Kreager. Oxford: Oxford University Press.

Coale, A.J. and S.C. Watkins, ed., 1986. *The Decline of Fertility in Europe. The Revised Proceedings of a Conference on the Princeton European Fertility Project.* Princeton: Princeton University Press.

Costa-Foru, Xenia. 1945. *Cercetarea monografica a familiei.* Bucuresti: Fundatia Regele Mihai I.

Davis, Kingsley. 1963. "The Theory of Change and Response in Modern Demographic History," *Population Index* 29, no. 4, 345-366.

Georgescu, D.C. 1940. *La fertilité différentielle en Roumanie.* Bucureşti: Institutul Central de Statistică.

Ghetau, V. 1997. *Evolutia fertilitatii in Romania. De la transversal la longitudinal.* Bucuresti: CIDE.

Hajnal, John. 1982. "Two Kinds of Preindustrial Household Formation Systems," *Population and Development Review* 8, no. 3, 449-94.

Hirschman, Charles. 1994. "Why Fertility Changes," *Annual Review of Sociology* 20, 203-33.

Hitchins, Keith. 1994. *Rumania 1866-1947*. Oxford: Clarendon Press.

Lesthaeghe, Ron and Chris Wilson. 1986. "Modes of Production, Secularization, and the Pace of the Fertility Decline in Western Europe, 1870-1930," *The Decline of Fertility in Europe. The Revised Proceedings of a Conference on the Princeton European Fertility Project*. Princeton: Princeton University Press.

Madison, Angus. 1995. *Monitoring the World Economy, 1820-1992*, Paris: OECD.

Serbu, G.R. 2000. "Evoluția fertilității populației feminine din R.P.R. în perioada 1900-1960," *Populație și societate* 4-5, 2-9.

Sklar, June. 1974. "The Role of Marriage Behavior in the Demographic Transition: The Case of Eastern Europe around 1900," *Population Studies* 28, no. 2, 231-47.

Stahl, Paul H. 2000. *Triburi si Sate din Sud –Estul Europei*. Bucuresti: Paideia.

Todorova, Maria N. 1993. *Balkan Family Structure and the European Pattern: Demographic Developments in Ottoman Bulgaria*. Washington: American University Press.

Watkins, Susan.1991. *From Provinces into Nations: Demographic Integration in Western Europe, 1870-1960*. Princeton, N.J.: Princeton University Press.

– 13 –
Reporting the People's War
Ottawa (1914-1918)

Jeff Keshen

It was Canada's first total war. It defined politics, economics, and the ideological milieu. But until recently, nearly all works on Canada's home front in the Great War have kept analysis to the macro level, removing the conflict from day-to-day life to focus on matters such as the war's role in building Canadian nationalism, as well as, conversely, national cleavages. This is now changing as demonstrated by recently published works on World War I Toronto and a comparative study of the Great War experience in Guelph, Medicine Hat and Trois-Rivières.[1] Still, as historians Jay Winter and Jean-Louis Major wrote in 1999 in an international context: "Whereas the history of nations at war has produced a literature of staggering proportions, the history of communities at war is still in its infancy."[2] This paper examines Ottawa. Despite being Canada's capital, it remains a blank slate when it comes to local wartime analysis. And in telling some of that story, my aim is to demonstrate the potential of the popular press as a historical source.

Incorporated as a city in 1854, by the time of the Great War Ottawa remained a modest place of just under 6,000 acres and some 100,000 souls. It had 16 lumbering firms - reflecting its economic roots - but its largest employer was the federal government with a payroll of approximately 5,000.[3] Its population was nearly half Catholic, and that group divided roughly two to one in favour of French over Irish, though both nationalities were congregated in the working-class slums of Le Breton Flats and, especially for the French, Lowertown. Those of Anglo-Protestant, Scottish, and Irish-Protestant background lived in more genteel areas, namely the districts comprising Upper Town, or, if part of the elite, the village of Rockcliffe Park.[4]

Yet, despite these, and other, divisions, more people came to feel part of a holistic community during the crisis of war. In describing this process, and the tapestry of other forces on the local scene, the historian could turn to numerous sources such as church, municipal government, school board, and private organizational records. But in gauging dominant opinions and trends,

---

[1] See Ian H.M. Miller, *Our Glory and Our Grief: Torontonians and the Great War* (Toronto: University of Toronto Press, 2002), and Robert Rutherdale, *Hometown Horizons: Local Responses to Canada's Great War* (Vancouver: University of British Columbia Press, 2004).

[2] W. John McDermott, Review of Jay Winter and Jean-Louis Major, eds., "Capital Cities at War: Paris, London, Berlin, 1914-1919," *Urban History Review* 27, no. 2 (March 1999): 72.

[3] *Canadian Printer and Publisher* (1914): 56-57; City of Ottawa, *Annual Report* (1914): 27-33.

[4] John Taylor, *Ottawa: An Illustrated History* (Toronto: James Lorimer & Company, 1986), 164-66, 211, 214.

171

especially before the appearance of public opinion polls, the mainstream press trumps all.

Over the late nineteenth century, newspapers transformed from rather modest tracts financially supported by political parties into independent big businesses. Between 1908 and 1914, the combined circulation of Canadian dailies soared from 1.073 million to 1.744 million. Readership expanded with a burgeoning urban population - increasing from 2 to 3.2 million between 1901 and 1911 - and a more educated public - by 1911, 85 per cent literate. Also critical was improved transport by road and rail, cheaper postal rates, the introduction of high-speed printing presses, and new wire services like Reuters and the Canadian Press.[5]

Increasingly, newspaper publishers focused on building circulation to attract advertising. By the Great War, advertising constituted more than half the revenue of major circulation-based Canadian dailies, especially since their price was kept low to maximize readership. Also to attract customers, what became the mainstream, or popular, press adopted attention-grabbing headlines, shorter stories, easier-to-read fonts, more photographs, and specialized features such as sports and women's pages.[6] By no means did such newspapers shun partisanship, but this moderated by the early twentieth century, often being confined to the editorial pages so as not to alienate large numbers of potential readers. This is not to suggest that the mainstream press captured the views of all. To the contrary, by virtue of what they covered and/or how they covered it, they often further marginalized or discredited ideas, voices and groups, namely those considered unconventional, dangerous, or destabilizing. Also, the popular press sometimes sought to mould public opinion. But such influence – if it did exist – derived from already having successfully connected to, and then utilizing, ideas and assumptions permeating the community.

In describing Ottawa's wartime's story, this paper relies on the two major English-language sources, the *Citizen* and *Journal*, and the principal French-language newspaper, *Le Droit*.[7] These tracts sought out a mass audience. Except on the basis of language, they were not designed for a particular constituency, as would be smaller-scale, specialized publications put out, for example, by a religious group, or trade or fraternal association.

The *Journal*, started in 1885, was owned and published - ultimately for more than 60 years - by the wealthy and well-connected P.D. Ross, once vice-president of the Ottawa Board of Trade. The *Citizen* was part of

---

[5] Robert S. Prince, "The Mythology of War: How the Canadian Daily Newspaper Depicted the Great War" (PhD diss., University of Toronto, 1998), 42; Minko Sotiron, *From Politics to Profit: The Commercialization of Canadian Daily Newspapers, 1890-1920* (Kingston and Montreal: McGill-Queen's University Press, 1997), 39; *Canadian Printer and Publisher* (1914): 278.

[6] Sotiron, *From Politics to Profit*, 4, 71-72, 77-80; Prince, "Mythology of War," 12; George Fetherling, *The Rise of the Canadian Newspaper* (Toronto: Oxford University Press, 1990), 108.

[7] The Ottawa *Free Press* had been in business since 1869, but was a victim of rising wartime costs. In late-1916, it was absorbed by the Ottawa *Journal*. Prince, "Mythology of War," 59; J. Brian Gilchrist, *Inventory of Ontario Newspapers, 1793-1986* (Toronto: Micromedia Ltd., 1987), n.p.

Canada's first newspaper chain, started by William Southam and that, by 1914, also included the Hamilton *Spectator*, Calgary *Herald*, and Edmonton *Journal* [8] The *Journal* was originally Liberal in its perspective, but by the Great War had given that mantle over to the *Citizen*, and increasingly leaned Conservative. But these were not political tracts of the last century. Neither received funding from political parties. Indeed, the *Citizen* made a point on its masthead each day with the quote: "An Independent, Clean Newspaper for the Home, Devoted to Public, Not Party Service." Their circulation numbers were impressive: in 1914, the *Citizen* distributed 17,923 copies daily and the *Journal* 12,553, and by 1918, with hunger for war news, those figures reached 28,526 and 27,884 respectively.

On the French side, *Le Temps*, which was supported financially by Ontario's Tory government (and even justified its introduction of Regulation 17 in 1912 that banned French-language instruction past grade two in publicly-financed schools) was disregarded by francophones as a party tract. After a precarious seventeen-year existence, it went bankrupt in early 1916. *Le Droit* better reflected this constituency. Started in March 1913 largely to protest Regulation 17, within two years it had built a readership of 7,000. In attracting advertisers, it emphasized its strong roots in the community with some 300 shareholders "recruited among the most influential [francophone] business men," as well as, in reflecting a religious population, its ownership by the Pères Oblats d'Ottawa.[9]

In analyzing newspapers, one could adopt a quantitative approach, classifying and then counting the number of times various topics are addressed. However, this is not well suited to such a vast domain as the Great War that involved a tremendous array of crucial subjects first appearing at different times, in various-sized stories and on front and inside pages. As such, this paper adopts what communication theorists refer to as a "qualitative" approach, where the researcher, presented with a mass of evidence, uses their judgment to identify dominant patterns, factoring in not only the frequency of topics, but also their prominence in newspapers and the descriptive language used.[10]

Ottawa newspapers, particularly the Anglo press, projected a just and popular conflict. Germany was "militaristic" and "unchristian"; its leaders bent on a mad desire for worldwide conquest; while its soldiers who committed all manner of atrocities also revealed the Teutonic character on the battlefield. By contrast, Canadian, and Allied, troops acquitted themselves "bravely," and always according to civilized, if not gentlemanly, standards of warfare. Battle,

---

[8] Sotiron, *From Politics to Profit*, 94; W.H. Kesterton, *A History of Journalism in Canada* (Toronto: McClelland and Stewart, 1967), 95-96.
[9] *Canadian Newspaper Directory*, 1914-1919.
[10] See Jane Stokes, *How to do Media and Cultural Studies* (London: Sage Publications, 2003), 68-69; Susanna Horing Priest, *Doing Media Research: An Introduction* (London: Sage Publications, 1996), 181; Erica Burmen and Ian Parker, eds., *Discourse Analytic Research: Repertoires and Reading of Texts in Action* (London: Routledge, 1993), 1; and Roger Fowler, *Language in the News: Discourse and Ideology in the Press* (London: Routledge, 1991), 1-3, 52.

though perhaps frightening and certainly deadly – as could readily be discerned from long casualty lists – was also "dramatic," "vivid," and "thrilling."[11]

Such themes appeared as often in news stories as editorial pages, reflecting the fact that romanticized and patriotic notions about war were widely accepted as truths. The *Citizen* and *Journal* differed on many political issues, but not when it came to the war. For instance, both supported Robert Borden's Union, or coalition, government in the December 1917 federal election to secure the passage of conscription. As for local francophones, it is important to keep in mind that there were no violent protests against the draft, and rioters in Quebec City were sharply criticized by clergy and in the pages of *Le Droit*. Also local francophones were heavily involved in volunteer patriotic campaigns. This is not to deny tensions and anger. *Le Droit* vociferously denounced what it saw as Anglo bigotry symbolized in Regulation 17, and like an estimated eighty per cent of local francophones, backed anti-conscription Laurier Liberal candidates in the 1917 federal election. Yet, equally prominent as a theme was the need to defeat the "monstre Teuton," though not by compelling people to serve overseas.[12]

Official censorship certainly factored into what was presented. Yet, most Canadian newspapers, including Ottawa's main three, accepted the suppression of information that could conceivably hurt the war effort. Some dissenters were kept in line by the threat of a $5000 fine and/or five years in jail as stipulated in the *War Measures Act*, but Canada's Chief Press Censor was not being disingenuous when claiming that he perceived most of those running major Canadian newspapers as allies in the fight against Germany. Moreover, the fact that the war was overwhelmingly popular made it good business for the press to plug patriotism.[13]

In reporting on its locale, nothing was more front and centre in major Ottawa newspapers than the multitude of volunteer activities people undertook to support the war. Certainly portrayals could be exaggerated, though one must conclude that generally people made considerable sacrifices given the amounts raised for numerous patriotic drives, combined with the context of growing inflation and an average annual income of just $1,000. Yet in Canadian historiography, the only aspect of wartime volunteerism that has received significant attention is recruitment, no doubt because it was so central to the war effort and strongly linked to conscription. Here, literature shows that military regiments enjoyed significant autonomy in terms of how they attracted recruits, that is until volunteers dried up and lack of controls precipitated serious labour imbalances.[14] This pattern reflected a society where localism rather than centralized control was the norm, even well into the war effort - a

---

[11] Among the literally countless articles in major Ottawa newspapers exemplifying these, and similar, themes, are: *Le Droit*, 1 dec. 1914, 6; Ibid., 27 mars 1917, 6; Ottawa *Citizen* (hereinafter *Citizen*) 12 March 1915, 1; Ibid., 26 June 1915, 1; Ibid., 20 April 1917, 9; *Ottawa Journal* (hereinafter *Journal*) 2 June 1915, 7; Ibid., 17 Feb 1916, 1.

[12] *Le Droit*, 13 nov. 1917, 6; Ibid., 18 dec. 1917, 1, 6.

[13] See Jeffrey A. Keshen, *Propaganda and Censorship in Canada's Great War* (Edmonton: University of Alberta Press, 1996), chapter 3.

[14] See Paul Maroney, "The Great Adventure: The Context and Ideology of Recruiting in Ontario," *Canadian Historical Review* 77, no.1 (March 1996): 62-98.

pattern also evident with myriad other citizen-run patriotic initiatives that remained pervasive on the local scene.

Among the first launched was the Canadian Patriotic Fund. A national private charity with local branches across the country, it was to provide financial support to wives, parents, and/or families with a principal breadwinner in the military. The press emphasized that its campaigns spoke to both patriotism and community responsibility, and, as such, heralded the fact that in terms of what they were asked to do, Ottawans never proved wanting. Only weeks into the conflict, the national Patriotic Fund committee sought $350,000 in Ottawa, but collected $380,000. In 1915, there was no drive, but in 1916, with pressure building on the fund, Ottawa's target was raised to $400,000, and it delivered $525,000. In 1917, the numbers were $500,000 and $661,000 respectively, and in 1918, $500,000 and $580,000.[15]

The famed Montreal financier and philanthropist, Herbert Baxter Ames, managed the national Patriotic Fund executive on which sat a *"Who's Who* of Canadian society." This was replicated on the local scene where stewardship fell to business, professional, church, and municipal government leaders, people who provided prestige, contacts, and often substantive donations. For instance, the 87-year-old lumber baron, J.R. Booth, was named Honorary President of the first Ottawa campaign and donated $20,000. Fundraising teams were created: a dozen for the 1914 campaign, and twenty-five, containing more than 300 people, for the second drive. A prominent local citizen led each team, such as, for the first drive, local labour leader D.J. O'Donoughue and francophone alderman J.A. Pinard.[16]

The success of Patriotic Fund campaigns was built not only upon promoting self-sacrifice, but also by providing community entertainment. Besides grand and colorful parades to open each drive, public rallies and fundraising shows filled places like the Russell Theatre that, until appropriated by the Federal District Commission in 1928 for the Confederation Square development, was the largest and premier venue for live entertainment.[17] Ottawa's mainstream press, particularly Anglo newspapers, became one with the Patriotic Fund campaigns. The *Citizen* and *Journal* printed pledge cards for people to cut out and send to local headquarters committing themselves to a one-time, quarterly, or monthly donation. Through each of the four campaigns the press created a sense of drama to get people involved with front-page headlines like: "Hurrah for the Capital! At 2 pm. $350,000 [of the $400,000 target for the second drive] Was in Sight."[18] Newspapers printed the names of donors and the amount they gave and often made special mention of minority groups to promote the idea that this was a drive uniting all. Among those quoted was Father E.J. Cornett of St. Joseph's Catholic Church, who proclaimed: "If we cannot go to the front the least that can be expected of us is to do our share towards providing for the wives and children of the brave men

---

[15] Philip H. Morris, *The Canadian Patriotic Fund – A Record of its Activities from 1914 to 1919* (Ottawa: The Mortimer Company, 1919), 150-51.
[16] *Citizen*, 25 Jan. 1916, 1; *Journal*, 31 Jan. 1916, 1; *Le Droit*, 6 mars 1918, 8.
[17] Taylor, *Ottawa*, 140.
[18] *Journal*, 26 Jan. 1916, 1; *Citizen*, 27 Jan 1916, 1.

taking our place in the trenches."[19] Also frequently cited and praised as a community leader was the Jewish department store owner, A.J. Frieman, a team captain for the second Patriotic Fund drive - this in a city where Jews were barred from numerous social clubs.[20]

With the profusion of war charities, starting in 1917, the annual drive of the Patriotic Fund was combined with an appeal from the Red Cross, the latter receiving twenty per cent of the total. The Red Cross was well established, well known and well respected as a philanthropic organization, its roots stretching back more than a half-century to the Crimean conflict. Before the end of August 1914, an Ottawa Branch of the Red Cross was established in an Upper Town house made available by Canada's High Commissioner to Britain, Sir George Perley, next to his own. The Governor-General served as the branch's honourary patron and its executive included the likes of Senator James Robertson and the department store owner A.E. Rae.[21] The branch attracted assistance from Ottawans of myriad background; in September 1915, the *Journal* identified volunteers linked to 84 local organizations, including churches of every Christian denomination, the Murray Street Synagogue, the Ottawa branch of the Société St-Jean-Baptiste, the Women's Christian Temperance Union, and the Royal Ottawa Golf Club.[22] A local Women's Red Cross Auxiliary was established by the end of 1914, and organized sections for fundraising; to buy and provide material for volunteers to make clothing; and to collect, sort and pack items for shipment abroad.[23] Ottawa's popular press strongly promoted these efforts, on several occasions even listing contributions such as: "Mrs___, 2 grey shirts."[24]

Like the Patriotic Fund, the Red Cross developed a variety of fundraising techniques. Starting in October 1914, it initiated Red Cross Relief Days, essentially a one-day blitz in which volunteers went out into the community to collect cash and in return provided donation tags. For one such day, A.E. Rae of the branch executive offered five per cent of Saturday sale receipts, and prominent local women, such as Mayor McVeity's wife, acted as store department managers, an event that raised $1,800.[25] Starting in 1915, Red Cross volunteers directed their energies into two annual four-day nationwide drives in the spring and autumn, the latter being co-ordinated throughout the Empire by the British Red Cross and ending on Trafalgar Day - October 21 - which commemorated Nelson's naval victory over Napoleon in 1805. For the first Trafalgar Day campaign, Ottawa met its goal of $50,000 out of the national target of $1.5 million, a ratio 2.5 times greater than its percentage of Canada's population. The grass roots - even if led by local elites - helped ensure that virtually no one escaped the call to give. Local Boy Scouts, some 350 strong by 1915 - the membership growing by twenty per cent in wartime due to the group's quasi-military appeal – blanketed city streets. Once again,

---

[19] *Journal*, 24 Jan. 1916, 2; Ibid., 27 Sept. 1915, 12; *Le Droit*, 22 jan. 1916, 7.
[20] *Citizen*, 25 Jan. 1916, 1.
[21] *Citizen*, 2 Sept. 1914, 11.
[22] *Journal*, 25 Sept. 1915, 4.
[23] *Citizen*, 9 Sept. 1914, 10; Ibid., 6 Nov. 1915, 10.
[24] *Journal*, 21 May 1915, 12.
[25] *Citizen*, 12 Sept. 1914, 12.

teams solicited funds door-to-door. In churches, special Red Cross envelopes were handed out, and in school classrooms, Red Cross coin boxes were passed around.[26]

Other fundraising strategies relied as much on creating an atmosphere of fun as sacrifice. Over the winter of 1915, Ottawa's Red Cross benefited to the tune of nearly $3,000 from a new, lighted, toboggan chute that cost five cents per run, and a nearby teahouse.[27] Other undertakings were more exclusive such as "Red Cross Bridge" parties that became something of a craze among middle- and upper-class women. One such event in 1915 at the prime minister's residence hosted by Lady Borden netted over $500.[28]

Ottawa's community war effort revolved not only around helping men overseas and their families at home. There were also thousands in khaki training in their midst, principally at the Lansdowne Park fairgrounds about a thirty-minute walk from the central core. While the press acknowledged problems such as drunk and disorderly conduct by men on leave,[29] this barely registered compared to reports on positive interaction between civilians and trainees. Stories described Ottawans thronging city streets to cheer military parades or going on a day's outing to witness training exercises and sham battles.[30] Military sporting teams participated in city baseball, soccer, rugby/football, and hockey leagues.[31] Military bands played in venues such as public parks. Trainees organized and starred in often elaborate live shows, typically to build up regimental funds. For instance, the April 1916 "Assault-at-Arms" performance by the 77th Regiment included soloists and a military chorus, vaudeville skits, fancy drill (including with bayonets), and various feats of physical prowess, such as gymnastics displays.[32]

The press highlighted community generosity toward trainees. Amongst the most active in this regard, namely in furnishing recreational equipment, was the Ottawa Branch of the Sportsmen's Patriotic Association. Started in November 1915, it grew to 2,000 members, in part because its initiation fee was only twenty-five cents. Its press accolades also reflected its very popular and successful community fundraising events, including, starting in 1916, its annual Victoria Day Grand Military and Athletic Carnival at Lansdowne Park. For an entrance fee of fifty cents, visitors were treated to a "monster parade" of soldiers; inter-regimental track and field competitions; competitive pontoon building; and evening dances with prizes awarded for the "best one-step, two-step and waltz."[33]

Also very much involved in entertaining and servicing soldiers was the Salvation Army, the Knights of Columbus and, most prominent with its 18,000 members nationwide, the YMCA. For trainees in Canada, and

---

[26] *Citizen*, 19 Oct. 1915, 2; *Journal*, 27 Oct. 1915, 13.
[27] *Citizen*, 18 Dec. 1915, 5; *Journal*, 7 Jan. 1916, 1.
[28] *Journal*, 13 Oct. 1915, 8.
[29] *Le Droit*, 9 mars 1915, 3; Ibid., 6 mai 1915, 3; *Journal*, 23 Nov. 1915, 10.
[30] *Journal*, 23 April 1915, 10; Ibid., 10 Sept. 1915, 14; *Citizen*, 18 Feb. 1915, 1; Ibid., 9 April 1915, 6; Ibid., 14 May 1915, 2; Ibid., 29 July 1915, 2.
[31] *Citizen*, 20 July 1916, 8; Ibid., 27 July 1916, 8; *Journal*, 3 Aug. 1918, 4.
[32] *Journal*, 15 April 1916, 24.
[33] *Citizen*, 17 May 1916, 9; Ibid., 20 May 1916, 10; *Le Droit*, 23 mai 1916, 2.

Canadians in khaki overseas, the YMCA arranged live shows and movies, and provided sporting equipment, dry canteens, and mobile refreshment booths serving tea and coffee. At Lansdowne Park, the Y's recreational tent also provided board and card games, stationary for letter writing, and books, magazines and newspapers.[34]

So critical were citizen-run ventures in supporting the war effort that in the opening stages of the Second World War, the federal government created a new Department of National War Services (NWS), one of whose main goals was to coordinate the activities of citizen volunteers. Also, reflecting the leading role women volunteers had played during the Great War, in 1940, as part of NWS, a Women's Voluntary Services Division was established. Indeed, this leadership role women assumed was another theme clearly articulated in the pages of Ottawa's popular press in the Great War. Yet, in much of the historiography, women's volunteerism is downplayed for being non-threatening to patriarchy because the tasks - besides being unpaid - often connected to traditional domestic roles (such as knitting) and reflected the stereotype of women as self-sacrificing and nurturing. But it was also the case that volunteerism got many women out of the house more than ever and instilled within them a sense of pride and importance from running extensive operations and in providing services presented as critical to the war effort. Ottawa's two major Anglo newspapers introduced a special page detailing women's wartime voluntary services. And though newspapers noted many factors linking to the achievement of female suffrage during the Great War - namely the federal government's desire to increase the pro-conscription vote, women's performance of new, and demanding, paid work, and their leading role in the successful campaign for wartime prohibition - it was through patriotic volunteerism, in which women made up some seventy-five per cent of participants, that they achieved greatest acclaim.[35]

Some women's groups seemed everywhere, generating extensive and laudatory press coverage. One was the Imperial Order Daughters of the Empire (IODE). A nationwide organization founded in 1900, and united ideologically by a pro-British and Imperialist ethos, it increased from one to two branches in wartime Ottawa. Its mostly middle- and upper-class membership was fast off the mark when it came to war-related volunteer work. In the opening weeks of the conflict, the Laurentian Chapter, whose Honorary Regent was the Governor-General's daughter, Princess Patricia, played a leading role in raising three times more than the $100,000 sought nationwide for the Duchess of Connaught's Hospital Ship Fund.[36]

Growing in popularity from its wartime activities, in 1915 Ottawa's IODE opened a new Madeleine de Verchères branch under the directorship of Mrs. Thomas Casgrain, the wife of Canada's Postmaster-General. Named to encourage the participation of French-Canadians, it set up operations in the Banque Nationale building, encouraged its members to take French lessons,

---

[34] *Citizen*, 30 Aug. 1915, 5; *Journal*, 8 Oct. 1915, 9.
[35] Miller, *Our Glory and Our Grief*, 134.
[36] Nancy Sheehan, "The IODE, the Schools and World War I," *History of Education Review* 13, no. 1 (1984): 37-38.

and convinced Lady Laurier to serve as Honourary Regent. Although inroads among francophones remained modest, such was not the case when it came to the branch's impact on the war effort. In a typical month, it shipped overseas over 5,000 rolled bandages, 3,200 surgical sponges, 1,200 surgical masks, and 7,000 cigarettes.[37]

IODE fundraising efforts also provided many social activities. Some were exclusive such as a 1915 gala dinner and dance to raise money for the 77th's regimental fund where Ottawa's "finest" young women, as well as Prime Minister and Lady Borden, joined officers in full dress uniform.[38] Probably the IODE's most prominent event, aimed at the general public and started in 1915, was its annual Christmas bazaar held in the cavernous Arcade Building where shoppers could purchase a wide variety of new and used items donated by individuals and area merchants, all at booths manned by IODE members and society leaders, including Lady Borden. Browsing shoppers were entertained by local glee clubs and could partake in games of skill such as "Kill the Kaiser."[39]

Yet, among community organizations, press reports leave the unmistakable impression that when it came to volunteer patriotic work, the Ottawa Women's Canadian Club was perhaps the most important group - male or female - on the local scene. Founded in 1904 and with nearly 1,300 members by 1918,[40] its leadership and membership, like the IODE's, was mostly drawn from the middle- and upper-class. Its president was Mrs. W.T. Herridge, wife of the moderator of Canada's Presbyterian Church. Whatever other groups were doing to do to help win the war, the Women's Club seemed to be doing more, raising as much as $50,000 per year.[41]

Before the end of October 1914, its members were assisting soldiers' wives making claims from the Patriotic Fund, providing them with short-term emergency financial assistance, and, to alleviate loneliness and strain, arranged entertainment for them and their families.[42] Also in the opening months of the war it established a Soldiers' Comfort Committee that sent gifts overseas, particularly to formations with a concentration of Ottawans.[43] Perhaps its most prominent activity - at least in terms of the press coverage generated - was the provisioning of comforts for Canadian POWs. Started in 1915, volunteers were soon preparing thousands of packages each month. Much of this was financed through the Club's "adopt a POW" campaign which cost contributors $2

---

[37] *Journal*, 1 Nov. 1915, 9; Ibid., 9 Nov. 1915, 9; *Citizen*, 24 Feb. 1915, 11; Ibid. 21 Feb. 1917, 13.

[38] K. Weatherbee, *From the Rideau to the Rhine and Back. The 6th Field Company and Battalion Canadian Engineers in the Great War* (Toronto:The Hunter-Rose Co., Limited, 1928), 33; *Journal*, 17 Dec. 1915, 8.

[39] *Journal*, 14 Nov. 1916, 5; Ibid. 6 Dec. 1916, 7; *Citizen*, 31 Oct. 1917, 5.

[40] *Citizen*, 5 June 1918, 5.

[41] *Journal*, 10 Dec. 1915, 2; Ibid., April 1918, 5; *Citizen*, 21 April 1918, 28.

[42] *Citizen*, 26 Oct. 1914, 11; Ibid., 31 Dec. 1914, 2; Ibid., 18 Jan. 1915, 10; *Journal*, 23 April 1915, 8.

[43] *Journal*, 29 Sept. 1915, 8; Ibid., 26 Oct. 1915, 2; *Citizen*, 2 Dec. 1915, 13.

monthly. Newspapers assisted by printing donor lists, detailing how many POWs people adopted, and for what duration.[44]

The Club also raised money through lectures and luncheons. Among sell-out performances for its 1915 season was an address by Major Stetham, an Ottawan who returned home legless, but nevertheless provided a "rousing" address on "Canada's heroes" in action.[45] Among Club events that year with particular appeal to Ottawa's social set was a Japanese night at the swank three-year-old Chateau Laurier hotel. Japanese lanterns lighted the hall leading into the main ballroom where "ladies were fetchingly attired in dainty Japanese costumes."[46] The Club also organized events for the entire community, most prominent, starting in June 1915, its annual three-day street bazaar. Stretching for three blocks, the first installment had twenty booths where people could sample national dishes of the Allied nations, while watching military bands and jugglers, and at night participate in a lighted street dance.[47]

Mainstream newspapers detailed the fact that prior to large-scale state intervention, citizen groups had mobilized thousands behind myriad patriotic causes. The spirit forged by these activities would prove indispensable to government as it became obliged to introduce new, and significant, obligations upon citizens. Among the more prominent examples was food conservation, which in June 1917, came under the direction of a new Food Controller's Office. Soldiers and civilians overseas had to be fed but the war had devastated European crops, while at home, military recruitment and the lure of well-paying urban war jobs had created, by mid-1917, agricultural labour shortages of some 36,000 in Western Canada, and nearly the same in Ontario.[48]

There can be little doubt about the enthusiasm to pitch in, including by the press. Ottawa's main newspapers printed instructions on how to can food and "patriotic recipes" that eliminated the use of scarce items. Rule-breakers were publicly shamed in newspapers,[49] while those like Ottawa's Local Council of Women were praised for actions such as resolving to no longer serve meals larger than three courses.[50]

The flip side to conservation was production. By 1917, over 200 Ottawans had headed West to assist on wheat fields, though economics, not just patriotism, played a part as the federal government heavily subsidized transport, and wages at $75 monthly plus room and board, was some fifty per cent higher than local agricultural labour rates.[51] Still, there was also plenty of local need and Ottawa newspapers seemed to adopt the role of recruiting agent, stressing that "unless some measures are taken to relieve the situation, many a farm will go untilled."[52] In 1917, 350 federal civil servants got involved,

---

[44] *Citizen*, 13 July 1915, 11; *Journal*, 26 Oct. 1916, 5.
[45] *Journal*, 1 Nov. 1915, 8.
[46] *Citizen*, 16 Oct. 1915, 13.
[47] *Citizen*, 28 June 1916, 14.
[48] *Citizen*, 23 Aug. 1917, 7.
[49] *Le Droit*, 14 mars 1917, 6; *Citizen*, 13 July 1917, 5, 14; Ibid., 14 Sept. 1918, 12; *Journal*, 20 Sept. 1917, 8.
[50] *Journal*, 22 Jan. 1918, 2.
[51] *Citizen*, 16 Aug. 1916, 2.
[52] *Citizen*, 7 May 1917, 2.

something also encouraged by the federal government which provided an extra week's paid holiday if it was used to supply farm labour.[53] Young people also pitched in, most as *Soldiers of the Soil*, a federal-provincial program established in early 1918 to attract 25,000 high school boys to assist on farms during the spring through autumn period. Within a few days of the program being announced, Ottawa met its quota of 250 lads, some of whom, no doubt, were enticed by the fact that those approved often started in April and were given credit for the full school year as long as they had been passing to that point.[54]

Closer to home, thousands of Ottawans, particularly women, cultivated backyard "war gardens." Larger initiatives came from churches and schools, and the Ottawa Vacant Lot Association organized a city-wide effort. Founded in advance of the 1917 growing season, its directors mostly came from the Ottawa Horticultural Society, though also included W.E. Harper, Secretary-Treasurer of the Ottawa Land Association, a property development firm that provided much of its 300 acres of vacant land in the city.[55] Application forms for lots were printed *gratis* by Ottawa newspapers. Demand consistently exceeded the supply of lots, which peaked at 300 in 1918, but this still left a waiting list of 400.[56] Preference was given to those who provided revenues to war charities. For example, in 1917 about thirty members of the Ottawa Women's Canadian Club tended three vacant lots that returned several hundred dollars for its Soldiers' Comfort Committee.[57]

Patriotic volunteerism was not only crucial in helping to win the war, but also in preparing for the transition to peace. To provide medical care and retraining, and to decide upon appropriate pensions for veterans, the federal government created a Military Hospitals Commission (MHC) in July 1915. In February 1918, the MHC became part of the Department of Soldiers' Civil Re-Establishment that also devised strategy to aid veterans who were physically fit. However, government welfare was still managed with frugality in mind so as not to further drive up a war debt that ultimately reached $1.3 billion, and, as often said, to prevent excessive dependency upon the state by the repatriated.[58]

Ottawa newspapers gave extensive coverage to the development of policies, and initially accepted the government's line on their generosity and effectiveness. But as programs were increasingly tested and found wanting, the message changed to the idea that those who had sacrificed for Canada deserved better. One major area of grievance was pensions. Although improving over the course of the war, they remained cast as inadequate, especially in light of rising inflation. In 1916, the *Citizen* used the phrase "mean and insufficient" to describe government support of $216 per annum for a totally disabled, non-

---

[53] Ottawa's municipal government also adopted this policy. See COA, City Council Minutes, BOC Report #3, 17 June 1918, 214, item 3.
[54] *Citizen*, 28 March 1917, 6; Ibid., 26 March 1918, 3; *Journal*, 15 April 1918, 8.
[55] *Citizen*, 8 March 1917, 10.
[56] *Citizen*, 5 April 1917, 10; *Journal*, 8 April 1918, 4.
[57] *Citizen*, 8 Aug. 1917, 2.
[58] J.C. Hopkins, *Canada at War: A Record of Heroism and Achievement, 1914-1918* (Toronto: The Canadian Annual Review Limited, 1919), 214.

commissioned single soldier.[59] When it came to providing preferences to veterans for employment in the federal civil service, newspapers noted that many ended up as messengers, receiving what the *Journal* cast as the "misery" salary of $41.66 monthly.[60]

The flip side to such shortcomings, however, was that citizen groups again took on added importance and prestige. In late 1915, Ottawans formed a Citizen's Repatriation Committee with representatives from, among others, the Board of Trade, Allied Trades and Labour Association, Société St-Jean-Baptiste, and the St. Patrick's Society, to help arrange "welcome home" ceremonies for the wounded, and eventually multitudes demobilized with peace.[61] Early the next year, a local branch of the Soldiers' Aid Commission appeared. Although created out of a 1915 federal-provincial conference to encourage greater "provincial involvement in matters arising out of the war," it received only modest funding and administrative support from the Ontario government.[62] But Ottawa's branch remained significant, its members having links to 106 local clubs, charitable and fraternal societies, and professional, occupational, labour, and political groups. They assisted veterans in accessing federal programs; coordinated with schools and vocational institutes to arrange re-training; offered emergency financial support; and helped men find decent employment and accommodation.[63] The branch also organized picnics, concerts, and ceremonial dinners for returned men and often their families.[64] Moreover, in a major and ultimately successful campaign enthusiastically promoted in Ottawa newspapers, it played a leading role in mobilizing support to have a question placed on the January 1918 municipal ballot asking if the city government should devote as much as $40,000 to acquire a building to serve as national headquarters for the Great War Veterans Association and a veteran's club house - a hefty sum considering that a stately home in Rockcliffe Park then cost half that amount.[65] The vote was decisive, and in August, following remodeling, the twenty-two room stone mansion in Upper Town, purchased for $35,000, opened its doors in a grand ceremony that included military bands and honour guards.[66]

A few months later, on Monday, 11 November 1918, Ottawans awoke to church bells proclaiming the Armistice. Quickly they thronged city streets, lit bonfires, set off fireworks, blew whistles and horns, banged on tin pans and wash boilers, sang patriotic songs, danced with strangers, and gleefully burned the Kaiser in effigy. According to newspapers, things did not

---

[59] *Citizen*, 15 March 1916, 12; Ibid., 26 March 1917, 9.
[60] *Citizen*, 6 Jan. 1917, 16; *Journal*, 15 Jan. 1917, 16.
[61] COA, City Council Minutes, BOC Report #42, 8 Dec. 1916, 429, item 4; *Citizen*, 13 Feb. 1917, 5; Ibid., 18 June 1918, 7; *Journal*, 3 Dec. 1918, 1.
[62] *Citizen*, 28 Jan. 1916, 13.
[63] *Journal*, 3 Sept. 1916, 5; Ibid., 19 March 1917, 3; *Citizen*, 27 April 1917, 15; Ibid., 8 May 1918, 5.
[64] *Citizen*, 5 June 1916, 15; Ibid., 14 March 1916, 14; Ibid., 8 May 1918, 5; *Journal*, 5 Jan. 1918, 4.
[65] COA, By-Laws of the Council of the Corporation of the City of Ottawa for the Year 1917, By-Laws 4475, 4476, 3 Dec. 1917; *Journal*, 15 Dec. 1917, 5; Ibid., 5 Jan. 1918, 1.
[66] *Citizen*, 23 March 1918, 13; *Journal*, 8 Aug. 1918, 2.

peter out until 4 a.m. on Tuesday.[67] Ottawans celebrated, and soon in official ceremonies would bereave, as a community, because in so many ways they had fought the war as a community.

Nowhere is that process better captured than in the daily descriptions carried in the popular, or mainstream, press. Ottawa's major newspapers demonstrate that despite local divisions, including those created or exacerbated by the war, patriotic volunteerism linked social classes and ethnic groups; provided people with direction, purpose, and a sense of importance; enhanced the status of women; and for many, despite the stress of this period, generated considerable excitement and even fun.

Of course, historians must recognize the limits of newspapers as evidence, and use them appropriately. It is critical to determine exactly whom the source targeted, and by virtue of its circulation, if it had legitimacy in reflecting that community. It is also important to remember that mainstream newspapers marginalized or distorted voices, such as, in wartime, those of enemy aliens, pacifists and socialists. But it was also the case that Ottawa's major newspapers - that, as businesses, sought to reflect their community and build readerships - enjoyed a connection with multitudes on the local scene. *Le Droit* circulated 7,000 copies daily and was challenged by no other French newspaper, and the *Citizen* and *Journal* each distributed more than 25,000 copies in a city whose population barely topped 100,000. This does not equate with accepting the veracity of what these sources printed. Here, context again becomes crucial. For instance, censorship and patriotism played key parts in producing pages containing gross inaccuracies about the war, something the historian could verify by consulting other sources, such as unit war diaries. But on the other hand, patriotism and jingoism, which also encouraged the acceptance of censorship, reflected a wider milieu, something that can also be verified by turning to additional types of evidence.

As such, by linking newspapers with their appropriate context - namely their audience and what can be reasonably accepted as part of that group's perspective - they can provide a treasure trove of details, and, despite being a rather traditional source, often shed new light on old topics. Indeed, Ottawa's mainstream press underscores the fact that patriotic volunteerism has not been given its proper due in the historiography. It was not only fundamental in helping to win the war, but also in making, for many Canadians, the war *the best years of their lives*.

---

[67] Sandra Gwyn, *Tapestry of War: A Private View of Canadians in the Great War* (Toronto: HarperCollins, 1992), 483-84; *Le Droit*, 11 nov. 1918, 1, 4; *Citizen*, 12 Nov. 1918, 1.

– 14 –
Documents in Bronze and Stone
Memorials and Monuments as Historical Sources

Jonathan F. Vance

In 1925, in passing its verdict in the competition to design Winnipeg's civic war memorial, the judging panel declared for the winner with the following words: "The sentiment is simply and directly expressed in a manner about which no doubt can be felt and no questions need to be asked."[1] For these judges, the winning design was not open to interpretation; it had one meaning and one meaning only, and that meaning would endure for all time.

Nearly a century's worth of experience with commemoration later, it seems ludicrous to suggest that the meaning of a monument could be so static. Indeed, the design that the judges confidently asserted was self-evident now seems distinctly less so. However, provided one is familiar with the artistic vocabulary, Emmanuel Hahn's design *is* still decipherable – the central column is a cenotaph or empty tomb, an ancient form of funerary architecture that was popularized after the First World War, and the draped figures on either side represent Service and Sacrifice. Furthermore, any monument, as a communal artifact, is more static than we might imagine. It is a text, in that the iconography and the inscription do not change over time. In most cases, it remains on the same site in the urban space, although more than a few memorials have been moved, for a variety of reasons. Improving traffic flow is perhaps the most common reason – the war memorial in Windsor, Ontario, was moved when it became an obstacle to the redevelopment of downtown streets. However, we should also remember that the removal of monuments frequently coincides with regime change, and not only in the former Soviet bloc or, most recently, Iraq. Charles Withers has written persuasively of the proposed destruction of the monument to the 1st Duke of Sutherland, near Golspie in Scotland, on the grounds that he was one of the driving forces behind the ruinous Highland Clearances and should not be commemorated with such a heroic vocabulary.[2] Similarly, Courtney Workman has detailed the efforts to have the monument to suffragists Elizabeth Cady Stanton, Susan B. Anthony, and Lucretia Mott returned to the rotunda of the Capitol building from the basement, where it had been moved by opponents of the Nineteenth Amendment.[3] Finally, the debate that surrounded the erection of any monument

---

[1] Queen's University Archives, Emmanuel Hahn papers, series II, box 7, file 17-13, Report of Board of Assessors, 22 December 1925. For the strange story that saw Hahn's design replaced by a cenotaph designed by Gilbert Parfitt, see Victoria A. Baker, *Emmanuel Hahn and Elizabeth Wyn Wood: Tradition and Innovation in Canadian Sculpture* (Ottawa, 1997).

[2] Charles Withers, "Place, Memory, Monument: Memorializing the Past in Contemporary Highland Scotland," *Ecumee* 3, no. 3 (1996): 325-344.

[3] Courtney Workman, "*The Woman Movement*: Memorial to Women's Rights Leaders and the Perceived Images of the Women's Movement," in Paul A. Shackel, ed., *Myth,*

in the first place is part of the historical record, and can be subjected to traditional modes of analysis.

What makes the monument a particularly malleable kind of historical document, however, is its interaction with its setting, both social and physical. Civic groups might use the monument as a stage to air contemporary debates, in an attempt to overlay a new meaning on the old. Because they tend to occupy prominent sites in the public space, monuments often become magnets for individuals wanting to air causes quite unrelated to the monument itself. By the same token, many a monument became neglected and forgotten when urban change gradually transformed the busy thoroughfare on which it once sat into a rarely travelled road. Looked at in these terms, the monument is constantly changing in a way that a written document is not. A letter says the same thing whether it is held in the National Archives of Canada or the Archives of Ontario. A monument, however, changes dramatically when its physical space or its social usage changes.

All of this is certainly true for traditional monuments, so much so that it hardly bears pointing out. But a new genre of monuments – what scholars have called the postmodern monument[4] – adds another range of complexities to

---

Memory, and the Making of the American Landscape (Gainesville, FL: University Press of Florida, 2001), 47-66.

[4] See Susan Rubin Suleiman, *Risking Who One Is: Encounters with Contemporary Art and Literature* (Cambridge: Cambridge University Press, 1994); Roxanna Myrhum, "Art From the Ashes," *Harvard Political Review* 1 April 2002; Jacqueline Barbera, "Monuments and Meaning," *Contrapposto* [California State University, Chico], at http://www.csuchico.edu/art/contrapposto/contrapposto98/pages/%20essays/barbera.html

their use as sources for historical study. Such monuments, even if they do not always look very different, have very different characteristics from the traditional. A discussion of those features reveals the ways in which future historians will be challenged in trying to come to terms with the new memorials that adorn our landscape.

The first striking characteristic is interactivity. In a traditional monument, the space between the viewer and the structure was to be maintained as a buffer. The monument was not to be climbed on, leaned against, or touched – indeed complaints about people laying hands on memorials can be found in virtually any local newspaper from the last century. In this reasoning, the monument was there only to be looked at; in observing, one would reflect upon its meaning and lessons. Indeed, debates over the optimum height of the memorial revolved around symbolic considerations – how high should the individual or event be elevated in the collective memory? – as much as practical – the higher the statue was situated, the less likely it was that someone would try to sit on its lap. The tribute to Queen Victoria in Hamilton, Ontario, is typical – people took advantage of its convenient location in Gore Park to sit on it, but city administrators did all they could to discourage such shows of disrespect.

The postmodern monument takes a very different approach. It creates a memorial space which viewers are invited to enter, to interact with the different elements of the structure. That interaction, their response to the monument, becomes part of the monument itself – the viewer becomes an actor in the commemorative process, rather than simply a detached bystander to that process. A typical example is the memorial which is proposed for the victims of the 9/11 attack on the Pentagon, a landscaped park with benches representing each of the dead.[5] This is not a utilitarian memorial in the classic sense – it was not created to fill a pressing need for 184 benches on the lawn of the Pentagon. Rather, it is a memorial whose commemorative force lies in its inherent interactivity. Individuals physically enter into it, becoming an element of the memorial; the person sitting on the bench and reflecting upon 9/11 is a part, albeit a transitory one, of the memorial.

Secondly, there is a general reluctance to use lengthy inscriptions on postmodern monuments. Traditional memorials (and one could use virtually any Great War memorial for illustration) tended to value text, if not the names of the dead, then a list of the values for which they supposedly died – truth, honour, justice, liberty. The inscription on the war memorial in Chatham, Ontario – "This monument / lovingly and gratefully commemorates / the gallant men of / Chatham and Kent County / who in the Great War 1914-1918 / took up arms, or died / for God, for King and country / for loved ones, home and Empire / for the sacred cause of justice / and the freedom of the world" – certainly leaves nothing to the imagination, and no room for interpretation. This inscription, like so many others from the same era, exists to tell the viewer precisely what the monument means, and therefore what the First World War meant.

---

[5] For details of this project, see http://memorial.pentagon.mil/; and Alicia Bessette, "Inscription in the Earth," *Bryn Mawr Alumnae Bulletin* (summer 2003): 2-3.

QUEEN VICTORIA MONUMENT

Postmodern monuments tend to shy away from text, in the full knowledge that getting the right words can be highly contentious.[6] In a milieu in which every word must be negotiated between a welter of groups with an interest in any given monument, the fewer words the better. At the same time there is the realization that language itself, no matter how much effort is taken to make it bland and uncontroversial, will always admit of a contested meaning. A good example of this phenomenon occurs on the Vietnam Veterans Memorial in Washington, DC, dedicated in 1982. Often characterized as a postmodern monument, its inscription is nevertheless contested: "In honor of the men and women of the armed forces of the United States who served in the Vietnam War. The names of those who gave their lives and of those who remain missing are inscribed in the order they were taken from us. Our nation honors the courage, sacrifice, and devotion to duty and country of its Vietnam veterans. This memorial was built with private contributions from the American people. November 11, 1982." Here, one might be tempted to interrogate two specific portions of the text. The phrase "they were taken from us" begs an important question that the use of the passive voice dodges: who took them? – the North Vietnamese army and the Viet-cong, or the United States government? And the reference to "courage, sacrifice, and devotion to duty and country" brings to mind all the Big Words that Paul Fussell argued had been made irrelevant by the First World War, and that architect Maya Lin had tried so hard to avoid in

---

[6] See, for example, the controversy over the recent decision by Parks Canada to rewrite the text on the plaque commemorating the Frog Lake Massacre in 1885, discussed in the *Ottawa Citizen*, 10 July 1999.

her design.[7] Even a straightforward text like this, then, says much more than it seems to.

Perhaps ironically, a typical postmodern monument in this sense might be Canada's National War Memorial, which predates the Vietnam Memorial by some forty years. In an echo of the tradition of inscribing memorials to individuals with only their surname (for example, Birmingham's monument to James Watt, one of the pioneers of the steam engine, bears a one-word inscription: "Watt"[8]), Vernon March's Ottawa memorial has only the dates of the Great War, to which the dates of subsequent conflicts have been added. The reason for this choice may have been practical – March had such trouble with well-meaning observers critiquing the figures that he may have been reluctant to tackle an inscription.[9] Furthermore, dates are inherently bilingual, an important consideration on a memorial to be raised to the dead of a bilingual nation.[10] Perhaps the planners felt that, by 1939 when the monument was unveiled, no words were necessary. Finally, it may have been a conscious decision to enable the memorial to be more inclusive – when the monument has no words, it invites the viewer to provide their own text – although it is difficult to imagine the government of the time thinking in these terms.

---

[7] See Paul Fussell, *The Great War and Modern Memory* (Oxford: Oxford University Press, 1975), 21-22; Maya Lin quoted in "Vietnam Veterans Memorial: America Remembers," *National Geographic* 167, no. 5 (May 1985): 557.
[8] George T. Noszlopy, *Public Sculpture of Birmingham, Iincluding Sutton Coldfield* (Liverpool: Liverpool University Pres, 1998), 32.
[9] See Jonathan F. Vance, "The Great Response: Canada's long struggle to honour the dead of the Great War," *The Beaver* 76, 5 (1996), 28-32.
[10] I am grateful to Galen Perras for his thoughts on this point.

Finally, traditional memorials relied heavily on allegorical content. Every design element had a specific meaning, every allegorical figure could be understood. Everyone knew what the broken chain or the laurel wreath meant, everyone could recognize the angel or the lion. Everyone, for example, would know what was meant by the memorial at the Lawrence Sheriff School in Rugby, England, a small statue of St. George slaying the dragon. There was a constancy in the meaning of allegorical and iconic symbols which meant that, even without the inscription which reads "There are dragons still," the monument itself was not open to interpretation. How could one possibly misinterpret the meaning of the Sheriff School's? It was, therefore, possible for Colin McIntyre to subtitle his 1990 book *How to Read a War Memorial*, because such memorials had a vocabulary that could be deciphered fairly easily, provided one had a rudimentary knowledge of contemporary iconography.[11]

Contrast this with a typical postmodern monument, like the one which honours the Women's Royal Canadian Naval Service (the Wrens) in Galt, Ontario. There is no vocabulary there, only a single figure of a woman in naval uniform. The Sheriff School's memorial can only mean one thing, but this memorial can almost mean anything – from a traditional celebration of martial values and the defence of the nation, to a critique of old-fashioned notions of heroism and courage and a lament at the masculine perpetuation of

---

[11] Colin McIntyre, *Monuments of War: How to Read a War Memorial* (London: Hale, 1990).

conflict. Or, it can mean nothing – it can simply be a Wren. It is up to the viewer to bring to this memorial whatever interpretation they wish. In the postmodern monument, iconography has given way either to realism (as in Galt) or abstraction (as in the new Canadian War Memorial at Green Park in London, England) – either way, there is no longer a vocabulary, or at least not one that can be understood without detailed descriptive notes from the sculptor or an art critic.[12]

The combined effect of these three characteristics is to ensure that each postmodern monument is not one but many. The interactivity, absence of words, and lack of allegorical elements all invite viewers to bring their own meaning. If one hundred people visit one single monument, they will have one hundred different responses; in effect, because the response is integral to the commemorative intent, this means the single monument becomes one hundred different monuments. Here, again, the Vietnam Memorial is instructive. If a still grieving widow approaches the wall and lovingly runs her fingers over one name, the memorial takes on a specific meaning. If a veteran in full dress uniform approaches the wall and throws a crisp salute at another name, the memorial takes on entirely different meaning. In between these two will be

---

[12] See, for example, Paul Gough's interpretation in, "Canada, Conflict & Commemoration: An Appraisal of the New Canadian War Memorial in Green Park, London and Reflection on the Official Patronage of Canadian War Art," *Canadian Military History* 5, no.1 (1996): 26-34.

countless other shades of meaning.

Of course, one might argue that even traditional memorials drew forth a myriad of responses, which is perfectly true. If we look at a photograph of any war memorial unveiling from the 1920s or 1930s, we have no way of knowing what every single person in attendance thought of the monument, or what meanings they elected to draw from it. We can, however, interpret the meaning that the monument's creators *intended* it to elicit. Traditional monuments were didactic, instructing passers-by what to remember, the person or the event, but also how to remember it. Whether or not people chose to remember it in that way is another matter. The important point is that these memorials attempted to direct a response. As a result, the memorial becomes very useful to the historian. If it does not reveal what a community thought about an event (although I would argue that it *can* tell us quite a bit on that score[13]), at the very least it reveals what elites *wanted* that community to think about an event.

The postmodern memorial, in contrast, makes a virtue of *not* trying to direct a response. It still tells you what to remember, but says nothings about how to remember it. Such monuments attempt to permit multiple meanings, and even shifting meanings. They may be constructed of the same bronze or stone, but they strive for a degree of impermanence that almost contradicts the materials of which they are made. Where the traditional memorial tried to tell a story, the postmodern memorial provides a space in which people can tell their own story. The traditional monument was text; the postmodern monument is context. The Irish Hunger Memorial, in Battery Park, New York, for example, simply acts as a stage (a reproduction of a rural Irish landscape, complete with cottage and stone walls), while a collection of poems, songs, recollections, recipes, speeches, and declarations inscribed all over the monument provides an ever-changeable script.[14] On that stage and with that infinitely manipulable script, every viewer can perform their own commemorative act, each of which will be different because each personal response to the physicality of the memorial will be unique.

---

[13] Sarah Farmer's *Martyred Village: Commemorating the 1944 Massacre at Oradour-sur-Glane* (Berkeley: University of California Press, 1999) describes how locals rejected and ultimately ignored the memorial raised by regional elites, which they felt did not adequately express the meaning of the massacre.

[14] For details of the memorial, see http://www.bstterypsrkcity.org/ihm.htm

The combination of these three characteristics provides significantly greater challenges for the historian who intends to use the postmodern monument as source material. We can still take clues from the monument's location and from the debates which surrounded its erection. There is much to be learned, for example, from the debate over the placing of the memorial to tennis star and philanthropist Arthur Ashe, on Monument Avenue in Richmond, Virginia, which revolved around the politics of commemorating an African-American in a memorial space which, until then, had been largely reserved for whites, and white heroes of the Confederacy at that.[15] But we can no longer "read" a monument in the way that we once could, because the postmodern monument consists of two inextricably intertwined and mutually dependant parts: the physical monument itself, and the response of each viewer to it. If we try to read such a monument through a traditional analytic approach, we will be getting only half the story, and perhaps not the most important half at that.

However, if certain avenues of enquiry are much less revealing when applied to the postmodern monument, others have been opened up. We could learn a great deal from an analysis of the artifacts that are left at the Vietnam Veterans Memorial and catalogued by the National Parks Service. We could interview people about their responses to the memorial to the victims of the Oklahoma City bombing, a field of empty chairs, each representing one of the victims, and two monumental arches, which signify the before-and-after of the tragedy. We could even set up a camera and see how people interact with the

---

[15] See Sarah Shields Driggs, Richard Guy Wilson, and Robert K. Winthrop, *Richmond's Monument Avenue* (Chapel Hill: University of North Carolina Press, 2001), 87-96.

Famous Five Monument on Parliament Hill in Ottawa. Such approaches might reveal much about the human role in the postmodern commemorative process, an element which was simply not a factor in traditional modes of memorialization.

This, in turn, will demand a different kind of inter-disciplinarity from the historian. To work with traditional monuments, one was advised to become familiar with art history, classical studies, literary theory, and historical geography, in addition to the usual historical modes of analysis. Those skills are still required, but increasingly one will have to turn to conceptual models from anthropology, sociology, psychology, and cultural theory. In short, historians will have to focus less on the structure of the memorial itself, and more on the way humans interact with that memorial.

The one thing that we must keep in mind, though, is that commemoration remains a deeply politicized act. An armada of historians have convinced us that there is no such thing as an apolitical monument.[16] However, the postmodern monument propagates the fiction that it *is* possible to create an apolitical memorial. By stripping a monument of its meaning and letting viewers superimpose their own meanings, it holds the promise that we can somehow create a non-politicized monument.

This, of course, is nonsense. The very absence of an attempt to direct a response is, in itself, a kind of direction. In this context, we might return again to the Vietnam Veterans Memorial, which was defended by its most vociferous supporters as completely apolitical. As Jan Scruggs, the memorial's key organizer, put it, "The Memorial says exactly what we wanted to say about

---

[16] See, for example, James M. Mayo's persuasive *War Memorials as Political Landscape: The American Experience and Beyond* (New York: Praeger, 1988).

Vietnam – absolutely nothing."[17] For some opponents, this was precisely the problem; sculptor Frederick Hart's criticism was that the design was fatally flawed because "Lin's sculpture is intentionally not meaningful."[18] For other opponents, the wall had all too much meaning – it was the black gash of shame, the memorial to losers. Ironically, it was the right-wing critics of the wall who were correct: the wall *is* highly political (although not in the way they argued it was[19]), every bit as political as Frederick Hart's realistic sculptural grouping of soldiers. In a second level of irony, this grouping, which was added to assuage the complaints of traditionalists, has been seen by Wall supporters as a politicization of their ostensibly apolitical memorial.

Rather than going deeper into this rather circular argument that raged in Washington in the late 1970s and early 1980s, it is simply sufficient to make one observation: the very fact that both sides debated the issues so passionately affirms that the apolitical monument is a chimera. The very act of erecting a monument, regardless of its form, constitutes a political statement. But there is a key difference which has crept into the commemorative process of late. The traditional monument wore its politics openly, for all to see – it made no bones about the agenda it was seeking to push. The postmodern monument, on the other hand, hides its politics carefully; not only must they be teased out of the debate that surrounds it, but they are also ever-changing. This, perhaps, provides the ultimate challenge to future historians in this field: by inviting viewers to bring their own interpretations to the commemorative process, the postmodern monument can be all kinds of politics simultaneously.

---

[17] Quoted in Fred Turner, *Echoes of Combat: Trauma, Memory, and the Vietnam War* (Minneapolis: Anchor Books, 2001), 178.

[18] Quoted in Albert Boime, *The Unveiling of the National Icons: A Plea for Patriotic Iconoclasm in a Nationalist Era* (Cambridge: Cambridge University Press, 1998), 319.

[19] Turner argues that, with the wall, "the war's sharp edges have been sanded down and the conflict, now smoothed into a traditional tale of national altruism, has been slipped safely into the library of American myths." Turner, *Echoes of Combat*, 184.

– 15 –

The Evidence of Omission in Art History's Texts

Katherine Romba

Historians have long sought the assistance of written texts when examining the visual and material evidence of a culture, considering what is said in the writings of the time to be an important indicator of pertinent issues, themes, and perspectives regarding the object.

Art historians are no exception. They have looked to artists and architects - like Wassily Kandinsky and Le Corbusier - as well as to theorists and critics - like Charles Baudelaire and Clement Greenberg - for elucidation of the content and meaning of art and architecture. In addition, the rise in archival research has taken art historians beyond conventional, published accounts like the treatise or manifesto to such documents as personal correspondence and annotated manuscripts in their search for greater insight into artistic works.

Although these interpretive texts often occupy a privileged place in the art historian's research, their role as direct indicators of meaning has not gone unchallenged. Some art historians have been spurred by critics such as Roland Barthes to treat the language of images as distinct from that of a written text, and have explored the slippery relationship between the two.[1] Others have explored the mediated nature of the text, its capacity to misrepresent the intentions of the artist or the impressions of the observer, and the fissure between theory and actual practice.[2]

In addition, the work of some historians of art and material culture has compromised the status of the interpretive text as an important source of evidence altogether. Some, influenced by the integration of semiotics into the field of art history, treat the image itself like a text, and analyze it using written works not as sources or explanations but as linguistic parallels, comparing the visual language of paintings to the literary styles of the time.[3] Others have moved the focus away from artistic intentionality and placed it instead on the meaning projected by an object's consumers, users, and observers, and have concomitantly shifted the focus from the artist's explicatory text to the evidence offered by field studies and by physical cues taken from the art or artifact itself.[4] Finally, still others who study artifacts have posited a distinction

---

[1] This and other approaches can be found in the journal *Word and Image*, established in 1985 as "a journal of verbal/visual inquiry." For Roland Barthes' position on the relationship between word and image, see in particular his essay "The Rhetoric of the Image" in Stephen Heath, trans., *Image, Music, Text*, (London: Fontana/Collins, 1977).

[2] See Reyner Banham's *Theory and Design in the First Machine Age* (Cambridge: MIT Press, 1960).

[3] See Maria A. Schenkeveld's *Dutch Literature in the Age of Rembrandt: Themes and Ideas* (Amsterdam and Philadelphia: J. Benjamins, 1991).

[4] See Dell Upton, "Form and User: Style, Mode, Fashion, and the Artifact" in Gerald L. Pocius, ed., *Living in a Material World: Canadian and American Approaches to Material*

between art and artifact, asserting that while the intended meaning of an artwork can be elucidated in the artist's explanatory writings, the unconsciously embedded meaning of the artifact must be revealed through other means, such as through the visual metaphors communicated by an object.[5]

Since the 1990s, a new approach to the interpretive text has emerged. With this recent approach, the written text remains an important indicator of meaning; however, now the text's importance resides not with what is said but with what is *omitted* - or, more precisely, what lacks verbal articulation in explicit, literal terms. Historians take as the crux of their project the issue of why certain topics that are patently significant to the art under consideration have been excluded from the interpretive texts.[6] For example, Alina Payne, in her recent essay "Reclining Bodies: Figural Ornament in Renaissance Architecture,"[7] poses the question of why the figural ornament so prominent on Renaissance architectural facades "escapes" Renaissance architectural theory and "disappears into some form of collective blind spot[?]" By examining the literary tradition of Renaissance architectural theory, she deduces that this omission stems from the fact that Renaissance architectural theory takes as its literary model Vitruvius's famous architectural treatise *De architectura*. Vitruvius, an architect of the Roman empire, omitted ornament from his text, claiming that it was the concern of sculptors and painters, whose responsibility it was to dress the architectural framework in suitable ornament. Also impacting Renaissance theory was classical rhetoric, which Vitruvius himself found germane to the principles of architecture and which thereafter had a long history as a model for architectural theory. Classical rhetoricians had treated ornament as a distinct area of literary investigation worthy of its own "body of theory and critical vocabulary," and Renaissance architects followed suit, separating out discussions of ornament from their own writings on architectural "composition," presenting ornament as its own internally cohesive endeavour.

Payne asks if this omission from architectural theory truly means that Renaissance architects failed to consider figural ornament - including the caryatids, masks, terms, and reclining bodies of the facade - an integral part of their architectural designs. Using a formal analysis of the Renaissance facade, Payne argues that this reluctance on the part of architects to discuss ornament actually evinces a separation between theory and practice, and belies the actual integrated nature of ornament within the entire architectural vision. Payne

---

Culture (St. John's: Institute of Social and Economic Research, Memorial University of Newfoundland , 1991), 156-69.

[5] See Jules David Prown, "On the 'Art' in Artifacts" in Pocius, ed., *Living in a Material World*), 144-155.

[6] Unlike some historians who continue to comb the archives for new revelatory texts, these historians have turned to familiar textual sources with a fresh eye. As historian Mark Wigley describes it: "Rather than bring new archival material to the surface, it is a matter of looking at the evidence lodged in the public record, sitting right there in front of us, nestled between the lines of the all too familiar literature." Mark Wigley, *White Walls, Designer Dresses: The Fashioning of Modern Architecture* (Cambridge: MIT Press, 1995), xv.

[7] Alina Payne, "Reclining Bodies: Figural Ornament in Renaissance Architecture," in George Dodds and Robert Tavernor eds., *Body and Building: Essays on the Changing Relation of Body and Architecture* (Cambridge, Mass.: MIT Press, 2002).

claims that the figural sculpture plays an integral role in the architectural project by expressing symbolically the tectonics of structure. Thus, the sculpture "could and did slide between the artificial barriers" constructed by the architectural theory.

Frederic Schwartz similarly considers an investigation into the omissions of art theory a key to better understanding the constructed nature of the text. In *The Werkbund: Design Theory and Mass Culture before the First World War*,[8] Schwartz takes as the object of his investigation the collaboration of artists with industry in Weimar, Germany, and takes as his prime texts the writings of one of the premiere proponents of this collaboration, Walter Gropius, the founding director of the Bauhaus school of design. He questions why Gropius focuses his writings merely on "the production of commodities," with a "willful blindness to the rest of the object's life: its distribution, exchange and consumption[?]"[9] Schwartz claims that to answer this question one must examine an earlier body of theory on art and industry, that of the Deutscher Werkbund, an association of artists and industrialists, to which Gropius' writings were in many ways merely a conclusion. The Werkbund, the first major German artistic institution to recognize mechanized production as capable of artistic merit, produced a body of theory that gradually transformed the framework of the theoretical discourse to suit its aims. Gradually dropped from discussion were troublesome issues like the alienation of the workers, who were relegated to an industrial division of labour, and the estrangement of the consumer, who no longer knew the source of the goods. Terms like "industry" which still carried ambivalent messages for the future of artistic design were replaced with more neutral jargon like "technology." Not only Werkbund art theorists but also cultural critics and sociologists colluded in this effort. By the late teens and 20s, when Gropius was writing his Bauhaus manifesto and pedagogical statements, the discourse on art and industry had been cleanly stripped of its unsavoury attributes. When Gropius wrote of a new design approach combining "technology and art," he was contributing to an existing mythology of industrialization, in which industry was a new, praiseworthy system of production based on standardization, functionality, and objectivity.

As one final example I will turn to the work of architectural historian Mark Wigley. Wigley takes as his text the historiography of modern architecture, and, as his object, modern architecture itself. In his book *White Walls, Designer Dresses: The Fashioning of Modern Architecture*, Wigley points out that the ubiquitous white wall of the 1920s, which has become inseparable from modern architecture's identity, is rarely mentioned in the history of this architecture. Rather than provide some elucidation on modern architecture's penchant for the white wall, the histories tend to focus instead on modern architecture's new technology and functionality. He says that the white wall is "almost always looked at in passing, lightly, obliquely, held in the periphery of the discourse, if not the blind spots that occupy its center."[10] To

---

[8] Frederic J. Schwartz, *The Werkbund: Design Theory and Mass Culture before the First World War* (New Haven: Yale University Press, 1996).
[9] Ibid., 2.
[10] Wigley, *White Walls*, xv.

locate the reason for this omission he deconstructs the historical narratives of modern architecture that have appeared since the 1930s. Like Schwartz, he attempts to trace textual biases and boundaries back to their original formation, and finds that the theories and manifestos by architects of the 1920s already showed the seeds of the historiography's discursive framework. The modern movement in architecture was already portrayed as a style of cohesion and permanence due to its secure foundation in function, objectivity, and technology, and was contrasted to the fleeting "fashionable" styles of the nineteenth and early twentieth centuries. Wigley also discovers that popularizing texts on architecture - books written for a lay audience - provide some of the most telling accounts, for they articulate what the professional literature will not: that although modern architecture's austere white uniform contributes to a compelling sense of order and unity within this new architectural movement, certain pitfalls accompany the white surface, particularly the possibility that the omnipresent layer of paint will be associated with the superficiality and trendiness of fashion. Wigley concludes that "ignoring [the white wall] is one way of ignoring the internal contradictions that are at once the source of the strength of the architecture and the point of its greatest weakness."[11] Wigley claims that the historians of modern architecture, who often took a personal interest in promoting this architecture, attempted to "efface" the white wall because it was too closely associated with that which was considered unstable, evasive, or even regressive - fashion and the superficiality of the surface.

These three historians - Payne, Schwartz, and Wigley - have ultimately examined different material and achieved different conclusions, and yet the crux of each project is the same: identifying and interpreting textual omissions in order to achieve a better understanding of the constructed nature of the meanings attributed to art and architecture. The purpose of this essay is not to advance one historian's particular methodology over another but rather to expand generally on the validity of the "unarticulated" as compelling textual evidence.

As the preceding scholarship shows, blind spots in a text can ostensibly result from a variety of factors, including the structural or epistemological constraints of a theoretical discourse, as well as an attempt to represent a consistent ideological position. Alina Payne contends, for example, that the content of Renaissance architectural theory, ideally a reflection of architectural concerns, was shaped by the authority of both Vitruvius and antique rhetoric. Frederic Schwartz posits that Walter Gropius' pedagogical theories of design for the Bauhaus were just as much an expression of his own vision as they were Gropius' adoption of an ideological position and discursive framework already formulated by Werkbund theorists. And Mark Wigley argues that the historiography of modern architecture subscribed willingly to the propaganda originally put forth by the architects of the 1920s and to their obfuscation of one of modernism's exposed weaknesses.

To identify which factor or factors contribute to a textual omission, historians have, of course, examined closely the text itself. What is being said

---

[11] Ibid., xxi.

and what *is not*? But to ultimately gain perspective on why an omission occurs and what it means, historians have expanded the reach of their research beyond both the text and the object. The factors which contribute to textual omissions often only come to light when one situates the text in a broader context, when one examines the larger discourse within which it operates, or the political, economic, social, or cultural thought of the time, or even the biographical details of the text's author. Alina Payne, for example, investigates Renaissance architectural theory's reception of Vitruvius and classical rhetoric to gain a better perspective on the Renaissance architect's blind spots. Frederic Schwartz examines an earlier discourse on industry and art as well as sociological texts for perspective on Walter Gropius' theory of design. And Mark Wigley turns to popular texts on architecture to locate what the professional literature has cautiously omitted from its own theory.

Although these approaches to interpretive texts continue to put textual sources in the foreground of historical research, some scholars have combined verbal and non-verbal evidence with successful results. Alina Payne, for example, ultimately resorts to a more traditional tool of art historical research, a formal analysis of the art object itself, in order to more securely identify the intended role of Renaissance sculpture within the composition of the architectural facade. Examining the manner in which figural sculpture like standing and reclining nudes interact with the architectonic framework, she concludes that this sculpture was not intended to be original art in its own right, as is often the case with the religious statues found in the niches of Gothic facades, but rather was ornament created specifically to enhance the architecture, decorative devices which "allowed texture, light, shade, and movement to enhance the tactility of the architectural elements of the facade."[12] Specifically, the organic forms of the sculpture provide accents to the structural composition, like accentuating the swelling of a column, "and so enhance the carrying message of a pilaster or the heavy inert weight of a pediment."[13]

Using some of the strategies adopted in the aforementioned case studies, I examined in my PhD dissertation the texts by some well-known theorists of modern architecture, such as Hermann Muthesius, as well as by some important though now obscure writers, like Joseph August Lux. My area of research was German architectural theory from the Wilhelmine period (1890-1918) and specifically that theory which describes and analyzes the growing role of industrial materials in architectural design. The launching point of my investigation was the question of why this architectural theory lacks any substantial response to contemporary cultural criticism, which described at length industry's pernicious role in artistic culture.

My research began with establishing exactly what the architectural theory *did* say about industrial materials. During the Wilhelmine period, the majority of the architectural discourse on new materials focuses on iron - the first major industrial building material - and the changes it effects on architectural aesthetics. For instance, Hermann Muthesius, one of the most famous spokesmen for the Deutscher Werkbund, saw "new principles of

---

[12] Payne, "Reclining Bodies," 108.
[13] Ibid., 112.

design" and "expressive modern form"[14] embodied in the engineered iron structures of bridges, railway terminals, and exhibition buildings. Friedrich Naumann, another founding member of the Deutscher Werkbund, claimed that "the new iron constructions are the greatest artistic experience of our time,"[15] and Joseph August Lux, an editor and writer on the arts, predicted that "a new architecture is in the coming, the architecture of iron, which imparts to the modern age its stylistic character."

The fact that early modern architects and theorists would envision iron as effecting great formal and aesthetic change is not in itself odd. What does stand out as unusual however is that the architectural theorists - self-appointed protectors of German culture - would neglect to respond to growing debates on industrialization, and appear to be, on the whole, dismissive of the notion that industry and mechanized production could cause greater cultural alienation, even though such a view was in high circulation at the time.

Sociologists like Georg Simmel and Werner Sombart, cultural critic Julius Langbehn, and British art reformers like John Ruskin and William Morris (whose writings had been translated into German since the turn of the twentieth century) had all well explored the notion that industry could be a major impediment to a direct, authentic expression of culture. For these writers with cultural concerns, industrial materials and industrial production ran afoul of traditional notions of cultural expression, whose standard was still the handcrafted works of premodern society. The fact that industrial materials were no longer accessible to the tools and hands of the artist and artisan, and that factory production consisted of a division of labour, suggested to these theorists that the object produced would no longer satisfy the conventional standards of cultural expression, which included the personality of the maker, the traces of human engagement, and the inner spirit of the people.

As a response to this critical literature, one finds from the architectural theory only glib assurances, like Joseph Lux's statement that "the general public should view the work and progress of technology not as an impediment to culture, but rather as a tremendous bearer of culture,"[16] or blithe repudiations, like Friedrich Naumann's enthusiastic claims that "all our [modern] culture is made from iron hands" and that "the character of the period is found in the technology of metal."[17]

In an attempt to better understand this curious stance taken by the architectural theorists, I began a more rigorous examination of the cultural criticism itself. Had it definitively rejected the cultural role of industry, as I had originally thought? Or, conversely, had indeed the architectural theorists completely repudiated the cultural criticism? Would I be able to discern a deeper discursive relationship between the two bodies of theory?

This latter assumption was, in fact, proved correct: the more closely I read the cultural criticism, the more I detected a pronounced and sophisticated

---

[14] Hermann Muthesius, *Style-Architecture and Building-Art* (Santa Monica: Getty Center for the History of Art and the Humanities 1994), 79.
[15] Friedrich Naumann, "Die Kunst im Zeitalter der Maschine," *Schweizerische Bauzeitung* XLIV, no. 10, (1904): 113.
[16] Joseph August Lux, *Ingenieur-Aesthetik* (Munich, 1910), 2.
[17] Naumann, "Die Kunst im Zeitalter der Maschine," 113, 115.

response to it by architectural theorists. In their promotion of iron, the architectural theorists had refuted the conclusions of the cultural critics by immersing iron in a rhetoric of premodern values, presenting this industrial material in terms of the very subjectivity, personality, and feeling promoted in the cultural literature.

The strategy taken up by architectural theorists was one of bypassing a conspicuous stance against the cultural criticism in favour of a more subtle and insidious approach. What to the historian of the twenty-first century may at first appear to be architectural texts with egregious omissions are upon closer inspection actually vigourous articulations of a position, whose effect on an educated Wilhelmine audience would not likely have been lost. Indeed, the greater one's familiarity with the cultural writings of the day, the greater one's ability to perceive what the contemporary reader would have experienced: a text whose subtle yet compelling rhetoric portrayed industrial materials and industrial production as continuing to possess the values of premodern cultural expression. By infusing their discussion of industrial aesthetics with the poignant terms and symbols associated with the erstwhile, crafted arts, the architectural theorists in fact portrayed iron as a medium of pre-industrial cultural values. These texts, which surely would have appealed more to the heart than to the mind, provided the hope - however irrational - that iron would be no less than stone and wood a material of such premodern cultural ideals. Far from being sources of alienation, industrial materials would be direct, intimate expressions of German culture.

For example, in 1902 Hermann Muthesius made the following claims regarding industrial production: "The existence of the tool is certainly a given of our culture. The machine is, however, only an improved tool," and "The machine must be, like every improved tool, a blessing rather than a curse for mankind."[18] Such statements appropriate the poignant premodern symbol of the tool, as portrayed by socio-political writers like Karl Marx, who described the tool in *Das Kapital* as a natural, organic extension of the handcrafter. Marx contrasted the tool to the machine, which had subjugated factory workers, making them its own appendages. Muthesius' confident portrayal of the machine as merely an improved tool also drew on the strident, premodern visions of British art reformers like John Ruskin, who had characterized the tooled material as expressing - as he phrased it in *The Stones of Venice* - the "personality, activity, and living perception" of the handcrafter. Muthesius transposes the premodern symbolism of the tool into the service of modern industry in order to portray the machine and its products as capable of expressing human engagement. For example, he concludes that industrial structures like the iron bridge - far from being culturally mute and impregnable - have a "modern sensitivity recorded in them," express the "audacity and power of the human spirit," and "mirror the sensibility of our time, just as the richly acanthus-laden cannon barrel did the seventeenth century or the carved and gilded sedan chair the eighteenth century."[19]

---

[18] Muthesius, *Style-Architecture*, 90-91.
[19] Ibid., 79, 92.

Not only the symbols but also the normative ideals of premodern society played an important role in this rhetoric. In his book *Ingenieur-Aesthetik*, Joseph August Lux applied the typically premodern quality of personal expression to industrial forms. By the time of the book's publication in 1910, sociologist Georg Simmel had already expounded repeatedly on the cultural implications posed by industry, in particular the loss of a sense of the artist's personality. For example, in his essay "Persönliche und sachliche Kultur" (personal and objective culture), published in 1900,[20] Simmel contends that the more the methods of labour are divided and mechanized, "the less the personality of the labourer can be expressed through them, the less the hand of the labourer can be recognized in the product." By way of contrast, Simmel argues that the machine affects the product not as "an individualized personality but only as the executor of an objective, prescribed task." A decade later, Simmel continues this notion, claiming that art "has such an immeasurable cultural value precisely because it is inaccessible to any division of labour, because the created product preserved the creator to the innermost degree."[21]

Joseph August Lux seems to respond directly to Simmel himself when he claims regarding modern engineering, "It is a false belief that objectivity (*Sachlichkeit*) leads to impersonality (*Unpersönlichkeit*). On the contrary. Objectivity itself allows for far-reaching personal differentiation."[22] In fact, Lux claims that the contemporary carriage house, containing a whole range of modern vehicles, is a veritable "portrait gallery."

This leads me to another type of omission - an omission that is actually a coded message. Sometimes the operative question is not why something was edited out, but rather how language has been manipulated to include layers of meaning. As is the case with true omissions, several factors can lead to this encoding. As the texts of Hermann Muthesius and Joseph August Lux have shown, some writers must have wished to defy clear logic and appeal instead to the emotions, biases, and hopes of the reader. Such a strategy was a savvy recourse by the authors of the Wilhelmine architectural theory, for German sociologists and British art reformers (among others) had laid out in compelling detail the drawbacks of industrialization for society and culture. Through countless leaps in logic, using the poignant symbols and language of pre-industrial production, these architectural theorists were able to portray industrial materials as the new sites of premodern cultural values.

To say that a text has been encoded suggests conscious intention on the part of the author. However, the unconscious agency of the author can be implicated as well. Another possible interpretation of textual omissions, not illustrated here, uses the tools of psychoanalytic theory and posits the notion

---

[20] Georg Simmel, "Persönliche und sachliche Kultur," *Neue Deutsche Rundschau* 11, 7, 3rd and 4th Quarters in 2 Bd. (1900), 700-712.

[21] Georg Simmel, "On the Concept and the Tragedy of Culture," in *Georg Simmel, Georg Simmel: The Conflict in Modern Culture* (New York, 1968), 45-46; originally published as "Der Begriff und die Tragödie der Kultur," in Georg Simmel, *Philosophie der Kultur: Gesammelte Essais* (Leipzig, 1911), 245-77.

[22] Lux, *Ingenieur-Aesthetik*, 52.

that the unconscious plays a determining role in the composition of a text. Particularly useful for historians in this respect may be Jacques Lacan's work, which contends that the unconscious communicates in a disguised linguistic form. In order to outmaneuver the censorship of the Ego, the unconscious articulates its desires using literary devices such as metaphor and metonymy rather than literal meaning.[23]

Whether by identifying blind spots or encoded meanings, historians of "omissions" have developed a new means of interpreting familiar texts. Although this approach has changed the types of questions asked regarding a text, the answers are in many ways familiar. They continue to tell historians more about the creator's perspective and intentions as well as about the meanings ascribed to cultural objects over time and by various people and groups. They also continue to highlight the mediated and constructed nature of these meanings. In this way, the evidence of "omission" is merely a new approach to a larger, established project of discerning what interpretive texts say, how, and why.

---

[23] Madan Sarup, *An Introductory Guide to Post-Structuralism and Postmodernism* (Athens, Georgia: University of Georgia Press, 1993), 9.

– 16 –

Images
Mode(s) d'emploi

Mélanie De Groote

L'image est un mode d'expression fixé dans le temps et dans l'espace. Bien lue, elle fournit des éléments de compréhension sur une époque et un endroit donnés. Les qualités des images n'ont pas échappé aux historiens. Encore faut-il pouvoir les lire et les regarder, bien voir pour bien comprendre. Dans notre contribution, nous nous proposons de mettre en évidence les atouts et difficultés du discours iconographique comme source historique. Les historiens exploitent de plus en plus les témoignages figurés, essentiellement dans le secteur de l'histoire des mentalités. Les images portent en elles des signes de leur époque et de leur contexte de création et de diffusion. Elles permettent d'accéder au regard et à l'environnement visuel de leurs contemporains. Elles posent cependant de nombreuses difficultés épistémologiques et typologiques que nous soulevons et contribuons à résoudre dans ces quelques pages.

Après avoir développé une méthode d'analyse propre, nous exposerons une application concrète de nos réflexions sur la base d'un document spécifique, à savoir une fresque monumentale de Louvain-la-Neuve (Belgique) réalisée par un artiste wallon, Claude Rahir, et intitulée *Petites histoires d'une grande Université* (1984). Cette œuvre témoigne d'une atmosphère et d'un contexte particuliers à l'issue du déménagement de l'Université catholique de Louvain à Louvain-la-Neuve et Louvain-en-Woluwe suite au conflit linguistique qui l'a secouée. *L'affaire de Louvain* a fait couler beaucoup d'encre et a produit de nombreux documents figurés. Ces documents nous introduisent dans un passé flou et ambigu et nous permettent d'en saisir la portée émotionnelle, mais aussi événementielle. Dans ce contexte, la fresque de Claude Rahir témoigne de l'histoire et d'un héritage en perdition à l'usage des plus jeunes et de la mémoire collective ou individuelle.

Les images comme sources pour l'histoire

Bien que les ouvrages de critique historique s'attardent encore très peu sur le sujet, le terrain de l'analyse iconographique n'est ni vierge, ni en friche. Nous devons les premiers pas méthodologiques aux historiens de l'art (écoles allemande et autrichienne) et à leurs rapports privilégiés avec le monde des images. Dans la première moitié du XXe siècle, Erwin Panofsky fonde l'iconologie, science qui interprète le contenu et les conditions d'émergence des œuvres d'art. La sémiotique développera ses théories exposées dans *Essais d'iconologie* (1939). À partir des années cinquante, Ernst Gombrich utilise la psychologie expérimentale, les théories de la perception visuelle et les conventions sociales et historiques pour l'analyse artistique[1].

Les images contribuent progressivement à construire une histoire appelée histoire culturelle, histoire des mentalités ou encore histoire des représentations. L'histoire des mentalités est exploitée dès 1929 par l'école française des *Annales* et ses fondateurs, Lucien Febvre et Marc Bloch. Leurs efforts seront poursuivis par leurs successeurs[2]. Avec eux, l'histoire s'écarte du politique pour s'intéresser à l'économique et aux idées, aux structures mentales des sociétés (pratiques collectives, symboliques, représentations mentales). Les historiens des *Annales* privilégient la longue durée et la régularité sur l'histoire événementielle et singulière. Ils s'ouvrent aux autres sciences humaines. Les centres d'intérêts dominants des générations postérieures d'historiens des *Annales* deviennent l'économique, le social et le culturel[3].

Les images s'intègrent légitimement aux autres sources de l'histoire des mentalités dans la mesure où elles révèlent, à qui sait les lire, les visions du monde, les structures et les conjonctures sociales. Les mythes, les légendes, les représentations mentales, les symboles, les croyances conduisent l'historien des mentalités à une perception raisonnée des sociétés et des hommes[4]. L'image nous parle d'une époque et nous familiarise avec sa culture. À travers les documents iconographiques, nous nous imprégnons d'une société donnée et percevons progressivement son mode de vie, ses valeurs, ses aspirations, ses préoccupations, sa sensibilité, son système de pensée, ses représentations mentales, ses mythes, etc.[5]. Les images nous ouvrent des portes sur le passé à travers le regard de contemporains, elles sont le miroir des sociétés[6]. Le champ d'exploitation des images est très large, elles peuvent enrichir de nombreuses recherches historiques. Elles contiennent des informations de formes, de détails, de gestuelles difficilement décelables dans les autres types de sources (paysage, vêtements, mobilier, architecture, pratiques quotidiennes, vie intime, techniques, objets, etc.). Elles nous permettent d'accéder directement au réel, sans l'intermédiaire d'autres témoins. Les images portent en elles les besoins, les fantasmes, les opinions, les stéréotypes, les aspirations d'une époque et d'un espace donnés.

Les images sont des outils d'appréhension du passé : elles ne se limitent plus à corroborer une histoire déjà écrite, mais contribuent à la construire et en

---

[1] Laurent Gervereau, *Les images qui mentent : histoire du visuel au XXe siècle*, Paris, Seuil, 2000, p. 18.

[2] Nous n'entrons pas dans les débats relatifs à l'école des *Annales*, sujet trop éloigné de nos préoccupations immédiates. Nous exposons seulement les éléments pertinents pour nous dans la démarche de ces historiens et susceptibles de nourrir notre réflexion.

[3] Paul Ricoeur, *La mémoire, l'histoire, l'oubli*, Paris, Seuil, 2000, pp. 238-244.

[4] Ibid., p. 247.

[5] Dominique Serre-Floersheim, *Le passé réfléchi par l'image ou Comment décrypter notre histoire par l'image*, t. 2 : *Le 17e et le 18e siècles*, Les Éditions d'Organisation, Paris, 1995, pp. 11-13.

[6] L. Van Ypersele, « La caricature et l'histoire », dans L. Courtois et J. Pirotte (dir.), *Image de la Wallonie dans le dessin de presse (1910-1961). Une enquête dans la presse d'action wallonne*, Fondation wallonne P.-M. et J.-F. Humblet, Louvain-la-Neuve, 1993, p. 113.

sont à l'origine. Elles sont historiquement intéressantes au moins à deux titres : elles renferment non seulement des informations relatives à leurs codes et à leur histoire propre (histoire des techniques, des supports, des styles, etc.), mais aussi des indices sur leur temps (histoire des mentalités et des représentations)[7]. Le support, le format, les matériaux, le style et les techniques de composition d'une image sont inhérents à l'époque et au lieu de production. Ils renferment des informations très riches à leur sujet[8].

Les images sont des sources complexes. Le regard de l'historien sur les images n'est pas celui de leurs contemporains[9] : nous voyons le passé avec un ancrage dans l'ici et le maintenant. Les images sont produites dans un espace-temps et un but précis, pour un public particulier. Leur usage doit être nuancé, elles naissent toutes d'un dessein plus ou moins avoué et répondent à des commandes, à des genres qui déterminent leur message. L'historien doit retrouver les effets produits à l'époque et ultérieurement, transcender les frontières du temps et de l'espace.

La part de réalité qu'elles révèlent à des yeux avertis ou non est très relative, directement perceptible ou non. L'intérêt historique de certains documents semble d'emblée plus évident que d'autres, mais toutes les images intéressent les historiens car elles sont toujours en relation avec la réalité. Elles sont le produit et le dépositaire d'une époque et d'une société précises. Elles témoignent de leur existence dans le monde et de leur relation au monde[10]. Chaque image renferme une portion d'histoire à déterminer. Les images modifient ou déforment la réalité, mais ne sont pas en mesure de l'évacuer. Klee résume bien notre point de vue lorsqu'il dit : l'art ne reproduit pas le visible, il le rend visible[11]. Les images ne reproduisent pas le passé, elles le rendent visible.

Les images nous permettent d'accéder à l'image de la réalité, pas à la réalité elle-même[12]. Elles créent l'illusion du réel et procèdent de choix humains et techniques. Les images nous livrent une portion choisie de la réalité, un montage, une production de l'esprit, une vision personnelle du monde, pas sa copie conforme. Elles ne sont ni objectives, ni totalisantes. Elles font toujours l'impasse sur le contexte et le hors-champ[13]. La subjectivité de l'auteur et les contraintes techniques s'interposent entre le lecteur et la réalité[14]. L'artiste nous livre sa réalité, pas la réalité. Dans son acte créateur, il est influencé par le monde qui l'entoure et par ses expériences personnelles. Les images traduisent le rapport de l'homme au monde et à son époque. Les choix de l'artiste révèlent une part d'histoire (les contraintes techniques et sociales, les pressions, les tendances, les déterminismes historiques et sociaux qui pèsent

---

[7] N. Journet, « L'iconographie, témoin de l'histoire? », dans *Sciences Humaines*, Hors-série : *Le monde de l'image*, n° 43 (déc. 2003/jan.-févr. 2004), p. 56.
[8] D. Serre-Floersheim, op.cit., p. 16.
[9] Ibid., pp. 26-27.
[10] Ibid., p. 16.
[11] Ibid., p. 24.
[12] L. Van Ypersele, op. cit., p. 113.
[13] L. Gervereau, op. cit., p. 475.
[14] L. Hamm, *Lire les images*, Armand Colin, Paris, 1986, p. 22.

sur lui), mais aussi sa vie intérieure (son insertion dans l'histoire, dans un lieu, une société, une époque)[15]. L'image est une expression individuelle d'expériences collectives. Le vécu collectif sert de base à la création imagière[16]. L'esprit critique et le jugement de l'historien nous font passer de la « petite histoire », celle de l'artiste, à la « grande histoire », celle de la collectivité[17].

Une méthode d'analyse

Les analyses requièrent de la rigueur, du systématisme et de la méthode. Il faut cependant admettre que l'objectivité est une utopie dans une approche des images qui en appellent aux sens et aux émotions. Toute démarche historique se heurte au mirage d'une objectivité absolue : l'historien ne peut faire complètement l'impasse sur sa subjectivité et sa sensibilité. Son expérience, ses valeurs, son environnement intellectuel, social, politique et économique orientent sa démarche. La critique historique est le garde-fou de l'historien. Elle le maintient dans un cadre scientifique, mais n'évacue pas son humanité.

À la subjectivité de l'historien, ajoutons un autre constat. Une analyse de sources iconographiques n'a pas de prétentions globalisantes. Les analyses et les interprétations sont réductrices et parcellaires au regard de la complexité et de la multitude des images. Les études sont partielles et circonstanciées, elles n'abordent jamais toutes les images et n'ont pas de pouvoir de généralisation. L'accumulation des recherches et leur croisement permettront d'embrasser une histoire de plus en plus complète. Les images ouvrent le champ de la macro et de la microhistoire, la compréhension du global et du particulier.

La première étape d'une analyse est l'identification et la définition des sources, de la méthode d'exploitation, des outils d'analyse et d'interprétation, ainsi que des objectifs et du questionnement. La période, le vecteur et le thème des sources déterminent l'analyse, ses outils et son questionnement[18]. Chaque image, chaque corpus appellent une méthode et des outils propres. La méthode de base que nous proposons fonctionne pour de nombreuses recherches, mais les images provoquent chacune un regard et un questionnement spécifiques, déterminés par leur environnement, mais aussi par le chercheur, son regard, son vécu et sa relation avec la source, les réactions provoquées et ses affinités avec certains aspects de la démarche.

Le chercheur doit partir des images et les regarder très longuement à toutes les étapes de l'analyse. Les images et le corpus requièrent une longue observation. Bien regarder et bien voir c'est déjà comprendre. Le regard s'exerce par la théorie, mais surtout par la pratique. Il faut procéder de façon systématique, avec curiosité et imagination.

Notre approche repose sur cinq étapes essentielles : identification des sources, approche intuitive, contextualisation, inventaire et description, interprétations. Une synthèse reprend les résultats de chacune de ces opérations et les expose sous forme de bilan.

---

[15] D. Serre-Floersheim, op.cit., pp. 27-29.
[16] Ibid., p. 30.
[17] Ibid., pp. 13-15.
[18] L. Gervereau, op. cit., p. 23.

Première étape : Identification du document
Le premier contact avec le document passe par sa carte d'identité. Elle renferme des informations qui serviront de base à l'étude et à l'interprétation des sources : titre, auteur(s), date(s), type, support, techniques, dimensions, lieu(x), éléments textuels ou sonores joints. Établir la carte d'identité est une opération de critique externe classique : on interroge le document d'un point de vue extérieur sans entrer dans son contenu. Tous ces éléments sont des indices de son époque de création et de réception[19].

L'auteur est parfois difficile à identifier. On distingue l'auteur intellectuel qui a conçu l'image, l'auteur matériel qui l'a techniquement réalisée et l'auteur officiel qui prend la responsabilité de sa diffusion[20]. Les images connaissent plusieurs dates importantes à relever : date de conception, date de création, date(s) de diffusion. L'analyse et l'interprétation de la source tiennent compte de ces différentes périodes qui marquent le projet et sa réception. De même, les lieux de création, de publication et de conservation figureront dans l'analyse. Des diffusions successives provoquent chacune des réactions spécifiques à l'espace et au temps qui les conçoit et les reçoit.

Le type, le support et les dimensions du document agissent également sur la réception du message : une publicité, une caricature ou un roman-photos ne sont pas reçus de façon identique. Il en va de même pour les techniques de création et de diffusion qui répondent à des contraintes personnelles (maîtrise ou non d'une technique de dessin, par exemple), sociales et techniques. Les éléments textuels et sonores présents sur ou autour de l'œuvre informent sur l'orientation de l'image déterminée par les diffuseurs (signature, titre[21], légende, commentaire, article, support auditif, etc.). À ce stade, le chercheur se contente de les relever. Leur analyse intrinsèque relève de la description et de l'interprétation.

Une fois la carte d'identité établie, le document est soumis aux critiques d'authenticité et de restitution. La critique d'authenticité doit détecter les retouches ou trucages éventuels, leurs proportions et les intentions de l'auteur. Cette tâche est compliquée par les techniques numériques qui rendent les manipulations invisibles. La critique d'authenticité détermine si le document est effectivement ou non ce qu'il prétend être. Qu'il soit authentique ou non n'est pas problématique tant qu'on a identifié clairement sa vraie nature. Un faux doit être pris en compte comme témoin de l'histoire et objet d'étude. Il contient toujours une part d'histoire. S'il a été diffusé, il a participé à créer l'information et à influencer les mentalités de son époque. Il s'est intégré dans un environnement visuel. Son étude doit se demander pourquoi il a été manipulé, quelles étaient le(s) but(s) poursuivi(s) par l'émetteur. Les images ne mentent pas, mais leur utilisation peut être usurpée par manipulation du contenu (retouche ou trucage) ou par apposition d'un texte erroné ou abusif.

---

[19] D. Serre-Floersheim, op.cit., p. 16.

[20] J. Pycke, *La critique historique : un long chemin à parcourir entre le témoignage et la synthèse*, coll. « Pédasup », Academia-Bruylant, Louvain-la-Neuve, 2000 (3ᵉ éd.), pp. 72-76.

[21] Le titre sur l'œuvre n'est pas toujours le titre donné par l'auteur et repris plus haut dans l'analyse.

L'historien doit définir la nature du document et déjouer le piège des apparences. Les images ne constituent pas d'emblée la preuve de ce qu'elles montrent.

La critique de restitution recense les originaux et les copies d'une source. L'arbre généalogique du document permet de détecter les copies et de déterminer la filiation d'un original. La chronologie de la source (iconographie source, iconographie première, iconographie seconde) offre, entre autres choses, de distinguer le direct télévisuel, du différé et d'images d'archives. L'historien travaille de préférence sur base de documents originaux car les copies sont souvent de moindre qualité : les couleurs, par exemple, supportent mal le passage de l'original à la copie. Dans le cas où les copies sont plus facilement disponibles, il s'assure de leur conformité et des modifications apparues lors du copiage. Le document qui l'intéresse est celui qui a été transmis. Les aménagements opérés sur des images originales pour s'adapter au public sont des modifications volontaires, frauduleuses ou non, dont il tiendra compte. Les modifications involontaires comme la mauvaise résolution n'entrent pas dans son étude si elles n'ont pas rencontré de public.

Deuxième étape : Approche intuitive

Cette étape introduit l'affectivité et l'esthétisme reçus des images, ainsi que la dimension du plaisir et de la curiosité[22]. L'historien jette un regard présent sur le passé. Sa sensibilité modifie son regard et, indirectement, son approche. Les réactions spontanées et premières offrent une vision naïve et inconsciente de l'image. L'analyse a tendance à effacer les premières impressions et les sensations affectives, esthétiques et le plaisir suscités par l'image. Or, la lecture des images passe par la subjectivité de l'observateur et une analyse historique d'image doit être à la fois sensible et intelligente[23]. À ce stade, on consigne librement les premières impressions, jugements, opinions et interprétations personnels sur l'ensemble de l'image. En fin de parcours, ces éléments sont repris et intégrés à l'interprétation et à la synthèse finales.

Troisième étape : Contextualisation

Le contexte permet de retrouver le sens des images et rend leurs éléments identifiables et intelligibles[24]. La remise en contexte permet de dépasser le stade des intuitions, de relier les faits et leurs représentations. Localiser et dater le document le situe dans un contexte précis, inscrit son message dans une époque avec ses habitudes, ses modes, ses sensibilités et permet d'en percevoir toute la portée. Le contexte en amont concerne la création et la production des images; le contexte en aval, leur réception et leur consommation. Entre les deux, il y a leur diffusion. Le contexte de création et de production des images est riche en informations et donc en éléments explicatifs. L'image est un produit mixte où chaque acteur de l'offre intervient sur le résultat final (commanditaires, concepteurs, réalisateurs et producteurs). Il est essentiel de déterminer l'influence et les intentions de chacun. En cours de réalisation, les

---

[22] L. Hamm, op. cit., p. 26.
[23] D. Serre-Floersheim, op.cit., pp. 32-33.
[24] R. Arnheim, *La pensée visuelle*, Paris, Flammarion, 1976, p. 150.

influences qui s'exercent sur les auteurs sont nombreuses. Elles sont d'ordres technique, stylistique, thématique, biographique, économique, politique, géographique, culturel. On recherche l'idéologie, les habitudes, les automatismes qui régissent le comportement de l'auteur et du public, ainsi que les liens qui unissent l'artiste au thème représenté. La création d'une image et sa diffusion subissent des pressions (autocensure, censure politique, groupes de pression, censures déontologique, éthique, psychologique, sociale, morale, etc.), des contraintes et des conventions propres aux techniques, au budget, au milieu, aux modes et à l'époque.

Les moyens mis en œuvre pour diffuser et faire circuler les images déterminent en partie leur impact sur la société. Le diffuseur, le canal et l'étendue de la diffusion sont les éléments pris en compte pour évaluer le contexte de diffusion. Ils permettront de mesurer le poids des images sur une société donnée en fonction de la force de leur diffusion.

Le contexte de réception pèse sur l'offre imagière et sur le sens des images. Le créateur entretient une certaine connivence avec son public[25]. Pour jauger le destinataire, on évalue son nombre, son profil et ses réactions. De quel milieu provient-il? Quels sont ses influences et son état d'esprit avant, pendant et après lecture de l'image? Quels ont été les usages sociaux du document-source?

Quatrième étape : Inventaire et description

L'inventaire de ce qui est donné à voir relève de la dénotation. On procède de façon systématique du premier au dernier plan et de gauche à droite. Avec la plus grande neutralité possible, en se gardant de toute interprétation[26], on inventorie et on décrit les éléments constitutifs de l'image (procédés picturaux, composition, éléments iconiques, scripto-iconiques et textuels). La description doit être aussi objective que possible, même si cette étape est déjà en partie culturelle et connotée. Une bonne description dépend d'une observation approfondie et systématique. L'analyse prend appui sur cette base descriptive qui ouvre la compréhension de l'image et de son message. À l'issue de cette étape, on relève la thématique globale et le sens premier qui se dégagent de l'image.

Cinquième étape : Interprétations

La phase consacrée aux interprétations marque le passage d'une analyse naïve qui inventorie les éléments à une analyse structurale qui relève le rapport entre eux[27]. Le stade ultime de l'analyse repose sur les étapes précédentes. Retrouver les différentes connotations d'une image est un travail d'imagination et de symbolisation[28] qui repose sur la connaissance du contexte. La perception et le déchiffrement des images se fait à travers la subjectivité du spectateur. On cherche à pénétrer et à reconstituer les impressions de l'époque que l'on

---

[25] L. Van Ypersele, op. cit., p. 113.
[26] On avance avec prudence dans la description qui constitue déjà un méta-langage.
[27] Roland Barthes, « La rhétorique de l'image », *Communications*, n° 4 (1964), p. 43.
[28] B. Cocula et C. Peyroutet, *Sémantique de l'image. Pour une approche méthodique des messages visuels*, Delagrave, Paris, 1986, p. 39.

complète avec un regard contemporain et le savoir des livres. On intègre aussi impressions et sentiments personnels.

L'affaire de Louvain peinte par un artiste wallon

Nous avons étudié une peinture murale de Claude Rahir intitulée *Petites histoires d'une grande Université* et située à Louvain-la-Neuve (Belgique), rue de la Lanterne-Magique. Les éléments issus de la fresque que nous évoquons sont accompagnés d'un numéro en indice dans le texte. Nous vous invitons à vous reporter à l'annexe pour les visualiser sur une reproduction de la peinture de Claude Rahir.

Deux communautés linguistiques, Flamands et Francophones, pour une seule université en terre flamande : voilà en quelques mots exposée la problématique de l'*affaire de Louvain*. Unilingue depuis sa fondation, l'Université catholique de Louvain[29] se bilinguise lentement. Sa flamandisation commence timidement en 1911 par le dédoublement progressif des cours jusque-là dispensés exclusivement en français. La première moitié du XXe siècle à Louvain est traversée d'incidents et de révoltes étudiantes réclamant l'homogénéité culturelle de la Flandre. Durant les années soixante, la tension entre les deux communautés linguistiques atteint son apogée. Des événements nationaux y contribuent et annoncent la fédéralisation du pays. Sur le front louvaniste, les Francophones ne sont pas avantagés : engorgement progressif de la ville sous une démographie étudiante en pleine croissance; étudiants flamands plus nombreux que les étudiants francophones dès 1960-61; professeurs flamands préférés à leurs collègues francophones pour leur bilinguisme.

La situation dégénère complètement le 16 janvier 1968 : les positions des Flamands et des Francophones sont devenues inconciliables. Le combat s'étend aux autres villes flamandes et s'élargit aux luttes contre l'Église et le capital au pouvoir par un front ouvrier. L'Église de Belgique se divise; le gouvernement démissionne. Lors des élections législatives du 31 mars, les partis traditionnels reculent au profit des formations fédéralistes et le gouvernement ouvre la voie au transfert de la section francophone hors de Flandre. En 1970, la loi promulgue l'existence de deux universités autonomes : l'Université catholique de Louvain (UCL) et la Katholieke Universiteit Leuven (KUL). Le 1er février 1971, le roi Baudouin pose la première pierre de Louvain-la-Neuve, ville nouvelle qui accueillera l'UCL en Wallonie. Le conflit linguistique entre Flamands et Wallons, ainsi qu'une surpopulation étudiante et un contexte politique en crise ont eu raison de l'Institution et forcé la section francophone à déménager dans le Brabant wallon et dans la périphérie de Bruxelles, pour la Faculté de médecine. Les 800 premiers étudiants et les premiers habitants

---

[29] La fondation de l'Université de Louvain remonte à 1425. L'institution est supprimée en 1797 par l'occupant français. En 1817, une université d'État est ouverte à Louvain. En 1834, Malines voit l'érection d'une université libre catholique qui retrouvera les murs de Louvain en 1835, peu après la fermeture de l'Université d'État. L'Université catholique de Louvain est née sur les fondations de l'ancienne Université de Louvain fondée en 1425.

s'installent à Louvain-la-Neuve en octobre 1972. En 1979, la dernière Faculté, celle de Philosophie et lettres, emménage.

Dans ce contexte perturbé, Claude Rahir, un artiste wallon, commence une peinture murale à Louvain-la-Neuve, le 15 mars 1984, soit cinq ans après la fin du déménagement. Son projet s'inscrit dans les préoccupations des créateurs de Louvain-la-Neuve qui souhaitent développer la ville culturellement et réclament « plus de couleur et moins de minéral dans cette ville déjà dominée par la brique et – modérément, nous y avons veillé – par le béton[30] ».

Claude Rahir est né en 1937 à Verviers. Depuis ses études[31], il s'est installé à Louvain. Instituteur de formation, il a enseigné au lycée *Virgo Sapiens* à Louvain avant de se lancer dans une carrière d'artiste. Ses ambitions ont pris forme dans un atelier prêté par l'Université, dans lequel il organise des cours d'art pour les enfants et des expositions. Lorsque l'UCL est transférée, il obtient de nouveaux locaux à Louvain-la-Neuve.

Pour professionnaliser son art, il a suivi des cours de peinture (Institut supérieur des beaux-arts Saint-Luc à Liège), de sculpture (Académie de Louvain) et de mosaïque (Ravenne, Italie). Son œuvre renferme des mosaïques murales, des bas-reliefs, des sculptures, des arrangements de jardins et fontaines en matériaux bruts, des peintures monumentales. Ses compositions comptent souvent plusieurs centaines de mètres carrés. Il exerce son art à travers le monde et travaille généralement à ciel ouvert, au vu de tous. Il a également produit des œuvres bibliographiques et des livres d'art. Ses efforts ont été couronnés de nombreux prix.

Nous retrouvons deux peintures murales de Claude Rahir à Louvain-la-Neuve (*Les âges de la vie*, 1976, place Agora; *Petites histoires d'une grande Université*, 1984, rue de la Lanterne-Magique), ainsi qu'une fresque et une mosaïque à Louvain-en-Woluwe (cliniques universitaires Saint-Luc). Ce n'est pas un hasard, car Claude Rahir est proche de l'Université[32].

En tant que muraliste, il participe à l'évolution d'un genre qui remonte, de loin, aux grottes préhistoriques et aux tombeaux pharaoniques; de près, au muralisme mexicain des années 1920. Du fait de sa fonction décorative, la peinture monumentale s'est toujours accommodée des monuments publics, mais aussi des habitations privées, à l'instar de la tapisserie et du vitrail. Sa diffusion est favorisée par l'aspect économique : la peinture murale permet de couvrir de grandes surfaces à moindres frais. La fresque[33] fait physiquement et chimiquement corps avec son support. Les matériaux de recouvrement employés sont des matériaux architecturaux. En Italie, beaucoup de monuments étaient construits pour recevoir des fresques, chose beaucoup moins courante au XXe siècle, où une fresque vient souvent cacher un mur gris et un espace sombre.

---

[30] M. Woitrin, *Louvain-la-Neuve/Louvain-en-Woluwe : le grand dessein*, éd. Duculot, 1987, p. 221.

[31] Après une année en Philosophie à l'UCL, il entreprend avec succès une formation d'instituteur à Louvain.

[32] Il a fait des études à Louvain et fréquentait beaucoup de professeurs de l'Université au lycée *Virgo Sapiens*. De plus, l'UCL lui a procuré successivement deux ateliers.

[33] Le terme « fresque » englobe aujourd'hui une réalité abusive. Il s'agit à l'origine d'une technique de peinture (*fresco*) à base de chaux, de sable et de pigments.

Le muralisme renaît en Amérique latine, dans la première moitié du XXe siècle, et particulièrement au Mexique où, sous les pinceaux révolutionnaires de Rivera, Orozco et Siqueiros, il devient un art expressionniste national et populaire, inspiré de la peinture murale précolombienne. Les thèmes muraux mexicains sont réalistes et d'inspiration idéologique : épisodes héroïques de l'histoire du continent, travail et luttes sociales. À la fois art et idéologie, le muralisme allie des traditions picturales mexicaines à des composantes esthétiques marxistes-léninistes. Le muralisme du XXe siècle atteindra les États-Unis (Stuart Davies et Ben Shan) et l'Europe. L'art mural américain des années septante est souvent collectif et exprime les combats sociaux, ethniques et raciaux. En France, il critique la société de consommation et les politiques. Le muralisme s'adapte aux exigences du temps et de l'espace : d'une peinture épique populaire et didactique, il est devenu art de rue décoratif, souvent dépourvu de message idéologique. L'idéologie en moins, Claude Rahir est un digne héritier de Rivera dont on retrouve les thèmes (actualité, folklore, références personnelles, portraits officiels) et le style (patchwork très coloré et réaliste). L'auteur se charge d'une mission de témoin et met en scène une société et son temps.

Le projet de Louvain-la-Neuve part d'une initiative de l'artiste. Un mur immense de 60 mètres de long sur 13 mètres de haut (superficie totale de 668 m^2) l'inspirait depuis quelques temps déjà. Cette énorme surface grise et triste n'attendait que ses pinceaux. Elle se trouvait à un endroit stratégique devant un espace ouvert à l'entrée de la ville et était visible des hauteurs et de la voie ferrée.

L'artiste a d'abord photographié le mur. Il a tiré de son cliché un poster sur lequel il a peint un projet pour le premier tiers du mur et l'a soumis aux autorités de l'Université. Ses faibles exigences financières (il ne demandait que l'équivalent du prix pour repeindre le mur en blanc), ainsi que le thème de la murale ont suscité un avis favorable. S'il a bénéficié d'une totale indépendance dans l'expression de son art, l'institution gardait entière liberté quant à l'avenir du mur. Aussi, en 1987, il est décidé que la construction d'un bâtiment pour l'IAG (Institut d'administration et de gestion) est devenue prioritaire. La réalisation des fondations commence en 1988. En 1991, la nouvelle construction recouvre plus de 90 p. cent de la murale. Maigre consolation pour l'artiste, elle est protégée par une couche de frigolite et constitue le premier vestige archéologique de Louvain-la-Neuve.

Le premier tiers de la composition suivait un plan préalablement soumis aux autorités académiques. La deuxième partie, soit les deux derniers tiers, s'est construite au jour le jour, selon la vie sur le site, des coups de cœur et des enquêtes auprès des facultés. Claude Rahir a également invité les étudiants à inscrire sur son œuvre quelques vers d'un poème d'amour de leur choix.

La peinture murale monumentale requiert des techniques et des matériaux particuliers. Claude Rahir emploie de la peinture pour bâtiment. Il choisit une couleur de base qui recouvre environ 70 p. cent de la surface à peindre. Dans ce cas-ci, la tonalité principale est le rouge, décliné en clairs, foncés, carmin, vermillon, orange, etc. Les couleurs complémentaires sont en l'occurrence les verts (20 p. cent), les jaunes (5 p. cent) et les bleus (5 p. cent).

L'artiste travaille dans une nacelle suspendue au mur. Cette technique l'oblige à peindre par bandes verticales de 6 mètres, sans possibilités de retouches, ni de recul. Il n'a pas l'occasion de quadriller une si grande surface pour organiser ses traits. Mais, à Louvain-la-Neuve, le béton était marqué tous les 40 cm par les points de serrage du coffrage qui lui ont fait office de quadrillage. Il descendait de la nacelle et faisait un polaroïd de la surface à peindre, polaroïd sur lequel il dessinait son projet à l'aide des repères du serrage. Il reportait ensuite ses traits sur le mur.

La fresque marquerait le plus distrait des passants à plus d'un titre : sa nature même de peinture murale; sa superficie ($668m^2$); sa situation; les tons criards; la thématique. Elle se regarde, ou se « lit », instinctivement de gauche à droite et de haut en bas, comme une bande dessinée qui raconterait l'histoire de l'Université. Un premier coup d'œil nous renvoie une œuvre monumentale, aux couleurs vives et accrocheuses, agressives selon certains. Des portraits, des bâtiments, des paysages et des citations se dégagent de l'énorme patchwork constitué par des éléments directement ou indirectement liés à l'Université et à la vie à Louvain, Louvain-la-Neuve et Louvain-en-Woluwe. La composition est constituée de « flashs » et d'épisodes symboliques ou simplement représentatifs des patrimoines matériel, culturel et intellectuel louvanistes et néolouvanistes. Elle renferme également des représentations de la Wallonie.

La murale se compose de deux « chapitres » principaux : l'Université à Louvain et l'UCL en Wallonie et à Bruxelles. Le premier tiers évoque l'Université ancienne dès sa fondation. La murale est structurée par des événements, des bâtiments et des hommes qui ont fait l'histoire de l'Université à Louvain. La partie qui lui est consacrée est plus courte et plus dense que la suite de la peinture. La deuxième partie de la fresque recouvre deux tiers du mur. Elle fait état de la vie et des recherches à l'UCL francophone. Claude Rahir intègre l'histoire des facultés et de l'Université à l'histoire et au patrimoine de la Wallonie. Le mode de réalisation des deux parties influe sur l'aspect global de la fresque. La partie ancienne a été pensée et couchée sur papier avant sa réalisation. La seconde a été travaillée au quotidien, par bandes verticales, pour répondre aux contraintes matérielles du mur et de la nacelle. Aussi, le début de la murale est-il construit et dense, alors que la suite est plus instinctive et plus aérée.

D'emblée, nous relevons des éléments en rapport direct avec l'institution et d'autres plus proches de l'auteur. Nous envisageons les éléments constitutifs de la fresque comme faisant partie d'un tout et les traitons en fonction de leur place et de leur signification dans cet ensemble. Parcourons rapidement la composition de Claude Rahir en commençant par la première partie consacrée à l'Université ancienne, avant de décrire la seconde partie qui exprime la vie des étudiants à Louvain-la-Neuve et Louvain-en-Woluwe.

Première partie : L'Université ancienne

Le pape Martin V_1 inaugure la fresque et l'histoire de l'Université. Il est représenté assis sur un trône. Il porte la tiare et le manteau de pourpre. C'est ainsi que les papes sont systématiquement représentés à partir du Xe siècle. Il tient sur ses genoux un document qui serait la bulle de fondation de l'Université de Louvain délivré par ses soins le 9 décembre 1425. La fresque s'ouvre naturellement sur l'acte fondateur de l'Université.

La première partie évoque l'Université ancienne à travers ses personnalités (autorités$_{11}$, professeurs$_{12}$, étudiants$_{14}$), ses bâtiments (Hôtel de ville$_2$, Halles$_{10}$) et son temps (Léonard de Vinci$_4$, Christophe Colomb$_5$). Claude Rahir s'est inspiré de documents anciens comme un dessin attribué à Jean van Eyck^{34} (Jean IV$_3$), une gravure de Gramaye^{35} (les Halles$_{10}$), une peinture de Pieter Bruegel l'Ancien^{36} (*Danses de noce*$_{15}$).

La *Sedes sapientiae*$_{16}$ ou *Siège de la sagesse*, haute de 10 mètres, domine largement la composition. Elle est, depuis 1909, l'emblème de l'Université et est toujours la patronne de l'UCL et de la KU Leuven. Elle fait la charnière entre les deux parties de la fresque.

Deuxième partie : les perspectives de l'UCL après le transfert

La seconde partie de la fresque est consacrée à la Wallonie et aux sites de Louvain-la-Neuve et de Louvain-en-Woluwe. Nous y avons relevé cinq thématiques essentielles :
- Le patrimoine wallon (les charbonnages et l'industrie sidérurgique$_{19}$, les richesses naturelles de la Wallonie$_{20}$, son patrimoine architectural$_{30}$ et culturel$_{32}$);
- L'espace et la conquête spatiale$_{17}$ témoignent d'un contexte scientifique et d'une émulation de la recherche à l'échelle mondiale, mais aussi d'un intérêt particulier de la part de Claude Rahir;
- La recherche à l'UCL et dans les facultés (le développement des relations nord/sud$_{24}$ et la faculté des Sciences agronomiques, le chanoine Georges Lemaître et la théorie du « Big bang »$_{25}$, le cyclotron$_{22}$, le cardinal Mercier$_{27}$ et la doctrine philosophique rénovée de saint Thomas, etc.);
- Les bâtiments et l'architecture particulière de Louvain-la-Neuve$_{29}$ et de Louvain-en-Woluwe$_{31}$, deux villes construites de toutes pièces pour accueillir les étudiants francophones;
- La vie sur le site de Louvain-la-Neuve$_{23}$.

La fresque comprend plus de 60 éléments textuels de l'Antiquité à 1984, à savoir 35 citations, trois extraits de partitions musicales, une formule mathématique et des indications complémentaires à caractère descriptif. Les 35 citations proviennent de 22 pays différents répartis sur quatre continents (Afrique, Asie, Amérique et Europe). Les textes sont retranscrits dans la langue et l'alphabet du pays correspondant. Ils sont souvent accompagnés du nom de l'auteur, de sa nationalité, parfois du titre et de la date de l'extrait. Ils ont été choisis par Claude Rahir, par des gens de passage ou par des étudiants.

On le constate, la fresque de Claude Rahir est très riche. Elle possède plus d'une centaine d'éléments visuels distincts. L'ensemble prend vite sens pour le passant qui capte des bribes à chacun de ses passages et reconstitue son

---

[34] *Jean IV, Duc de Brabant de 1415 à 1427*, dessin attribué à Jean van Eyck, Rotterdam, Musée Boymans-van Beuningen.
[35] Gravure extraite de J. B. Gramaye, *Antiquitates illustrissimi ducatus Brabantiae*, 1610, KUL, BC.
[36] *Danses de noce*, peinture sur bois (119 x 157 cm), 1566.

imaginaire universitaire. La fresque avait un impact d'autant plus fort qu'elle était facilement compréhensible, en tout ou en partie. Son sujet et l'expression de ce sujet sont en effet très abordables. L'image est multilingue, elle marque davantage que les textes et est plus vite perceptible. Le choix des couleurs, les jeux de perspectives et de proportions font qu'une image reste plus ou moins longtemps en mémoire : la prégnance d'une forme est sa capacité à capter l'attention et à résister aux perturbations[37]. Dans ce cas-ci, les couleurs vives et le gigantisme de l'œuvre interpellent.

Claude Rahir a peint sa vision de l'Université, en fonction de son vécu et de ses lectures. Sa source d'inspiration principale est un ouvrage consacré au 550e anniversaire de la fondation de l'Université de Louvain[38]. Il a aussi rencontré des membres de l'UCL qui lui ont confié souvenirs et documents.

Le titre de la murale, *Petites histoires d'une grande Université*, évoque les partis pris de l'auteur. Le contenu n'est pas encyclopédique, mais épisodique, voire anecdotique. L'auteur a procédé à des choix arbitraires qui relèvent de ses sources et de ses affinités. Le titre traduit également une grande estime pour l'institution représentée.

La plupart des éléments visuels choisis par l'auteur sont récurrents dans l'iconographie universitaire : la *Sedes Sapientiae*$_{16}$, les Halles de Louvain$_{10}$, les gloires de l'Université (Vésale$_8$, Erasme$_7$, Mercator$_6$, etc.), la bibliothèque des Sciences de Louvain-la-Neuve$_{28}$, etc. L'image transmise est conforme à celle véhiculée par l'Université lorsqu'elle se met en scène ou se représente à l'occasion d'un anniversaire, d'une publication, d'un doctorat *honoris causa*. Au fil des siècles, l'Université s'est créé une image sur la base des événements et des personnalités de son histoire et à partir des lieux qui ont abrité cette histoire. Elle les exploite afin qu'ils servent au mieux ses intérêts, sa reconnaissance et son rayonnement.

La *Sedes sapientiae*$_{16}$ domine la murale. Elle réalise la jonction, ou le relais, entre Louvain et Louvain-la-Neuve, entre la Flandre et la Wallonie, entre la KUL et l'UCL. Elle marque une certaine continuité entre ces paires. La Flandre est à gauche, elle représente le passé et 550 ans d'histoire commune. La Wallonie est à droite, elle incarne le présent de 1984 et l'avenir de l'UCL. L'Université à Louvain-la-Neuve et Louvain-en-Woluwe s'inscrit dans la continuité de l'Université de Louvain fondée en 1425 et revendique son héritage commun. Il y a un jeu de rejet et d'attraction entre Louvain et l'UCL. La fresque est une affirmation de l'identité de l'UCL par rapport aux Flamands, dans un contexte de frustration et d'exacerbation des spécificités de chacune.

La toponymie, le nom des auditoires, le folklore et les traditions universitaires (cortège académique$_{12-14}$) sont des référents historiques qui enracinent l'Université dans la durée. L'UCL s'accroche à un passé qui dort à 30 km à peine, mais qui semble si lointain. L'architecture moderne abrite une institution vieille de « 575 ans ». En déménageant de Louvain, les Francophones ont définitivement perdu le prestige patrimonial et culturel, d'autant qu'au fil des générations, le souvenir de Louvain s'affaiblit et tend à

---

[37] B. Cocula et C. Peyroutet, op. cit., pp. 15-17.
[38] *L'Université de Louvain (1425-1975)*, Presses universitaires de Louvain (UCL), Louvain-la-Neuve, 1976.

disparaître. Les étudiants parlent maintenant de « Louvain » pour désigner « Louvain-la-Neuve », par opposition à « Leuven », une université flamande. Nous pouvons craindre que les générations futures finissent par ignorer que leur Université tire sa source en Flandre, à Louvain (Leuven). Le passé de l'UCL est plus perceptible dans la vieille ville flamande qui en est profondément marquée jusque dans la pierre.

Au milieu de cette pauvreté mémorielle, la fresque de Claude Rahir témoigne de la richesse du patrimoine de l'Université depuis 1425. Le passé de l'Université est à Louvain, c'est là qu'elle puise ses racines, mais son présent et son avenir sont en Wallonie. La murale permet à l'UCL de se raccrocher à son passé commun avec la KUL et d'en assumer l'héritage. Elle s'adresse aux étudiants et ravive le souvenir de leurs racines. En 1984, elle voulait les réconforter et les rapprocher de Louvain qu'ils avaient dû quitter sous la pression flamande. Claude Rahir veut asseoir Louvain-la-Neuve sur des fondations, donner une âme à ce que certains appellent encore parfois « la ville sans âme » et l'inscrire dans une continuité historique.

Le discours iconographique est en lui-même suffisamment explicite pour ne pas nécessiter un soutien textuel. Les textes ne sont pas indispensables pour la compréhension de la fresque. Ils orientent le parcours du passant et le guident sur les pas de l'artiste. Ils précisent le sens et accentuent le message de la murale. L'image est ici autosuffisante, pour autant que le spectateur ait quelques connaissances de l'Université et de la Wallonie. Texte et image ont des fonctions et des codes propres, mais dans ce cas précis, on ne sort pas forcément du cadre de notre analyse basée essentiellement sur l'image. En effet, on peut reconnaître un caractère iconique aux alphabets étrangers (arabes, asiatiques, cyrillique) et aux autres langages (mathématiques ou scientifiques). Ils apparaissent comme une image d'un monde étranger, d'une culture scientifique ou ethnique lointaine et signifient l'altérité, la science ou l'excellence.

La fresque fait cependant l'impasse sur les crises rencontrées par l'Institution, les guerres et *l'affaire de Louvain*. Les XVIIe, XVIIIe et XIXe siècles sont également absents de la murale. L'artiste n'a pas trouvé dans ces siècles de possibilités suffisamment illustratives, rien ne lui parlait ou ne l'inspirait pour cette période. Par ailleurs, des bâtiments emblématiques et certaines célébrités de l'Université ne sont pas représentés alors qu'ils apparaissent traditionnellement lorsque l'Université affirme son identité. Le peintre a forcément dû choisir. Ses choix sont orientés par les sources à sa disposition, par ses souvenirs d'étudiants, ses sensibilités et par des éléments plus symboliques ou anecdotiques. Quoi qu'il en soit, il n'a jamais prétendu à l'exhaustivité, seulement à la représentativité et à l'exaltation. La composition se veut profondément positive, tout concourt dans ce sens : les couleurs vives, le choix des illustrations, certains symboles (phénix$_{18}$, colombes$_9$, fleurs$_9$), les formes tout en rondeur. Claude Rahir a peint une image rassurante et positive.

Bilan

Petites histoires d'une grande Université exprime l'état d'esprit aux lendemains du transfert de l'UCL en Wallonie et à Bruxelles. Les Néolouvanistes sont toujours nostalgiques du prestige et de la beauté de la ville de Louvain. Louvain-la-Neuve n'a pas l'âme et l'histoire de la vieille cité, mais ses habitants se consolent par sa modernité (« -la-Neuve ») et son ouverture sur le monde.

Claude Rahir transmet l'exaltation positive de l'époque. Le projet de l'UCL en région francophone a été porté à bout de bras par des ambitieux déterminés à faire rayonner l'Université et la ville, à l'inscrire dans une continuité, à lui donner une histoire, à la légitimer. La fresque a contribué à asseoir l'institution dans une continuité historique et a participé au rayonnement de l'Université (Michel Woitrin[39], en visite officielle en Asie, a d'ailleurs offert à ses hôtes un poster de la murale pour figurer l'UCL). Malheureusement, les étudiants d'aujourd'hui ne soupçonnent pas la richesse qui dort derrière le mur mitoyen.

L'université dessinée par Claude Rahir ne reflète pas strictement la réalité. Elle est embellie et positivée à l'excès. Elle alimente le message que l'Université aime à répandre d'elle-même, avec des vides historiques et des licences mythologiques ou poétiques. Elle chante la gloire de l'UCL et de ses membres. Inconsciemment ou pas, l'artiste est tributaire de l'Institution et reflète son auto-représentation historique classique.

La murale provenait de motivations strictement personnelles et n'avait alors suscité que peu d'égard de la part des autorités (inauguration intime, disparition rapide). Elle avait surtout l'avantage de cacher une grande surface de béton peu joyeuse. Maintenant, nous la regardons avec nostalgie. Tout comme pour les événements des années 60-70 et la naissance des sites de Louvain-la-Neuve et de Louvain-en-Woluwe, les circonstances tendent à s'effacer derrière une reconstitution plus lyrique des faits. L'histoire de l'Université traverse les siècles à son insu, parfois elle les guide.

Les priorités et les voies d'exposition de l'Université ont évolué. Les préoccupations de Louvain-la-Neuve et Louvain-en-Woluwe à leurs débuts sont de montrer l'Université par la culture. Les deux jeunes sites souffrent d'un sentiment d'infériorité par rapport à leur grande sœur flamande (ils garderont d'ailleurs de nombreux référents à Louvain dans la toponymie jusque dans le choix du nom des deux nouvelles villes) et doivent faire leurs preuves. Aujourd'hui, l'accent est mis davantage sur la science et l'excellence européenne. Une constante : l'Université a toujours offert une certaine visibilité à ses contemporains dont elle cherche une reconnaissance et une légitimation historique et/ou scientifique.

Conclusion

L'image est un principe d'action et de transformation sociale et culturelle, individuelle et collective. Elle fait surgir le réel sur un mode et des codes qui lui sont propres. Elle nous informe sur le regard d'une époque et ses systèmes de représentation. À ce titre, notamment, elle représente pour nous une source pertinente et riche. Mais l'historien doit se méfier des apparences : l'image ne se limite pas à ce que l'on voit ou à ce qu'elle montre. De nombreux facteurs, individuels ou collectifs, personnels ou culturels, viennent orienter la lecture qui en est faite, consciemment ou pas. Nous regardons ce que notre société, notre culture, notre environnement nous ont appris à

---

[39] Administrateur général de l'UCL à l'époque.

regarder. Les images obéissent à des codes dont la lecture et le décodage sont fonction de l'espace-temps de création, de diffusion et de réception. À chaque étape, les images accusent de nouvelles significations en circulant.

Les fabricants d'images exploitent leurs caractéristiques et leurs modes d'action. Le récepteur n'est pas toujours conscient de leurs pouvoirs et de leurs actions sur lui. Qu'elles le poussent à l'achat, à l'adhésion ou à la séduction, le lecteur doit rester vigilant et lucide devant un média si pervers et subtil. Nous voudrions encourager l'enseignement des codes et des fonctionnements des images. Nous voudrions en particulier que les enfants et la jeunesse deviennent un public averti et puissent agir et choisir en connaissance de cause, après l'exercice d'un esprit critique affûté par une éducation adaptée à notre monde contemporain.

Vous l'aurez compris, notre travail poursuivait trois objectifs : sensibiliser les historiens aux intérêts d'exploiter les documents figurés au même titre que les sources traditionnelles; promouvoir l'apprentissage de la lecture des images dès le plus jeune âge dans l'enseignement officiel; élaborer une méthode d'analyse des sources iconographiques. Les deux premiers découlent d'un constat et de préoccupations personnelles. Le troisième répond aux besoins de nos recherches. Ces objectifs ne pourront se réaliser complètement sur le court terme et nécessiteront l'investissement de nos lecteurs. En effet, pour convaincre nos collègues et changer, ou faire évoluer, les travaux historiens, il faudra que nos convictions soient relayées par des professeurs et des chercheurs reconnus par leurs pairs.

De Groote, *Images : mode(s) d'emploi*

Annexe : *Petites histoires d'une grande Université*[40]

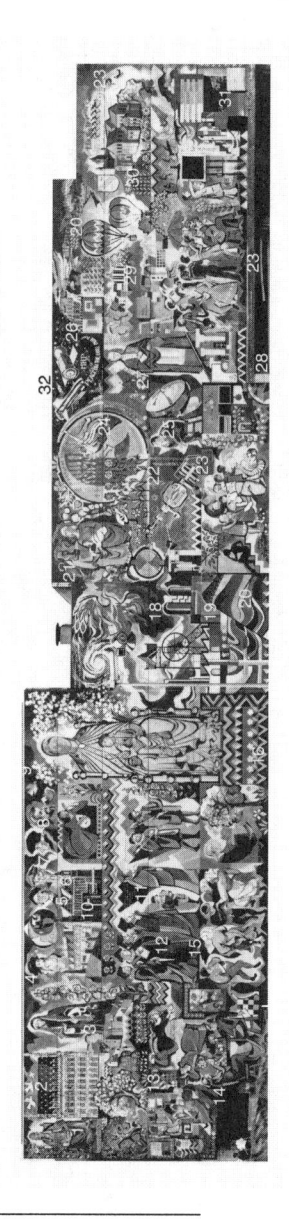

---

[40] Claude Rahir, *Petites histoires d'une grande Université*, peinture murale, 60m x 13m, Louvain-la-Neuve, 1984.

What do the Radio Program Schedules Reveal?
Content Analysis versus Accidental Sampling in Early Canadian Radio History

Anne F. MacLennan

Although content analysis is used extensively in the field of communications, it has been applied only sporadically to broadcasting history. Most of the standard works on Canadian radio history are nationalistic in tone and make reference to the threat of American programming without quantifying its impact for assessment. Extensive content analysis of Canadian radio program schedules during the 1930s in Vancouver, Montreal, and Halifax questions some of the long-held historical misconceptions about Canadian radio. While judgmental samples and the representations of lobbyists to government commissions would be considered suspect and completely unsuitable for a contemporary study, these remain the standard sources for most discussion of Canadian radio in the 1930s. This paper addresses the chronic misuse of these types of sources, due to the lack of readily available statistics for early Canadian radio programming.[1]

Hovering between the humanities and social sciences, the discipline of history is frequently perceived as less rigorous within the larger discussions of social science research. While the vast majority of historical work is differentiated from social science due to its narrative and comparative styles, recent work in the field evades this type of classification opting instead for more interpretive and positivistic approaches. The use of grounded theory and interpretative approaches, however, are more consistent with history's narrative style, relying upon the critical and interpretive powers of individual historians. Alternatively, vast numbers of historians are more closely allied with disciplines that follow a more positivistic approach, favouring representative sampling and discipline-specific methods. The interplay between the field of communications and history and their interdisciplinary natures allows for many methodological possibilities that have yet to be fully explored.

Additionally history has long been associated with a reliance on accidental sampling.[2] In fact the very nature of the field and its area of investigation make it dependent on the remains of society and what previous generations have deemed fit to preserve or leave behind. Much of the useful material evidence with regard to daily life has been destroyed, particularly in very present-oriented matter, such as broadcasting. Broadcasting, particularly

---

[1] Anne MacLennan, "Circumstances Beyond Our Control: Canadian Radio Program Schedule Evolution During the 1930s" (PhD. diss., Concordia University, 2001).
[2] Michael Del Balso and Alan D. Lewis, *First Steps: A Guide to Social Research*, 2nd ed. (Toronto: Nelson Thomson Learning, 2000), 86; Arthur Asa Berger, *Media and Communication Research Methods: An Introduction to Qualitative and Quantitative Approaches* (Thousand Oaks: Sage Publications, 2000), 139-40; W. Lawrence Neuman, *Social Research Methods: Quantitative and Qualitative Approaches*, 5th ed. (Boston: Pearson Education Inc., 2003), 418-20.

in its early years, was highly prized by contemporaries for its immediacy and currency. Unfortunately the repercussion of this valued immediacy was that most programs that Canadians listened to in the 1930s were not preserved, but simply dispersed into the ether.[3] Thus most research with regard to early Canadian radio has focussed on the legislative and political discussion precipitated by commercial broadcasters, the Canadian Radio League, and the federal government. Assumptions about the threat of Americanization, the power of broadcasters, and the greed of advertisers figured heavily in discussions of this new medium, without any evidence of their links to potential listeners through program selection. In an effort to recapture the fragments that remain, content analysis of program schedules permits a reconstruction of the basic programming trends and developments in Canadian radio during the 1930s.

The need for content analysis to support other selective and theoretical research in the field has been long recognized in works such as Gérard Laurence's *Le contenu des médias électroniques* and Paul Rutherford's *When Television Was Young: Primetime Canada 1952-1967*.[4] British communications historian and theorist, Paddy Scannell, has appealed for more research "solidly underpinned by detailed, empirical historical knowledge" in order to broaden a field that is very theoretical.[5] Despite these early examples and pleas, this technique tends to be overlooked in this area of historical research.

The international literature surrounding radio history is also profoundly limited when compared to that covering print media or television. American researcher Michele Hilmes argues that the neglect of radio arises from a "consensus-shaped, and unproblematic reflection of a pluralistic society, rather than the conflicting, tension-ridden site of the ruthless exercise of cultural hegemony ... [over] alternative popular constructions that oppose and resist it."[6] Robert McChesney echoes this sentiment in *Telecommunications, Mass Media, and Democracy: The Battle for the Control of U.S. Broadcasting, 1928-1935,* and objects to the neglect and trivialization of the movement for radio reform.[7] His meticulous examination of the records of the principals in the battle for the control of broadcasting, tracks the unevenly matched contest between network broadcasters and a variety of groups that questioned the inevitability of network commercial broadcasting. The very discussion of the battle fought by these groups, however ineffectual, countered the conception

---

[3] Although the term "ether" is not technically correct it is historically appropriate, because the electromagnetic spectrum was widely referred to as the ether during the 1930s.

[4] Gérard Laurence, *Le contenu des médias électroniques* (St. Hyacinthe: Edisem, 1980); Paul Rutherford, *When Television Was Young: Primetime Canada 1952-1967* (Toronto: University of Toronto Press, 1990).

[5] Paddy Scannell, "History and Culture," *Media, Culture & Society* 2 (January 1980): 1.

[6] Michele Hilmes, *Radio Voices: American Broadcasting, 1922-1952* (Minneapolis: University of Minnesota Press, 1997), xvii.

[7] Robert W. McChesney, *Telecommunications, Mass Media, and Democracy: The Battle for the Control of U.S. Broadcasting, 1928-1935* (New York: Oxford University Press, 1993).

that commercialization of American radio was the only possibility available for the development of the medium. Although the American networks managed to exercise cultural hegemony over broadcasting in the United States, commercial broadcasting did not seize absolute control in Canada. Canadian historians quickly focused on government intervention in the form of the creation of a national network, defining it as inevitable. Consequently the overwhelming focus on this national network has resulted in only fragmentary coverage of the remaining history of early Canadian radio.

The narrative of early Canadian radio history draws from a variety of disciplines, former broadcasters, and nostalgic literature.[8] The first major academic work in Canadian broadcasting history was Frank W. Peers' *The Politics of Canadian Broadcasting, 1920-1951*. His *The Public Eye: Television and the Politics of Canadian Broadcasting, 1952-1968* completes the early national survey of broadcasting.[9] The early literature was imbued with a sense of the national importance of the establishment of the Canadian Broadcasting Corporation (CBC). Peers writes "... the political choices in the 1930's were nearly all national in character - bound up with the feeling that Canada must have an identity of its own, that its communications should not be subordinate to or dependent on the enterprise or the industry of another country."[10] The expanding threat of American cultural imperialism is an underlying assumption in the early literature. Peers canonizes Graham Spry and Allan Plaunt and their lobbying efforts at the Canadian Radio League to move the Conservative government to create the Canadian Radio Broadcasting Commission (CRBC). Peers' ideas are crystallized in the assertion that "a unique Canadian system of broadcasting endures ... it reflects values different from those prevailing in the British or American systems. It not only mirrors Canadian experience, but helps define it."[11]

Peers' thesis that public broadcasting mirrored and defined national identity has been accepted with little criticism. Increased Canadian dependence upon American political and economic policies, with cultural domination looming threateningly on the horizon, has provoked a number of studies concentrating upon the purely national aspects of Canadian broadcasting.

---

[8] Among the reminiscences are: Bill McNeil and Morris Wolfe, *The Birth of Radio in Canada: Signing On* (Toronto: Doubleday Canada Limited, 1982); T. J. Allard, *Straight Up: Private Broadcasting in Canada, 1918-1958* (Ottawa: The Canadian Communications Foundation, 1979); Sandy Stewart, *From Coast to Coast: A Personal History of Radio in Canada* (Toronto: CBC Enterprises, 1985); Sandy Stewart, *A Pictorial History of Radio in Canada* (Toronto: Gage Publishing Limited, 1975); and Warner Troyer, *The Sound and the Fury: An Anecdotal History of Canadian Broadcasting*. (Toronto: Personal Library Publishers, 1982).

[9] Frank W. Peers, *The Politics of Canadian Broadcasting, 1920-1951* (Toronto: University of Toronto Press, 1969). The officially commissioned British survey is Asa Briggs, *The History of Broadcasting in the United Kingdom*, 4 vols. (London: Oxford University Press, 1961-1979). The American equivalent is Erik Barnouw, *A Tower in Babel: A History of Broadcasting in the United States to 1933* (New York: Oxford University Press, 1966) and *The Golden Web: A History of Broadcasting in the United States 1933-1953* (New York: Oxford University Press, 1968).

[10] Peers, *Politics of Canadian Broadcasting*, 284.

[11] Ibid., 3.

Austin Weir's history and dense memoir, *The Struggle for National Broadcasting in Canada*, and Margaret Prang's "The Origins of Public Broadcasting in Canada," gave equal weight to public broadcasting's inevitable role as a cultivator of national identity.[12] Prang viewed the adoption of public broadcasting, however flawed, as an expression of Canadian nationalism, specifically the "defensive expansionism" that came into being to counter the threat of American culture, and as an extension of John A. Macdonald's National Policy. More recently Michael Nolan's *Foundations: Alan Plaunt and the Early Days of CBC Radio* pursued a similar nationalist train of thought.[13] Nolan depicted Plaunt as a product of the surge of post-war nationalism during the 1920s. The fundamental assumption of an American threat that could only be countered with a Canadian national network remains unquestioned in the wider discussion of twentieth century Canadian history.

The shared specific concern of these works was indeed government action to promote Canadian broadcasting in the face of the threat of Americanization, a theme pursued by employing conventional sources such as government reports, private papers, and newspaper editorials.[14] These traditional works and their nationalistic perspective long dominated the literature unchallenged.[15] Standard surveys of Canadian history have relied on and reiterated the interpretations of Peers, Weir, and Prang. Thus, the nationalistic interpretations of radio's past forged in the 1960s have been reinforced with repetition.

Newer works stress alternative perspectives rather than novel approaches. Marc Raboy's *Missed Opportunities: The Story of Canada's Broadcasting Policy* judges the broadcasting system to be the result of interaction between the social pressure of public service broadcasting and pressure from financial interests to preserve Canada as a distinct entity from the United States.[16] He argues that there is a blurring of the concept of "national"

---

[12] Peers worked as a CBC producer, program organizer and supervisor of public affairs programs in radio and television. E. Austin Weir, *The Struggle for National Broadcasting in Canada* (Toronto: McClelland and Stewart, 1965). In May 1929, Weir was appointed head of the radio department of the Canadian National Railways' national network of radio stations. By 1937 Weir became Commercial Manager of the CBC and Superintendent of the CBC Press and Information Services. Margaret Prang, "The Origins of Public Broadcasting in Canada," *Canadian Historical Review* 46 (March 1965):1-31.

[13] Michael Nolan, *Foundations: Alan Plaunt and the Early Days of CBC Radio* (Toronto: CBC Enterprises, 1986); Michael Joseph Nolan, "Alan Plaunt and Canadian Broadcasting" (PhD. diss., University of Western Ontario, 1983), 377.

[14] Mary Vipond, "'Please Stand By for that Report': The Historiography of Early Canadian Radio," *Fréquence/ Frequency* 7-8 (1997): 13-17.

[15] Other general studies that accept this traditional view of radio history include: Albert A. Shea, *Broadcasting the Canadian Way* (Montreal: Harvest House, 1963); E. S. Hallman with H. Hindley, *Broadcasting in Canada* (Don Mills: General Publishing Company Limited, 1977); Herschel Hardin, *A Nation Unaware: The Canadian Economic Culture* (Vancouver: J. J. Douglas Ltd., 1974); and David Ellis, *Evolution of the Canadian Broadcasting System: Objectives and Realities 1928-1968* (Ottawa: Minister of Supply and Services, 1979).

[16] Marc Raboy, *Missed Opportunities: The Story of Canada's Broadcasting Policy* (Kingston and Montreal: McGill-Queen's University Press, 1990), xii.

and "public" interest, making the broadcasting system an instrument of the state called "administrative broadcasting," which serves to combat the internal threat of Quebec nationalism. Raboy, however, uses traditional sources and the familiar themes of regulation and national broadcasting to emphasize the failure to provide alternatives to a capitalist or administrative broadcasting structure and the neglect of Quebec within that structure.

Michel Filion also discusses broadcasting from the Quebec perspective in *Radiodiffusion et société distincte: Des origines de la radio jusqu'à la Révolution tranquille au Québec*.[17] His broad survey essentially argues that the radio experience of French Canadians was distinct from that of their English-speaking counterparts in the "rest of Canada." Despite Filion's criticism of the traditional literature, he makes use of Peers, Weir, and the same government reports and committee proceedings for his research. He contends American programs presented no threat to Quebec culture in what he calls the "free market" period before 1932, nor were they a substantial threat in the "hybrid" period that followed. Although previous researchers may have been remiss in not belabouring such an obvious point, Filion's basic premise that Quebecers were more loyal to their culture and better at developing indigenous cultural products for the new media than other provinces is a contention not supported by this content analysis.

As an aural medium in a province that holds language to be its most distinctive element, American programs had little chance of penetration in unilingual French-speaking areas. Filion largely excludes the Montreal area and the presence of a large English-speaking population in Quebec, which presents a huge exception to his analysis. Alternatively it could be argued that the building of a national radio broadcasting network helped to broaden the base of both public and private broadcasting in the province, undoubtedly fostering and strengthening a distinct *québécois* culture. Despite this new perspective the use of traditional source material yields no new information with regard to programming.

More recent literature on early Canadian broadcasting has consisted of retrieving interesting strands of inquiry from the mass of remaining unexplored areas, largely stemming from the work of Mary Vipond. She overcame the obstacle of a lack of readily available resources by a close study, in part, of departmental files and correspondence relating to the regulation of radio broadcasting in the records of the Department of Marine and Fisheries. Vipond's *Listening In: The First Decade of Canadian Broadcasting 1922-1932* shifts the focus away from the establishment of the CRBC and CBC to examine the *ad hoc* development of broadcasting practices and private radio prior to the establishment of a national network.[18] This study of the interplay and interdependence of the triangular relationship between manufacturers, broadcasters and their customers, and the audience, breaks new ground as the most complete study to date on the emergence of Canadian radio broadcasting a full decade prior to the intervention of public broadcasting in any form. This

---

[17] Michel Filion, *Radiodiffusion et société distincte: Des origines de la radio jusqu'à la Révolution tranquille au Québec* (Laval: Éditions du Méridien, 1994).

[18] Mary Vipond, *Listening In: The First Decade of Canadian Broadcasting,1922-1932* (Kingston and Montreal: McGill-Queen's University Press, 1992).

willingness, as in much of the international discourse, to forgo a strictly political discussion of radio has helped to widen the assessment of radio's role and impact.[19]

The content analysis that forms the background for the findings presented in this work is confined to the 1930s, a developmentally important decade for the medium of radio in Canada. The decade is defined by the change to broadcasting from exclusively private Canadian broadcasters and some American affiliates to the introduction of the CRBC and the CBC. A full daily broadcasting schedule became routine in the "thirties," and radio grew to be one of the central popular entertainment media in North America. Within the confines of this decade the majority of Canadian radio stations moved to a new level of development, fully diversifying their schedules in the face of two monumental challenges: American commercial broadcasting and the establishment of Canadian network broadcasting.

An analysis of the radio program schedules drawn from the newspapers of three major Canadian cities, Halifax, Vancouver, and Montreal, not only reveals a shared pattern of development but also regional and local differences as well as national and American influences. The cities represent the East Coast, West Coast, and a linguistically diverse central city. Moreover they encompass locations marked by differing influences: a strong impact of Canadian national networks in one city; a small independent competitive market in another; and a broadcasting environment characterized by American affiliation in the third. By studying these different media markets, it is possible to trace the contribution of a variety of environments and factors to the development of Canadian radio stations throughout the decade. The full schedule available to listeners employed for this content analysis includes the products of local stations and the American stations listed in the evenings, which present a realistic picture of the Canadian broadcasting environment.

The stratified random sample encompasses Sunday, 29 December 1929 to Saturday, 6 January 1940. Three weeks of program schedules yearly were drawn from the *Vancouver Sun, Montreal Gazette,* and *Halifax Herald* to pinpoint the impact of annual changes and to assess gradual trends. Although a sample of one week yearly may have illustrated the same patterns, this larger sample leveled out any abnormalities, bringing the results closer to the norm by providing a much more reliable picture of the radio schedule in the 1930s. Models for this work are extremely rare; thus a combination of contemporary

---

[19] Vipond, "'Please Stand By for that Report'," 23; Mary Vipond, "Financing Canadian Public Broadcasting: License Fees and the 'Culture of Caution'," *Historical Journal of Film, Radio and Television* 15 (1995): 285-300; Mary Vipond, "London Listens: The Popularity of Radio in the Depression," *Ontario History* 88 (March 1996): 47-63; Mary Vipond, "The Beginning of Public Broadcasting in Canada: The CRBC, 1932-36," *Canadian Journal of Communication* 19 (1994): 151-71; Mary Vipond, "The Continental Marketplace: Authority, Advertiser, and Audiences in Canadian News Broadcasting, 1932-1936," *Journal of Radio Studies* 6 (1999): 169-84; Mary Vipond, "Desperately Seeking the Audience for English Canadian Radio," in Michael D. Behiels and Marcel Martel, eds., *Nation, Ideas, Identities: Essays in Honour of Ramsay Cook* (Toronto: Oxford University Press, 2000), 86-96.

and current compilations of radio programs formed a guide for categorization in this analysis.[20]

The earliest content analysis of radio programming was American sociologist William Albig's study "The Content of Radio Programs, 1925-1935."[21] Albig's non-random judgmental sample was quite small, limited in scope to a study of only seven American radio stations. The work remains the background for more contemporary discussions such as Christopher Sterling and John Kitross' *Stay Tuned: A Concise History of American Broadcasting*, which is the only content analysis from the period in existence aside from presentations to the Federal Communications Commission.[22]

One of the most interesting findings of this content analysis is that contrary to popular expectations and beliefs, the establishment of the CBC not only promoted the growth of Canadian radio programming, but also provided a convenient vehicle for American programs. Detailed investigation reveals the strengths and weaknesses of the early Canadian radio schedules and the areas vulnerable to expanding American content. By including all the stations in the schedules, the development of Canadian radio can be evaluated alongside its American competition, emphasizing areas of neglect and development resulting from the interaction of an assortment of variables at work. Content analysis begins to fill in some of the *lacunae* in the literature of Canadian radio history especially with regard to the assessment of programming trends or the impact of American broadcasting on the Canadian environment. Throughout the 1930s, Canadian radio stations employed consistent strategies for development and a few core areas of programming to distinguish themselves in what was

---

[20] Harrison B. Summers, comp., *A Thirty-Year History of Programs Carried on National Radio Networks in the United States 1926-1956*, orig. ed. 1958 (New York: Arno Press Inc., 1971). Similar, although not as comprehensive, information is also available in promotional material from the networks, which published lists of their popular sponsored and sustaining programs. NBC, *NBC Network Programs* (NBC, June 1938); NBC, *NBC Network Programs* (NBC, November 1938). The categories employed by Gladstone Murray were "(a) Music - (1 - serious, 2 - popular); (b) Talks and Dialogue; (c) Dramatic; (d) Variety (comedy, etc); (e) News; (f) Special Events; (g) Religious and Devotional; (h) Children's Programs; (i) Educational; (j) Sport; and (k) Women's Programs. Canada, House of Commons, Special Committee on Radio Broadcasting, *Minutes of Proceedings and Evidence* (Ottawa: King's Printer, 1939), 302. Jon D. Swartz and Robert C. Reinehr, *Handbook of Old-Time Radio: A Comprehensive Guide to Golden Age Radio Listening and Collecting* (Metuchen, New Jersey: The Scarecrow Press, Inc., 1993); John Dunning, *On the Air: The Encyclopedia of Old-Time Radio* (New York: Oxford University Press, 1998); Frank Buxton and Bill Owen, *The Big Broadcast, 1920-1950* (New York: Viking, 1972); Vincent Terrace, *Radio's Golden Years* (San Diego: Barnes, 1981). The categories used were: adventure; crime and mystery; astrology; children; comedy; drama; drama anthology; education; exercise; games; music; dance music; religious music; news; opera; quiz; religious; serial drama; special; sports; sustaining; talk; talk and information; variety; women; and unidentified. Percentages of programs refer to identified programming unless otherwise specified.
[21] William Albig, "The Content of Radio Programs, 1925-1935," *Social Forces*, 16 (March 1938): 338-49.
[22] Christopher H. Sterling and John M. Kitross, *Stay Tuned: A Concise History of American Broadcasting*, 2nd ed. (Belmont, Calif.: Wadsworth Publishing Company, 1990), 120.

becoming an increasingly homogenized network broadcasting environment dependent on network-generated programs. While Canadian programming on Canadian stations was overwhelmingly dominant at the beginning of the decade, a significant shift occurred by 1939. The ultimate impact of network broadcasting during the 1930s is revealed in Table 1.1 below.

Table 1.1 Percentage of American Content on Radio Program Schedules on Canadian Stations in Halifax, Montreal and Vancouver, 1930-1939

City	1930	1939
Halifax	0.25	22.57
Montreal	4.42	23.43
Vancouver	2.42	16.85

The technological context and economic boundaries of radio guaranteed the enduring influence of the American radio industry, due to the range of signals and the inability to block them. The network system that evolved in the United States and the demise of most independent stations may not have been inevitable. The early development of disparate broadcasting markets in Halifax, Montreal, and Vancouver illustrate that local and Canadian programming had appeal and that independent stations were viable. The CBC's decision to incorporate American network programming into its schedule made a powerful impact. The use of American network programs by the CBC in turn seemed to influence other Canadian radio stations to do the same, thereby changing the overall balance within Canadian broadcasting.

From its earliest days in the 1920s, Canadian radio stations were never judged in isolation, but in comparison with the easily available and more highly developed offerings of the American radio industry. This became even more the case in the 1930s, as the American networks reached near complete domination of radio in that country. Many Canadians listened to American network programs directly on powerful border stations, and by 1930 four Canadian stations in Montreal and Toronto became American network affiliates. As American affiliates these Canadian stations possessed an increasingly diversified program schedule, and were able to branch out into several new genres of programming.

The evolution of Canadian radio program schedules was also affected in the 1930s by the arrival of the public broadcasting networks, first the CRBC and then its successor the CBC. As in the United States, the Canadian networks offered local stations the possibility of increasing and diversifying their programming by affiliation. For those stations without affiliation, again as was the case with the American networks, the CRBC and CBC provided both comparison and competition. The fact that the CBC also picked up some of the most popular American network programs only exacerbated the competitive environment within which independent local Canadian stations struggled to survive. The role of the CBC within the larger historical literature is characterized as "fostering ... Canadian ideals and culture" as the CRBC was described at its conception in the final report of the Special Committee on

Radio Broadcasting.[23] The reality of the CBC and the effect of its commercial policies were far removed from these early hopes. The lofty ideals and rhetoric of those who created the public broadcaster have remained part of the popular conception of the CBC; few realize that from its inception the CBC has also served, ironically, partially to facilitate and encourage the entry of American programming into Canada.

The disparities among the Halifax, Montreal, and Vancouver broadcasting environments are immediately apparent. Halifax was dominated by a single station, which became an affiliate of the CRBC and then the CBC. Montreal dealt effectively with the challenge of linguistic duality in part by the early American network affiliation of its two major stations. Vancouver was marked by its collection of competitive independent stations, somewhat removed from the direct impact of network broadcasting until the last years of the decade. Each station in turn employed similar strategies to deal with the challenges of the decade in order to diversify, survive, and preserve a local voice. Nevertheless the larger challenges of American network broadcasting and the development of a Canadian national network had a cumulative effect in each city that was remarkably similar.

Operating independently at the outset of the decade, Halifax stations took years to incorporate even the minutest quantities of American content into their schedules. Without American network affiliation, Halifax area stations would seem to have been prime candidates for the use of electrical transcriptions. However, Table 1.2 indicates that availability of the technology to employ electrical transcriptions did not provide sufficient enticement to the stations to make an active use of American programs.

The CRBC first delivered American programming directly to Halifax through CHNS in 1933. This was limited largely to orchestral music and the occasional serial. Even with these additions American content remained restricted to only 3.03 per cent of the schedule that year. The CRBC's introduction to the Halifax broadcasting environment through CHNS constituted neither dramatic nor lasting change. In 1936 when three stations in the region, CFCY, CJLS, and CHNS, became part of the CBC network of radio stations, variable quantities of American content were introduced to the Halifax schedule.

Between 1937 and 1938, the American programming on CHNS jumped almost three-fold, from 5.32 per cent of the schedule to 14.47 per cent. Broadcast hours remained consistent, while American content increased, most drastically in serialized dramas. American content also continued to be drawn from music, variety shows, children's programming, and comedy. As a CBC affiliate the station's access to and adoption of American programming grew, but more importantly for the first time it supplanted rather than merely supplemented the station's Canadian offerings. By 1939 American programming was well entrenched in the CHNS schedule growing to 21.53 per cent. CHNS seemed to be competing with the CBC's new network station, CBA in Sackville, by offering more American programming beyond that of the

---

[23] Canada, Dominion Bureau of Statistics, General Statistics Branch, *The Canada Year Book 1933* (Ottawa: King's Printer, 1933), 732.

CBC schedule, thus distinguishing itself from its new competitor. By virtue of its longer broadcast day CHNS offered a greater quantity of American programs to the Halifax audience than CBA, though such programming constituted a slightly smaller proportion of the entire CHNS schedule.

Table 1.2 Percentages of Broadcast Duration of American Programs on Canadian Radio Stations in the Halifax Radio Program Schedule, 1930 to 1939

Station	1930	1931	1932	1933	1934	1935	1936	1937	1938	1939
CBA	-	-	-	-	-	-	-	-	-	23.88
CBC	-	-	-	-	-	-	-	-	22.6	-
CFCY	-	-	-	-	-	-	8.87	7.94	10.8	-
CHNS	0.28	0	0	2.01	4.09	3.03	5.72	5.32	14.5	21.53
CJLS	-	-	-	-	-	-	8.15	3.45	18.5	-
CKIC	0	0	0	-	-	-	-	-	-	-
CNRA	0	-	-	-	-	-	-	-	-	-
CNRH	0	0	0	-	-	-	-	-	-	-

CKAC and CFCF were American affiliates from 1929 and 1930 respectively, thus making American content a fixed presence in the schedules of local Montreal radio stations throughout the decade. American programming on CKAC remained minimal until 1934 when it was faced with additional competition from CHLP (a French-language station) and CRCM (a CBC station), both entering the Montreal market the previous year. Whether the potential threat of these new stations was real or imagined, within a year of their arrival both CKAC and CFCF had almost doubled their American content from the year before. CHLP displayed a very limited interest in making American programs a part of its standard schedule. As a CRBC station, CRCM employed American content sparingly in its schedule. The very presence of competition, even on a part-time basis, reinforced and added to the use of American programming in the Montreal broadcasting market as a whole.

In Montreal the CRBC was forced to build its own station since the existing profitable stations would not make time in their schedules for the Commission's programming. Music was the only major component of American programming employed by CRCM, thus posing no immediate threat to the American affiliates. American content almost doubled on CKAC and CFCF during the first year of CRCM's operations, thereby preserving their positions as providers of such programming. The levels of American content on these Montreal stations subsided slightly when it became obvious that CRCM would employ limited quantities of musical programming from the United States as indicated in Table 1.3. The launch of two CBC stations in Montreal in 1937 precipitated the next rise in American content in the city's radio program schedule. Immediately upon its establishment CBM began making use of a diversified selection of American programs. For the first time the American affiliates were faced with the prospect of competing for American programs with another Montreal station. CFCF was forced out of its former position of preeminence in the realm of American serial drama. The extensive use of American programs by the CBC intensified the competition. By 1939 this greater proportion of American content became a permanent feature of the Montreal schedule.

The CBC may well have been serving its mandate by making American programs more available across the country. C.D. Howe, the Minister of Transportation, in an address to the Canadian Association of Broadcasters declared: "The Canadian Broadcasting Corporation is one in which the shareholders are the listeners, and the corporation's business is to give the listeners what they desire."[24] The network's performance was at odds with Corporation Chairman Leonard Brockington's description of the CBC as relying on American content solely for sophisticated programming and to provide financing for Canadian programming. The intensive use of American serial dramas and vaudeville-style performances did not fit Brockington's description. Ironically, CBM's arrival in Montreal seemed to have stimulated greater use of American programming on many of the city's stations, itself included, contrary to the stated goals of the CBC network then, and the assumptions of historians since.

Table 1.3 Percentages of Broadcast Duration of American Programs on Canadian Radio Stations in the Montreal Radio Program Schedule, 1930 to 1939

Station	1930	1931	1932	1933	1934	1935	1936	1937	1938	1939
CBF	-	-	-	-	-	-	-	20.8	23.3	18.3
CBM	-	-	-	-	-	-	-	13.6	21.9	22.4
CBO	-	-	-	-	-	-	-	20.8	29.5	-
CFCF	2.06	34.54	19.2	19.64	38	34.5	37.9	55.5	44	43.2
CHLP	-	-	-	2.37	0.5	6.2	1.59	10.4	4.77	2.16
CHYC	17.39	10	0	-	-	-	-	-	-	-
CKAC	6.38	9.62	5.44	12.69	23.3	18.6	27.8	31.3	20.3	19.2
CKCL	2.15	-	-	-	-	-	-	-	-	-
CKCO	-	-	-	-	-	-	2.45	-	-	-
CKGW	44.75	30.24	33.5	-	-	-	-	-	-	-
CNRM	0	0	-	-	-	-	-	-	-	-
CRCM	-	-	-	6.72	9.9	6.28	5.36	19.4	-	-
CRC0	-	-	-	3.08	-	5.77	5.17	17.1	-	-
CRCT	-	-	-	27.92	38.5	31.7	-			

---

[24] *Ottawa Evening Citizen*, 8 Feb. 1938, 7.

The incorporation of American programming into the Vancouver radio program schedule differed from what happened in Montreal and Halifax in two ways. First, no Vancouver station ever acquired an American affiliation. Second, because the CRBC and CBC had their own station in the city, no opportunities for affiliation to the Canadian network were available to the other local stations. The city's existing stations had only irregular access to American programs, which was reflected in their fluctuating use of American content.

The constant presence of American border stations may also account for the meager offerings on the Canadian side. In the first few years of the decade, American programming was quite limited, as shown in Table 1.4. At any one station it might amount to the inclusion of only one regular program. Availability determined the selection of American programs. Without network affiliation the programs chosen did not always reflect the basic network successes, such as comedy, that tended to be the immediate foci of affiliates. Electrical transcriptions, which were not driven by network priorities, were one of the main sources of American programming on Vancouver radio stations.

The appearance of CRBC stations in the Vancouver radio program schedule added to the negligible amount of American content. It was composed primarily of musical programs - such as those of the New York Philharmonic Orchestra - which constituted 76.92 per cent of that total. The other local independent stations made diminished use of American programming rather than increasing it, partly due to the expense and the lack of affiliation opportunities.

Increased use of American programming on local stations coincided with the arrival of the CBC station CBR in 1937. By the end of 1937 American content reached 9.36 per cent of CBR's schedule, a pattern paralleled by other local stations. In 1938, CBR led the way with the greatest quantity of American programming in the market, with 21.65 per cent of its schedule comprised of such content. Although significant in Vancouver, it fell well below the 29.21 per cent on the total CBC network schedule. Despite the fact that CBR had less American content than some other CBC stations, it stood in marked contrast to the other independent Vancouver stations that had employed even more limited quantities of American programs. All Vancouver stations, however, scheduled a much greater proportion of American content at the end of the decade than had been the case prior to the arrival of CBR.

American programming grew slowly in Vancouver's schedule. The lack of easy access to American programming through network affiliation was the major factor restraining the growth of American shows in Vancouver. As independents, Vancouver stations sparingly selected their American programs from those distributed through electrical transcription only. Once the local independent stations were faced with the prospect of competing with a full-time Canadian network station they selected American programs to assist in their diversification of the program schedules. The addition of the Canadian network station forever altered the market by making the inclusion of American programs a standard component of local offerings.

Table 1.4 Percentages of Broadcast Duration of American Programs on Canadian Radio Stations in the Vancouver Radio Program Schedule, 1930 to 1939

Station	1930	1931	1932	1933	1934	1935	1936	1937	1938	1939
CFCT	0	-	-	-	-	-	-	-	-	-
CFJC	-	-	-	10.7	-	-	-	-	-	-
CHWK	-	0	-	10.7	-	-	-	-	-	-
CJOR	0	0	7.36	5.46	0	1.21	10.2	12.19	16.7	29.28
CKCD	-	-	-	-	-	0	1.1	0	0	5.7
CKFC	0	-	0	0	0	0	0.53	0	18.7	6.32
CKMO	7.54	4.97	0	0	0	0	3.66	3.13	3.22	6.74
CKOV	-	-	-	10.4	-	-	-	-	-	-
CKWX	2.13	7.73	6.44	2.56	0	0	3.89	2.61	28.6	8.43
CNRV	0	2.34	0	-	-	-	-	-	-	-
CRCV	-	-	-	4.98	3.67	9.25	5.89	4.24	-	-
CBR	-	-	-	-	-	-	-	9.36	21.7	39.05

The clear consistency in the growth and development of Canadian radio stations was evident despite divergent local circumstances. By the end of the decade there was a marked rise in the incorporation of American programs in the schedules of Canadian stations; American content amounted to 22.57 per cent in Halifax, 23.43 per cent in Montreal, and 16.85 per cent in Vancouver. Notably, American content reached approximately the same levels in the cumulative program schedules in all three cities despite their varied local circumstances. In Halifax, the CBC station CBA and the CBC affiliate CHNS aired 23.88 per cent and 21.53 per cent American programming respectively. In Montreal, a standard of approximately 20 per cent American content seems to have been set, with CBF contributing 18.29 per cent, CBM 22.39 per cent and CKAC 19.20 per cent. The major exceptions to this standard were CFCF at 43.19 per cent and CHLP at 2.16 per cent. In Vancouver, there was quite a range of usage of American material. Most stations provided fairly small amounts of American programming, with CKCD at 5.7 per cent, CKFC at 6.32 per cent, CKMO at 6.74 per cent, and CKWX at 8.43 per cent. The greater rates of incorporation of American content in the schedule were employed by CJOR at 29.28 per cent and CBR at 39.05 per cent, bringing the average to 16.85 per cent of the total program schedule. Despite the distinct routes that each city's stations took with respect to their incorporation of American content, the results were similar. In each city the introduction of added American content through the local CBC station or affiliate provided the foundation for the legitimization and standardization of its use within the schedules of virtually all Canadian radio stations.

The impact of network programming was perhaps unavoidable; the immediate increase and pervasive invasion of American network programs that accompanied the arrival of the CBC, however, indicates that at the very least the new network potentially accelerated the process of homogenization toward a North American culture. The resistance to such assimilation by Vancouver stations, CHNS in Halifax, until it became a CBC affiliate, and French-language stations in Montreal demonstrated that the process was not inevitable or necessary. The barrier to the assimilation of these stations into the larger North American culture may have been the lack of ability or means. However, content analysis of the program schedules reveals that the CBC forever altered the course of broadcast media in Canada by making it an inextricable part of a mixture dependent on both American and Canadian network programming.

– 18 –
Television as Historical Source
Using Images in Cultural History

Caroline-Isabelle Caron

Let us reflect on the state of historiography in Canada and the usual reluctance of Canadian historians, whether English- or French-speaking, to use audio-visual sources in their research. Whereas they readily use all forms of textual sources, oral sources, and even some iconographic sources, historians shy away from film and television. They rarely refer to these productions for purposes other than as illustrative and teaching tools. Historians do not readily analyze audio-visual sources in Canada. They leave them to specialists of film and communication studies.

In my research on Quebec cultural history I have purposefully looked at representations of the past, in the form of commemorations,[1] and representations of the future, in the form of science fiction (Caron, 2003a; 2003b), to get a better sense, a closer glimpse if you will, of Quebec's collective *encyclopedia*, in Umberto Eco's sense of the word (Eco, 1995: 95-106). I use *encyclopedia* as the sum of the experiences and representations possessed by a person, and more generally, by a collectivity, which enables them to understand their world, and act and react to various experiences.

When attempting to assess the Americanization of Quebec popular culture, a look at television and movies, where the place of American-made and made-for-American products is enormous, is self-evident. In the last third of the twentieth century, the place of such products in Quebec culture has become very large. However, without looking farther than statistics, one cannot fully understand the cultural affect of these products on Quebec culture. By looking at television schedules and movie returns only, by looking at the statistical position of these foreign products on the Quebec market, one can conclude as to their presence in the market, their proportion of the actual viewing public. We can conclude as to how much they are viewed. However, we cannot conclude as to their actual effect, their influence on Quebec culture. To understand, beyond statistics, *how* they were viewed, an analysis of how they have been understood historically is necessary. Just knowing how much American television Quebecers have been watching since 1953 is not enough (Atkinson, 1999).

I want rather for us to reflect on audio-visual products phenomenologically, not only as cultural works that are produced and broadcast and that contain meanings to be decoded and analyzed. Rather, let us look at them as products that are actually viewed by an audience. These works contain cultural signs - visual, textual, oral, and narrative - which are heard,

---

[1] My current research project focuses on commemorative feasts and celebrations in Nova Scotia's Acadian communities, with particular attention on local events and community organizations, between 1800 and 1960.

seen, and understood by real people. Identifying and contextualizing these signs enables us to better understand historically how they are understood. Further, identifying and contextualizing how these signs were *later* repeated and referred to in popular culture enables us to understand how they were appropriated by the broader culture. To understand the impact of American television on Quebec culture, one must look at how it was received.

The question of audience perception of a cultural product can be addressed in two ways. First directly, by asking questions to a chosen sample. This works well in sociological and communications research, when one is looking for immediate perception of cultural products, when one wants to identify how a product is understood right then.[2] This is of little help when one is looking for the long-term influence of any given cultural product, i.e., for historical research. Rather, the second way of looking at audience perception is more useful for this purpose. One must look at audience perception indirectly, by looking at the re-appropriation of a cultural product.

This allowed in my research for the understanding of how a product had been integrated into the common vocabulary of a culture. With American audio-visual products, the question of appropriation becomes interesting because one must take into account the mediation resulting from the dubbing of the shows. Because the dubbed products are not quite the same as the originals, the result of their acculturation should effect their place in the common culture.

In my research, I have focused on one of the most historically known and influential, and most widely watched American television series ever: *Star Trek: The Original Series* (*TOS*), starring William Shatner as Captain Kirk. I looked at how *TOS* has been integrated in Quebec culture since its first showing in French in the Montreal-dubbed version entitled *Patrouille du Cosmos* in the early 1970s. I not only used the professional productions themselves (i.e., the series and the movies in both English and French), but also professional works of Quebec popular culture that refer to it (shows, series, movies), as well as amateur and semi-professional productions (such as fan fiction, fan movies, and shorts produced for the *Kabarets KINO*). I then expanded my research to other American-made and made-for-Americans series and movies to confirm my conclusions (Caron, 2004). For the purposes of this paper, however, I will focus only on *Trek*.

After a careful analysis of the 79 episodes of *TOS* and *Patrouille du Cosmos*, my conclusions were startling. Comparing the English and French versions, I found fundamental and influential differences between what Americans had been watching and listening to and what Quebeckers had. Through dubbing, a different cultural product had been created. Stories had been reoriented, dialogues re-written, characters altered, jokes "re-funnied" and values shifted. In short, Quebeckers were not watching the same show as their American counterparts. They were watching a show that was uniquely *Québécois*, even though the original product was foreign. This dual nature of

---

[2] On methodologies for identifying television audiences and publics, see Proulx, 1998. For an example of a comparative reception study, in the case of *Dallas*, see Katz and Liebes, 1991. For Trek audiences, see Tulloch and Jenkins, 1995.

Patrouille du Cosmos gave it a paradoxical influence on Quebec culture (Caron 2003b: 247-8).

In *Patrouille du Cosmos*, characterization is the result of several factors, only some of which are inherent to the original English version. The dubbing actors' performances, their stage direction, French-language dubbing traditions, and the allusions made in the translated dialogues all alter the viewers' ultimate perception of the characters and stories. Kirk in French is not the same as in English; neither are the other members of the *Enterprise*'s crew.

One striking change is a consequence of the way the characters are played by the dubbing actors. In French-speaking countries, dubbing is done with the *bande rythmo* method in which the source text is divided into one-minute segments, shown to the dubbing actors on a screen at the top or bottom of which is a timing indicator and a scrolling band. On the band is the dubbed text, as well as indications for rhythm, tone, accentuation, and emphasis. As the text scrolls past the timing indicator, the actors know when exactly to pronounce which syllable and make which sound. The result is usually a very tight lipped synchrony. Often, however, the outcome will also be a flattening of the general tone of the acting performance, as the actors are never acting more than a minute of dialogue at a time. It can also lead to overacting. As a result, the dubbers' acting performance is not always believable, or simply not very inspired, no matter how good the translated text (Pommier, 1988: 105-6). Most *Patrouille du Cosmos* episodes suffer from this kind of flattening.

If that often means the acting is somewhat uninspired, it also results in an impression that the characters are stoic and unemotional. In *Patrouille du Cosmos*, Starfleet officers are not easily moved or excited by the situations around them. Kirk's grandiloquent speeches are spoken in a poised and reflective tone. Spock's original neutral, logical tone is sometimes nothing short of somber. Scotty's exited commentaries are transformed into determined analyses and cynical retorts.

The French dubbing tradition also significantly alters spoken dialogues because French-speaking audiences as a whole insist on linguistically and stylistically correct dialogue (Luyken, 1991: 138). This has significant consequences. In a large proportion of French-language-dubbed audiovisual media, the level of the spoken language is quite high. The language used is what is known as *Français international*, a version of the language devoid of regional indicators, in which accent and phrases are neutral and standardized, so that the geographical origins of the speaker cannot be identified. There is also a social (class) component to International French as the speakers are assumed to be well educated.

In *Patrouille*, characters speak International French. The result is that most audible regional indicators in the original dialogue are erased. There is no difference to be heard between characters that originally spoke with various British or American accents. The end result of all this is that the *Enterprise*'s crew speak in a manner that implies an extensive education, some degree of refinement, great psychological strength in the face of danger, and an underlying uniformity of social provenance, even if some accents remain.

The ultimate effect of these dubbing changes is striking. Though French-speaking audiences watch William Shatner act in his (now famous) over-the-top way, they hear the poised vocal tone, intonations and careful enunciation of the recently deceased Yvon Thiboutot. The actor's movements and facial expressions don't always fit what is being said. In other words, Thiboutot's acting does not match Shatner's.

Dubbing research has long since proven that dubbing is not only a simple translation, but also a means of cultural transposition (Leppihalme). The objective of dubbing is first to make a television show or a movie understandable to the target audience, by transposing it into the target audience's language, but also into the target audience's culture. Cultural referents not understandable by the target audience need to be replaced. In short, the point is to make the product feel natural to the target audience, often by hiding the foreignness of a foreign movie or television series. Dubbing is also a means of making a cultural product acceptable to the target audience. Sometimes that means altering characters, character names,[3] values, or even entire storylines for the target audience not to be offended.

My analysis of the *Star Trek* series and especially the movies clearly supports this assertion (Caron 2002). *Star Trek: Generations* and *Star Trek: First Contact* were the first Trek movies that were dubbed in French both in France and in Quebec. Comparing the Paris and Montreal-made versions revealed just how culturally centered dubbed versions are. Dubbers replaced American cultural referents by French or Quebec ones in the movies. Dialogues were significantly altered (by the addition of jokes or profanity), character personalities and provenances were transformed, though differently in each country, but always different from the original American.

The flip side of hiding the foreignness of a movie is that dubbing can be used as a nationalist tool (Danan, 1991; Plourde, 1999). In some countries, such as France, dubbing can be used to assert cultural supremacy over the original culture, especially if that culture is American.

There are overt and less overt ways of doing this. The French dubbing tradition is notorious in its replacement of American cultural referents with European ones. Even in the case of Star Trek, where most of the cultural referents do not even exist in real life, those few referents that are identifiably American are nationalized. Starfleet ranks, loosely based on American Navy ranks, were replaced in the Paris-made versions with French Marine ranks (see Table 1). In the same vein, the characters use the French custom of addressing whoever is in command as "Commandant." The Montreal-made version, on the other hand, favours lip-synchrony and the characters address each other with ranks loosely similar to the original English-language titles (see Table 1).

Looking at the dubbed versions of the series and movies allowed me to determine how dubbing affected the original products and understand the nature of the changes. The next step was to look at how *Star Trek* has been appropriated into Quebec culture. If dubbing changed the very nature of the original American show, it is expected that the way the show has been understood in Quebec culture would be different.

---

[3] For example, Mr. Sulu was renamed Mr. Kato in Japan because the original name was not Japanese despite the purported origin of the character.

Through dubbing, *Star Trek* was made intelligible to Quebec viewers of *Patrouille du Cosmos*. Parts of *Star Trek* lore are not part of Quebec's common culture the way they are in the U.S. Of course, Spock's ears and Kirk's active libido are known; they are part of Quebec's collective encyclopedia because they were not changed by the dubbing process. So are many of the purely visual vocabularies of the show: the shape of a vessel with primary and secondary hulls, and warp nacelles, for example. Quebeckers know and are capable of using and recognizing these elements as references known to all. However, because of dubbing, purely textual and oral elements of *Star Trek* were not appropriated. There is no equivalent to "Beam me up!" However, Vulcans are referred to as "bourriques" (asses) in the show. That mental image has had lasting cultural affects. The filter of dubbing erased original linguistic markers from *Star Trek* but replaced some of them with linguistic markers unique to *Patrouille du Cosmos*. Only the visual referents and some (but not all) of the narrative structures remain in the dubbed version of the original.

Table 1: Starfleet Ranks in the American, French and Quebec versions of *StarTrek: Generations* and *Star Trek: First Contact*

Starfleet	French Marines	Starfleet (Quebec)
Ensign	Enseigne de vaisseau 2e classe	Enseigne
Lieutenant, j.g.	Enseigne de vaisseau 1ère classe	Lieutenant
Lieutenant	Lieutenant de vaisseau	Lieutenant
Lieutenant Commander	Capitaine de corvette	Lieutenant Commandeur
Commander	Capitaine de frégate	Commandeur
Captain	Capitaine de vaisseau	Capitaine

Source: Caroline-Isabelle Caron, "Moving Words, Hiding Nations: Cultural Transfers and Nationalism in the French-language Translations of Star Trek Motion Pictures." Presented at the Populat Culture Association / American Culture Assiciation conference, Toronto, Ont., 2002.

The best way to know the cultural effect of these numerous changes is to look for actual references to *Star Trek* in Quebec popular culture and its cultural products. Focusing on text only would be counterproductive. However, by enlarging the search to all forms of media, and especially to film and television, the references become numerous. Audio-visual productions from Quebec amateurs and professionals from the movie shorts produced for the highly celebrated *Kabarets KINO*, to the plays, shows, and movies of Claude Meunier (such as *La Petite Vie)*, to the extremely popular science fiction satire series, and now movie, *Dans une galaxie près de chez vous*, contain innumerable references to *Trek*. These references pop up in visuals, themes, narratives and dialogues, and are by no means obscure to audiences. They are understood. The recent and continued media frenzy around *Dans une galaxie près de chez vous*, is proof enough: journalists have repeated *ad nauseam* that the show spoofs *Star Trek* (Bérubé, 2004; Cauchon, 2004). Let us look at a fan movie first.

In 1992, a group of audiovisual media and communications students at the Cégep de Jonquière (Qc) chose for their two-year project to write, produce, and shoot an original 28-minute episode of *TOS*. Entitled *Le Juge*, the episode was written by Daniel Lavoie (who plays Spock) and directed and produced by Éric Bernard (who plays McCoy). It features all of the main characters, as well as Klingons, a mysterious and beautiful female alien, and an omnipotent being standing in judgment of humanity. The episode is a mix of several familiar storylines and decors taken from various episodes of *Star Trek*. At first glance, *Le Juge* looks like an homage to *TOS*. Sets, costumes, camera movements, and angles have been very carefully and successfully reproduced. Original music and sound effects were also used. Visually, it is extremely close to *TOS*. However, this is misleading. In reality, *Le Juge* is an episode of *Patrouille du Cosmos*. Éric Bernard stated in an interview: "With a small budget and a lot of time, I was able to produce a 30-minute *Star Trek* episode in FRENCH. It looked cheezy and the effects are bad also ... like the original series ..." (Original emphasis, Faries, 2000: 1).

The dialogues are very well written in irreproachable International French. They include all of the expected features of *Trek*, including an opening monologue. The actors, though all amateurs and not all talented, try their best to reproduce the characteristics of their respective characters. And there lies the paradox. They must emulate the physical acting styles and typical body movements of William Shatner, Leonard Nimoy, and DeForest Kelley, while imitating the vocal performances of Yvon Thiboutot, Régis Dubost and Michel Georges. The best actor in the group is Carl Poulin, who plays Kirk. An examination of his performance is very revealing. Poulin's physical movements are pure Shatner. However, his poised vocal tone, his intonations, and his careful enunciation are strikingly reminiscent of Thiboutot. The result is similar to watching *Patrouille du Cosmos*.

The performances are all a little off, not only because of their amateurism, but also mainly because fluctuating synchrony is an inherent feature of *Patrouille du Cosmos*. Clearly, *Patrouille du Cosmos*' main characteristic is the result of the dubbing process; otherwise Bernard, Lavoie and the others would not have attempted to reproduce it so closely. They have assimilated these elements and presented them on the screen, both as fans and as members of the Quebec audience.

Le Juge's familiar storyline and paradoxical acting prove that the effect *Patrouille* has had on its audience is more about form than about content. *Patrouille* is a common vocabulary that can be spoken and acted. It is a cultural allusion in and of itself. When reproduced in the visual and audible spirit of the original (i.e., "cheezy"), the result is undeniably a hybrid of two cultural worlds, and (more or less) unintentionally comedic. To understand the actual cultural impact of this paradoxical cultural product, let us look at the most popular science fiction show written and shot in Quebec today.

From 1999 to 2001, the space adventure/slapstick comedy/satire *Dans une galaxie près de chez vous* was the only Quebec-made science fiction program on Quebec television. It targeted the early adolescent viewers of the youth cable network Vrak.tv, but attracted a vast and diverse adult audience as well. On 9 April 2004, the movie *Dans une galaxie près de chez vous* was released and in a month grossed more than two million dollars, a feat rarely achieved by Quebec movies. During its three seasons and 65 episodes, as well as in the movie, *Dans une galaxie* presents the adventures of Capitaine Charles Patenaude and his crew aboard the Planetary Federation vessel *Romano Fafard* (from Earth's number one power, Canada!) in the 2030s. The opening narration states their mission: to find a suitable planet to which the human population can escape Earth, now deprived of its ozone layer, and to go "là où la main de l'homme n'a jamais mis le pied (where man's hand has never laid foot)."

The series has all the expected characteristics of a spaceship show. It has an opening narration stating the ship's mission. Many episodes have stereotypical storylines that refer back to classic American science fiction, from *Star Trek* (of course) to *Star Wars* and *Forbidden Planet*. The vessel *Romano Fafard* may look like it was made out of tin cans, but it also has all the features of a Starfleet ship, with primary and secondary hulls, and a warp nacelle. It has a multicultural and mixed crew, but of various intellectual capacity and dexterity, all of them prone to pie-in-the-face physical comedy, yet as idealistic and dedicated as the crew of the *Enterprise*. In short, this is not simply another *Red Dwarf*. *Dans une galaxie* is clearly spoofing dubbed classic science fiction. Mainly, however, it is spoofing *Patrouille du Cosmos* (not *Star Trek*) on several levels.

Capitaine Charles Patenaude (played by Guy Jodoin) is a dashing officer, ready to run into danger to accomplish his mission. Patenaude expresses himself in poised, yet pathos-filled, long-winded speeches. His accent and vocabulary are perfect International French. He only breaks from this when he speaks in aside, where he uses Quebec dialect in order to emphasize a scene's gags. Patenaude mentions proverbs, poets and philosophers, though in ridiculous combinations. Physically, his movements are grand and theatrical. In short, he speaks and moves like a captain should; that is he moves and speaks like Kirk does in *Patrouille du Cosmos*. The major difference is that here the comedic effect is intentional and exaggerated.

The audiovisual vocabulary of *Patrouille* appears in *Dans une galaxie* for the same reason (but for the opposite effect) than in *Le Juge*. In order to be a recognizable science-fiction spoof, *Dans une galaxie* must first be recognizable as a science-fiction show. It therefore contains recognizable elements of the best-known science-fiction show to have played on Quebec television. Because the audio and visual elements of *Patrouille* are not perfectly coherent, because the costumes and makeup (especially when seen today) are somewhat silly, the effect may be comedic. Using this, the writers and producers of *Dans une galaxie près de chez vous* built a comedy and a satire of the entire science-fiction genre.

This aspect of *Patrouille du Cosmos* (and classic science-fiction television in general) is constantly used in Quebec television in order to produce a comedic effect. *TOS* references in Quebec television and movies are always used in order to produce a laugh. As a cultural allusion, *Star Trek* equals ridicule.

The primary reason for this is that it is known as a dubbed product. Dubbed science-fiction television and movies, like all dubbed television and movies, are paradoxical cultural products. At once, they are foreign, yet not, because they sound familiar. Because of the vagaries and exigencies of dubbing, they also always look and sound - in short feel - a little off. A Quebec audience will be looking at foreigners (i.e., Americans) but listening to French or Québécois speakers; their true foreignness and alien-ness is linguistically hidden, but still visually present. Dubbed cultural products are inherently paradoxical, even more so when a Quebecer is watching, say, an American movie dubbed in France. Then, he hears Americans who speak like French persons, not Québécois, not like *Us*.

It is no surprise, then, that Quebec audiences which have been fed a steady dose of dubbed American television and films, including science fiction, have appropriated it in a paradoxical way. It was inevitable. Viewers are constantly aware of dubbing, always aware of the hidden - or the not so well hidden - foreignness of the viewed products. As such, Quebec audiences have over time necessarily distanced themselves from dubbed cultural products as they were watching them. There is a constant awareness of the *Other* behind the dubbing. This *Other* has a dual form; it is both the disembodied voice of the dubber and the voiceless body of the original actor. At a very basic level, viewing dubbed cultural products leads to a very basic form of cultural criticism, hence the prevalence of comedy or children's programming with sci-fi content in Quebec. When science fiction is always associated with foreign, dubbed and therefore unintentionally funny/inane programming, why would that not influence the genre as it is perceived in the target culture, in this case Quebec?

At the end of this very long walk through my research, let us go back to historiography. Though this particular research focuses on recent enough phenomena that many historians would argue it is more sociological than a legitimate study of the past, I want to argue here that it illustrates the potential usefulness of using television and movies as primary sources for the study of Quebec cultural history. By using these media as more than illustrations, I was able to dive into the collective encyclopedia of Quebec. By looking farther than mere statistics about television and movies, I got a look at how American culture has truly influenced Quebec culture over the last thirty years. The conclusions are very comforting rather than grave, quite the contrary to what many cultural historians, sociologists and media specialists have stated in the last decade.

In short, if I had not analyzed the substance of the American-made and made-for-American shows and movies viewed in Quebec and especially of how they were understood, integrated and appropriated into popular culture, I could not conclude that the Americanization of Quebec culture is not as grave a phenomenon as many have posited (Atkinson, 1999). Dubbing filters reorient American cultural products in very significant ways. It nationalizes them. As such, Quebec culture changes, adapts, and does become more North American, but no more than it becomes more Japanese by watching dubbed animé, whose presence on Quebec television is almost as old as *Star Trek*'s. There is a use for such an approach in history and in historiography. *Aurore l'enfant martyre* and similar movies could be an interesting look at the encyclopedia of the mid-century clerical class in Quebec, for instance.

References

Atkinson, Dave (1999), "L'américanisation de la télévision : qu'est-ce à dire ?" *Variations sur l'influence culturelle américaine.* Ed. Florian Sauvageau (Sainte-Foy : Presses de l'Université Laval), 59-72.

Bérubé, Stéphanie (2004), "Culte du 3e type," *La Presse*, 3 avril, C1-C3.

Caron, Caroline-Isabelle (2002), "Moving Words, Hiding Nations : Cultural Transfers and Nationalism in the French-language Translations of Star Trek Motion Pictures." Presented at the Populat Culture Association / American Culture Assiciation conference, Toronto (ON)

Caron, Caroline-Isabelle (2003a), "Diversity in Outerspace? : The Uniformisation of Human Cultures in the Star Trek Universe." Presented at the Populat Culture Association / American Culture Assiciation conference, New Orleans (LA).

Caron, Caroline-Isabelle (2003b), "Translating Trek: Re-writing an American Icon in a Francophone Context," *Journal of American Culture*, 26, no. .3 (Sept. 2003): 329-55.

Caron, Caroline-Isabelle (2004), "Looking at Them but Listening to Us," presented at 25th International Conference on the Fantastic in the Arts, Fort Lauderdale (FL).

Cauchon, Claude (2004), "Le Romano Fafard en cinérama," *Le Devoir*, 3-4 avril: E1-E2.

Danan, Martine (1991), "Dubbing as an Expression of Nationalism." *Meta,* 36, 3, 605-614.

Eco, Umberto (1985), *Lector in Fabula. Le rôle du lecteur ou la coopération interprétative dans les textes narratifs.* (Paris : Grasset).

Faries, Michael A. (2000), " Intererview with Éric Bernard," http://www.space1999.org/features/articles_interviews/ericbernard_interview1.html.

Katz, Elihu and Tamar Liebes (1991), "Moyens de défense et vulnérabilités : typologie de la réaction des téléspectateurs face aux émission de télévision importées." Eds. Dave Atkinson, Ivan Bernier and Florian Sauvageau. *Souveraineté et protectionisme en matière culturelle. La circulation internationale des émissions de télévision à la lumière de l'expérience canado-américaine* (Sainte-Foy: Presses de l'Université Laval), 147-159.

Leppihalme, Ritva (1997), *Cultural Bumps: An Empirical Approach to the Translation of Allusions* (Clevedon *et al.* : Multilingual Matters Ltd.).

Luyken, Georg-Michael (1991), *Overcoming Language Barriers in Television: Dubbing and Subtitling for the European Audience* (Manchester : European Institute for the Media).

Plourde, Éric (1999), "Le doublage de The Simpsons : divergences, appropriation culturelle et manipulation du discours." Thesis U. de Montréal.

Pommier, Christophe (1988), *Doublage et postsynchronisation* (Paris : Dujarric).

Proulx, Serge, ed. (1998), *Accusé de réception. Le téléspectateur construit par les sciences sociales* (Québec : Presses de l'Université Laval).

Tulloch, John and Henry Jenkins (1995), *Science Fiction Audiences: Watching Doctor Who and Star Trek* (London: Routledge).

"Wie es eigentlich gewesen?"
Early Film as Historical Source?

Michel S. Beaulieu

It is a phrase, a "dirty" one to use my grandmother's vocabulary, which is a mere whisper in the hollowed halls of academia in North America. But, on exceptionally cold winter nights, it can still be faintly heard – haunting and taunting – the hordes of structuralists, post-structuralists, modernists, and post-modernists that can be found huddled in every nook and corner of university campuses:

wie es eigentlich gewesen (as it really happened)[1]

It is a belief, an incantation as E.H. Carr suggests, that while "not a very profound aphorism [it] had an astonishing success."[2] This sentence embodied for nearly a century the activity performed by academic historians. Leopold Von Ranke, the man who dared utter such a blasphemous phrase, is considered by many such as Mark Gilderhus to have "more than anyone transformed history into a modern academic discipline, university based, archive bound, and professional insofar as the leading proponents underwent extensive postgraduate training."[3] However, despite having written over 60 volumes of published work in his lifetime and his notions of objectivity fuelling a century of discourse on the nature of history, he is nearly forgotten today.[4]

---

[1] The best known utterance of this phrase can be found in the preface to his book *Geschicten der Romanischen und Germanischen Völker von 1494 bis 1514*, (*Histories of the Latin and Germanic Nations from 1494-1514*). The full phrase reads: "History has been assigned the office of judging the past, of instructing our times for the benefit of future years. This essay does not aspire to such high offices; it only wants to show how it had really been – *wie es eigentlich* gewesen." See Gay and Wexler, *Historians at Work*, vol. 3, 16; Georg G. Iggers and Konard von Moltke, eds., *Leopold von Ranke, Theory and Practice of History*, (New York: Bobbs-Merrill Co., Inc., 1973), 137.
[2] E.H. Carr, *What is History?* (New York: Vintage books, 1961), 5.
[3] Mark T. Gilderhus, *History and Historians: A Historiographical Introduction*, 3rd ed. (New Jersey: Prentice Hall, 1996), 47.
[4] Although reasonably accurate, this is a broad generalization. There are historians still aware of Ranke's contributions and advocate his ideas as they relate to the empiricist tradition. See, for example, G.R. Elton's aptly entitled *Return to Essentials* (Cambridge: Cambridge University Press, 1991).

According to Roger Wines, one reason for this neglect is the relative inaccessibility of Ranke's work to English-speaking readers.[5] The other, though, is more theoretically and ideologically based. Most familiar with Ranke today know him as the founder of scientific history – something as a discipline we have tried to distance ourselves from.[6] It is, though, another of Ranke's concepts, integral to his notion of achieving history "as it really happened," which still forms the basis of historical research and inquiry: the centrality of facts to the writing of history.[7]

On the surface, film would seem to be a document which provides the objective facts from which Ranke's complete history can be written. As Beth August argues, film is unique as it has the ability to "capture visual reality and act as a recorder and preserver of those images."[8] However, this paper is not intended to argue the validity of Ranke's notions of history, or for that matter those put forward by any objectivists – nor is it intended to add yet another voice to the chorus of criticism against him. In fact, one underlying belief of this paper is that, as Carl L. Becker argues, inherent in all historical work "the actual past is gone; and the world of history is an intangible world, recreated in our minds."[9] Instead, the intent of this examination is to provide a platform for a dialogue on the use of filmic sources in the writing of Canadian history and its role not as a recorder of "history as it really happened," but as another "fact" of the past historians should consult. Separated into two parts, the first is a discussion of motion pictures as a complex and multi-faceted document underutilized and understudied as a bona fide source by historians.

---

[5] Roger Wines, *Leopold von Ranke: The Secret of World History* (New York: Fordham University Press, 1981), 16.

[6] Allan Nevins, for example, recommends Ranke to those historians "who want systematized erudition, inexorable logic, a scientific attention to the arrangement of facts in neat categories." See Allan Nevins, *The Gateway to History* (rev. ed., 1962), 42 in Peter Gay, ed., *Styles in History* (New York: W.W. Norton and Company, Inc., 1974) (reprint 1988).

[7] This is in part demonstrated by Ranke's 1844 statement that, "I see the time approaching when we shall base modern history, no longer on the reports even of contemporary historians, except insofar as they were in possession of personal and immediate knowledge of facts; and still less on work yet more remote from the source; but rather on the narratives of eyewitnesses, and on genuine and original documents." Quotation from Ranke, Introduction to the *History of the Reformation in Germany* SW I:X translated and quoted in Wines, *Leopold von Ranke: The Secret of World History*, 8. Another version also appears in Gay, *Style in History*, 74.

[8] Beth August, "Film for the Historian," in E. Bradforth Burns, ed., *Latin American Cinema: Film and History* (Los Angeles: University of California, 1975), 97.

[9] Carl L. Becker, "What are Historical Facts?," in Ronald Nash, ed., *Ideas in History*, Vol. 2, *The Critical Philosophy of History* (New York: E.P. Dutton and Co., 1969), 185. This also closely resembles a similar expression by Charles A. Beard. See his "That Noble Dream," *American Historical Review* XLI (1935).

The second is an example of the rich evidentiary nature of a film produced in Port Arthur and Fort William, Ontario, in 1913. I have chosen to examine silent film because it is a "closed chapter." The analytical tools, though, remain the same and are equally relevant to other types.

Scene 1: Towards a Methodology

Can films be viewed through the same lens as other historical "facts?" Quite simply, the answer is yes. The position of film as the most viable, prestigious, and influential form of mass communication of the twentieth century enshrines its importance.[10] As John E. O'Connor argues, "film and television demand recognition as forces in twentieth century society and culture, so they must also be recognised as shapers of historical consciousness."[11] Interestingly, the idea of including films as part of historical methodology is not unique by any means. Since the birth of motion pictures,[12] historians have discussed the value of film as a historical document.[13] For example, as early as 1895 suggestions were made by W.K.L. Dickson, the man responsible for the development and perfection of Thomas Edison's first motion picture machine, that,

> The advantages to students and historians will be immeasurable. Instead of dry and misleading accounts, tinged with the exaggerations of the chronicler's minds, our archives will be enriched by the vitalized pictures of great national scenes, instinct with all the glowing personalities which characterised them.[14]

Considering the role that film has played in the hundred years since its invention, not considering it a "fact" worthy of the same analysis as other "artefacts" of the past is a failure to, as E.H. Carr suggests, "bring into the

---

[10] Paul Audley, for example, suggests the importance of film as part of his argument in *Canada's Cultural Industries: Broadcasting, Publishing, Records and Film* (Toronto: James Lormier and Company, 1984), 21.

[11] John E. O'Connor, ed., *Image as Artifact: the Historical Analysis of Film and Television* (Malabar, Florida: Robert E. Krieger Publishing Company, 1990), 2.

[12] That motion pictures were "born" is a much used, but wholly inaccurate, phrase. Motion pictures were the culmination of a millennia of technological achievements and adaptations. For a brief synopsis of the idea, see Charles Musser, *The Emergence of Cinema: The American Screen to 1907* (Berkely: University of California Press, 1994), 1-91.

[13] See Boleslaus Matuszewski, *Une nouvelle source de l'histoire* (Paris, 1898) quoted in Martin A. Jackson, "Film as a Source Material: Some Preliminary Notes Toward a Methodology," *Journal of Interdisciplinary History* IV, no. I (Summer 1973): 73.

[14] W.K.L. and Antonia Dickson, *History of the Kinetograph, Kinetoscope, and Kinetophongraph* (New York, 1895), 51-52 quoted in John B. Kuiper, "The Historical Value of Motion Pictures," *American Archivist* 31, no. 4 (October 1968): 385.

picture all known or knowable facts relevant, in one sense or another, to the theme in which he is engaged and to interpretation proposed."[15]

Why then do historians continue to not consult filmic evidence? According to Warren Susman, the main problem is that "not all historians are comfortable with such sources: they appear too slippery, too easily manipulated."[16] This belief, though, is largely based on misconceptions and misunderstanding. Films are no different from any other type of factual document. While they are unique in that they are dependent on technology for their creation and viewing, they can be examined in much the same way that E.H. Carr suggests any work of history should: "when we take up a work of history, our first concern should be not with the facts which it contains but with the historian who wrote it."[17]

In Canada, historians have long been fascinated by motion pictures and their possible use in research and teaching. As early as 1941, Charles W. Jeffries commented in the *Canadian Historical Review* that "people nowadays get much of their information and their conceptions of life, past and present, through media other than books, lectures, and sermons, the long-standing established sources of instruction."[18] Yet, despite this acknowledgement and a continuing belief by academics that the culture of Canada is in grave peril, historians have for the most part continually neglected the history of film.[19] As

---

[15] Carr, *What is History?*, 32.

[16] Warren I. Susman, "Film and History" Artifact and Experience," *Film and History* 15, no. 2 (1985): 26.

[17] Carr, *What is History?*, 24.

[18] Charles W. Jeffries, "History in Motion Pictures," *Canadian Historical Review* 22, no. 4 (December, 1941): 361.

[19] Despite the contention by those such as Robert Craig Brown and Ramsay Cook that early twentieth century Canada was transformed "by more than number and size," little attention has been given to anything beyond agriculture, immigration, industrialization, and national expansion in Canadian historiography. Little discussion of the cultural fabric of Canada is discussed and, in contrast to comparable American studies, the handful of general histories on the period often discuss the history of film as part of the greater discussion on art, literature, and, as does John Herd Thompson and Allen Seager, the serious threat of the "northbound tidal wave of American mass culture, radio programs, professional spectator sports, and magazines." See Robert Craig Brown and Ramsay Cook, *Canada 1896-1921: A Nation Transformed* (Toronto: McClelland and Stewart, 1974), 1 and John Herd Thompson and Allen Seager, *Canada, 1922-1939: Decades of Discord* (Toronto: McClelland and Stewart, 1985). For examples of film's inclusion in the discussion of Canada's cultural history see Alan Smith, *Canada: An American Nation* (Kingston and Montreal: McGill-Queen's University Press, 1994); David H. Flaherty and Frank E. Manning, *The Beaver Bites Back?, American Popular Culture in Canada* (Kingston and Montreal: McGill-Queen's University Press, 1993); Paul Audley, *Canada's Cultural Industries: Broadcasting, Publishing, Records and Films* (Toronto: J. Lorimer, in association with the Canadian Institute for Economic Policy, 1983); Ian Lumsden, ed., *Close the 49th Parallel, Etc: The Americanization of Canada* (Toronto: University of

David Frank has recently commented, "there are not many standard titles on the history of Canadian film ... [and] Film Studies in Canada seem to have been largely nationalistic in spirit, rather like the older studies of broadcast history."[20]

The situation is even more complicated for those undertaking an examination of film prior to the establishment of the National Film Board of Canada in 1939. Despite being written over 20 years ago, Peter Morris' *Embattled Shadows* remains the only comprehensive book-length study of the period. It is therefore not surprising that Morris' introductory statement that "the study of Canadian film history is still in an embryonic state," is as apt today as when it was first written.[21] In fact, despite a shared belief by many film scholars like Chris Gittings that "*Embattled Shadows* is not exploited as much as it could be in our syllabus and research," there has been little forward movement in the field.[22] In no way is this lack of scholarship reflective of the

---

Toronto Press, 1970); and John H. Redekop, ed., *The Star Spangled Beaver* (Toronto: Peter Martin Associates Limited, 1971).

[20] David Frank, "Short Takes: The Canadian Worker on Film," *Labour / Le Travail* 46 (Fall 2000): 417. Frank fails to acknowledge, though, that some such as Gene Walz have long recognized that the history of film in Canada "is not monolithic or orderly or continuous; it is not, therefore, easily chronicled." Walz argues that many of the major contributions to Canadian film history that remain unrecognized are so "because film history in Canada is not the history of industry, but of many industrious people and organisations, separated by both space and time and rarely if ever united in grandiose, common enterprise." In the most clearly articulated statement of its kind in Canadian film historiography, Walz provocatively calls for "a chorus of voices engaged in the kind of painstaking, cross-country chronicling of every nook, cranny and anything else that might relate" to the history of film in Canada. For film historians "to fill in the blanks in our past," Walz states they "must not only rediscover the contributions to our film culture that have been overlooked or forgotten ... [but] also reappraise the positions of those people and institutions already recognised." See Gene Walz, ed., *Flashback: People and Institutions in Canadian Film History* (Montreal: Mediatexte Publications Inc., 1986), 11-12.

[21] Peter Morris, *Embattled Shadows* (Kingston and Montreal: McGill-Queen's University Press, 1978, reprint 1992), 1.

[22] Christopher Gittings, *Canada's National Cinema* (New York: Routledge, 2002), 3. The exception is the work performed by film historians in Quebec. A number of historical works have been published in the last 10 years that delve somewhat into the early history of film in that province. Notable are the works by Germain Lacasse, André Gaudreault, and Pierre Véronneau. See Germain Lacasse and André Gaudreault, "The Introduction of Lumière Cinematographe in Canada," Madeleine Beaudry trans., *Canadian Journal of Film Studies* 5, no. 2 (Fall 1996): 113-23; André Gaudreault, Germain Lacasse, and Pierre Sirois-Trahan, *Au pays des ennemis du Québec pour une nouvelle histoire des début du cinema au Québec* (Québec: Nuit Blanche, 1996); Germain Lacasse, "Cultural Amnesia and the Birth of film in Canada," *Cinema Canada* no. 108 (1984): 16-17.; Germain Lacasse and Serge Duigou, *L'Historiographe (Les débuts du spectacle*

abundance of filmic material available throughout Canada. Extensive caches of rich and largely unexplored documents are known to exist in the film collections of municipal, provincial, and federal institutions and archives throughout the country. Additionally, countless films are in the hands of private individuals and lay forgotten in attics and barns from coast to coast. This lack of scholarship is problematic, as contextualizing any early films that a historian would hope to use is extremely difficult.

In contrast, it should not be surprising that the American preoccupation with motion pictures has permeated scholarship in the United States to a much larger extent than in Canada. Paula Marantz Cohen's *Silent Film and the Triumph of the American Myth*, for example, argues that the United States defined the motion picture and vice versa. The "alliance between film and America," Cohen states, "was the result of more than economic opportunity and available human and natural resources, though it drew on these factors for support. It rested on film's ability to participate in the *myth of America* as it was elaborated in the course of the nineteenth century."[23]

In terms of scholarship, whether the "myth of America" is real or imagined is irrelevant. There can be no doubt those motion pictures were an integral part of creating, sustaining, and developing how America perceived itself in the early twentieth century. This fact alone has caused it to become part of any historical discussion on the period and led to an increasing body of scholarship on the use of film as a historical source. John E. O'Connor and Martin Jackson's formation of the Historian's Film Committee in the early 1970s, for example, enshrined a place for a dialogue on film and history in the American Historical Association.[24]

Since the establishment of the AHA Committee, a plethora of material has been written on historical approaches to film, mainly through the committee's journal, *Film & History: An Interdisciplinary Journal of Film and Television*. One of the most notable monographs is the aptly titled *Film History: Theory and Practice*, by Robert C. Allen and Douglas Gomery.[25] Its

---

cinématographique au Québec) (Montreal: Cinémathèque québécoise, 1985). For Véronneau see *Self Portrait: Essays on the Canadian and Québec Cinemas*, translated and expanded with Piers Handling (Ottawa: Canadian Film Institute, 1980), and *Le success est au film parlant français: histoire du cinema au Québec* 1 (Montréal: La cinémathèque québécois/Le muse du cinema, coll. Les dossiers de la cinémathèque, no. 3, 1979), 1.

[23] Paula Marantz Cohen, *Silent Film and the Triumph of the American Myth* (New York: Oxford University Press, 2001), 6.

[24] Recently, a special edition of *Perspectives*, the AHA's newsletter, focused entirely on film and the issue of history and drew the participation of notable film scholars such as Robert Rosenstone and Kathryn Fuller, to mainstream historians such as Richard White. See *Perspectives* 37, no. 4 (April 1999).

[25] The authors stated intention was to produce a work that would "(1) place film history within the context of historical research in general; (2) acquaint the reader with specific

examination of the methods, approaches, successes, and short-comings of film history as a discipline remains the most concise and articulated discussion in English. *Film History* is, in many ways, a manual designed to assist film historians in coming to grips with this subject. The study attempts to demonstrate that the writing of history "is not the passive transmission of facts, but an active process of judgement – a confrontation between the historian and his or her material."[26] For historians this is not new, but, in the case of film history, the "fact" that judgment is being passed on is, in terms of historical evidence, an unconventional one. However, Allen and Gomery's work does not address one key issue: the use of film in writing history, rather than the writing of film history.

John E. O'Connor's edited collection *Image as Artifact* is the best attempt so far to form, as the contributors intended, a "coherent and comprehensive methodology to the study of film,"[27] and to "identify the specific way in which the historian's tools best apply to the study of moving images."[28] It advocates two stages of historical analysis of what it terms "a moving image artefact." The first is to gather information on the content, production, and reception of the film strictly as a document. While many aspects of the film become evident simply through viewing it, O'Connor and the contributors to the collection suggest attention needs to be paid to additional aspects of the film, namely:

> A close study of the content of the film itself – the images which appear on screen and the sounds on the soundtrack and the ways they are brought together to convey meaning; the social, cultural, political, economic, and institutional background of the production and the conditions under which it was made; and the ways in which the film ... was understood by its original audience.[29]

The second stage involves examining the material gathered in stage one in relation to what can be "reduced to four frameworks of historical inquiry."[30] These "frameworks" are categorized as, in no order of importance:

---

and, in some cases, unique problems confronting film historians; (3) survey the approaches that have been taken to the historical study of film; and (4) provide examples of various types of film historical research." See Robert C. Allen and Douglas Gomery, *Film History: Theory and Practice* (New York: Knopf, 1985), iv.

[26] Ibid., 43.
[27] O'Connor, *Image as Artifact*, 6.
[28] Ibid., ix.
[29] Ibid., 6, 10-26.
[30] Ibid., 7.

> Framework 1: The Moving Image as Representation of History;
> Framework 2: The Moving Image as Evidence of Social and Cultural History;
> Framework 3: Actuality Footage as Evidence for Historical Fact;
> Framework 4: The History of the Moving Image as Industry in Art Form.

It is important to understand, as O'Connor suggests, that "these four categories are not meant to be rigid or limiting in any way ... in practice, there will *always* be overlap among the four; *no one of them can or should be applied without reference to the others.*"[31]

While not entirely a separate framework, one aspect of the compilation that deserves separate mention is the need for the historian to use film in relation to other forms of records. Anticipating O'Connor's collection, Christopher H. Roads, once Deputy Director and Keeper of the Department of Records, Imperial War Museum, suggested in 1966 that regardless of how one views film as a document its "value and use ... as historical evidence can be appreciated only if the prospective user has a broad grasp of the circumstances surrounding its creation, preservation, and accessibility as well as its general character, and, therefore, its relationship with other classes of records."[32]

Keeping in mind both Allen and Gomery's approach to the writing of history, and the methodology advocated by O'Connor, what follows is a brief study of a film made in and about Fort William and Port Arthur, Ontario, in 1913. This is intended to provide an example of how historians can use film to complement and enrich traditional documents. Unlike the case study of *The Plow that Broke the Plains*, that follows the theoretical discussion in *Image as Artifact*, the following incorporates O'Connor's and his colleagues' strategies rather than compartmentalizing them.[33]

Scene 2: Port Arthur and Fort William: Canada's Keys to the Great Lakes

Like many parts of Canada during the early twentieth century, the residents of Port Arthur and Fort William viewed their progress and future development as synonymous with the desire to replicate the prosperity of the

---

[31] Ibid., 8. Each of these categories receives extensive attention in individual chapters representing contributions by various leading film historians. See 27 to 107 for Framework 1, 108 to 168 for Framework 2, 169 to 216 for Framework 3, and 217 to 284 for Framework 4.

[32] Christopher H. Roads, "Film as Historical Evidence," *Journal of the Society of Archivists* (October 1966), 183.

[33] O'Connor's "Case Study" is organized by subheadings of each stage and method of historical inquiry. While useful as a demonstration, it is not consistent with the format of most historical scholarship.

United States.³⁴ As demonstrated in the following article that appeared in the *Weekly Herald* in 1898, the potential of the region was often framed in comparison to major American metropolises:

> We [at the Lakehead] are subsisting upon delicacies procured from the far points of the compass. We stand in the gateway to the ocean ... We are nearer London, England, than New York City. We look toward the South and we can almost see the smoke rising from the modern London – Chicago. We go north and return with millions from our Klondyke ... Some fine morning we will awake to find this the centre of a busy, mighty people; we have all the industrial possibilities of any country ... While other communities totter and fail, ours will stand. Our growth has been that of the oak; when it reaches its maturity it will be known for its strength.³⁵

The city that both Port Arthur and Fort William were most frequently compared to was Chicago: "like Chicago, Port Arthur was located both as to water and railway communications to become the national distribution point of this country and the metropolis of the West."³⁶ Similarly, another article in 1910 attempted to draw a direct parallel between the harbours of Port Arthur and Fort William and that of Chicago. According to the *Port Arthur Daily News-Chronicle* "the two cities at the head of Lake Superior have a greater Western tributary and have greater harbour facilities than Chicago" had when it began to boom.³⁷

In many ways the development of the Lakehead in the early twentieth century was reminiscent of Chicago's between 1820 and 1890. The growth and economic success of Chicago and its outlying regions were natural choices for emulation. The business elite of the Lakehead and the provincial government of Ontario saw that Chicago, like the Lakehead, began as a fur-trading outpost that entered the mid-nineteenth century with a bleak outlook.³⁸ However, the industrialization and continental policies of the American government spurred a

---

³⁴ Greg Scott, for example, demonstrates that communities along the St. Lawrence also viewed their potential through an American lens. See "The Chicago of the Dominion?: The Development of Port Franks, Ontario," *Ontario History* XCV, no. 1 (Spring 2003): 22-37.
³⁵ *Weekly Herald*, 18 Nov. 1898 quoted in Thorld J. Tronrud, *Guardians of Progress: Boosters and Boosterism in Thunder Bay, 1870-1914* (Thunder Bay: Thunder Bay Historical Museum Society, 1993), 9.
³⁶ *Port Arthur Daily News-Chronicle*, 21 March 1906.
³⁷ *Port Arthur Daily News-Chronicle*, 2 Feb. 1910.
³⁸ See Dominic A. Pacyga and Ellen Skerret, *Chicago: City of Neighbourhoods* (Chicago: Loyola University Press, 1986), chapter 1, for a brief description, with visuals, of the early settlement of the river area now known as "the loop."

period of railway growth. From its modest two tracks in 1850, by 1856 more than 3,000 miles of track were providing the roadbed for 58 passenger and 38 freight trains daily.[39] Chicago's position as the focus of this transcontinental network allowed the hinterland fort of 1820 to develop into the railway capital of both the United States and the world by 1871.[40]

The railway's effect on the development of the region was profound. In addition to the maintenance and supply yards required, with the railroads came an influx of settlers, businesses, and investment. Drawn by the city's growing position as a major world wheat handling centre, Chicago's function as "a railway hub allowed it to become the great interchange through which the mid-western agricultural bounty was collected for movement to the east.[41] The growth of Chicago's prominence in the railroad industry "was only rivalled by its growth in the Lake Traffic."[42] The construction of canals, dredging, and a variety of other improvements assisted "Chicago to branch out like the arteries of a growing organism, knitting the agricultural settlements and trade centers into an economic unit and joining the Chicago Region with the outside world."[43]

Such beliefs were not an isolated phenomenon, but rather part of an experience known as "Boosterism." Prevalent in the late nineteenth and early twentieth century, Thorold J. Tronrud, for example, contends that "at its simplest level, boosterism describes that wide range of initiatives taken by business groups, individuals and municipal governments to promote their communities ... it was an ideology of growth which defined spirit and self-image of the community as a whole."[44] Similarly Alan Artibise demonstrates that boosters measured "their city's growth in qualitative terms [by the] number of rail lines, miles of streets, dollars of assessment, size of population, and value of manufacturing and wholesale trade."[45] Interestingly, of all the booster techniques utilized in the early twentieth century, moving pictures, arguably

---

[39] Harold M. Mayer and Richard C. Wade, *Chicago: Growth of a Metropolis* (Chicago: Chicago University Press, 1969), 40. See also Perry Duis, *Challenging Chicago: Creating New Traditions* (Chicago: Chicago Historical Society, 1976) for a discussion on the modernization and development of Chicago.

[40] Mayer and Wade, *Chicago*, 35, 40.

[41] Duis, *Challenging Chicago*, 9, and Irving Cutler, *Chicago: Metropolis of the Mid-Continent*, 3d. ed. (Dubuque, Iowa: The Geographic Society/Hunt Publishing Company, 1982), 201.

[42] Mayer and Wade, *Chicago*, 42.

[43] Daniel H. Burnham, Jr. and Robert Kingery, *Planning the Region of Chicago* (Chicago: Chicago Regional Planning Association, 1956), 81.

[44] Tronrud, *Guardians of Progress*, 5.

[45] Alan Artibise, "Boosterism and the Development of Prairie Cities, 1871-1913" in Alan Artibise, ed., *Town and City, Aspects of Western Canadian Urban Development* (Regina: University of Regina Press, 1981), 213.

one of the most influential media, has been little researched.[46] The ability of moving pictures to reach both literate and non-literate audiences was only matched by photography, and, as with photographs, early audiences believed that what they saw on screen was an actual depiction of life.[47]

In manner, appearance, and purpose the earliest moving pictures made in, or about, the Lakehead were part of the same booster tradition that developed this image of the West. Primarily travelogues and industrial films, the moving pictures made between 1911 and 1926 used images and text to highlight the twin cities as both the Canadian Chicago of the North and a haven for adventurers.[48] The idea of producing films at the Lakehead also followed the evolution of that medium in North America. An interesting facet of early production was the correlation between permanent theatres and an increase in film production.[49] Beginning as early as 1900, residents of Port Arthur and Fort William had been active participants in the growing continental movie-going culture.[50] In fact, film historians such as Peter Morris argue that the impact of the establishment of permanent theatres was so profound that most film histories originate from this point.[51]

Yet beyond exceptions, such as the Holland Brothers, Ernest Ouimet, George Scott, and James Freer, it was not until 1911 that domestic production companies in Canada began to make films. Most of these companies were of two types: makers of fiction films for the American market or those claiming to be producing "all Canadian" drama, but in reality making only a scenic or promotional film.[52] At the Lakehead, early moving pictures highlighted the same industries that had made Chicago the metropolis it had become by 1910,

---

[46] Tronrud in *Guardian's of Progress* does briefly mention the use of films, but as it was not specifically the scope of his work no analysis of the film is included.

[47] For a discussion of photography's use see David Mattison, "In Visioning the City: Urban Historical Techniques Through Historical Photographs," *Urban History Review* 13 (1984): 43-51; M.F. Fox, "Bird's-Eye Views of Canadian Cities: A Review," *Urban History Review* 4 (1977): 38-45, and Jim Burant, "Visual Records and Urban Development," *Urban History Review* 12 (1984): 57-63.

[48] This was preceded by the use of panoramic photographs to highlight the prosperity and potential of regions. See Joseph Earl Arrington, "William Burr's Moving Panorama of The Great Lakes, The Niagara, St. Lawrence, and Saguenay Rivers," *Ontario History* LI, no. 3 (1959) for a brief, but interesting, example.

[49] Peter Morris briefly discusses this in his *Embattled Shadows: A History of Canadian Cinema, 1895-1939* (Montreal and Kingston: McGill-Queen's University Press, 1978).

[50] For a discussion of this phenomenon in the United States see Kathryn Fuller, *At the Picture Show: Small Town Audiences and the Creation of a Movie Fan Culture* (New York: Smithsonian Institute, 1996), and Douglas Gomery, *Shared Pleasures: A History of Movie Presentation in the United States* (Madison: University of Wisconsin Press, 1992).

[51] Morris, *Embattled Shadows*, 27.

[52] Ibid., 46.

and the boosters imagined a similar historical development for Port Arthur and Fort William.

The image portrayed by the early filmmakers and the aspects of Canadian society they focused on were constructed as self-fulfilling prophecies. Prosperity, modernity, security, and productivity were the themes of the earliest essay films made in Canada. In the Canadian West, a region where boosterism was the most prevalent, "new ideas and perceptions evolved out of previous ones"[53] and, just as at the Lakehead, the image of the prairies was one of a "new and better society ... a garden of abundance in which all material want would be provided and where moral and civic virtues would be perfected."[54] The films made at the Lakehead during this period attempt to depict such an imagined community with varying success.

At the turn of the twentieth century, James Whalen was one of the key industrial figures at the Lakehead who imagined the region as the next metropolis of the North. A consummate booster for the cities of Port Arthur and Fort William, he was involved in almost all aspects of the regional economy. His fortune was built upon the natural resources of the area and his continued success relied upon the prosperity of local industry, real estate, and shipbuilding in which he had invested heavily.[55] Whalen also had an interest in moving pictures, building the Lyceum theatre in 1908. Realizing the potential of film, he purchased the Commercial Motion Picture Company of Montreal in 1911 to show his vision of the region and promote his business interests. The result was *Port Arthur and Fort William: Canada's Keys to the Great Lakes* which was intended "to be the grandest booster film made to that date at the Lakehead."[56]

Like William Van Horne, the man responsible for financing James Freer's films, Whalen was a great believer in modern promotional methods. His *Port Arthur and Fort William: Canada's Keys to the Great Lakes* was an attempt to show how, like the Chicago of the nineteenth century, the twin cities

---

[53] R. Douglas Francis, *Images of the West: Changing Perspectives of the Prairies, 1690-1960* (Saskatoon: Western Prairie Producer Books, 1989), xvii.
[54] Ibid., 106.
[55] For more information on the life of James Whalen see Raymond Furlotte's brief examination, *The James Whalen Empire* (Thunder Bay: Thunder Bay Hydro, 1990).
[56] *Port Arthur and Fort William, Ontario: Keys to the Great Lakes*, 45m., Commercial Motion Picture Company of Canada, 1913, 45mm (James Whalen Collection, National Archives of Canada). The film itself remains the earliest moving picture made at the Lakehead still in existence. It is also the longest film of its type still in existence in Canada and one of the most interesting examples of boosterism by a Lakehead resident. The only moving picture to precede "Port Arthur and Fort William: Canada's Keys to the Great Lakes" was "The Making of A Loaf of Bread." Shot in 1907 by a British entrepreneur, it was purported to have been funded from Ottawa and eventually shown in London, England. However, the only discussion of this film occurs in *Guardians of Progress* and a newspaper clipping from the *Morning Herald*, 22 October 1907.

were indeed the keys to the great West and all the economic promise held therein. Filmed between 1911 and 1913, the Whalen Film, as it was referred to locally, also served to highlight his financial interests as the footage focuses primarily on his companies, properties, and investments. Within the film are scenes depicting the region in a manner reminiscent of the newspaper articles of the time.

Contained within the first glimpses of the cities are all the aspects a booster would wish to demonstrate to his audience. Behind the breakwater stands the harbour, in defiance of nature and protecting the residents of the Lakehead from the fury of Lake Superior. The spectator is made aware, through images and title cards, of the breakwater, the Prince Arthur Hotel, the Canadian Northern railway station, and a variety of grain elevators.

The importance of Port Arthur's harbour is the first part of the region to get attention. The icebreaker *James Whalen* is shown opening up the harbour to allow "some of the 62 steamships clearing from winter-berths, sailing east with grain cargoes" to get underway.[57] Each ship clearing port is briefly highlighted with its name and size stated for the audience.[58] The film establishes that all of the ships are going to feed the multitudes in the East. A variety of scenes further demonstrates the amount of water traffic in the region. Intended, like the street scenes, to show a thriving water system, the footage is oddly self-defeating as many vessels in each shot merely go back and forth in front of the camera.[59] Also shown is the reason why many of these ships used the harbour for a winter berth. One of the region's prominent companies, Whalen's Western Dry-Dock and Shipbuilding Company, is the focus of scenes. The largest of its kind in Canada at the time, the dry-dock's continued operation rested on the success of the harbour and the business generated from the thriving cities of Port Arthur and Fort William.[60] Included with these exterior shots are those filmed inside showing the technology used by, and skills of, the workers.[61]

The film also examines a number of the region's other important industries, including grain elevators and grain handling, one the region's main economic activities. Initially introduced in the third shot of the film, grain

---

[57] As no format exists for the citation of title cards in silent films, TC (for title card) followed by its sequence in the film will be used. *Port Arthur and Fort William, Ontario: Canada's Keys to the Great Lakes*, TC 1.

[58] These ships include the steamers *Fitzgerald* and *A.E. Stewart* and an unknown whaleback.

[59] The tug *James Whalen* can clearly be seen doing this a number of times.

[60] Bruce Muirhead, "The Evolution of the Lakehead's Commercial Transportation Infrastructure," in Thorold J. Tronrud and A. Ernest Epp, eds., *Thunder Bay: From Rivalry to Unity* (Thunder Bay: Thunder Bay Historical Museum Society, 1995), 84-85.

[61] The footage also contains images of some of the 1,200 men the dry-dock employed. They are shown in the midst of constructing a number of vessels. See *Port Arthur and Fort William, Ontario: Canada's Keys to the Great Lakes*, TC 6.

elevators are prevalent throughout. From the beginning of the film when King's Elevator is introduced, the prominent role of the elevators is frequently referred to. The Canadian Northern Elevator is introduced with a title card careful to point out that it was one of the largest in the world, and that its capacity was being expanded.[62] Similarly, the Ogilvie Elevator and Flour Mills, Empire Elevator, Grand Trunk Elevator, and Canadian Pacific Railway Elevator are used as focal points for many of the street scenes, panoramas, and harbour shots of Fort William.[63] Often at the end of a street, or the largest landmark in the skyline, their importance is apparent even without the title cards that inevitably pay tribute to their capacity and importance.[64]

As the largest and most predominant structures in the area, the elevators were used as a platform from which some of the spectacular panoramas found in the film were shot, which outline the expanse of industrial, commercial, and residential areas in the twin cities. Not unlike early Edison street scenes, much of the remaining footage is taken from a streetcar moving through downtown areas of Port Arthur and Fort William. The inclusion of the street railway is no coincidence as both cities were always quick to point out that they, not Toronto, Kingston, or Montreal, had Canada's first publicly owned street railway.[65] These scenes are intended to demonstrate the activities prevalent in the cities. As well, downtown cores are shown, with a special focus on commercial activity. Even the expansion of these core areas is highlighted as the film also shows excavation for the Whalen office building, then underway.

Port Arthur and Fort William: Keys to the Great Lakes also emphasizes services that only a modern and urban centre could provide. Union Station and the CPR tracks in Fort William show, in addition to their economic connotations, the communication and passenger service that enabled the region to keep abreast of what was occurring elsewhere in the world. Schools, churches, political figures, and other trappings of a good and moral society are also included. Like many of the films depicting Chicago and other American cities, the street scenes of Fort William include the fire department leaving the central fire hall. While the film shows older horse-drawn carriages, it gives

---

[62] *Port Arthur and Fort William, Ontario: Canada's Keys to the Great Lakes*, TC 9.

[63] The panoramic, or bird's eye, view, of cities was a common technique. See M.F. Fox's review of "The Bird's Eye Views of Canadian Cities: An Exhibition of Panoramic Maps (1865-1908): A National Archives of Canada Exhibition (July-November 1976)" *Urban History Review 4* (1977): 38-45, and David Mattison's examination of historical photographs in "In Visioning the City: Urban History Techniques Through Historical Photographs," *Urban History Review* 13 (June 1984): 43-51.

[64] For the Empire Elevator see *Port Arthur and Fort William, Ontario: Canada's Keys to the Great Lakes*, TC 34.

[65] For more information on the street railway see F.B. Scollie, "The Creation of the Port Arthur Street Railway, 1890-95," *Papers and Records*, Thunder Bay Historical Society, xviii (1990): 40-58 and Mark Chochla, "Sabbatarians and Sunday Street Cars," Ibid., xvii (1989): 25-36.

prominence to the city's new automobile, a relatively recent mass-market product which symbolized the future.

Highlighted in Whalen's film are many of the industrial and commercial accomplishments of the Lakehead. The region's dependence on natural resources is tempered by the increasing amount of industry generated by the dry-docks and other large operations. The street scenes and panoramic views of the city clearly show its urban layout. Anticipated to be shown at industrial exhibitions throughout North America, the scenes and shots described were carefully selected to demonstrate to the rest of the continent that the twin cities at the head of Lake Superior had all the potential of Chicago and other major American cities and contained a natural beauty and resources they did not.

While the vision of James Whalen was not the vision of everyone in the community, no greater force impacted how the communities of Fort William and Port Arthur, Ontario, imagined themselves in the first decades of the twentieth century than boosterism. Whalen, though, was not the first in Canada to use moving pictures to promote his business interests. As early as 1908, companies had been formed with the purpose of producing films to be shown at fairs and industrial exhibitions. Many of these films were made under the auspices of provincial governments and railway companies. In 1908, the Urban Company of Montreal was contracted by the government of British Columbia to make films to show "the advantages and resources of British Columbia to the outside world."[66] And, like James Freer almost a decade before, the CPR and CNR, with backing from the federal government, continued to produce moving pictures to attract immigrants to the regions serviced by their trains. While *Port Arthur and Fort William: Keys to the Great Lakes* was a citywide event when it "premiered" at the Lyceum theatre in Port Arthur in 1913, there is no indication that it had much success elsewhere.[67]

Scene 3: The Historian and Film

How many graduate students dread the discovery, right before orals or external evaluations, of the publication of one more source, its inclusion considered paramount to the demonstration of knowledge? Yet, the vast majority of dissertations, or scholarly monographs for that matter, have neglected to consult an important fact – film. Some still may argue as Neil Postman that "all forms of serious public discourse are threatened by the influence of the mass media."[68] But Postman is only partially correct. Motion pictures were an expression of the twentieth century. Peter Gay argues that

---

[66] Morris, *Embattled Shadows*, 36.
[67] The film "premiered" with prizes being handed out to those who could identify themselves. See Furlotte, *James Whalen Empire*, 5.
[68] O'Connor, *Image as Artifact*, 4.

Ranke "recognised that history is a progressive discipline."[69] An embrace of film as an integral part of historical scholarship is merely a next step in the progress of the discipline.

Developed just prior to 1900, it is an ever-present chronicler of individuals and events that shaped the last century – and continues to do so into the twenty-first, and, as such, film adds to, and complements the breadth of, evidentiary materials available to the historian. It is time historians turned to the ever-increasing and rich cache of "facts" found in the archives and even video stores the world over. For, if one were to take E.H. Carr to heart and accept his belief that "the historian without his facts is rootless and futile,"[70] then as a profession we have failed. Carr contends that "the duty of the historian to respect his facts is not exhausted by the obligation to see that his facts are accurate. He must seek to bring into the picture all known or knowable facts relevant, in one sense or another, to the theme in which he is engaged and to interpretation proposed."[71] Film should not replace the sources traditionally used by historians, but its inclusion can bring us a step closer to reaching Ranke's unattainable goal of history "as it really happened."

---

[69] Gay, *Styles in History*, 72.
[70] Carr, *What is History?*, 35.
[71] Ibid., 32

Evidence of What?
Changing Answers to the Question of Historical Source as Illustrated by Research Using the Census

Chad Gaffield

Surprisingly and in repeatedly unexpected ways, historians have continued to debate in recent decades the central question of their craft: how can the past be described and explained? At each stage of the debate, the answers to this question have reflected and contributed to larger epistemological discussions across the disciplines. The following discussion examines selected aspects of the twists and turns of recent historical debate by using the example of research on census enumerations. From the time of the "new social history" of the 1960s and 1970s to the cultural history of the 1980s and 1990s, scholars have focused on census enumerations for quite different reasons and in quite different ways. At the core of this research have been changing answers to the question of evidence: census enumerations are evidence of what? In examining the different ways that scholars have addressed this question, particular attention will be paid to the interactions of historians with scholars in other disciplines across the social sciences and humanities. This analysis will focus on Canadian research although scholars in other countries especially the United States and Great Britain have similarly continued to debate how census enumerations can support historical interpretations.

Before the 1960s, researchers did not view the census as a valuable historical source for analysing Canadian history. In contrast, the government officials who actually administered the census at the start of each decade since the mid-nineteenth century believed that they were creating a permanent record about Canadian society that would, in fact, be used by future researchers to analyse the patterns and trends of social, economic, cultural, and political change. As a result, government record-keepers and archivists were charged with preserving census enumerations and, despite pressures of space and resources, they did so to a considerable extent including the substantial microfilming in the early 1950s of original manuscript census schedules reaching back into the nineteenth century.[1]

The conviction of census officials and archivists that the Canadian census should be preserved for historical study proved to be justified during the 1960s when scholars turned to the census for two key reasons: to study evidence of behaviour and to learn about the historically "anonymous." Under

---

[1] While the decennial census began in 1851-52, earlier enumerations date from the mid-seventeenth century. The history of the Canadian census and its availability for research is summarized in the *Report of the Expert Panel on Access to Historical Census Records* (Ottawa: Ministry of Industry, 2000). The Expert Panel included Chad Gaffield, Gerald LaForest, Lorna Marsden, John McCamus, and Richard Van Loon (chair).

the leadership of Michael Katz, David Gagan, and a few other researchers, the census came to be seen as a way to move beyond the literary sources that characteristically underpinned the established historical scholarship.[2] These sources were now criticized as only providing "impressionistic" evidence of the thoughts, ambitions, and claims of a small number of official and unofficial leaders. The census promised to enable interpretations based not on the ideas of a minority but rather on the behaviour of the whole society. Partly as a rejection of the "history of ideas" and intellectual history that had gained considerable favour among historians by the 1950s, the new compelling questions in historical debate concerned what was being done across populations rather than what was being written by elites.

The pioneering studies drew upon the social sciences both for concepts and methods. Sociology, for example, offered ways to study occupational structure while anthropology provided methods for analyzing family and household structures and networks. The basic approach was to count individual responses to the census enumeration questions and to inter-relate them with the responses of other individuals as listed in the same dwelling, neighbourhood, and community. The census thus became associated with quantitative history as the evidence of individual behaviour was counted up to identify patterns within class, ethnicity, and gender similarities and differences.

At the time, the research possibilities seemed endless. Each census during the nineteenth century provided an increasing number of responses to an increasing number of questions ranging from those focused on personal attributes such as age, sex, and birthplace to those dealing with the means of living such as occupation and agricultural production. The ability to examine the manuscript census returns that were made available by the 92-year confidentiality policy allowed researchers during this period to move from the 1851-52 to the 1861, 1871, and 1881 enumerations. As a result, researchers could not only examine one historical moment but could also compare patterns as well as follow individuals from one census to the next. In this work, a North American version of micro-history became the preferred research strategy of scholars using the census as evidence of the historically anonymous. Focused on specific communities, townships, or cities micro-history sought to increase the level of interpretation and understanding by reducing the level of observation. Unlike local histories, micro-historical research treated the analysis of individuals and groups in a particular time and place not as an end in itself but rather as a means of understanding larger historical changes familiar elsewhere as well.[3] By systematically examining the responses to

---

[2] Michael B. Katz, *The People of Hamilton, Canada West: Family and Class in a Mid-Nineteenth-Century City* (Cambridge: Harvard University Press, 1975), and David Gagan, *Hopeful Travelers: Families, Land, and Social Change in Mid-Victorian Peel County, Canada West* (Toronto : University of Toronto Press, 1981).

[3] Chad Gaffield, "The Micro-History of Cultural Relations: Prescott County and the Language of Instruction Controversy," paper presented to the Canadian Historical Association, June 1984. The European version of micro-history is discussed in Carlo Ginzburg, "Microhistory—Two or Three Things That I Know About It," *Critical Inquiry* 20, no. 1 (1993): 10-35.

census questions for certain enumeration districts, scholars sought to enhance their grasp of generalized social and economic transformations.

In unprecedented ways, scholars claimed to be rewriting the history of modern society by describing significant features of the lives of both the "famous" and "anonymous." Micro-histories emphasized the value of studying popular behaviour rather than elite perceptions, and they challenged established understandings of key features of the nineteenth century especially urbanization, commercial development, and early industrialization. In this way, the census became a familiar source in detailed studies of the specific and diverse ways in which social and economic change occurred during the nineteenth century.

One example of the robust and often surprising results of the census-based, micro-historical studies of the 1970s was the conclusion that fertility rates declined during the later nineteenth century in both rural and urban areas. Although the pattern of this decline varied considerably across the communities under study, the discovery of significantly changed fertility rates seemed to justify the enthusiasm for the "new social history."[4] Not only did the decreasing family size reflect a major behavioural change that was not documented in the maligned literary sources but it occurred despite the absence of any official or unofficial support among leadership groups. In this way, the declining fertility rates that accelerated the growth of mass schooling, new domestic relations, and numerous other social and economic reconfigurations encouraged scholars to continue studying the ways that historical change occurred from the "bottom-up."

Moreover, the study of fertility further motivated scholars to undertake micro-historical studies since the initial research projects revealed considerable variation in the ways and extent to which family size declined across different groups and settings. This diversity suggested that questions of family size were addressed within webs of relationships radiating out from the domestic to larger communities. By focusing on specific cities or townships, scholars believed that it would be possible to incrementally move toward comprehensive understandings by comparing patterns of behaviour across time and space. The manuscript census seemed to be an ideal source for such comparisons since each enumeration required responses to the same questions across different communities. Scholars were often frustrated by the fact that census officials did not simply add but also sometimes changed the wording or definition of specific questions from one enumeration to the next but, in comparison to other historical sources, the manuscript census seemed to offer rich evidence of mass behaviour to an extent that far surpassed other sources.

But soon some nagging concerns moved from footnotes to the top of the research agenda of many scholars including some of those who had been most enthusiastic about census-based micro-histories. This transition gained speed during the late 1970s and through the 1980s and was propelled by

---

[4] An earlier example is R.M. McInnis, "Childbearing and Land Availability: Some Evidence from Individual Household Data," in R.D.Lee, ed., *Population Patterns in the Past* (New York: Academic Press, 1977), 201-28. More generally, see the chapters in Charles Tilly, ed., *Historical Studies of Changing Fertility* (New Jersey: Princeton University Press, 1978).

research results that raised questions about each of the key distinguishing characteristics of the new social history. In the case of studies of declining fertility, for example, the complexity of behavioural patterns motivated scholars to focus increasingly on the possibility that attitudes, perceptions, and values played key roles in explaining the diverse trajectories across different groups. The continuing inability of researchers to fully explain fertility patterns by interrelating factors such as religious identity, occupation, and wealth inspired greater attention to changing ideas and priorities about which the census seemed to provide no evidence.

Similarly, the repeated research finding that, with only limited exceptions, family size was declining at least to some extent across diverse communities during the later nineteenth century suggested that a macro-level process was unfolding in these years. Scholars increasingly suspected that this process involved conceptual changes that lead to changed behaviour.[5] These historiographical developments called into question the conviction that the key to understanding historical change involved systematic study of mass behaviour through micro-historical research on sources such as the manuscript census. Rather, interest turned to the possibility that social and economic change had to be explained in terms of perceptions and attitudes that transcended the particularities of specific communities and that had to be apprehended through study of what was said and written.

In this way, the research findings produced during the late 1960s and 1970s undermined the perceived value of the concepts and methods borrowed from the social sciences. In turn, these research findings encouraged the scholarly rehabilitation of the literary sources so thoroughly disparaged just a few years earlier. The result was that the new social history unexpectedly helped fuel the rise of the influence of the humanities on historians, and the popularity of cultural history during the 1980s and 1990s. This trend was reinforced by an increasing scepticism about the ability of the manuscript census to even provide reliable evidence about mass behaviour. The initial tendency to take at face value the responses to the various census questions written on the enumeration forms gave way to growing doubt that these forms deserved to be studied at all. Using a vocabulary of errors, inaccuracies, pitfalls, biases, and limitations, researchers increasingly documented the difficulties of carrying out a census in settings like nineteenth century Canada. Historical debate moved from early skirmishes among researchers about the usefulness of specific census questions to full-blown battles about the evidentiary value of any enumeration for understanding the "anonymous," specific communities or social and economic transformations.[6]

---

[5] See Peter Gossage, *Families in Transition: Industry and Population in Nineteenth-Century Sainte-Hyacinthe* (Montreal and Kingston: McGill-Queen's University Press, 1999), and Kevin McQuillan, *Culture, Religion and Demographic Behaviour: Catholics and Lutherans in Alsace, 1750-1870* (Montreal and Kingston: McGill-Queen's University Press, 1999).

[6] Examples include Alan A. Brookes, "Doing the Best I Can: The Taking of the 1861 New Brunswick Census," *Histoire sociale / Social History*, 9, no. 17 (1976): 70-91, and Normand Fortier, "Les recensements canadiens et l'étude de l'agriculture québécoise 1852-1901," *Histoire sociale / Social History*, 17, nos. 33-34 (1984): 257-287.

The increasing questions about how successfully census enumerations were conducted helped to discourage researchers from undertaking projects that would pursue the interpretations offered by scholars such as Katz and Gagan. Although some substantial efforts did continue during the 1980s, more and more researchers turned away from the study of popular behaviour in specific settings based on the census. Instead, increasing attention came to be focused on ideas, those in positions of influence, and macro-level developments. Unlike the earlier history of ideas and intellectual history, however, the new cultural history followed the "linguistic turn" toward the view that reality is not perceived but rather is constructed by mental processes. This view attributed an unprecedented scholarly importance to the articulation of thoughts not only as expressed in written form but also in all human creations. While some scholars argued that historical understanding could never move beyond the analysis of the various articulations of human thought, most historians engaged cultural history as a new strategy to address the same questions that attracted attention during the earlier "new social history" especially those posed in terms of the origins of modern societies. This new strategy characteristically made three assumptions: that culture significantly explains behaviour; that those in positions of official and unofficial power primarily cause historical change; and that larger forces significantly frame the histories of local areas. Clearly, these assumptions contrasted markedly with the previous emphases on what people did more than what they said, on the possibility of historical change originating "bottom-up," and on the need to lower the level of observation in order to increase the level of explanation.

Surprisingly, perhaps, given the rapidly changing scholarly orientation, the census soon became a focus of historical research once again. Now, however, the census was defined as providing evidence of elite perspectives, values, and ambitions. In this view, it was the census questions and not the answers that were of foremost historical interest. Census enumerations were examined not as offering ways to reveal the hidden histories of communities but rather as evidence of state projects in which those in leadership positions attempted to enhance their power over large jurisdictions.[7] Rather than depicting enumerators writing down the information provided by householders to questions of general importance, scholars now described how census officials imposed elite conceptions on the rest of society by designing both the questions and acceptable answers. While researchers in the 1960s and 1970s had focused on the "taking" of the census, other scholars in the 1980s and 1990s wrote about the "making" of the census.[8] Each enumeration was

---

[7] Benedict Anderson, *Imagined Communities: Reflections on the Origins and Spread of Nationalism* rev. ed. (London: Verso, 1991), and related works such as Theodore M. Porter, *The Rise of Statistical Thinking* (Princeton: Princeton University Press, 1986), and Ian Hacking, *The Taming of Chance* (Cambridge: Cambridge University Press, 1990).

[8] Bruce Curtis, "On the Local Construction of Statistical Knowledge: Making up the 1861 Census of the Canadas," *Journal of Historical Sociology*, 7, no. 4 (1994): 416-34, and his award-winning *The Politics of Population: State Formation, Statistics, and the Census of Canada, 1840-1875* (Toronto: University of Toronto Press, 2001). Also see Patrick A. Dunae, "Making the 1891 Census in British Columbia," *Histoire sociale / Social History*, 31, no. 62 (1998), 223-39.

studied not as evidence of behaviour but rather as evidence of elite political, economic, cultural, and social ideas. And rather than counting responses to census questions, researchers studied the questions themselves as illustrations of the ways in which governments were attempting to increase and solidify their power. In this way, the census came to be associated with "qualitative" research as well as with the "quantitative" research of the earlier new social history.[9]

During the 1990s, some scholars remained fully attached to epistemologies associated with quantitative or qualitative, micro or macro, social or cultural approaches. Toward the end of the decade, however, many researchers were attempting to go beyond such dichotomies. Two questions were at the heart of their efforts: how to build on the strengths of both the new social history and of the subsequent cultural history to develop an integrated socio-cultural epistemology, and how to use micro-historical convictions to underpin macro-historical interpretations. The pertinence of these questions arose from a growing conviction that ideas and behaviour had to be studied in holistic ways since they were inherently interrelated in the histories of individuals and groups. Similarly, historians increasingly perceived deep connections between the histories of the "anonymous" and the "famous" with differential flows of influence both up and down, depending upon the historical context including the relevant distributions of power and influence.[10]

In the case of the census, by the late 1990s the result was new efforts to examine various enumerations as providing evidence of individual lives that were both linguistically-constructed and materially-based. The census was now seen as enabling insights about diverse perceptions and realities relating to specific communities as well as larger jurisdictions.[11] Scholars agreed with the importance of analyzing the enumeration process and census questions as related to elite priorities and perceptions but they also increasingly emphasized that census officials could not simply ask whatever they liked; enumerations depended upon, at least to some extent, a shared grid of understanding about both the questions and the expected answers. Such understanding was not always obtained, of course, but rather than viewing the contradictory and confused results in these cases as indications of the inadequacy of the census as a historical source, scholars began seizing upon such results as opportunities to

---

[9] For examples of work between the mid-1980s and mid-1990s, see the special issue of *Histoire sociale / Social History*, 28, no.56 (November 1995), guest-edited by Kris Inwood and Richard Reid including their discussion in "Introduction: The Use of Census Manuscript Data for Historical Research," 300-311. Also, see Robert P. Swierenga, "Historians and the Census: The Historiography of Census Research," *Annals of Iowa* 50, no. 6 (1990): 650-73 and, more recently, David I. Kertzer and Dominique Arel, eds., *Census and Identity: The Politics of Race, Ethnicity, and Language in National Censuses* (Cambridge: Cambridge University Press, 2002).

[10] For one example of the changing perspectives, see Chad Gaffield, "Children, Schooling, and Family Reproduction in Nineteenth-Century Ontario," *Canadian Historical Review* 72 (1991): 157-91.

[11] An early effort to move in this direction was Gordon Darroch and Lee Soltow, *Property and Inequality in Victorian Ontario: Structural Patterns and Cultural Communities in the 1871 Census* (Toronto: University of Toronto Press, 1991).

probe the mentalities of those being enumerated by reading the schedules "against the grain."

In the same way, researchers tended to move away from the idea that the census enumerations only provided evidence of the ability of those in power to impose their concepts and to define individuals and groups according to their own preferences. Rather, the census suggested a sense of inadequacy and ignorance among officials as well as a sense of comfort and control.[12] In other words, the convictions of both the new social history and the subsequent cultural history seemed warranted. But the first question remained: how could the census be read as providing evidence in keeping with integrated socio-cultural approaches to historical change?

The second question probed connections between the deep complexity of specific times and places and the overall similarity of key historical trajectories related to the expansion of mass schooling, declining fertility, and other features of social, economic, cultural, and political transformation in numerous (though certainly not all) societies. Scholars became increasingly convinced that particular times and places were characterized by both a specificity and a generality within which such specificity had to be contextualized.[13] As researchers acquired increased appreciation of the diversity and complexity of everyday life, they also repeatedly concluded that larger forces determined the limits within which the ideas and behaviours of individuals and groups had to be situated. In other words, micro-history and macro-history represented different but interrelated observational levels.[14]

One way to pursue the ambition of an integrated socio-cultural and micro-macro approach to historical evidence is to apply the concept of multi-authored sources. In this concept, each source is created by numerous authors in direct and indirect ways. The appropriate analysis of the census, for example, can be seen to depend upon understandings of the multi-layered political, social, economic, and cultural contexts within which enumerations took place. In recent years, scholars have paid greater and greater attention to the challenge of developing such understandings as they have become increasingly convinced of the complexity and diversity of the ways in which censuses were conceptualized, and how specific questions were formulated and responses given. Specifically, the nineteenth and early-twentieth century census in Canada can be analyzed in terms of eight distinct authors:

---

[12] Peter Baskerville and Eric W. Sager, "The Census as Historical Source," in Baskerville and Sager, *Unwilling Idlers: The Urban Unemployed and their Families in Late Victorian Canada* (Toronto: University of Toronto Press, 1998), 195-216. Also see Peter Baskerville and Eric Sager, "Finding the Work Force in the 1901 Census of Canada.," *Histoire sociale / Social History,* 28, no. 56 (1995): 322-39.

[13] Chad Gaffield, "La région: une combinaison spécifique d'éléments non spécifiques," in Fernand Harvey ed., *La région culturelle: problematique interdisciplinaire* (Québec: Institut québécois de recherche sur la culture, 1994), 27-31.

[14] In this spirit, see Ruth Sandwell, "Rural Reconstruction: Towards a New Synthesis in Canadian History," *Histoire sociale / Social History* 27, no. 53 (1994): 1-32.

1) the international community of census officials and advisors who developed approaches within their own jurisdictions by sharing, comparing, and debating their plans and experiences;
2) the politicians who consistently approved the census but who also argued about and influenced its design and operation;
3) the religious leaders who supported, contested, and affected the census in numerous ways;
4) the business and community leaders who sought to profit from the census for their own purposes;
5) the journalists who created and reflected elite and popular interest in the census through considerable coverage especially in enumeration years;
6) the census bureaucracy in Ottawa who prepared for and followed up each enumeration including the editing, revising, and compiling of results;
7) the enumerators who conducted the census;
8) the respondents whose statements affected to varying degrees what was written on enumeration forms.

Certainly, these authors as well as others contributed to the content of each census in vastly different ways and to significantly different extents depending upon their positions of influence and involvement. And, of course, the visible results of such authoring in the extant census documents are a profound simplification of the input of the diverse influences. By viewing the census as a multi-authored source, an emphasis is placed on the importance of contextualizing the enumeration process and the specific questions and other writing on actual census schedules. Each enumeration resulted from complex interactions of "authors" both directly and indirectly involved in census work. In this view, the administrative history of each census enumeration becomes crucial to the appropriate analysis of the evidence produced in various communities as well as in centralized offices. The important questions range from decisions about when and whom to enumerate to form design, census questions, respondent reaction, and subsequent administrative processes. Research on such questions sheds light on the diverse and competing concepts, definitions, and objectives that are associated with each census enumeration at the various levels from the interactions at specific dwellings to international discussions.[15]

Beyond analyzing the roles of the multiple authors of census enumerations is the challenge of interpreting the traces of this authorship on the actual documents. One way to address this challenge is to systematically consider the criteria that appear to underpin each evidentiary trace under examination. In this approach, the ambition is not to evaluate census questions, responses, or the enumeration process in an abstract way but rather to relate this

---

[15] Chad Gaffield, "Linearity, Non-Linearity, and the Competing Constructions of Social Hierarchy in Early Twentieth-Century Canada: The Question of Language in 1901," *Historical Methods* 33, no. 4 (2000): 255-260; Gordon Darroch, "Constructing Census Families and Classifying Households: 'Relationship to Head of Family or Household' in the 1901 Census of Canada," *Historical Methods* 33, no. 4 (2000): 206-10; and Bettina Bradbury, "Single Parenthood in the Past: Canadian Census Categories, 1891-1951, and the 'Normal Family'," *Historical Methods* 33, no. 4 (2000): 211-17.

evidence to the criteria used in their creation. Five questions can be posed about each of the groups of authors in this regard:

1) What are the (often) competing and distinct criteria being used by different individuals, groups and institutions in determining the census objectives, enumeration process, questions, responses, and subsequent handling and analysis:
2) Why are these criteria being used and not others?
3) How do the various criteria change over time?
4) Why do these changes in criteria occur and not others?
5) What are the consequences of the use of various criteria for different individuals, groups and institutions?

By posing questions about the diverse and competing criteria that underpin the multiple authoring of the census, scholars are moving beyond the notion of "right" and "wrong" census questions or responses just as they are abandoning distinctions between "qualitative" and "quantitative" evidence. Viewing sources such as the census as multi-authored makes clear that the key epistemological question is when to take a realist stance rather than how to choose between constructivist and realist perspectives. Similarly, this approach enables analysis of the embeddedness of individual and collective histories within larger contexts that go beyond specific communities.

Questions about authorship and criteria can be posed in the case of the census to a vast array of sources from the actual enumeration schedules to the archives of administrative history to newspapers and records of political debate. The challenge is to situate and relate each of these sources within their historical setting; in other words, to contextualize them by identifying their interconnections.[16] At the same time, it should be emphasized that the ability to interrelate the linguistically-constructed and materially-based character of historical documents will never do justice to the full complexity of the past. Nonetheless, the move toward socio-cultural epistemologies that attempt to contextualize different observational levels promises to build effectively upon the significant research findings that have so considerably enhanced our historical understandings since the 1960s.

The example of the changing ways in which research using census enumeration schedules has unfolded in recent decades emphasizes that metaphysical and epistemological questions are indeed at the heart of historical debate. Although most scholarly writing reports, compares, and contests specific research findings, it is the use of new concepts, new sources, and new research strategies that changes the larger context within which specific historical studies are undertaken. It is often argued that such innovations come from outside the discipline of History where researchers are characteristically depicted as theoretically weak and methodologically unimaginative. In recent decades, for example, sociologists, anthropologists, philosophers, and literary

---

[16] This approach is being used to construct the Canadian Century Research Infrastructure that will be composed of diverse databases related to the 1911-1951 period. See http://www.canada.uottawa.ca/ccri.

scholars have all claimed to have had significant impacts on the changing ways in which historians practice their craft. The dominant image of historical debate since the 1960s is of a discipline being driven by external forces beginning with the social sciences and moving to the humanities by the 1980s.

In contrast, the preceding discussion suggests how surprising research findings in recent decades inspired historians to reconceptualize historical change and to develop new ways of addressing historical questions. Such innovations have certainly taken place in light of developments in other disciplines but the result has been more of an exchange among social scientists and humanists than a borrowing by historians; indeed, the greater influence may be from History to the other human sciences which have become increasingly preoccupied with the importance of change over time.[17] One conclusion is that, in order to practice interdisciplinarity, we cannot only exchange concepts and methods but must also study the same sources whenever appropriate; no particular type of evidence is the property of a particular discipline. In this sense, one way to move historical debate forward toward socio-cultural and micro-macro approaches is to encourage interdisciplinary encounters through a focus on the same sources and on the key question: evidence of what?

---

[17] In the case of sociology, see Peter Wagner, "As Intellectual History Meets Historical Sociology: Historical Sociology after the Linguistic Turn," in Gerard Delanty et al., eds., *Handbook of Historical Sociology* (London: Sage, 2002), as well as the stimulating essays of Andrew Abbott, *Time Matters: On Theory and Method* (Chicago: University of Chicago Press, 2001).

Contributors
Collaborateurs

Michel S. Beaulieu is currently a doctoral candidate in the Department of History at Queen's University. His recent work includes the edited collection *The Lady Lumberjack: An Annotated Collection of the Writings of Dorothea Mitchell* (2004), the restoration and completion of the 1930s film *The Fatal Flower* (1930; 2004), and a forthcoming article in the *Canadian Journal of Film Studies* on professional filmmaking at the Lakehead in the late 1920s.

Cristina Bradatan is an Assistant Professor in the Department of Sociology at the University of Central Florida. Her areas of interest are ethnicity, migration, and family dynamic in Eastern Europe.

Caroline-Isabelle Caron is an Assistant Professor at Queen's University. She specializes on the cultural history of Francophones in Canada in the 19th and 20th centuries. She published on contemporary American cultural influences in Québec television. She also will be publishing in 2005 a book on commemorations and representations of ancestry in Acadie and Quebec entitled *Se trouver des ancêtres. Un parcours généalogique nord-américain, 19e-20e siècles*. She is currently working on a project looking into local commemorations and historical festivals in Acadian communities of Nova Scotia since 1880.

Mélanie De Groote est assistante de recherche à l'Université catholique de Louvain (Belgique). Elle travaille sur l'histoire des universités belges, sur les mouvements étudiants ainsi que sur les sources orales et iconographiques. Elle réalise actuellement une thèse de doctorat sur les rapports entre l'engagement étudiant dans les années 60-70 et d'autres formes d'engagement dans la vie active.

Laura E. Ettinger, Assistant Professor of history at Clarkson University, Potsdam, New York, is the author of *Modern Midwives: The Birth of Nurse-Midwifery in America* (forthcoming, Ohio State University Press), as well as several articles. Her interests include gender and the professions, the culture of childbirth, the structure of American health care, and oral history.

Kouky Fianu est professeur agrégé au Départment d'histoire de l'Université d'Ottawa. Elle travaille sur l'histoire des pratiques sociales d'écriture dans la France médiévale, et plus particulièrement sur l'histoire du notariat à Orléans, entre les XIIIe et XVe siècles.

Chad Gaffield is Professor of History and holds a University Research Chair at the University of Ottawa. His current research focuses on the socio-cultural history of language and identity in 19th and 20th century Canada. The Royal Society of Canada awarded Gaffield the J. B. Tyrrell Historical Medal for 2004.

Lisa Helps holds an MA from the University of Victoria and will be pusuing a doctoral degree in History. Her areas of interest include the connections among bodies, spaces and gendered, classed, racialized and colonial relations of power and how each of these relates to the making of modern Canada in the late 19th and early 20th centuries.

James Hull is a member of the Department of History at Okanagan University College and an Associate Scholar of the Institute for the History and Philosophy of Science and Technology. He is the author of numerous papers on the history of science and industry.

Jeff Keshen is a Professor in the Department of History at the University of Ottawa. Among his publications are *Propaganda and Censorship during Canada's Great War* and *Saints, Sinners and Soldiers: Canada's Second World War*.

Samy Khalid est doctorant au Département d'histoire de l'Université d'Ottawa. Ses recherches portent sur l'immigration suisse au Canada et plus particulièrement sur la construction identitaire et les représentations de la citoyenneté chez les migrants.

Vadim Kukushkin holds a doctorate in Canadian history from Carleton University and is currently a Grant Notley Postdoctoral Fellow at the University of Alberta. He specializes in the ethnic and immigration history of Canada with a focus on 20th-century immigrants from Eastern Europe. He is the author of several articles and co-editor, with R. C. Elwood, of *Mikhail Klochko: Soviet Scientist, Cold-War Defector, Canadian Storyteller* (Penumbra Press, 2002).

Susan Lamb is completing her PhD in the History of Medicine at the Institute of the History of Medicine, The Johns Hopkins Medical School, Baltimore, Maryland. She received her MA in History from the University of Toronto.

Barbara Lorenzkowski is an Assistant Professor of American history at Nipissing University. Her work explores questions of ethnicity and modernity, community and nation, public culture and trans-nationalism. She is the author of several articles and book chapters, including the prize-winning "A Platform for Gender Tensions" in the *Canadian Historical Review* in 1998.

Anne F. MacLennan is a Sessional Assistant Professor at York University and a recent PhD graduate in History from Concordia University. Her dissertation *Circumstances Beyond Our Control: Canadian Radio Program Schedule Evolution During the 1930s* is under revision for publication as a monograph and she is researching qualitative aspects of early broadcasting.

Charlotte Masemann recently defended her PhD thesis, "Garden Produce in Medieval Ghent and Lübeck," at the Centre for Medieval Studies at the University of Toronto. She currently teaches as a sessional lecturer in the History Department of Carleton University.

Sylvie Perrier est professeure adjointe au Département d'histoire de l'Université d'Ottawa. Intéressée aux pratiques sociales du droit, elle travaille présentement sur le remariage dans la région toulousaine au XVIIIe siècle et est l'auteure du livre *Des enfances protégées. La tutelle des mineurs en France (XVIIe-XVIIIe siècles* (Presses universitaires de Vincennnes, 1998).

Katherine Romba is currently completing her doctorate in art history at the Institute of Fine Arts, New York University. Her dissertation examines expressions of modern cultural identity in German architectural theory. An article related to the work in this anthology will also appear in the *Rutgers Art Review*.

Robert Strong received his PhD in Creative Writing and Literary Studies from the University of Denver. In 2004, he held a Mellon research fellowship at the Massachusetts Historical Society. He currently teaches at St. Lawrence University in Canton, New York.

Jonathan F. Vance holds the Canada Research Chair in Conflict and Culture in the Department of History at The University of Western Ontario. He is the author of many books and articles, including *Death So Noble: Memory, Meaning, and the First World War* (1997) and *High Flight: Aviation and the Canadian Imagination* (2002).

Hubert Watelet est professeur émérite de l'Université d'Ottawa et ancien codirecteur de la revue *Histoire sociale / Social History*. Ses publications ont d'abord porté sur l'industrialisation européenne des XIXe et XXe siècles, et notamment sur l'industrie minière, les petites entreprises et l'archéologie industrielle. Aujourd'hui, il s'intéresse davantage à l'histoire socio-culturelle et celle des sentiments d'une part, mais aussi à l'épistémologie de la connaissance historique et l'historiographie.